PRAISE FOR

Coming Apart

"Charles Murray . . . has written an incisive, alarming, and hugely
frustrating book about the state of American society."
—Roger Lowenstein, *Bloomberg Businessweek*

"Charles Murray has an unparalleled talent for persistently
forcing the most explosive issues of American politics into
the center of the political debate."
—Thomas Edsall, *New York Times*

"Step forward Charles Murray . . ., whose new book, *Coming Apart*,
offers by far the best available analysis of modern American
inequality—and a much-needed antidote to the campaign
for a European America."
—Niall Ferguson, *Newsweek*

"*Coming Apart: The State of White America, 1960–2010*
brims with ideas about what ails America."
—*The Economist*

"A timely investigation into a worsening class divide
no one can afford to ignore."
—*Publishers Weekly*

"[Charles Murray] argues for the need to focus
on what has made the U.S. exceptional beyond its
wealth and military power . . . religion, marriage,
industriousness, and morality."
—*Booklist* (starred review)

Coming Apart

Coming Apart

The State of
White America
1960–2010

CHARLES MURRAY

CROWN
FORUM

NEW YORK

CROWN FORUM with colophon is a registered trademark of Random House, Inc.

Originally published in hardcover in slightly different form in the United States
by Crown Forum, an imprint of the Crown Publishing Group, a division of
Random House, Inc., New York, in 2012.

Library of Congress Cataloging-in-Publication data is available upon request.

ISBN 978-0-307-45343-3
eISBN 978-0-307-45344-0

Printed in the United States of America

Book design: Chris Welch
Cover design: Base Art Co.
Cover photographs: (champagne flute)
Thomas Northcut/Photodisc/Getty Images; (crushed can) iStockphoto

5 7 9 10 8 6 4

First Paperback Edition

To Catherine,
my touchstone

Contents

Part III

Why It Matters

Coming Apart

November 21, 1963

IN RETROSPECT, a single day often comes to demarcate the transition between eras. Never mind that the Continental Congress voted to declare the colonies' independence on July second and that the document probably wasn't signed until August. The Fourth of July, the day the text of the Declaration of Independence was adopted, will forever be the symbolic first day of the new nation. In the twentieth century, December 7, 1941, became the symbolic end of an America that held the world at arm's length and the beginning of America the superpower. November 22, 1963, became the symbolic first day of what would be known as the Sixties and of the cultural transformation that wound its course through the subsequent decades. The symbolic last day of the culture that preceded it was November 21, 1963.

IT WAS A THURSDAY. New York City saw a trace of rain that day, with a high of fifty-six, ending several days' run of late-autumn sunshine. As dusk fell at CBS headquarters at 485 Madison Avenue, Walter Cronkite was in the anchor chair for *The CBS Evening News*. Just a year and a half into his job, Cronkite was not yet the nation's Uncle Walter. He wasn't even the nation's leading anchorman. His ratings had lagged behind those of Huntley and Brinkley on NBC from the beginning, and the shift in September from a fifteen-minute program to a half-hour program had done nothing to close the gap.

There wasn't much news to spice up the broadcast this evening. The day had produced one good human-interest story: Robert Stroud, the Birdman of Alcatraz, had died in his sleep at the federal prison in Springfield, Missouri, that morning. But otherwise, the news was humdrum. The Senate Armed Services Committee had approved President Kennedy's nomination of Paul Nitze to be secretary of the navy. House minority leader Charles Halleck held a press conference in which he said that he did not see how the president's civil rights bill could get to the floor of the House before the Christmas recess—no surprise, given the many ways in which the all-powerful Rules Committee, dominated by southern Democrats, could delay the process. On Wall Street, the Dow industrials had dropped more than 9 points, more than 1 percent of the Dow's opening 742. Nobody was especially worried, however. The October figures for housing starts and durable goods had just come out, providing more evidence that the economy was on the upswing.

CBS might have been number two in evening news, but it was number one in prime-time programming. The Neilsen ratings that week placed eight CBS programs in the top ten, led by *The Beverly Hillbillies* with a rating of 34.9, meaning that 34.9 percent of all American homes with a television set were watching it. Since 93 percent of American homes had a television set by 1963, the upshot was that the same program was being watched in almost a third of all the homes in the United States. Those same staggering numbers went deep into the lineup. All of the top thirty-one shows had ratings of at least 20. By way of comparison, the number one show in the 2009–10 season, *American Idol*, considered to be a gigantic hit, had a rating of 9.1.[1]

The explanation for the ratings of 1963 is simple: There wasn't much choice. Most major cities had only four channels (CBS, NBC,

ABC, and a nonprofit station of some sort) at most. People in some markets had access to just one channel—the monopoly in Austin, Texas, where the lone station was owned by Lady Bird Johnson, was the most notorious example.

The limited choices in television viewing were just one example of something that would come as a surprise to a child of the twenty-first century transported back to 1963: the lack of all sorts of variety, and a simplicity that now seems almost quaint.

Popular music consisted of a single Top 40 list, with rock, country, folk, and a fair number of Fifties-style ballads lumped together. No separate stations specializing in different genres, except for country music stations in a few parts of the nation. Except in university towns and the very largest cities, bookstores were small and scarce, usually carrying only a few hundred titles. No Amazon. If you didn't see a movie during the week or two it was showing in your town, you would probably never see it. No DVDs. With television, you either saw a show the night it played or waited until it was repeated once during the summer. No TiVo.

People drove cars made in the United States. Foreign cars from Europe were expensive and rare. Cars from Japan had just been introduced in 1963, but had not been greeted with enthusiasm—"made in Japan" was synonymous with products that were cheap and shoddy. You might see an occasional sports car on the road—Ford's Thunderbird or Chevrolet's Corvette—but the vast majority of customers chose among sedans, convertibles, and station wagons made by General Motors, Ford, or Chrysler.

The typical American city of 1963 had appallingly little choice in things to eat. In a large city, you would be able to find a few restaurants serving Americanized Chinese food, a few Italian restaurants serving spaghetti and pizza, and a few restaurants with a French name, which probably meant that they had French onion soup on the menu. But if you were looking for a nice little Szechuan dish or linguine with pesto or sautéed fois gras, forget it. A Thai curry? The first Thai restaurant in the entire nation wouldn't open for another eight years. Sushi? Raw fish? Are you kidding?

ON THIS THURSDAY, November 21, television's prime-time lineup included *The Flintstones*, *The Donna Reed Show*, *My Three Sons*, *Perry Mason*, and *The Perry Como Show*, but it was the fourteenth-rated show, *Dr. Kildare*, that made *Time* magazine's recommended viewing. The story that week involved a pregnant unmarried teen who had gotten an abortion. She was so psychologically shattered by the experience that even Dr. Kildare couldn't help. He had to refer her to a psychiatrist in another CBS program, *The Eleventh Hour*, for an episode that would air a week later.

She shouldn't have gotten pregnant in the first place, of course. Getting pregnant without being married was wrong, and if a girl did get pregnant then she and the boyfriend who had gotten her in that fix were supposed to get married. If she didn't get married, she should put the baby up for adoption. These were conventional views shared across the political spectrum. As of 1963, Americans continued to obey those norms with remarkable consistency. The percentage of births to single women, known as "the illegitimacy ratio," had been rising worrisomely among Negroes (the only respectful word for referring to African Americans in 1963). But among whites, the illegitimacy ratio was only 3 percent, about where it had been throughout the century.

Marriage was nearly universal and divorce was rare across all races. In the 1963 Current Population Survey, a divorced person headed just 3.5 percent of American households, with another 1.6 percent headed by a separated person. Nor did it make much difference how much education a person had—the marriage percentages for college grads and high school dropouts were about the same.

Not only were Americans almost always married, mothers normally stayed at home to raise their children. More than 80 percent of married women with young children were not working outside the home in 1963.[2] When Americans watched *The Adventures of Ozzie and Harriet* (it was still going strong in 1963, at twenty-sixth place in the ratings), they were looking at a family structure that the vast majority of them recognized from their own experience, whether they were white or black and whether they were working class, middle class, or rich.

An irony of *Ozzie and Harriet* was that the real Harriet Nelson was herself a working mother (she was a show-business veteran who played herself on the show). Another irony: It wasn't clear that Ozzie did work—or at least the show never disclosed what Ozzie did for a living. But he had to be doing something. Rich or poor, it was not socially respectable to be adult, male, and idle. And so it was that 98 percent of civilian men in their thirties and forties reported to government interviewers that they were in the labor force, either working or seeking work. The numbers had looked like that ever since the government had begun asking the question.

Whether television was portraying loving traditional families or pointing with alarm to the perils of breaking the code, television was a team player. It was taken for granted that television programs were supposed to validate the standards that were commonly accepted as part of "the American way of life"—a phrase that was still in common use in 1963.

The film industry chafed under that obligation more than the television networks did, but it mostly went along. Few relics of a half century ago seem more antiquated than the constraints under which filmmakers operated. If filmmakers in 1963 wanted the approval of the Production Code of the Motion Picture Association of America, which almost all of them still did, the dialogue could not include any profanity stronger than *hell* or *damn*, and there had better be good dramatic justification even for them. Characters couldn't take the name of the Lord in vain, or ridicule religion, or use any form of obscenity—meaning just about anything related to the sex act. Actors couldn't be seen naked or even near naked, nor could they dance in a way that bore any resemblance to a sexual action. The plot couldn't present sex outside marriage as attractive or justified. Homosexuality was to be presented as a perversion. Abortion? "The subject of abortion shall be discouraged, shall never be more than suggested, and when referred to shall be condemned," said the code.[3]

There had been pushes against the Production Code before November 1963. Movies like *Elmer Gantry* and *Lolita* had managed to get code approval despite forbidden themes, and a few pictures had been released without approval, notably *Man with the Golden Arm*, *Anatomy of a Murder*, and *Some Like It Hot*. A British production that made every sort of licentiousness look like fun, *Tom Jones*, had opened in October. But the top-grossing American-made movies of 1963— *How the West Was Won*, *Cleopatra*, *Bye Bye Birdie*, *The Great Escape*, *Charade*—still fit squarely within the moral world prescribed by the Production Code.

Freedom of expression in literature was still a live issue. A federal court decision in 1959 had enjoined the Post Office from confiscating copies of *Lady Chatterley's Lover*, *Tropic of Cancer*, and *Fanny Hill* sent through the mails, but many state laws were still on the books. Just a week earlier, a court in Manhattan had heard a case testing a New York State law that prohibited selling any book that "exploits, is de-voted to, or is made up of descriptions of illicit sex or sexual immoral-ity." Did *Fanny Hill* fall into that category? Without a doubt, said the three-judge panel. It was well written, the court acknowledged, but "filth, even if wrapped in the finest packaging, is still filth."[4]

Part of the reason for these widely shared values lay in the religios-ity of America in 1963. A Gallup poll taken in October asked as two of its background questions the interviewee's religious preference and whether he or she had attended church in the last seven days (note the wording in 1963—"church," not "church or synagogue" or "wor-ship service"). Only 1 percent of respondents said they did *not* have a religious preference, and half said they had attended a worship ser-vice in the last seven days. These answers showed almost no variation across classes. Poor or rich, high school dropout or college graduate, the percentages of Americans who said they were religious believers and had recently attended a worship service were close to identical.[5]

Hollywood had especially elaborate restrictions on the way that criminal activity could be portrayed, amounting to a stipulation that movies must always show that crime doesn't pay. But to most Ameri-cans, that didn't seem odd. By 1963, crime had been low for many years. In large swaths of America, doors were routinely left unlocked, children were allowed to move around the neighborhood unsuper-vised, and, except in the toughest neighborhoods of the largest cities, it seldom occurred to someone walking alone at night to worry about muggers.

The nation's prisons held only a fraction of the inmates they would hold by 2010, but clearance rates for crimes and the probability of prison time if convicted for a felony were both high. And so we have this paradox compared to later years: Crime was low and few people had ever been in prison, even in low-income neighborhoods, but most of the people in those neighborhoods who regularly committed crimes ended up in jail. People weren't being naive to believe that crime didn't pay. By and large, it really didn't.

As for illegal drugs, we cannot put hard numbers to the prevalence of use—surveys on drug use wouldn't begin until the late 1970s—but there certainly wasn't much happening that attracted the attention of the police. In 1963, there were just 18 arrests for drug abuse violations per 100,000 Americans, compared to 1,284 per 100,000 for drunkenness.[6] As of 1963, people drank like fish and smoked like chimneys, but illegal drugs were rare and exotic.

America still had plenty of problems on November 21, 1963. The greatest of all, the one that had been eating at the vitals of the American body politic ever since the founders couldn't bring themselves to condemn slavery in the Declaration of Independence, was the status of African Americans. In 1963, the South was still such a thoroughly segregated society that whether the segregation was de jure or de facto didn't make much practical difference. In the North, the laws supporting segregation were gone, but neighborhoods and schools in urban areas were segregated in practice. The racial differences in income, education, and occupations were all huge. The civil rights movement was the biggest domestic issue of the early 1960s, and it was underwritten by a moral outrage that had begun among blacks but was rapidly raising the consciousness of white America as well.

The status of American women in 1963 had not yet led to a movement, but there was much to be outraged about. Almost as many girls as boys had enrolled in college in the spring of 1963, but thereafter the discrepancies grew. That same year, there were 1.4 male college graduates for every female, two master's degrees awarded to males for every one that went to a female, and eight PhDs that went to males for every one that went to a female. Worse than that were the expectations. Teaching and nursing were still two of the only occupations in which women received equal treatment and opportunity, and the women who did enter male-dominated professions could expect to put up with a level of sexual harassment that would prompt large summary damage awards in the 2000s. The vast majority of men took it for granted that women were expected to get married, cook the meals, keep the house clean, raise the children, and cater to the husband. Women who didn't were oddballs.

Pollution was a dreadful problem in many urban areas. The smog in Los Angeles was often a visible miasma hanging over the city, and less visible pollution was just as dangerously a presence in the nation's lakes and rivers.

And there was the problem that within a year would become a focal point of national domestic policy: poverty. The official poverty line didn't exist yet—it was in the process of being invented by the economist Mollie Orshansky and her colleagues at the Social Security Administration—but when that definition of poverty was retrospectively calculated for 1963, it would be determined that almost 20 percent of the American people were below the poverty line. And yet poverty was still on the periphery of the policy agenda. The reason was more complicated than obtuseness or indifference, and it goes to the strategic optimism that still prevailed in 1963: Poverty had been dropping so rapidly for so many years that Americans thought things were going well. Economists have since reconstructed earlier poverty rates using decennial census data, and determined that 41 percent of Americans were still below the poverty line in 1949.[7] A drop from 41 percent to under 20 percent in just fourteen years was a phenomenal achievement. No one knew those numbers yet, but the reality of the progress they represent helps explain why the average American wasn't exercised about poverty in 1963. Things had been getting better economically in ways that were evident in everyday life.

That kind of progress also helps explain why, if you took polling data at face value, America didn't have a lower class or an upper class in 1963. In the responses to a Gallup poll taken that fall, 95 percent of the respondents said they were working class (50 percent) or middle class (45 percent). A great many poor people were refusing to identify themselves as lower class, and a great many affluent people were refusing to identify themselves as upper class. Those refusals reflected a national conceit that had prevailed from the beginning of the nation: America didn't have classes, or, to the extent that it did, Americans should act as if we didn't.

AS WALTER CRONKITE ended the broadcast on November 21 with his newly coined sign-off, "That's the way it is," he had no way of knowing that he was within hours of a career-changing event. The grainy videotape of the special bulletins, with Cronkite's ashen face and his carefully dispassionate voice saying that the news was official, the president was dead, fiddling with his glasses, trying to hide that he was blinking away tears, would become the iconic image of how the nation got the news.

Nor could he, nor any of his audience, have had any way of knowing how much America was about to change, in everything—its politics, economy, technology, high culture, popular culture, and civic culture.

The assassination was to some degree a cause of that change. On November 21, 1963, Kennedy was not an unusually popular president. The image of JFK's presidency as Camelot came later, through Theodore White's interview of Jackie Kennedy a few weeks after the assassination. In the weeks just before the assassination, Gallup put his job approval rating at 58 percent—not bad, but hardly spectacular in that unpolarized era—and the *New York Times'* number one nonfiction best seller was Victor Lasky's highly critical *J.F.K.: The Man and the Myth*. Apart from his only average political clout when he died, Kennedy was disinclined by temperament and beliefs to push for radical change. Then an accident of history brought a master legislator to the White House at a time when national grief and self-recrimination hobbled his political opposition. It is surely impossible that anything resembling the legislative juggernaut that Lyndon Johnson commanded would have happened if Kennedy had been in the Oval Office. No one knows how Vietnam would have played out if Kennedy had lived, but it could hardly have been worse than the trauma that Johnson's policies produced.

In other ways, the assassination provides a marker coinciding with changes that were going to happen anyway. Many of the landmark reforms of the 1960s were produced by Supreme Court decisions, not the president or Congress, and the activist supermajority on that court was already established. Seven of the judges sitting on the court when Kennedy died were there throughout the next six years of historic decisions.

A sexual revolution of some sort was inevitable by November 21, 1963. The first oral contraceptive pill had gone on the market in 1960 and its use was spreading rapidly. Of course sexual mores would be profoundly changed when, for the first time in human history, women had a convenient and reliable way to ensure that they could have sex without getting pregnant, even on the spur of the moment and with no cooperation from the man.

A revolution of some sort in the fortunes of African Americans was inevitable. The civil rights movement had been intensifying for a decade and had reached its moral apogee with the March on Washington on August 28, 1963, which filled the Mall with a quarter of a million people and concluded with Martin Luther King Jr.'s "I Have a Dream" speech. The precise shape of the legislation and regulatory regime to implement the revolution were probably different under Johnson than they would have been under Kennedy, but momentum for major change in 1963 was already too great to stop.

Something resembling the War on Poverty would probably have been proposed in 1964, no matter what. Michael Harrington's *The Other America* had appeared in the spring of 1962 proclaiming that 40 to 50 million Americans were living in poverty, and that their poverty was structural—it would not be cured by economic growth. Kennedy had read the book, or at least some laudatory reviews of it, and ordered the staff work that would later be used by Johnson in formulating his War on Poverty. How many programs Kennedy could have actually passed is another question, but Harrington's thesis was already being taken up by the liberal wing of the Democratic Party and would have become part of the policy debate even without the assassination.

Other movements that would have sweeping impact on American society were already nascent in 1963. Early in the year, Betty Friedan had published *The Feminine Mystique*, seen now as the opening salvo of the feminist movement. Rachel Carson's *Silent Spring* had appeared in 1962 and become a *New York Times* best seller, setting off public interest that would lead to the environmental movement. Ralph Nader had written his first attack on the auto industry in the *Nation*, and two years later would found the consumer advocate movement with *Unsafe at Any Speed*.

The cultural landscape of the Sixties was already taking shape in 1963. Bob Dylan's "Blowin' in the Wind," "A Hard Rain's a-Gonna Fall," and "Don't Think Twice, It's All Right"—all theme songs for what we think of as the Sixties—had been released six months before Kennedy died. In November 1963, the Beatles had played for the queen, were the hottest group in England, and were planning their first U.S. tour.

And history had already swallowed the demographic pig. The leading cohorts of the baby boomers were in their teens by November 21, 1963, and, for better or worse, they were going to be who they were going to be. No one understood at the time what a big difference it could make if one age group of a population is abnormally large. Everyone was about to find out.

THIS BOOK IS about an evolution in American society that has taken place since November 21, 1963, leading to the formation of classes that are different in kind and in their degree of separation from anything that the nation has ever known. I will argue that the divergence into these separate classes, if it continues, will end what has made America America.

To forestall misinterpretation, let me spell out what this book does *not* argue.

First, I do not argue that America was ever a classless society. From the beginning, rich and poor have usually lived in different parts of town, gone to different churches, and had somewhat different manners and mores. It is not the existence of classes that is new, but the emergence of classes that diverge on core behaviors and values—classes that barely recognize their underlying American kinship.

Second, I do not make a case for America's decline as a world power. The economic dynamics that have produced the class society I deplore have, paradoxically, fostered the blossoming of America's human capital. Those dynamics will increase, not diminish, our competitiveness on the world stage in the years ahead. Nor do I forecast decline in America's military and diplomatic supremacy.

But the American project was not about maximizing national wealth nor international dominance. The American project—a phrase you will see again in the chapters to come—consists of the continuing effort, begun with the founding, to demonstrate that human beings can be left free as individuals and families to live their lives as they see fit, coming together voluntarily to solve their joint problems. The polity based on that idea led to a civic culture that was seen as exceptional by all the world. That culture was so widely shared among Americans that it amounted to a civil religion. To be an American was to be different from other nationalities, in ways that Americans treasured. That culture is unraveling.

I focus on what happened, not why. I discuss some of the whys, but most of them involve forces that cannot be changed. My primary goal is to induce recognition of the ways in which America is coming apart at the seams—not seams of race or ethnicity, but of class.

That brings me to the subtitle of this book and its curious specification of white America. For decades now, trends in American life have been presented in terms of race and ethnicity, with non-Latino whites (hereafter, just *whites*) serving as the reference point—the black poverty rate compared to the white poverty rate, the percentage of Latinos who go to college compared to the percentage of whites who go to college, and so on. There's nothing wrong with that. I have written books filled with such comparisons. But this strategy has distracted our attention from the way that the reference point itself is changing.

And so this book uses evidence based overwhelmingly on whites in the description of the new upper class in part 1 and based exclusively on whites in the description of the new lower class in part 2. My message: Don't kid yourselves that we are looking at stresses that can be remedied by attacking the legacy of racism or by restricting immigration. The trends I describe exist independently of ethnic heritage. In the penultimate chapter, I broaden the picture to include everyone.

As with all books on policy, this one will eventually discuss how we might change course. But discussing solutions is secondary to this book, just as understanding causes is secondary. The important thing is to look unblinkingly at the nature of the problem.

Part 1

The Formation of a New Upper Class

P ART 1 IS about the emergence of a new American upper class that is qualitatively different from any that the country has ever known.

Harvard economist Robert Reich was the first to put a name to an evolving new class of workers in his 1991 book, *The Work of Nations*, calling them "symbolic analysts."[1] Reich surveyed the changing job market and divided jobs into three categories: routine production services, in-person services, and symbol-analytic services. In Reich's formulation, the new class of symbolic analysts consisted of managers, engineers, attorneys, scientists, professors, executives, journalists, consultants, and other "mind workers" whose work consists of processing information. He observed that the new economy was ideally suited to their talents and rewarded them accordingly.

In 1994, in *The Bell Curve*, the late Richard J. Herrnstein and I discussed the driving forces behind this phenomenon, the increasing segregation of the American university system by cognitive ability and the increasing value of brainpower in the marketplace.[2] We labeled the new class "the cognitive elite."

In 2000, David Brooks brought an anthropologist's eye and a

wickedly funny pen to his description of the new upper class in *Bobos in Paradise*. *Bobos* is short for "bourgeois bohemians." Traditionally, Brooks wrote, it had been easy to distinguish the bourgeoisie from the bohemians. "The bourgeoisie were the square, practical ones. They defended tradition and middle-class values. They worked for corporations and went to church. Meanwhile, the bohemians were the free spirits who flouted convention." But by the 1990s, everything had gotten mixed up. "It was now impossible to tell an espresso-sipping artist from a cappuccino-gulping banker,"[3] Brooks wrote. Bobos belonged to what Brooks labeled "the educated class."

In 2002, Richard Florida, a professor of public policy at George Mason University, identified "the creative class," telling his readers, "If you are a scientist or engineer, an architect or designer, a writer, artist, or musician, or if you use your creativity as a key factor in your work in business, education, health care, law or some other profession, you are a member."[4] He celebrated the changes in the workplace, lifestyle, and social capital that accompanied the ascendancy of the creative class.

Reich, Brooks, Florida, and Herrnstein and I were all describing the changing nature of the people in the managerial and professional occupations of the upper-middle class. When I use the term *new upper class*, I am not referring to all of them, but to a small subset: the people who run the nation's economic, political, and cultural institutions. In practice, this means a fuzzy set in which individuals may or may not be in the upper class, depending on how broadly you want to set the operational definition.

The Narrow Elite

At the top are those who have risen to jobs that directly affect the nation's culture, economy, and politics. Some of them wield political power, others wield economic power, and still others wield the power of the media. I will call this subset the *narrow elite*. The narrow elite includes the lawyers and judges who shape constitutional jurisprudence, the people who decide how the news will be covered on national news programs, and the journalists and columnists whose bylines are found in the leading print media and on the Internet. It includes the top executives in the nation's largest corporations, financial institutions, foundations, and nonprofit organizations. It includes the producers, directors, and writers who create the nation's films and television dramas, the most influential scholars in the nation's elite universities and research institutes, and senior government administrators and politicians.

The narrow elite numbers fewer than a hundred thousand people, and perhaps only ten thousand or so. If this seems too small, think about the numbers for specific components of the narrow elite.

With regard to opinion media, for example, go to political websites that maintain a list of links to all the columnists on their respective sides of the political spectrum, make sure you've got a full representation of columnists from Left to Right, and add them up. Make a list of the influential talk show hosts from Left to Right. It is impossible to make the number of genuinely influential opinion writers and talkers larger than a few hundred. The top few dozen have much more influence than those below them.

With regard to constitutional jurisprudence, count up the judges on the circuit courts of appeals and the Supreme Court, and estimate the number of attorneys who argue cases before them. The influential actors cannot be made to number more than the low thousands, with the number of key figures no more than a few hundred. When it comes to formulating and passing legislation, the number of key actors at the federal level does not even consist of everyone in the House and Senate. A few dozen of them are far more influential than everyone else. In the corporate and financial worlds, the CEOs and financial heavy hitters whose actions affect the national economy are limited to the very largest and most strategically placed institutions. And so it goes throughout the narrow elite. The number of influential players is surprisingly small even for a country as sprawling and decentralized as the United States.

The Broad Elite

Construed more broadly, the new upper class includes those who are both successful and influential within a city or region: the owners and top executives of the most important local businesses and corporations; the people who run the local television stations and newspapers; the most successful lawyers and physicians; the most prominent faculty if the city has an important university; and the most powerful city officials.

The number of people who belong under the broad definition of the new upper class is a judgment call. At one extreme, we might choose to limit the definition to the top 1 percent of people working in managerial and professional occupations. There is an argument to be made for such a stringent restriction. In the military, flag officers—generals or admirals—constitute only about 0.4 percent of all military officers. In the executive branch of the federal government, positions reserved for the Senior Executive Service plus presidential appointments amount to about 1.3 percent of the civilian equivalent of military officers (GS-7 or higher). It could be argued that these include the vast majority of people who could be deemed "highly successful" in the military and the executive branch of government.

But 1 percent is perhaps too stringent. If we restrict the new upper class to the top 1 percent in the private sector, we're going to have nothing but chief executives of major companies, the most senior partners in the very largest and most influential law firms, and so on. There's also money to consider. If I were to limit the broad elite to the top 1 percent of those working in management and the professions, the mean family income of the new upper class as of 2009 would have been $517,700.

A plausible middle ground is the most successful 5 percent of the people working in the professions and managerial positions. In the military, the top 5.5 percent of officers in 2006 consisted of those with the rank of colonel or above.[5] The Senior Executive Service, presidential appointees, plus the GS-15s constituted the top 6.6

percent of employees with a GS-7 grade or higher. In the world of
business, 5.1 percent of all people classified as working in managerial
positions were chief executives. Not all chief executives qualify for
the new upper class and, in large corporations, senior executives just
below the CEO do qualify, but saying that the most successful 5 percent of businesspeople belong in the new upper class would seem to
be reasonable.

These considerations lead me to conclude that using the top 5 percent lets in just about everyone who is unequivocally part of the new
upper class, plus a large number of those who are successful but borderline. I hereby operationally define the new upper class as the most
successful 5 percent of adults ages 25 and older who are working in
managerial positions, in the professions (medicine, the law, engineering and architecture, the sciences, and university faculty), and in
content-production jobs in the media.[6] As of 2010, about 23 percent
of all employed persons ages 25 or older were in these occupations,
which means about 1,427,000 persons constituted the top 5 percent.[7]
Since 69 percent of adults in these occupations who were ages 25 and
older were married in 2010, about 2.4 million adults were in new-
upper-class families as heads of household or spouse.[8]

What's New About the New Upper Class

Every society more complex than bands of hunter-gatherers has had
an upper class and, within that upper class, an elite who ran the key
institutions. The United States has been no exception. But things are
different now than they were half a century ago. America's new upper
class is new because its members have something in common beyond
the simple fact of their success.

Insofar as Americans in the past used the phrase "upper class" at
all, it usually connoted the old-money rich of the Northeast United
States. The closest parallel to what I am calling the new upper class
used to be known as The Establishment. But The Establishment,
too, was identified with the Northeast, and its role was associated
with a few great corporate entities (predominantly the oil, steel, and

railroad giants), the staid financial world (it was still staid when people talked about The Establishment), and political influence discreetly exerted in paneled rooms behind closed doors. Insofar as members of The Establishment served in government, they were to be found primarily in senior posts in the Treasury Department, the State Department, and the Central Intelligence Agency. The Establishment had little to do with the film industry, television, journalism, high technology, rough-and-tumble entrepreneurialism, or rough-and-tumble politics.

As of 1960, the people who had risen to the top had little in common except their success. The world in which David Rockefeller, the biggest name in The Establishment, grew up could not have been more different from the world of the Jewish immigrants and sons of immigrants who built Hollywood and pioneered radio and television broadcasting. The men who were the leaders at CBS News in 1960 included the son of a farmer from Polecat Creek, North Carolina (Edward R. Murrow), the son of a Kansas City dentist (Walter Cronkite) who dropped out of college to become a newspaper reporter, and a Rhodes Scholar (Charles Collingwood).

Dwight Eisenhower's initial cabinet was called "nine millionaires and a plumber." But only two of them had been born into affluent families. The others included two sons of farmers, the son of a bank cashier, the son of a teacher, the daughter of the only lawyer in a tiny Texas town, and the son of parents so poor that he had to drop out of high school to help support them.

The Kennedy administration's early nickname was "Harvard on the Potomac," but his cabinet was no more elite than Eisenhower's had been. Attorney General Robert Kennedy was rich and Harvard-educated, and Treasury Secretary Douglas Dillon was a full-fledged member of The Establishment, but the others consisted of three sons of small farmers (a tenant farmer, in one case), and the sons of a sales manager of a shoe company, the owner of a struggling menswear store, an immigrant factory worker, and an immigrant who made his living peddling produce.[9] A narrow elite existed in 1960 as in 2010, but it was not a group that had broadly shared backgrounds, tastes, preferences, or culture. They were powerful people, not a class.

Americans still rise to power from humble origins. Harry Reid, the Senate majority leader as I write, was born to a miner and a laundress in Searchlight, Nevada, and grew up in poverty. John Boehner, the Speaker of the House, was one of twelve children born to the owner of a working-class bar, and took seven years to finish college while he worked to pay for it. Hilda Solis, President Obama's secretary of labor, was born to immigrant parents who met in citizenship class and worked on factory floors all their lives. It still happens. But along with the continuing individual American success stories is a growing majority of the people who run the institutions of America who do share tastes, preferences, and culture. They increasingly constitute a class.

They are also increasingly isolated. The new isolation involves spatial, economic, educational, cultural, and, to some degree, political isolation. This growing isolation has been accompanied by growing ignorance about the country over which they have so much power.

Such are the propositions to be argued in part 1.

1

Our Kind of People

In which is described the emergence of a new and distinctive
culture among a highly influential segment of American society.

O N SEPTEMBER 29, 1987, ABC premiered an hour-long dramatic series with the cryptic title *thirtysomething*. The opening scene is set in a bar. Not a *Cheers* bar, where Cliff the mailman perches on a bar stool alongside Norm the accountant and Frasier the psychiatrist, but an airy room, perhaps attached to a restaurant, with sunlight streaming in through paned windows onto off-white walls.

The room is crowded with an upscale clientele gathered for drinks after work, nattily uniformed servers moving among them. Two women in their late twenties or early thirties wearing tailored business outfits are seated at a table. A vase with a minimalist arrangement of irises and forsythia is visible in the background. On the table in front of the women are their drinks—both of them wine, served in classic long-stemmed glasses. Nary a peanut or a pretzel is in sight. One of the women is talking about a man she has started dating. He is attractive, funny, good in bed, she says, but there's a problem: He wears polyester shirts. "Am I allowed to have a relationship with someone who wears polyester shirts?" she asks.

She is Hope Murdoch, the female protagonist. She ends up marrying the man who wore the polyester shirts, who is sartorially correct by the time we see him. Hope went to Princeton. She is a writer who put a promising career on hold when she had a baby. He is Michael Steadman, one of two partners in a fledgling advertising agency in Philadelphia. He went to the University of Pennsylvania (the Ivy League one). Hope and Michael live with their seven-month-old daughter in an apartment with high ceilings, old-fashioned woodwork, and etched-glass windows. Grad-school-like bookcases are untidily crammed with books. An Art Deco poster is on the wall. A Native American blanket is draped over the top of the sofa.

In the remaining forty-five minutes, we get dialogue that includes a reference to left brain/right brain differences and an exchange about evolutionary sexual selection that begins, "You've got a bunch of Australopithecines out on the savanna, right?" The Steadmans buy a $278 baby stroller (1987 dollars). Michael shops for new backpacking gear at a high-end outdoors store, probably REI. No one wears suits at the office. Michael's best friend is a professor at Haverford. Hope breast-feeds her baby in a fashionable restaurant. Hope can't find a babysitter. Three of the four candidates she interviews are too stupid to be left with her child and the other is too Teutonic. Hope refuses to spend a night away from the baby ("I have to be available to her all the time"). Michael drives a car so cool that I couldn't identify the make. All this, in just the first episode.

The culture depicted in *thirtysomething* had no precedent, with its characters who were educated at elite schools, who discussed intellectually esoteric subjects, and whose sex lives were emotionally complicated and therefore needed to be talked about. The male leads in *thirtysomething* were on their way up through flair and creativity, not by being organization men. The female leads were conflicted about motherhood and yet obsessively devoted to being state-of-the-art moms. The characters all possessed a sensibility that shuddered equally at Fords and Cadillacs, ranch homes in the suburbs and ponderous mansions, Budweiser and Chivas Regal.

In the years to come, America would get other glimpses of this culture in *Mad About You*, *Ally McBeal*, *Frasier*, and *The West Wing*, among others, but no show ever focused with the same laser intensity on the culture that *thirtysomething* depicted—understandably, because the people who live in that culture do not make up much of the audience for network television series, and those who are the core demographic for network television series are not particularly fond of the culture that *thirtysomething* portrayed. It was the emerging culture of the new upper class.

Let us once again return to November 21, 1963, and try to find its counterpart.

The Baseline

The World of the Upper-Middle Class

Two conditions have to be met before a subculture can spring up within a mainstream culture. First, a sufficient number of people have to possess a distinctive set of tastes and preferences. Second, they have to be able to get together and form a critical mass large enough to shape the local scene. The Amish have managed to do it by achieving local dominance in selected rural areas. In 1963, other kinds of subcultures also existed in parts of the country. Then as now, America's major cities had distinctive urban styles, and so did regions such as Southern California, the Midwest, and the South. But in 1963 there was still no critical mass of the people who would later be called symbolic analysts, the educated class, the creative class, or the cognitive elite.

In the first place, not enough people had college educations to form a critical mass of people with the distinctive tastes and preferences fostered by advanced education. In the American adult population as a whole, just 8 percent had college degrees. Even in neighborhoods filled with managers and professionals, people with college degrees were a minority—just 32 percent of people in those jobs had college degrees in 1963. Only a dozen census tracts in the entire nation had adult populations in which more than 50 percent of the adults had college degrees, and all of them were on or near college campuses.[1]

In the second place, *affluence* in 1963 meant enough money to afford a somewhat higher standard of living than other people, not a markedly different lifestyle. In 1963, the median family income of people working in managerial occupations and the professions was only about $62,000 (2010 dollars, as are all dollar figures from now on). Fewer than 8 percent of American families in 1963 had incomes of $100,000 or more, and fewer than 1 percent had incomes of $200,000 or more.

This compressed income distribution was reflected in the residential landscape. In 1963, great mansions were something most Americans saw in the movies, not in person. Only the richest suburbs of New York, Chicago, and Los Angeles had entire neighborhoods consisting of mansions. The nature of the change since then can be seen by driving around suburban neighborhoods where the affluent of the 1960s lived, such as Chevy Chase, Maryland; Belmont, Massachusetts; or Shaker Heights, Ohio. Most of the housing stock remaining from that era looks nothing like the 15,000- and 20,000-square-foot homes built in affluent suburbs over the last few decades. No reproductions of French châteaux. No tennis courts. No three-story cathedral ceilings. Nor were the prices astronomically higher than the prices of middle-class homes. The average price of all new homes built in 1963 was $129,000.[2] The average price of homes in Chevy Chase offered for sale in the classified ads of the *Washington Post* on the Sunday preceding November 21, 1963, was $272,000, and the most expensive was $567,000. To put it another way, you could live in a typical house in one of the most exclusive neighborhoods in the nation for about twice the average cost of all houses built that year nationwide.

There was a difference between the houses of the upper-middle class and of those who were merely in the middle class. An upper-middle-class home might have four bedrooms instead of two or three, two bathrooms and a powder room instead of one bathroom, and two floors instead of one. It might have a two-car garage, maybe a rec room for the kids and a study for Dad. But it seldom bore any resemblance to a mansion. For an example of elite housing in 1963, download an episode of *Mad Men* that shows the Drapers' suburban home—that's the kind of house that the creative director of a major New York advertising agency might well have lived in.

The members of the upper-middle-class elite did not have many options for distinguishing themselves by the cars they drove. You could find a few Mercedeses and Jaguars in major cities, but even there they were a pain to keep up, because it was so hard to get spare parts and find a mechanic who could service them. Another factor was at work, too: Executives and professionals in 1963, especially outside New York and Los Angeles, were self-conscious about being seen as show-offs. Many people in the upper-middle class who could have afforded them didn't drive Cadillacs because they were too ostentatious.

Another reason that the lifestyle of the upper-middle class was not dramatically different from that of the middle class was that people who were not wealthy could get access to the top of the line for a lot less in 1963 than in 2010, in the same way that you could live in Chevy Chase for not that much more than you would pay for a house anywhere else. It seems paradoxical from the perspective of 2010. Day-to-day life wasn't cheaper then than it is now. In Washington newspaper advertisements for November 1963, gas was cheaper, at the equivalent of $2.16 per gallon, but a dozen eggs were $3.92, a gallon of milk $3.49, chicken $2.06 a pound, and a sirloin steak $6.80 a pound. The best-selling 1963 Chevy Impala cost about $26,600. At Blum's restaurant in San Francisco, not an expensive restaurant, you paid $12.46 for the hot turkey sandwich, $13.17 for the chef's salad, and $5.34 for the hot fudge sundae.[3] Pearson's liquor store in Washington, DC, had started a wine sale two days earlier, advertising its everyday wines at prices from about $6 to $12. All of these prices would have looked familiar, in some cases a little expensive, to a consumer in 2010.

But the most expensive wasn't necessarily out of reach of the middle class. In 1963, one of the most expensive restaurants in Washington was the newly opened Sans Souci, just a block from the White House and a great favorite of the Kennedy administration. The *Washington Post's* restaurant critic had a meal of endive salad, poached turbot, chocolate mousse, and coffee for a total of $44.91. The image of a luxury car to Americans in 1963 was a Cadillac. Its most expensive model, the Eldorado Biarritz, listed at $47,000. That same Pearson's advertisement selling *vin ordinaire* for $6 to $12 offered all the first-growth Bordeaux from the legendary 1959 vintage for about $50 a bottle (yes, I'm still using 2010 dollars).

And so there just wasn't that much difference between the lifestyle of a highly influential attorney or senior executive of a corporation and people who were several rungs down the ladder. Upper-middle-class men in 1963 drank Jack Daniel's instead of Jim Beam in their highballs and drove Buicks (or perhaps Cadillacs) instead of Chevys. Their suits cost more, but they were all off the rack, and they all looked the same anyway. Their wives had more dress clothes and jewelry than wives in the rest of America, and their hairdressers were more expensive. But just about the only thing that amounted to a major day-to-day lifestyle difference between the upper-middle class and the rest of America was the country club, with its golf course, tennis court, and swimming pool that were closed to the hoi polloi. On the other hand, there were lots of municipal golf courses, tennis courts, and swimming pools, too.

The supreme emblem of wealth in 2010 didn't even exist in 1963. The first private jet, the Learjet Model 23, wouldn't be delivered for another year. Private and corporate planes consisted mostly of Cessnas and Beechcrafts, small and cramped. Only a few hundred large private planes existed, and they were all propeller-driven. The owners of even the poshest of them had to recognize that an economy seat on a commercial DC-8 or Boeing 707 provided a smoother, quieter, and much faster ride.

The World of the Rich

Still, a private plane is a major difference in lifestyle, even if it is not a jet, and private planes did exist in 1963. Shall we look for a distinct upper-class culture among the wealthy?

In 1963, *millionaire* was synonymous with not just the affluent but the wealthy. A million dollars was serious money even by today's standards, equivalent to about $7.2 million in 2010 dollars. But there were so few millionaires—fewer than 80,000, amounting to two-tenths of 1 percent of American families.[4] The authentically wealthy in 1963 comprised a microscopic fraction of the population.

Some portion of that small number had no distinct preferences and tastes because they had made their money themselves after growing up in middle-class or working-class families. They hadn't gone to college at all, or they had attended the nearest state college. They might live in duplexes on Park Avenue or mansions on Nob Hill, but they were the nouveaux riches. Some acted like the stereotype of the nouveaux riches. Others continued to identify with their roots and lived well but not ostentatiously.

The subset of old-money millionaires did have something resembling a distinct culture. Besides living in a few select neighborhoods, they were concentrated in Boston, New York, and Philadelphia. They summered or wintered in a few select places such as Bar Harbor, Newport, and Palm Beach. They sent their children to a select set of prep schools and then to the Ivy League or the Seven Sisters. Within their enclaves, old-money America formed a distinct social group.

But besides being a tiny group numerically, there was another reason that they did not form an upper-class culture that made any difference to the rest of the nation. Those who hadn't made the money themselves weren't especially able or influential. Ernest Hemingway was right in his supposed exchange with F. Scott Fitzgerald.[5] In 1963, the main difference between the old-money rich and everybody else was mainly that they had more money.

Take, for example, the woman who was the embodiment of the different world of the rich, Marjorie Merriweather Post. Heiress to the founder of the company that became General Foods, one of the wealthiest women in America, she owned palatial homes in Washington, Palm Beach, and on Long Island, furnished with antiques and objets from the castles of Europe. She summered in the Adirondacks, at Camp Topridge, surrounded by her private 207 acres of forest and lakes. She took her sailing vacations on *Sea Cloud*, the largest privately owned sailing yacht in the world, and flew in her own Vickers Viscount airliner, with a passenger cabin decorated as a living room, probably the largest privately owned aircraft in the world.

Hers was not a life familiar to many other Americans. But, with trivial exceptions, it was different *only* in the things that money could buy. When her guests assembled for dinner, the men wore black tie, a footman stood behind every chair, the silver was sterling, and the china had gold leaf. But the soup was likely to be beef consommé, the main course was almost always roast beef, steak, lamb chops, or broiled chicken, the starch was almost certainly potato, and the vegetable was likely to be broccoli au gratin.[6] The books on the shelves of her libraries were a run-of-the-mill mix of popular fiction and nonfiction. She screened the latest films in the privacy of her homes, but the films her guests watched were standard Hollywood products. The wealthy had only a very few pastimes—polo and foxhunting are the only two I can think of, and they engaged only a fraction of the rich—that were different from pastimes in the rest of America. By and large Mrs. Post, like others among America's wealthy, spent her leisure time doing the same kinds of things that other Americans did. The wealthy just did them in fancier surroundings and had servants. The cultural differences that did exist were ones of manners—more refined from one point of view, snootier from another. The old rich had a different cultural style, but not different cultural content. They were curiosities, not an upper class that mattered to anyone but themselves.

The World of the Intellectuals

There is one other place we might look for a distinct elite culture in November 1963. Much of the *thirtysomething* culture had to do with the tastes and preferences of graduates of elite schools. Also, as I mentioned, there were a handful of census tracts in 1963 where people with college degrees already amounted to more than 50 percent of the adults—all of them near a few college campuses. So let us look for a distinctive culture among the intellectual elite in the one place where it was most likely to have already existed in 1963 if it existed anywhere: Cambridge, Massachusetts.

In 1963, Cambridge, home to Harvard University and the Massachusetts Institute of Technology as well as other colleges, was as close to an intellectual capital as the United States had. The faculties of both of Cambridge's premier institutions were full of academic superstars. MIT's undergraduates were selected for their exceptional mathematical and scientific talents. Harvard College by 1963 was a magnet for the nation's eighteen-year-olds with the highest SAT scores and the most glittering extracurricular accomplishments. The students in Harvard's and MIT's graduate schools were chosen from the cream of the graduating classes of other universities.

Within the campuses of both universities, life was different from ordinary America, amounting to a different culture in some ways—in the nature of the conversations, aesthetic sensibilities, attitudes toward religion, and political ideology, for example. The intellectual life within the universities was rich and intense. No one could attend more than a fraction of the dramatic productions, concerts, and guest lectures by famous public figures that occurred alongside the classes. Yet the culture that surrounded faculty and students outside the physical plants of Harvard and MIT was not much different from anywhere else.

I was at Harvard from September 1961 until June 1965. Harvard Square was different in some ways from Des Moines, Iowa, the city near the town where I grew up. Everybody in Cambridge seemed to drink their coffee with cream, whereas practically no one did in Des Moines. The Brattle Theatre was famous for its Bogart Festivals during reading period and had a little bar in the basement that probably didn't have a counterpart in Des Moines. The kiosk at the Harvard Square MTA station sold foreign magazines that couldn't have been bought in Des Moines. Just off the square was Cardullo's, a specialty shop that sold things like tinned pâté and Cadbury's chocolate, hard to get in Des Moines. There was live folk music at Club 47 on Mount Auburn Street, where Joan Baez had recently gotten her start. There were about ten times more bookstores within a few blocks of Harvard Square than in the entire city of Des Moines.

But that's about it. The coffee shops where you got breakfast in Cambridge and Des Moines were the same, and they were not Au

Bon Pain or European-style coffeehouses. They were places where the waitress poured your Maxwell House coffee from a glass pot into a white mug with one hand while she set down your plate of two eggs, bacon, hash browns, and white toast with the other. The rest of Cambridge's restaurants were the same as those in Des Moines. Within easy walking distance of Harvard Yard, I recall two Chinese restaurants, one spaghetti house (Formica tables, fluorescent lighting, paper cups for your Coke), two favorite sandwich shops (Elsie's and the newly opened Mr. Bartley's Burgers), a beer house that Harvard people dominated (Cronin's), and a working-class bar (Charlie's Kitchen) where students were tolerated but were a minority. The Würsthaus, a noisy German restaurant, was Harvard Square's closest approach to fine dining.

On the block adjacent to Harvard Square were a grocery store, a Woolworth's five-and-dime, and a hardware store. When your parents came to visit, they stayed at the Treadway Inn, a nondescript motel, or at the tired old Commander Hotel up Garden Street. The Harvard Coop sold the same goods as Younkers Department Store in Des Moines, except for the Harvard sweatshirts.

This is not to say that the faculty and students of Harvard and MIT shared the same tastes and preferences as everybody else in Cambridge. Rather, there weren't enough of them to impose their will. They were a majority in only a few neighborhoods. A few years earlier, in the 1960 census, just 18 percent of the adults in Cambridge had college degrees and Cambridge's median income was just $43,641. In 1963, the Harvard Square area had not yet begun to draw in young professionals who decided that they preferred Cambridge to the suburbs. The faculty and students of Harvard and MIT had not yet been reinforced by an influx of employees of high-tech industries and research organizations. Once you subtracted all the students, faculty, and university administrators living in Cambridge in 1963, most of the rest of Cambridge was a working-class and lower-middle-class community. The latent propensity to create a different culture existed, but the intellectuals of Harvard Square didn't have the critical mass to reshape the community in the ways that their tastes and preferences would reshape it when a critical mass materialized.[7]

The New-Upper-Class Culture

Over the next few decades, they got that critical mass, and the result was becoming visible by the late 1980s, when *thirtysomething* began. By the end of the 1990s, the new culture had fully blossomed.

Its mise-en-scène is captured in *Bobos in Paradise* by David Brooks's description of the transformation of Wayne, Pennsylvania, where he had attended high school in the late 1970s. Wayne is one of Philadelphia's famous Main Line communities. When Brooks had lived there, the business district had been an unremarkable place with a few restaurants with names like L'Auberge, a few tasteful clothing stores with names like the Paisley Shop, and a small assortment of pharmacies, grocery stores, and gas stations that tended to the day-to-day needs of the affluent residents of Wayne. By the time Brooks was writing in the late 1990s, all that had changed.

The town, once an espresso desert, now has six gourmet coffeehouses. . . . Café Procopio is the one across from the train station, where handsome middle-aged couples come on Sunday morning, swapping newspaper sections and comparing notes across the table on their kids' college admissions prospects. . . . A fabulous independent bookstore named the Reader's Forum has moved into town where the old drugstore used to be. . . . The artsy set can now go to a Made by You—one of those places where you pay six times more to decorate your own mugs and dishes than it would cost to buy flatware that other people have decorated—and to Studio B, a gift emporium that hosts creative birthday parties to ensure that self-esteeming kids become even more self-esteeming. . . . Sweet Daddy's sells gourmet jelly beans, spiced apple cider sorbet, and gelato in such flavors as Zuppa Inglese. . . . The Great Harvest Bread Company has opened up a franchise in town, one of those gourmet bread stores where they sell apricot almond or spinach feta loaf for $4.75 a pop. . . . If you ask them to slice the bread in the store, they look at you compassionately as one who has not yet risen to the higher

realm of bread consciousness. . . . To the west of town there is a
Zany Brainy, one of those toy stores that pretends to be an educational institution. It sells lifelike figurines of endangered ani-
mals, and it's driven the old Wayne Toytown, which carried toys
that didn't improve developmental skills, out of business.[8]

My ellipses have skipped over a lot more, but you get the idea—we're
looking at the community where Hope and Michael Steadman of *thirtysomething* moved when they reached their forties.

The new-upper-class culture is different from mainstream American culture in all sorts of ways. Some are differences in lifestyle that
individually are harmless but that cumulatively produce cultural separation between the new upper class and mainstream America. Still
others involve differences that consist of good things happening to
the cognitive elite that are not open to the rest of America.

Lifestyle Choices Tending Toward Cultural Separation

If you want to get a quick sense of just how visibly different the new
upper class is from mainstream America, attend parents' night at an
elementary school in a zip code with a median income at around the
national average and then attend parents' night at an elite private elementary school.

It starts in the parking lot. At the ordinary school, about half of the
cars will be American brands; at the elite private school, the over-
whelming majority will be foreign.[9] As you go inside and begin to
mingle, notice the ages of the parents. In the mainstream school, the
mothers of the children are mostly in their late twenties to mid-
thirties. In the elite school, you may see no mothers at all who are in
their twenties. Many are in their forties. With the men, the difference
is even greater, with even more of them in their forties and some in
their fifties. Or older.

Another visible difference is weight. In the mainstream school,
two-thirds of the parents are overweight and about a third of them
are obese (proportions that are consistent with the national distribution from the 2009 survey of obesity by the National Center for

Health Statistics).[10] At the elite private school, the parents are, on average, a lot thinner, and obesity is rare, because the new upper class pays a lot of attention to health and fitness. They may work out at their health clubs and be attractively lean or run marathons and look emaciated. They may do yoga for an hour a day or mountain bike on the weekends and swim on weekdays, but one way or another, they are fat much less often than a random assortment of Americans.

The Nature of the Evidence

As I describe these differences, most of the evidence must be qualitative. For the measures that are covered in the standard government surveys, the samples are not large enough to zero in on the top few centiles of the socioeconomic distribution. Much of the specialized quantitative information I need about the new elite's tastes and preferences exists, but I cannot get hold of it. Everybody who sells advertising has detailed data on the demographics of consumer preferences for BMWs versus Ford pickup trucks or Bud Lite versus Ketel One, but such data are proprietary. The best I can do is use the DDB Life Style data that were provided to Robert Putnam in the research for *Bowling Alone* and are now available to other scholars.[11] That database does not permit us to isolate the top few centiles—the highest income code is $100,000—but it does give a quantitative measure of the relationship between income, education, and a wide variety of tastes and preferences.

I also continue to draw heavily on the work of David Brooks and Richard Florida. Both *Bobos in Paradise* and *The Rise of the Creative Class,* along with their other books, have extensive documentation, some quantitative and some qualitative, for the generalizations they draw about the tastes and preferences of their Bobos and Creative Class, respectively, and my endnotes contain references to their discussions. My generalizations are consistent with theirs.

There is one other way to verify or reject the account you are about to read: your own experience. The people who read a book on American socioeconomic classes are self-selected for certain

traits that put most of you in a position to have observed the new
upper class at close hand. Judge for yourself whether my generalizations correspond to your experience.

The members of the new upper class are healthy in other ways.
They know their cholesterol count and often their percentage of body
fat. They monitor their diets, eating lots of whole grains, green vege-
tables, and olive oil, while limiting intake of red meat, processed
foods, and butter. Whatever the latest rage in vitamin supplements
may be, they know about it. Vegetarian and vegan restaurants find
their best markets in upper-class shopping enclaves. Some members
of the new upper class look upon fast food as an abomination and
never, ever take their children to McDonald's. For others, a Big Mac
or Popeyes fried chicken is an occasional guilty pleasure, but hardly
anyone in the new upper class approaches the about-once-a-week average of the rest of the population.[12]

When it comes to alcohol, the new upper class usually drinks wine
or boutique beers. Many of them are eager to hold forth at length on
the minutiae of either beverage, but they imbibe moderately. As for
smoking, do not try to light up when you visit an upper-class home
unless you want to become an instant social pariah. According to the
Centers for Disease Control, about a third of American adults still
smoke, but you wouldn't know it if you hang out with the new upper
class.[13]

In mainstream America, the statistics about the percentage of people who read a newspaper every day are depressingly low.[14] In contrast, the members of the new upper class are extremely well informed
about politics and current events of all sorts, and they tap into some
of the same sources wherever they may live throughout the nation.
Liberal members of the new upper class typically check the *New York
Times* website every day, while conservative members of the new
upper class check the *Wall Street Journal* every day—and large numbers on each side check the other side's paper of record as well. Magazines you might find on the coffee table of a new-upper-class home
include the *New Yorker* and the *Economist*, along with the occasional
Rolling Stone, *Fine Gardening*, and the *New York Review of Books*.

The new upper class is selective in its radio listening. Those who commute by car and are liberals probably listen to National Public Radio's *Morning Edition* on the way into work and *All Things Considered* on the way home—and a fair number of moderate and conservative members of the new upper class listen as well. They either listen to or know about Garrison Keillor—if you are in a gathering of the new upper class, you can use the phrase "all the children are above average" and be confident that almost everybody recognizes the allusion. Few members of the new upper class except political junkies listen to the genre that has come to dominate radio ratings, talk radio. The one acceptable exception is *Car Talk*.

Members of the new upper class don't watch much television.[15] If they watch television news, it is likely to be the PBS *NewsHour*. Many don't use the television for entertainment except to watch films. Others have a few series that they watch faithfully—in recent years, perhaps *House* or *Mad Men*. Satirical animated shows such as *The Simpsons* and *South Park* have some loyal followers among the new upper class. But these favorites are unlikely to account for more than half a dozen hours of viewing a week. Meanwhile, the average American watches about thirty-five hours of television per week.[16] Much of that viewing in mainstream America consists of material that is invisible to most of the new upper class—game shows, soap operas, music videos, home shopping, and hit series that members of the new upper class have never watched even once.

The new upper class does not often frequent bars with pool tables in them, bars that allow smoking, or bars with many wide screens showing professional sports. Males in the new upper class don't spend a lot of time watching professional sports on television even at home—maybe tennis if they play tennis themselves, or golf if they golf themselves, and maybe some of the games of their favorite baseball or football team. But sitting down in front of the TV at noon on Saturday and Sunday and watching sports for the rest of the afternoon is uncommon.

The new upper class and mainstream America don't take the same kind of vacations. Money comes into play here, but the vacations are also different in kind. For elite thirtysomethings who have not yet had children, the vacation might consist of backpacking into a remote lake in British Columbia or diving off Belize, whereas their age contemporaries in the working class and middle class already have children and are driving them to Disney World. Fortysomethings of the new upper class are likely to be attracted to a barge trip through Bordeaux or chartering a sailboat to cruise the Maine coast, not a trip to Las Vegas. New-upper-class and mainstream fiftysomethings might both choose to go on a cruise, but the new upper class would never consider booking a passage on one of the big liners with two thousand passengers. They take their cruise on a small all-suite ship accommodating just a hundred passengers, and it's going to the Galápagos.

For mainstream America, a trip to Europe, Asia, or South America is a big deal—something that many never do even once. For the new upper class, foreign vacations are a normal part of their lives. But the ties of the new upper class to the rest of the world do not depend on vacations. For many, foreign travel is a routine part of their working lives. Senior executives, consultants, and international attorneys are constantly on the move, visiting foreign clients and subsidiaries. Conferences and guest lectures may take the star academic overseas several times a year. Members of the new upper class in every occupational domain are likely to have coworkers and colleagues from around the world with whom they interact regularly, and professional relationships that often merge with personal friendships. Many in the intellectual wing of the new upper class feel more comfortable around their intellectual colleagues from other countries than they do with Americans who aren't intellectuals.

Cultural Separation in Family Life

A less visible but more fundamental kind of cultural separation involves the raising of children. In one sense, there is no separation. Put two mothers with children in strollers next to each other on a park bench, and they will probably be deep in conversation about naps and feeding schedules within moments, whatever their differences in age, race, or socioeconomic class. But Hope Steadman's relentless mothering in *thirtysomething* reflected a real phenomenon.

The children of the new upper class are the object of intense planning from the moment the woman learns she is pregnant. She sets about researching her choice of obstetrician immediately (if she hasn't already done it in anticipation of the pregnancy), and her requirements are stringent. She does not drink alcohol or allow herself to be exposed even to secondhand smoke during her pregnancy. She makes sure her nutritional intake exactly mirrors the optimal diet and takes classes (along with her husband) to prepare for a natural childbirth— a C-section is a last resort. She gains no more and no less than the prescribed weight during her pregnancy. She breast-feeds her newborn, usually to the complete exclusion of formula, and tracks the infant's growth with the appropriate length and weight charts continually.[17] The infant is bombarded with intellectual stimulation from the moment of birth, and sometimes from the moment that it is known that conception has occurred. The mobile over the infant's crib and the toys with which he is provided are designed to induce every possible bit of neural growth within the child's cerebral cortex.

By the time the child is a toddler, some new-upper-class mothers return to their careers, turning over daytime child care to a nanny (sometimes selected in part for the second language that the parents think the child should learn) or to a high-end preschool during the day. But many new-upper-class mothers put their careers on hold while the children are young, and sometimes until the children leave for college. The term *soccer mom* came into being at about the time that the post-1970s mothers in the upper-middle class had children in elementary school.

The childbearing and child-rearing practices of the new upper class are admirable in many ways. It would be wonderful if every pregnant woman were as meticulous about taking care of herself and the unborn child as new-upper-class women are. Some features of child rearing are universally accepted to be important for the development of children—basics such as open affection, verbal interaction with infants and toddlers, and consistent discipline. On these and other good parenting practices, social scientists find that, as groups, parents in the upper-middle class come out well ahead of parents in the middle and working classes.[18]

The downside is that new-upper-class parents tend to overdo it. The children in elite families sometimes have schedules so full of ballet classes, swimming lessons, special tutoring, and visits to the therapist that they have no time to be children. It is not urban legend, but documented fact, that some parents send their children to test-preparation schools for the entrance test to exclusive preschools.[19] The lengths to which some parents will go to maximize their child's chance to get into a prestigious college are apparently without limit. And the hovering behavior of these parents once the child has gone to college is so common that it has led to a phrase for them—"helicopter parents"—that is in common use among the administrators of America's universities. Considerable social science research has also found that elite parents' constant praise of their children can backfire, because it so often consists of telling children how smart they are, not of praising children for things they actually do. As a result, many children become protective of their image of being smart and are reluctant to take chances that might damage that image.[20]

Other mothers love their children just as much as upper-class mothers do, but their children experience different upbringings, with cultural implications in the long term. One major reason will be discussed in chapter 8: A much larger proportion of working-class than upper-middle-class children are raised in broken homes or never-formed homes. All by itself, that difference has pervasive implications for the child's socialization and for different social norms across classes.

Another source of cultural separation, mentioned earlier, is the advanced age at which women in the new upper class tend to have their babies. To be specific: In 2006, the mean age at first birth among all American women with fewer than sixteen years of education was 23.0. The mean age for women with sixteen years of education was 29.5. The mean for women with seventeen or more years of education was 31.1. These differences in age at first birth cut many ways. A mother in her thirties is more mature than a mother in her twenties, and maturity is statistically associated with better child-rearing practices. But the issue we're discussing now is cultural separation. The Little League functions differently (and has a different chance of functioning at all) when dads are thirtyish versus when dads are fifty-ish. The generation gap between a mother and her thirteen-year-old daughter is different when the mother is in her mid-thirties and when the mother is approaching fifty.

Perhaps the most general cultural difference—one that can be bad or good depending on individual cases—is that mainstream America is a lot more relaxed than the new upper class about their children. I don't mean that other American parents care less, but that, as a group, they are less inclined than upper-class parents to obsess about how smart their baby is, how to make the baby smarter, where the baby should go to preschool, and where the baby should go to law school. They buy the car seat that's on sale at Walmart instead of spending hours searching the web for the seat with the best test results in simulated head-on collisions. When their children get into trouble at school, they are less determined than upper-class parents to come up with reasons why it's the teacher's fault, not their child's.

One of the major preoccupations of upper-class parents during their children's teenage years, the college admissions process, is almost entirely absent in mainstream America. Only a small proportion of colleges in the United States are hard to get into. Everywhere else, all you have to do is apply and attach a halfway decent high school transcript and ACT or SAT score. Outside elite circles, there may be mild angst about whether children get into their first choice in the state university system, but no more than that. Most mainstream American parents lose no sleep whatsoever because their child's college is not in the top ten in the *U.S. News & World Report* rankings.[21]

Cultural Separation at Work

We have now come to a domain in which the life of much of the new upper class has changed fundamentally while the life of much of mainstream America has not. These changes are not restricted to the new upper class, applying more broadly to most people who work in managerial jobs and the professions. But they apply most lavishly to the people who have gotten farthest up the ladder.

Some lucky people in those occupations no longer have a set time to report to work and a specific place they have to be. They work out of their homes, using a computer, and if they feel like taking the laptop to the beach, there's nothing to stop them. For others, the constraints have been loosened. They work on a flextime arrangement, or combine some work at the office with some work at home.

For those who work at the office, that office has been reinvented.[22] The office of 1963, with desks for the underlings in the middle and private offices for the senior executives lining the outer walls, each with a secretary sitting outside the door, has nearly disappeared. Corporate offices around the country—not just the work spaces at trendy new companies like Google, but at Procter & Gamble, too—have been reorganized and rebuilt on principles that are supposed to maximize creative interaction. Sometimes everyone is in the same room, from the CEO on down, working without private offices. Sometimes the office is organized into teams that interact—*ensemble individualism* is one of the terms of art for this kind of structure. The feel of the physical work space is different from that of the traditional office, emphasizing high ceilings, availability of outside views to everyone (the boss no longer monopolizes the view with a corner office), abundant and well-appointed hangout spaces, bold colors, exposed structural elements, indirect lighting, and lots of artwork.[23]

The hierarchy and status signals of the traditional office have been stripped, or at least reduced, in the offices where the new upper class works. In many places, everyone is on a first-name basis. Dress codes have been relaxed or abandoned altogether. Instead of looking for organization men, corporations pride themselves on seeking out the free spirit and the eccentric, with the proviso that the free-spirited and eccentric also be really talented. If you are really talented, and if your job is one where creativity is essential, you've got it made. You are at the center of senior management's concern. What might make you happier? What support can be lavished upon you to free up your creativity? Above all, nothing must be done to cramp your style.

None of this means that the lucky people of the new upper class who work in these occupations are lolling about. The graduates of the top law schools who get those coveted jobs at the big New York and Washington law firms may get a starting salary in six figures, but they are also expected to put in sixty-plus hours every week. At one of the leading quant hedge funds, there's a reason that management maintains a room containing nothing but racks filled with every variety of candy, free for the taking: The firm's genius mathematicians tend to be around at all hours, needing a sugar high to keep going. The genius programmers at Apple and Google and Microsoft are notorious for pulling all-nighters when a deadline looms. But the elites who work those long hours live in a world where work has more of the characteristics of fun than ever before.

For the 82 percent of American adults who are not in a managerial position or in the professions, that revolution which is so celebrated in accounts of the transformed workplace has had hardly any effect on their lives.

Some of them are support staff in the offices where the new upper class work, and they get the advantages of being in a physical space that is more attractive and functional than it was a few decades ago. But support staff are still expected to be on the premises during working hours. Maybe they can work out a flextime arrangement, but beyond that their jobs are conducted very much as they always have been.

Other workplaces in America haven't changed even that much. The technological changes in hospitals have been sweeping, but the nurses, dietitians, respiratory therapists, and orderlies who work there do their jobs much as they always have, subject to the same constraints of hours and place that those jobs have always imposed (and the same is true, I should add, of physicians). The schools where K–12 teachers work have more audiovisual and computer equipment than they used to, but the teachers still usually sit at desks in front of classrooms of students and try to get them to absorb the day's material, and they have to be at the school from the time it opens until the time it closes. Police do the same things they've always done, with more help from the computer. Shop owners, plumbing contractors, insurance agents, and other people running their own small businesses are subject to the same constraints and routines that their occupations have always required. Save for their computers, the workplace revolution has largely skipped them.

In blue-collar occupations, some of the tools have changed. If you drive a delivery truck for FedEx, you use a handheld device that connects with a sophisticated computer tracking system that would have been unimaginable in 1963. But the structure of the world of work is usually the same. If you work in the produce department of Safeway, install drywall, cook in a restaurant, repair cars, or mine coal, you have a shift to work. There is a time to punch in and a time to punch out, and a physical location where you are to be during that time. The surroundings of the job are much as they ever have been. A construction site is still a construction site, an oil rig is still an oil rig, a farm is still a farm, a loading dock is still a loading dock. Some assembly lines have changed so that they are not quite as mind-numbingly boring as they used to be, but that has happened only in some industries, and American assembly lines have been disappearing anyway as manufacturing has moved overseas.

What About Politics?

I have given only the barest outline of the tribal customs and rites of the new upper class. I spent a paragraph on new-upper-class vacations, while David Brooks devotes eight pages of *Bobos in Paradise* to them. I didn't even mention sex; Brooks has another eight pages about that. I didn't mention religion; see all thirty-seven pages of his chapter 6. I gave a few pages to changes in the world of work; Richard Florida devotes the better part of an entire book to them. But the lacuna that is likely to be at the top of your mind is politics. The new upper class tends to be liberal, right?

There's no getting around it: At least for the narrow elite, every way of answering that question produces a yes. In chapter 3, I give politics a longer discussion, because it relates to the isolation of the new upper class. But that reality need not obscure another one: Most of the description of the elite culture in this chapter cuts across ideological lines. The details can be different. As a group, elite liberals are more exercised about being green than are elite conservatives. The dinner party given by a conservative hostess of the new upper class is more likely to feature red meat as the entrée than a dinner party given by a liberal one. The children of elite conservatives probably face a higher risk of a spanking for misbehavior than the children of elite liberals. But these differences are swamped by the ways in which people occupying the elite positions in America have adopted similar norms and mores. The essence of the culture of the new upper class is remarkably consistent across the political spectrum.

2

The Foundations of the
New Upper Class

*In which are described the conditions that led to the emergence of
the new upper class.*

FOUR DEVELOPMENTS TOOK us from a set of people who ran
the nation but were culturally diverse to a new upper class that
increasingly lives in a world of its own. The culprits are the
increasing market value of brains, wealth, the college sorting machine,
and homogamy.

At the Bottom of It All:
The Increasing Market Value of Brains

In the early 1990s, Bill Gates was asked what competitor worried him
the most. Goldman Sachs, Gates answered. He explained: "Software
is an IQ business. Microsoft must win the IQ war, or we won't have a
future. I don't worry about Lotus or IBM, because the smartest guys
would rather come to work for Microsoft. Our competitors for IQ are
investment banks such as Goldman Sachs and Morgan Stanley."[1]
Gates's comment reflected a reality that has driven the formation of
the new upper class: Over the last century, brains became much more

valuable in the marketplace. The evidence for that statement took two long chapters to present in *The Bell Curve*, but the reasons why it happened are not mysterious.[2]

The Effect of Cognitive Ability on Vocational Success

Cognitive ability is only one of many factors that explain why some people rise to the top of their professions. Assets such as industriousness, motivation, self-discipline, and interpersonal skills play crucial roles. But that truth is easily misinterpreted to mean that cognitive ability is unimportant.

The analogy originated by sociologist Steven Goldberg helps keep things in perspective: For the professions, creative work, and the management of large and complex organizations, cognitive ability plays the same role in determining success that weight plays in determining the success of offensive tackles in the National Football League. The heaviest tackle is not necessarily the best. In fact, the correlation between weight and performance among NFL offensive tackles is probably quite small. But to have a chance of getting the job, you had better weigh at least 300 pounds.[3] Similarly, the correlation of IQ scores with performance among those people who are attorneys, screenwriters, and biochemists is modest. But to be a top attorney, screenwriter, or biochemist, you have to be very smart in the ways that IQ tests measure.

First, the higher-tech the economy, the more it relies on people who can improve and exploit the technology, which creates many openings for people whose main asset is their exceptional cognitive ability. What was someone with exceptional mathematical ability worth on the job market a hundred years ago if he did not have interpersonal skills or common sense? Not much. The private sector had only a few jobs such as actuary that might make him worth hiring. His best chance was to go into academia and try to become a professor of mathematics. His options were not much wider in 1960. What is a person with the same skill set worth today? If he is a wizard programmer, as people with exceptional mathematical ability tend to be, he is worth six figures to Microsoft or Google. If he is a fine pure mathematician, some quant funds can realistically offer him the prospect of great wealth.

Second, the more complex business decisions become, the more businesses rely on people who can navigate through labyrinths that may or may not call upon common sense, but certainly require advanced cognitive ability. Consider the prospects for a lawyer. A hundred years ago, lawyers mostly practiced law for individual clients and made the amounts of money that individuals could afford to pay. Those who were corporate lawyers made corporate salaries—good, but not the stuff of dreams. As the size of business deals grew and regulatory law became more complex, the need for lawyers who never see the inside of a courtroom increased. Today, if a first-rate attorney can add 10 percent to the probability of getting a favorable decision on a regulatory ruling worth hundreds of millions of dollars, he is worth his many-hundreds-of-dollars-per-hour rate. If he can work out the multidimensional issues that enable the merger of two large corporations, he may be worth a commission of millions of dollars. The same thing happened in the financial industry, as technology has made possible new and complex—but also fabulously profitable— financial instruments.

Third, the bigger the stakes, the greater the value of marginal increments in skills. In 1960, the corporation ranked 100 on the Fortune 500 had sales of $3.2 billion.[4] In 2010, the 100th-ranked corporation had sales of $24.5 billion—almost an eightfold increase in constant dollars. That kind of supersizing in the corporate world occurred across the range—the corporation ranked 500 in 2010 was about eight times larger than the 500th-ranked corporation in 1960. The dollar value of a manager who could increase his division's profitability by 10 percent instead of 5 percent escalated accordingly.

To some degree, the demands on the cognitive skills of managers also grew over that half century because of the increasing complexity of choices that often accompanies huge size. But that's not the main point. Even if the skills required of the manager of a corporate division in 1960 and 2010 were the same, and raw brainpower did *not* play a more important role, cognitive ability is nonetheless an all-purpose tool. Given the same interpersonal skills, energy, and common sense, the manager with higher cognitive ability has an edge in increasing profitability by 10 percent instead of 5 percent—and that, combined with the larger stakes, also made brains worth more in the marketplace.

The Enabler: Wealth

Given that backdrop, it is no surprise that the people working in managerial occupations and the professions made a lot more money in 2010 than they had made in 1960, and that their growing wealth enabled the most successful of them, the members of the new upper class, to isolate themselves from the rest of America in ways that they formerly couldn't afford to do. Figure 2.1 shows the median income of families at various points on the income distribution, starting with those at the 25th centile and going all the way up to the 99th centile. The data are based on American families of all races and ages.

FIGURE 2.1.   **AMERICAN FAMILY INCOME DISTRIBUTION**

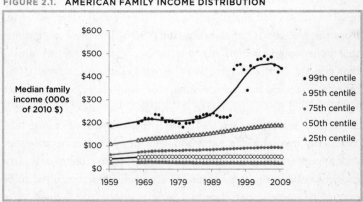

Source: Integrated Public Use Microdata Series (IPUMS). Unit of analysis is the family. The initial year is 1959 because the income variables in a decennial census or March Current Population Survey (CPS) interview refer to the preceding calendar year.

Shelves of books and academic articles have been written about the material in figure 2.1. Narratives can be told for every level. Real income for the bottom quartile of American families fell after 1970. The poor didn't actually get poorer—the growth of in-kind benefits and earned-income tax credits more than made up the drop in pretax cash income—but they didn't improve their position much either.[5] Real family income for families in the middle was flat. Just about all of the benefits of economic growth from 1970 to 2010 went to people in the upper half of the income distribution.

Centiles and Percentiles

Centile means the same thing as *percentile*. But in a text that often refers to percentages and percentage changes, using *centile* makes for clearer sentences.

The increase was most dramatic at the very top of the distribution. From 1960 through the early 1990s, the top centile of American families had incomes that began at around $200,000. Then in 1994–95, the bottom end of the top centile careened up from $233,000 to $433,000. Whether the change happened within that single year is open to debate—an analysis using IRS data shows the leap occurring from the late 1980s through the late 1990s—but there is no doubt that a phenomenal growth in top incomes occurred sometime during that period.[6] In the March 2010 Current Population Survey (CPS), reflecting income data for calendar year 2009, the 95th centile for working-aged Americans began at $199,000 and the 99th centile at $441,000. And remember: $441,000 is the *bottom* of the top centile.

The top five centiles are important for our purposes because they contain almost all of the new upper class. It is possible to draw that conclusion because of the nature of accomplishment required to be part of the new upper class as I have operationally defined it. In twenty-first-century American society, meeting that definition also means that you almost certainly have a family income that puts you into the top five centiles of family income ($199,000-plus).

For many of the positions that qualify you for the new upper class, $199,000 is far below the average. If you are a partner in a major law firm or the president of an important university or foundation, you are likely to be making several hundred thousand dollars a year. If you are the CEO of a major corporation, you are making millions per year in total compensation.

Even if you are in a position that doesn't allow you to become truly wealthy, your family's income was almost surely close to the top five centiles of income, and often deep into them. As of 2010 a cabinet officer made $191,300, a Supreme Court justice made $208,100, and the Speaker of the House made $217,400. Ordinary members of Congress made $169,300, and deputy secretaries and heads of major agencies made $172,200. And that's just the salary for the people holding those jobs, not their family's total income. Many of them have spouses who bring in large salaries as well. Furthermore, people often come to those positions after making a lot of money in their previous careers, and the value of the perks of high government office rival those of CEOs.

Other "poor" members of the new upper class are journalists, academics, and public intellectuals in general. David Brooks calls their plight *status-income disequilibrium*, a psychological condition that occurs, for example, when an eminent Columbia faculty member goes home after giving his speech at the Plaza Hotel to admiring Wall Street executives. While his audience is dispersing in their limos to their duplex cooperatives on the Upper East Side, he catches a cab home to his cramped apartment near the Columbia campus, his standing ovation still ringing in his ears, only to be told by his wife that the shower drain is clogged and he must take care of it before the children get up for school the next morning.[7] Brooks speaks to a disorienting reality that many well-known faculty members, journalists, and guests on the Sunday news shows can relate to. Their status is a lot higher than their income. But these same people have family incomes of more than $150,000 a year even if there's just one income (the big names make at least that much at major universities, newspapers, and think tanks). Even if they don't write best sellers, they often supplement their salaries with book advances and speaking engagements. If the spouse is also providing an income, their income can easily reach the top centile. Those who suffer from status-income disequilibrium feel strapped for money because taxes take a big chunk of their income, and most of them live in New York or Washington, where they have to spend much of the rest on housing, child care, and tuition for private schools. But they can feel poor only because their professions so often throw them in contact with the truly rich. With the rarest exceptions, even the poorest members of the new upper class are in the top few centiles of the American income distribution.

These observations are borne out by the incomes reported in the CPS. I have used the top 5 percent of people in managerial occupations and the professions as a working definition of the new upper class. In 2009, the cutoff for the 95th centile of family income for people working in those occupations was $287,000.

Wealth enabled the development of an isolated new upper class. It did so first by enabling the new upper class to become spatially isolated. The price of houses in a neighborhood screens the people who can live there. Even the Columbia professor, poor as he feels and cramped though his apartment may be, is living in a neighborhood priced so that only people in the top few centiles of income can afford to live there. The higher the price that a new-upper-class couple can pay, the more precisely they can define the kind of neighborhood in which they live. The higher the price that they can pay, the more privacy they can buy—in the form of a concierge and security guards in the lobby of their urban apartment building, a literally gated community, or a high-end suburb insulated from the rabble by distance.

Wealth also enabled the development of a distinctive lifestyle among the new upper class. Markets supply demand, and if there is a demand for the goods and services that underpin an alternative lifestyle, the market will provide those goods and services.

The Mechanism: The College Sorting Machine

The initial mechanism whereby people with distinctive tastes and preferences are brought together is the college sorting machine.

Exceptions like Bill Gates and Steve Jobs notwithstanding, almost everyone in the new upper class has finished college. But the simple possession of a bachelor's degree does not come close to capturing the complicated relationship between education and the nature of the new upper class. The key to understanding why the new upper class has formed and why it has such a distinctive culture is the interaction between high cognitive ability and education in general, and more specifically the interaction of high cognitive ability and elite colleges.

Cognitive Ability as a Natural Incentive for Segregation

The human impulse behind the isolation of the new upper class is as basic as impulses get: People like to be around other people who understand them and to whom they can talk. Cognitive segregation was bound to start developing as soon as unusually smart people began to have the opportunity to hang out with other unusually smart people.

The yearning for that kind of opportunity starts young. To have exceptional cognitive ability isolates a young person as no other ability does. The teenager with exceptional athletic ability who becomes the star quarterback has lots of people who are eager to be his friends even if he is shy or socially awkward. The teenager with exceptional interpersonal ability is one of the most well-liked kids in school— that's what exceptional interpersonal ability does for you. But the math star who possesses only average interpersonal ability is seen as an oddball. He has just one or two classmates he can talk to about what he's good at, if he's lucky, and he may have no one at all. The teenage girl with average interpersonal ability and exceptional verbal ability has the same problem. If she has fallen in love with the poetry of T. S. Eliot, she is hard-pressed to find anyone else who will understand why. Her classmates already don't get her jokes and are put off by her vocabulary. She knows that if she were to try to talk about *Ash Wednesday*, she would first get blank stares and then be teased unmercifully.

When cognitively talented children are forced to deal with that situation, they usually find ways to cope. They study topology or read *Ash Wednesday* in the privacy of their bedrooms. The boy learns to talk about sports with the other guys and the girl learns not to use vocabulary that will attract ridicule. Making that effort often produces surprising results, as the cognitively gifted children realize that the other kids are smarter and more interesting than they had thought. In all cases, the need to make the effort tends to encourage flexibility, maturity, and resilience among cognitively talented youth.

Still, it amounts to one of those things that people are glad they have done, but did only because they had to. Either they figure out a way to fit in or else they are lonely (see Sinclair Lewis's *Main Street* for the revenge of the lonely small-town smart boy). Those same young people would have jumped at the opportunity to be around other people like themselves. Over the last half century, the opportunities to do so opened up. The expansion of college education in general played the single most important role in that process. But another development was almost as important.

Cognitive Stratification Among Colleges

Cognitive stratification among colleges occurred extraordinarily fast.[8] As of 1950, elite colleges did not have exceptionally talented student bodies. By 1960, they did.

Before World War II, most of the freshmen in an elite college were drawn from the region's socioeconomic elite—from the Northeast for the Ivy League, the West Coast for Stanford and USC, and the South for Duke and Vanderbilt. Some of those students were talented, but many were academically pedestrian. In a study done in 1926, the average IQ of students at the most prestigious schools in the country, including Columbia, Harvard, Princeton, and Yale, was 117, barely above the 115 that has been the average of all college graduates, and denoting the 88th centile of cognitive ability.[9] That same year, the Carnegie Foundation conducted a study of all of Pennsylvania's colleges and universities, using the same measure of IQ that produced the 117 mean for the high-prestige schools. In Pennsylvania alone, ten colleges had freshman classes with mean IQs that put them at the 75th to 90th centiles, making those classes cognitively indistinguishable from those of the elite schools.

That situation persisted through the 1930s and 1940s. As late as

1952, the mean SAT verbal score (now known as the Critical Reading score) of incoming Harvard freshmen was just 583, above the national mean but nothing to write home about.[10] Then came the revolution. By 1960, the average SAT verbal score among incoming Harvard freshmen had jumped to 678. The progenitors of the revolution were aware of how momentous the shift had been. William J. Bender, Harvard's dean of admissions, summed up the preceding eight years. "The figures," he wrote, "report the greatest change in Harvard admissions, and thus in the Harvard student body, in a short time—two college generations—in our recorded history."[11] The average Harvard freshman in 1952 would have placed in the bottom 10 percent of the incoming class by 1960.

The same thing happened throughout the college system, as shown in figure 2.2. The colleges are representative of the ones clustered at various SAT verbal scores. The backdrop is the distribution of SAT scores in 1960 if all eighteen-year-olds had taken the test.

FIGURE 2.2.   **COGNITIVE STRATIFICATION AMONG COLLEGES AS OF 1960**

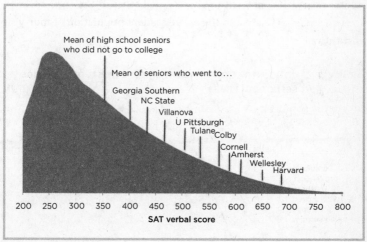

Sources: Siebel, 1962; College Entrance Examination Board, 1961. Adapted from Herrnstein and Murray, 1994.

Georgia Southern is representative of a school in the second tier of a state university system, while North Carolina State is typical of a large first-tier university as of 1960. Then come successively more selective private schools. But even among them, the differences in the mean verbal score of the incoming freshmen were substantial, with Harvard anchoring the high end.

The stratification became still more extreme during the 1960s. In 1961, 25 percent of Yale's entering class still had SAT verbal scores under 600. Just five years later, that figure had dwindled to 9 percent, while the proportion of incoming students with SAT verbal scores from 700 to 800 had increased from 29 to 52 percent.[12]

The situation at the end of the twentieth century may be conveyed through the work of Roger Geiger, who studied how the students in the top five centiles of test scores (1400-plus on the SAT or 30-plus on the ACT) were distributed among the nation's universities. Using data for 1997, he calculated the approximate numbers of such students who attended the top 35 public universities, the top 35 private universities, and 35 highly selective small colleges in 1997. Figure 2.3 shows the cumulative percentage of students with these high scores who were soaked up by just 105 colleges. I have extended the horizontal axis to 100 percent to give a visual sense of the concentration of such students relative to the entire student population of four-year institutions.

FIGURE 2.3.   CONCENTRATION OF TOP HIGH SCHOOL STUDENTS IN 105
SELECT COLLEGES

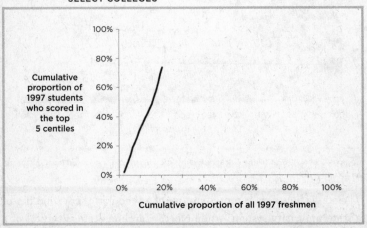

Source: Geiger, 2002, tables 3.2, 3.3, 3.4.

Together, just 10 schools took 20 percent of all the students in the United States who scored in the top five centiles on the SAT or ACT. Forty-one schools accounted for half of them. All 105 schools, which accounted for just 19 percent of all freshmen in 1997, accounted for 74 percent of students with SAT or ACT scores in the top five centiles.

Given this concentration of academic talent in a relatively few colleges and universities, the original problem has been replaced by its opposite. Instead of feeling sorry for the exceptionally able student who has no one to talk to, we need to worry about what happens when exceptionally able students hang out only with one another.[13]

What Are the Elite Schools?

There is no shortage of rankings of colleges and universities, with the *Barron's* and *U.S. News & World Report* lists being the most famous. You should think in terms of the usual suspects. At the top are the iconic schools—Columbia, Harvard, Princeton, and Yale. Right behind them (some would say beside them) are consensus high-prestige schools such as Stanford, Duke, MIT, the rest of the Ivy League, and some of what used to be known as the Seven Sisters, followed by another two or three dozen schools whose names are familiar to all parents who aspire to get their children into selective schools. The top twenty-five national universities and top twenty-five liberal arts colleges in the *U.S. News & World Report* rankings, which can be viewed online, include all of the schools that everyone agrees are elite, plus a few with less glittering reputations.[14]

The segregation of the college system now means that the typical classroom in a third-tier public university is filled with students who are not much brighter than the average young person in the nation as a whole, whereas the typical classroom in an elite school has no one outside the top decile of cognitive talent, and many who are in the top hundredth or thousandth of the distribution. Both sets of students are technically "college educated" when they get their BAs, but that's where the similarity stops. The cognitive pecking order of schools is apparent to everyone—to employers looking at applicants' résumés, to parents thinking about where they want their children to go to college, and to high school students thinking about how to best make their way in life.

Incentives on the demand side have interacted with incentives on the supply side. More and more of the best students want to go to the elite schools, and the elite schools, eager to maintain their status, search ever more assiduously to fill their incoming class with the best of the best. The competition on both sides to achieve the same end has proved to be irresistible. In the early 1990s, when Richard Herrnstein and I were writing *The Bell Curve*, he sat on the Harvard undergraduate admissions committee. One day when we were on the phone discussing the latest draft, he told me happily that Harvard had snagged more exceptionally qualified students for the next entering class than ever before. "But Dick," I said, "we're writing about all the problems that causes." Herrnstein, who loved Harvard, replied (with a smile, I am sure), "I want 'em all."

The Dominance of the Upper-Middle Class in Elite Schools

The concentration of high-ability students wouldn't be so bad if those students had only their ability in common. In the ideal of the meritocracy, the new Yale or the new Princeton is now peopled by all those lonely high school students I was just describing, gathered from small towns and inner cities, the children of bakers and bankers, nurses and insurance agents, showing one another how much they have to learn about the full spectrum of American life.

It didn't work out that way. The opening of elite schools to the academically talented of all backgrounds was not accompanied by socioeconomic democratization of those schools. On the surface, it looked as if things had changed. The proportion of students coming from socially prominent families dropped. The proportion that came from exclusive prep schools dropped. The de facto quotas on the number of Jews who would be admitted were dropped. Affirmative action increased the representation of African Americans and Latinos on elite campuses. The numbers of Asian American students increased manyfold through the force of their superb credentials.[15] But despite these changes, the student bodies of the elite schools were still drawn overwhelmingly from the upper-middle class. According to sociologist Joseph Soares's analysis in *The Power of Privilege*, consistent with other such analyses, 79 percent of students at "Tier 1" colleges as of the 1990s came from families in the top quartile of socioeconomic status, while only 2 percent came from the bottom quartile.[16] For Soares, these numbers are evidence of obvious bias against the most able students who are not from the upper-middle class and above. "Unless one believes that only rich people can be smart," he writes, "we have a staggering distance to travel to achieve a fair opportunity for all to reach every level of our educational system."[17]

The bias that Soares set out to investigate could occur in two ways. The first is that the pool of applicants is biased. The second is that the admissions process continues to give preferential treatment to the children of the affluent.

Soares presents compelling evidence that the applicant pool is biased. Using the National Educational Longitudinal Study (NELS), Soares demonstrates that the applicant pool is heavily loaded toward youths who come from the high-income professional class, especially those who come from the Northeast United States. In a logistic regression analysis of the NELS data that controls for other influences on the decision to apply, Soares finds that students with the same gender, race, and SAT scores are more than three times as likely to apply to a selective school if they come from one of those professional high-income families in the Northeast, and twice as likely if they come from a professional high-income family outside the Northeast.[18] Other things being equal, Asians were almost twice as likely to apply as non-Asians, and students from private schools were four times more likely to apply than students at public schools.[19]

So the applicant pool is skewed. But from among this pool, are admissions officers giving preferential treatment to those who possess the right cultural capital? Without doubt, certain applicants get an edge that has nothing to do with merit. In *The Price of Admission*, journalist Daniel Golden documents the ways in which elite schools manage to find room for the children of alums, big donors, celebrities, athletes, the elite college's own faculty, and wealthy parents whose estates might eventually make their heirs into big donors.[20] The question is this: What would the freshman class look like if all of these considerations were eliminated and the decisions were made purely on the basis of test scores, extracurricular achievements, teacher recommendations, and high school transcripts? Answer: Socioeconomically, the change in the class profile would range from minuscule to zero. The elite schools are turning away at least two-thirds and often 80 or 90 percent of their highly qualified applicant pool. The applicants on the cusp who would be admitted if all the preferential treatment were eliminated would still be dominated by children from the upper-middle class, because those are the young people who dominate the applicant pool.

When Soares turns his multivariate analyses to the admissions decisions, his results are notable for what they did not reveal. The most basic indicators of the socioeconomic status of the applicant—parental income and occupation—did not produce significant relationships with probability of admission after controlling for measures of the student's real abilities.[21]

The reason that upper-middle-class children dominate the population of elite schools is that the parents of the upper-middle class now produce a disproportionate number of the smartest children. For example, one of the basics for having a decent chance of getting into an elite school is a high SAT score, with "high" defined as at least 700 on the SAT verbal and SAT math. Among college-bound seniors who took the SAT in 2010, 87 percent of the students with 700-plus scores in the math and verbal tests had at least one parent with a college degree. Fifty-six percent of them had a parent with a graduate degree.[22] This is not a function of coaching—the dispassionate studies of coaching show average gains of only a few dozen points—but of ability to do well in a challenging academic setting.[23] That ability is reflected in the other measures—grades, teacher evaluations, and many types of extracurricular accomplishments—that admissions committees use.

In that glaring relationship of high test scores to advanced parental education, which in turn means high parental IQ, lies the reason that the tests aren't the problem and bias in the admissions process isn't the problem. The children of the well educated and affluent get most of the top scores because they constitute most of the smartest kids. They are smart in large part because their parents are smart.[24] That brings us to the role of homogamy.

The Perpetuator: Homogamy

Homogamy refers to the interbreeding of individuals with like characteristics. Educational homogamy occurs when individuals with similar educations have children. Cognitive homogamy occurs when individuals with similar cognitive ability have children.

The Increase in Cognitive Homogamy

Before the age of mobility, people commonly married someone from the same town or from the same neighborhood of an urban area. The events that threw people together seldom had anything to do specifically with cognitive ability. Similar cognitive ability was a source of compatibility between a young man and young woman, and some degree of cognitive homogamy existed, but it was a haphazard process.[25] Meanwhile, educational homogamy was high, because hardly anyone went to college. In large proportions of married couples, both had less than a high school education or both had a high school diploma.

As the proportion of college graduates increased, so did the possibilities for greater educational homogamy at the top, as college graduates found they had more potential marriage partners who were also college graduates. Drawing on the extensive technical literature and the CPS, sociologists Christine Schwartz and Robert Mare examined trends in "assortative marriage," as it is known in the jargon, from 1940 to 2003.[26] They found that homogamy has increased at both ends of the educational scale—college graduates grew more likely to marry college graduates and high school dropouts grew more likely to marry other high school dropouts.

For our purposes—trying to understand how the new upper class came to be—the effects of increased educational attainment may be seen in a simple measure. In 1960, just 3 percent of American couples both had a college degree. By 2010, that proportion stood at 25 percent. The change was so large that it was a major contributor to the creation of a new class all by itself.

But increased educational homogamy had another consequence that the academic literature on homogamy avoids mentioning. Increased educational homogamy inevitably means increased cognitive homogamy.

A college education, starting with admission and continuing through to graduation, is a series of cognitive tests.[27] To be able even to begin a major in engineering or the hard sciences, students have to be able to do advanced calculus, and that in turn requires logical-mathematical ability in roughly the top decile of the population. To be able to cope with genuine college-level material in the social sciences and humanities requires good linguistic ability—in the top quartile of the distribution if you're content with scraping by, closer to the top decile if you want to get good grades in a moderately demanding college.[28] To graduate means passing all these tests plus a general test for perseverance.

Which Comes First, Education or IQ?

Educational attainment is correlated with IQ, but education does not have much effect on IQ after the child enters elementary school. By that, I do not mean that the *absence* of any education after age 6 wouldn't make a difference, nor that exceptions do not exist. Rather, I mean that if a thousand children are administered a good IQ test at age 6, and those children then attend a wide variety of elementary and secondary schools, their IQs at age 18 will be very similar to what they were at age 6, and statistical analysis will not show that the children who went to the expensive private schools got an IQ boost as a result. This finding goes back to the famous Coleman Report in the 1960s.[29] Scholars still debate whether additional years of education are associated with increments in general mental ability or just increments in test scores, but no one contends that education routinely transforms average children into intellectually gifted adults.

The result is that each level of educational attainment—high school diploma, AA, BA, MA, and professional degree or PhD—implies a mean IQ for people attaining that level that has been remarkably stable among whites at least since the beginning of the 1980s. I must limit the numbers to whites as I present these data, because aggressive affirmative action has produced means for African Americans and Latinos at each level of educational attainment that are substantially lower and more variable than the white means.[30] But since we are talking about the new upper class, there are good reasons to think in terms of the white means—partly because African Americans and Latinos who enter the new upper class have passed a number of career tests signifying that they approximate the white means on cognitive ability for each level of educational attainment, and partly because the new upper class is still overwhelmingly white.[31]

Table 2.1 shows the evidence for these stable means. The data for persons reaching adulthood in the 1980s and 2000s come from the 1979 and 1997 cohorts of the National Longitudinal Survey of Youth (NLSY), which are used to establish national norms for the Armed Forces Qualification Test (AFQT), which measures the same cognitive abilities that IQ tests measure.[32]

TABLE 2.1. **MEAN WHITE IQ FOR LEVELS OF DEGREE ATTAINMENT IN THE NLSY-79 AND NLSY-97**

| | Years when subjects reached age 25 | |
	1982–89	2005–9
Mean IQ for persons completing no more than . . .		
No degree	88	87
High school diploma/GED	99	99
Associate's degree	105	104
Bachelor's degree	113	113
Master's degree	117	117
PhD, LLD, MD, DDS	126	124

Source: NLSY-79, NLSY-97. Sample limited to whites.

The stability of the scores over the three decades from the 1980s through the 2000s is remarkable, considering that the number of bachelor's degrees, expressed as a percentage of twenty-two-year-olds, increased from 22 percent in 1981 to 37 percent in 2008. But the country was also becoming steadily more efficient at getting the best students into college over that period, so that the greater size of the college population didn't mean a markedly less able population.

If the mean IQs at the higher levels of educational attainment have been stable, then the growth of two-degree couples has meant, inevitably, greater cognitive homogamy at the top. But that's just the beginning. The college sorting machine has also been at work.

College brings people together at the time of life when young adults are beginning to look around for marriage partners, and the college sorting machine brings the highest-IQ young women and young men together in the most prestigious schools. As if that weren't enough, graduate school adds another layer of sorting, so that the brilliant young woman who went to a state university goes to Harvard Law School, where she is brought into the elite pool. For the prospective members of the new upper class who don't find a marriage partner as an undergraduate or at grad school, the names of the schools they attended give them badges that signal their status to prospective mates. The substance of their education also sorts them into occupations that increase the likelihood that they will eventually marry people with similar characteristics.[33]

So it's not just that college graduates are likely to marry college graduates, but that graduates from elite colleges are likely to marry other graduates from elite colleges.[34] Back in the days when Harvard men and Wellesley women were more likely to be rich than to be especially smart, this meant that money was more likely to marry money. In an era when they are both almost certainly in the top centiles of the IQ distribution, it means that very smart is more likely to marry very smart.

Shared Culture

Put people with greater educational and cognitive similarity together, and you have the makings of greater cultural similarity as well. When one spouse is a college graduate in the top centiles of cognitive ability and the other is a high school graduate with modestly above-average cognitive ability, they are likely to have different preferences in books and movies, different ways of spending their free time, different friends, and differences in a dozen other aspects of life. Those differences carry with them a built-in measure of cultural dispersion within marriages. In 1960, two-thirds of families in managerial and professional occupations had that built-in educational heterogeneity. In 2010, when three-quarters of the most financially successful couples both had college degrees, the demand for the goods and services to supply the distinctive tastes and preferences of very bright and well-educated people had been concentrated.

Transmission of Cognitive Ability to the Next Generation

Another consequence of increased educational and cognitive homogamy is the increased tenacity of the elite in maintaining its status across generations. The adage "shirtsleeves to shirtsleeves in three generations" grew out of an observed reality: If the children and grandchildren are only average in their own abilities, money from a fortune won in the first generation won't keep them at the top of the heap. When the parents are passing cognitive ability along with the money, the staying power of the elite across generations increases.

Specific numbers can be attached to such statements. The stability of the average IQs for different levels of educational attainment over time means that we can predict the average IQs of children of parents with different combinations of education, and we can also predict where the next generation of the smartest children is going to come from.

On average, children are neither as smart nor as dumb as their parents. They are closer to the middle. This tendency is called regression to the mean. It exists independently of genes. Regression to the mean is a function of the empirically observed statistical relationships between the tested IQs of parents and children. Given the parameters in the note on page 366, the expected value of the IQ of a grown-up offspring is 40 percent toward the population mean from the parents' midpoint IQ.[35]

Suppose we have four white couples with the same level of education, plugging in the average IQs for those levels of education as given in table 2.1 (splitting the difference between the NLSY-79 and NLSY-97 figures when necessary). I add a fifth couple who both have degrees from elite colleges, with a midpoint IQ of 135.[36] Here is what we can expect as mean IQs of the children of these couples:

Parents' Educations	Expected IQ of the Child
Two high school dropouts	94
Two high school diplomas	101
Two college degrees (and no more)	109
Two graduate degrees	116
Two degrees from an elite college	121

These represent important differences in the resources that members of the next generation take to the preservation of their legacy. Consider first a college graduate who marries a high school graduate, each with the average cognitive ability for their educational level (113 and 99, respectively). Their expected midpoint IQ is 106. Suppose they have built a small business, been highly successful, and leave $5 million to their son. If their son has the expected IQ of a little less than 105, he will have only about a 50 percent chance of completing college even assuming that he tries to go to college. Maybe he inherited extraordinary energy and determination from his parents, which would help, but those qualities regress to the mean as well. Shirtsleeves to shirtsleeves in three generations is a likely scenario for the progeny of that successful example. Compare that situation with the one facing the son of two parents who both graduated from elite schools. If he has exactly the expected IQ of 121, he has more than an 80 percent chance of getting a degree if he goes to college. These percentages are not a matter of statistical theory. They are based on the empirical experience of both the 1979 and 1997 cohorts of the National Longitudinal Survey of Youth—if you had an IQ of 105 or one of 121 and entered college, those are the probabilities that you ever got a degree.[37]

In addition to those differing chances of graduation are qualitative differences between young people with IQs of 105 and 121. First, the

reasons that someone with an IQ of 105 doesn't finish college probably include serious academic difficulties with the work, whereas the
reasons a person with an IQ of 121 doesn't finish college almost certainly involve motivation or self-discipline—no one with an IQ of 121
has to drop out of college because he can't pass the courses. Second,
there is a qualitative difference in the range of occupations open to
those two young persons. The one with an accurately measured IQ of
105 cannot expect to be successful in any of the prestigious professions that are screened for IQ by their educational requirements (e.g.,
medicine, law, engineering, academia). It is unlikely that he can even
complete those educational requirements. Someone with an accurately measured IQ of 121 can succeed in any of them if his mathematical and verbal talents are both strong, or succeed in the ones
geared to his talents if there is an imbalance between mathematical
and verbal ability.[38]

Now think in terms of an entire cohort of children. Where will the
next generation of children with exceptional cognitive ability come
from? For purposes of illustration, let's say that "exceptionally high
cognitive ability" means the top five centiles of the next generation of
white children. More than a quarter of their parents may be expected
to have a midpoint IQ of more than 125.[39] Another quarter may be
expected to have midpoint parental IQ of 117–125. The third quarter
may be expected to have midpoint parental IQ of 108–117. That
leaves one quarter who will be the children of parents with midpoint
parental IQ of less than 108. Only about 14 percent of that top five
centiles of children are expected to come from the entire bottom half
of the distribution of white parents.

Therein lies the explanation for that startling statistic I reported
earlier about SAT scores: In 2010, 87 percent of the students with
700-plus scores in Critical Reading or Mathematics had a parent with
a college degree, and 57 percent had a parent with a graduate degree.
Those percentages could have been predicted pretty closely just by
knowing the facts about the IQs associated with different educational
levels and the correlation between parental and child IQ. They could
have been predicted without making any theoretical assumptions
about the roles of nature and nurture in transmitting cognitive ability

and without knowing anything about the family incomes of those SAT test-takers, how many test preparation courses their children took, whether they went to private schools, or how ingenious the educational toys in the household were when they were toddlers.

In an age when the majority of parents in the top five centiles of cognitive ability worked as farmers, shopkeepers, blue-collar workers, and housewives—a situation that necessarily prevailed a century ago, given the occupational and educational distributions during the early 1900s—these relationships between the cognitive ability of parents and children had no ominous implications. Today, when the exceptionally qualified have been so efficiently drawn into the ranks of the upper-middle class, and when they are so often married to people with the same ability and background, they do. In fact, the implications are even more ominous than I just described because none of the numbers I used to illustrate the transmission of cognitive ability to the next generation incorporated the effects of the increased educational homogamy of recent decades. In any case, the bottom line is not subject to refutation: Highly disproportionate numbers of exceptionally able children in the next generation will come from parents in the upper-middle class, and more specifically from parents who are already part of the broad elite.

3

A New Kind of Segregation

*In which I describe how the cultural divide between the new
upper class and the rest of America is being reinforced by
residential segregation that enables large portions of the new
upper class to live their lives isolated from everyone else.*

I N 2009, AMERICA'S leading scholar of residential segregation, Princeton's Douglas Massey, joined by coauthors Jonathan Rothwell and Thurston Domina, published a major study of American residential segregation over the course of the twentieth century.[1] The good news was that racial segregation had receded in the aftermath of the civil rights revolution. Racial segregation was still substantial, but the trend had been in the right direction for almost four decades. The bad news was that socioeconomic segregation had been increasing.

Massey and his colleagues focused on a comparison of households below the poverty line with households that had incomes at least four times the poverty line. Their evidence was not the stuff of headlines. The dissimilarity index for people below the poverty line and families four times above the poverty line in metropolitan areas increased from 0.34 to 0.42 from 1970 to 2000.[2] They also found that the isolation index of college graduates within census tracts increased from 0.19 to 0.36.[3] But if the numbers were obscure, the authors' summary judgment was clear enough: "During the late twentieth century, in other words, the well educated and the affluent increasingly segmented themselves off from the rest of American society."[4] They were reminded of a phrase coined by Robert Reich when he first described the new class of symbolic analysts back in 1991: "The secession of the successful."

The authors had used a modest definition of *affluence*. At least four times the median poverty line included 42 percent of American families in the 2000 census.[5] The authors had actually demonstrated that people in the middle class on up have distanced themselves from the poor. What about people in the neighborhoods that are *really* affluent and *really* well educated? As you are about to see, they didn't just separate themselves from the poor. They separated themselves from just about everyone who isn't as rich and well educated as they are.

A Tale of Three Cities

Austin, Texas

Austin, Texas, was still a small city when the census was taken in 1960, with a population of just 186,545. It was the state capital and home to the flagship campus of the University of Texas, which gave it some distinction. But Austin was otherwise like other small cities scattered around the state, with an economy based largely on receiving and shipping agricultural products from the surrounding farm country. Some local companies manufactured brick, tile, and bedroom furniture.

The capitol building and the campus were both in the middle of downtown. Austin's wealthiest citizens lived to the west of downtown and north of the Colorado River in four census tracts that comprised 16 percent of Austin's adult population.[6] The median family income in those affluent census tracts was $60,700—roughly the income of an experienced Austin public school teacher in 2010.[7] Thirty-five percent of residents ages 25 and older in those four census tracts had a bachelor's degree or higher—or to think of it another way, almost two out of three adults in Austin's most affluent neighborhoods did *not* have a college education.[8]

Four censuses later, in 2000, Austin had been transformed. The population had grown to 656,562, making Austin the sixteenth-largest city in the nation. The area adjoining downtown to the west was still the rich part of town, and had expanded even farther west by 2000, but it now housed a different demographic than it had forty years earlier, with a median income of $106,100. The median income in the richest zip code was $211,800.

Education had grown as much as income. Twelve zip codes had BA percentages above 60 percent. The increases in wealth and education went together. The top twelve wealthiest zip codes also boasted ten out of twelve of the best-educated zip codes.[9]

It wasn't just more money and more education in the west half of Austin that made the difference. Austin had become home to some of the trendiest and highest-tech industries in the country. Dell Computer, ranked 48 on the Fortune 500 that year, had its headquarters in Austin. So did Whole Foods Market, which had grown from one small natural food store to a nationwide chain and would enter the Fortune 500 in 2005. A partial list of new-economy companies that located some of their operations in Austin then or in the decade to follow includes Apple, Google, Freescale Semiconductor, Cirrus Logic, Cisco Systems, eBay, PayPal, Intel, National Instruments, Samsung, Silicon Laboratories, and Sun Microsystems. About eighty-five biotechnology companies would locate in Austin by 2010, making it a leading employer in that vibrant new industry.

The technical jobs offered by such employers required not just people with college educations but also very smart people. Occasionally that meant hiring the genius college dropout (the University of Texas had spawned its own exemplar in Michael Dell), but usually employers fished in the ponds where the biggest fish were the most numerous, which meant that the west side of Austin was swarming with executives who had been trained at Rice, Berkeley, Stanford, Duke, the Ivies, and other elite colleges. The Austin campus of the University of Texas had also been transformed. In 1960, it had been known mainly as a party school with a great football team. By 1985, its academic reputation had risen to the point that it was named one of the eight "Public Ivies" in a book listing the best state universities.[10]

Add to that the spouses. The growing educational homogamy since

1960 meant that most of the spouses were drawn from the same pond of the cognitively talented and well educated as the people being hired by the high-tech firms. Family life on the west side of Austin had been transformed in ways that money alone wouldn't produce.

Manhattan, New York

Seventeen hundred miles and a world away from Austin is Manhattan. In 1960 and 2000 alike, New York City was the nation's leading metropolis, and Manhattan was its crown jewel. Then as now, the emblem of New York's wealth was the Upper East Side, extending from Fifth Avenue to the East River between Fifty-Ninth Street and Ninety-Sixth Street.[11]

The rest of Manhattan's neighborhoods were a mélange. Directly north of Central Park was Harlem, the most famous black neighborhood in America. On the southeastern part of the island near the Brooklyn Bridge was the Lower East Side, home to Jewish and Italian immigrants in the early twentieth century and still a white working-class neighborhood in 1960. Scattered to the west and north were the financial district around Wall Street, avant-garde Greenwich Village, the meatpacking district, the garment district, plus a few dozen other ethnically, culturally, or economically distinctive neighborhoods.

Outside the Upper East Side, Manhattan was still predominantly a blue-collar town in 1960. This may not be a surprise for Manhattan north of Central Park, where 67 percent of adults had not completed high school and the median income was just $34,500. But the rest of Manhattan (excluding the Upper East Side) wasn't that much better educated or richer. A majority of adults had not completed high school and the median family income was $39,300. That was lower than the median for the nation as a whole. Apart from that, remember that these are 2010 dollars. Try to imagine raising a family in Manhattan on $39,300 a year.

Now consider the Upper East Side. To some degree, it was already a world apart in 1960. In the census tracts that ran from Fifth Avenue to Park Avenue, median family income was more than $150,000. The richest of all was the census tract across from the Metropolitan Museum of Art, with a median of $176,000. But the Upper East Side from Lexington Avenue to the East River wasn't wealthy. The median family income for the Upper East Side as a whole was just $55,400—far less than the salary of an experienced teacher in the New York City public schools in 2010.[12] Just 23 percent of adults on the Upper East Side as a whole had college degrees.

Fast-forward to 2000. The number of people living in Manhattan had not changed much in the intervening years, but the ways that they made their livings had changed a lot. In 1960, 40 percent of Manhattan's jobs had been industrial. By 2000, that 40 percent had shrunk to 5 percent. By 2000, 15 percent of all jobs in Manhattan were in the financial sector, another 15 percent fell into the category of "professional, scientific, and technical services," and another 9 percent were in a category labeled simply "information." That's 39 percent of all jobs.

That doesn't mean blue-collar work wasn't being done in Manhattan anymore. It just means that by the year 2000, people who lived in Manhattan south of the Nineties weren't doing them. Instead, Manhattan south of the Nineties had turned into an abode for a highly educated, highly paid professional, managerial, and technical class. Even excluding the Upper East Side, the median family income of Manhattan south of Ninety-Sixth Street had risen from the $39,300 of 1960 to $121,400 in 2000. The proportion of adults with college degrees had risen from 16 percent to 60 percent. Within the Upper East Side itself, the median family income had risen from the $55,400 of 1960 to $195,300. The proportion of adults with college degrees had risen from 23 percent to 75 percent.

At street level, life in New York still had the same crackling energy in 2000 as it had had in 1960. Visually, it was far more diverse, its sidewalks even more packed with people from around the world. To the casual eye, it also still seemed to have the same riotous diversity of activity, investment bankers brushing by ConEd workers and street vendors selling hot dogs to advertising executives. But the diversity existed only on the streets. As soon as people entered their office buildings or their apartments, they were surrounded by colleagues and neighbors who were in the top few centiles of education and income.

Newton, Iowa

Eleven hundred miles west of Manhattan, and another world away, is Newton, Iowa. In 1960, the census listed Newton's population as 15,381. It was the home of the Maytag Company, the washing machine manufacturer, ranked 326 that year in the Fortune 500 list of America's largest corporations.

We don't have educational and income data for the rich part of Newton in 1960 or 2000, because it was too small to have a census tract of its own. But Newton had affluent people—the Maytag Company paid its executives well—and southwest Newton was where almost all of them lived, including Fred Maytag II. His house was larger than others in southwest Newton, but not by a lot. It was notable mostly because it had a swimming pool.

Within three blocks of Fred Maytag's home in each direction lived the owner of the second-largest company in town (the Vernon Company), several Maytag executives, several physicians and attorneys, the publisher of the local newspaper, and two owners of local auto dealerships. Other residents within that three-block radius were the sheriff, whose wife gave piano lessons, the city employee who ran the town's waterworks, a couple of insurance agents, the proprietors of a drugstore, a dry-goods store, and a lumberyard, the high school band teacher, and many low-level white-collar workers and factory workers.[13] There was also the dilapidated house of a recluse known as Over the River Charlie, who kept chickens in his backyard.

Newton was my boyhood home, which I remember fondly, but the description of the people who lived within three blocks of Fred Maytag II is a factual statement of the mix of people in the affluent part of a town that contained one of the five hundred largest corporations in the country. It is a description that could be matched by many American towns and small cities that were home to industrial corporations as of 1960.

Forty years later, Maytag was still on the Fortune 500, at number 368. The corporate headquarters and the plants for manufacturing washing machines and dryers remained in Newton. But things had changed. The new president of the company had decided to live in an affluent neighborhood of Des Moines, thirty-six miles to the west, and other senior executives had followed his example. Those who remained in Newton congregated in high-end housing developments that were populated exclusively by people who could afford to buy the large homes in them, which meant no factory workers, no low-level white-collar workers, and no high school band teacher. Fewer senior executives showed up at the local Rotary and Kiwanis Club meetings, and they were less likely to serve on civic boards or charitable drives. Their spouses were not as active in Newton's school affairs and church affairs. Their children were less likely to attend Newton's public schools.

During the 1980s and 1990s, Maytag also found it increasingly difficult to attract top executive talent. In 1960, most of Maytag's executives had grown up in midwestern towns like Newton. In 2000, Maytag was competing for executive talent with corporations that hired from around the nation, and few of the people who were being recruited wanted to live even in Des Moines, Iowa's big city, let alone in a town of 15,000 surrounded by cornfields.

Elite Neighborhoods and the SuperZips

In different ways, Austin, Manhattan, and Newton all experienced the secession of the successful. But the essence of the change was not geographic separation. Yes, the new wealthy housing developments in west Austin were farther away from downtown Austin than the richest parts of Austin had been in 1960, and the Maytag executives living in Des Moines were certainly farther away from downtown Newton than their predecessors had been. But usually the differences between 1960 and 2000 were ones of density and resources within neighborhoods that had been "the best part of town" for decades.

The Traditional Elite Neighborhoods

America has neighborhoods that have been famous for a century: places like the Upper East Side in New York, Beacon Hill in Boston, and the North Shore of Chicago. To illustrate the magnitude of the change in density of advanced education and the magnitude of income that occurred over the last half century, I assembled data on median family income and percentage of adults with college degrees for fourteen of the most famous "best parts of town" in 1960, and what had happened to those same indicators by 2000. The results are shown in table 3.1.

All fourteen of these elite neighborhoods tell the same story. In 1960, college graduates were still a minority, usually a modest minority, in even the most elite places in the United States. Only Beverly Hills had a median family income greater than $100,000. Over the next forty years, these places, already fashionable in 1960, were infused with new cultural resources in the form of college graduates and more money to pay for the tastes and preferences of an upper class. These infusions were not a matter of a few percentage points or a few thousand dollars. The median income in these fourteen elite towns and neighborhoods went from $84,000 to $163,000—almost doubling. The median percentage of college graduates went from 26 percent to 67 percent—much more than doubling.

The Serendipitous Merits of Using 2000 Census Data

All of the zip code data in this chapter must be based on the 2000 census, because socioeconomic data on zip codes for the 2010 census were not released before this book went to press. I plan to add the 2010 values in any subsequent edition of *Coming Apart*. But in some ways, using the 2000 census has an advantage. I believe that the segregation of the new upper class will prove to be more extreme in 2010 than it was in 2000, but it was already extreme in 2000. The consequences of the segregation of the new upper class are not something for us to worry about in the future; these consequences have been working their way through our society for many years even now. The 2000 census numbers help make that point.

TABLE 3.1. ELITE PLACES TO LIVE IN 1960 AND WHAT HAPPENED TO THEM BY 2000

	Median percentage of adults with college degrees		Median income (000s of 2010 dollars)	
	1960	2000	1959	1999
New York				
The Upper East Side[a]	23	75	$55	$183
Lower Westchester County[b]	25	58	$87	$155
The Connecticut Corridor[c]	27	65	$90	$191
Boston				
Brookline	21	77	$69	$124
The Western Suburbs[d]	27	70	$75	$157
Philadelphia				
The Main Line[e]	25	64	$83	$140
Washington, DC				
Northwest Washington[f]	35	79	$88	$172
Lower Montgomery County[g]	42	77	$94	$176
McLean/Great Falls	26	74	$74	$180
Chicago				
The North Shore[h]	32	68	$95	$152
Los Angeles				
Beverly Hills[i]	19	56	$115	$158
San Francisco				
Lower Marin County[j]	26	69	$64	$158
Burlingame/Hillsborough	21	54	$89	$144
The Palo Alto Area[k]	28	65	$72	$157
Total	**26**	**67**	**$84**	**$163**

Sources: Bogue file of 1960 Census Tracts and 2000 Census zip code data from American FactFinder on the Census Bureau website.

a. From Central Park to the East River between Fifty-Ninth Street and Ninety-Sixth Street.

b. Eastchester, Greenburgh area, Harrison, Mamaroneck, Pelham, Rye (town and city), Scarsdale.

c. Darien, Greenwich, New Canaan, North Stamford, Westport.

d. Concord, Lexington, Needham, Newton, Newton Centre, Newton Highlands, Newton Lower Falls, Newton Upper Falls, Newtonville, Sudbury, Wayland, Wellesley, Wellesley Hills, Weston.

e. Ardmore, Bala Cynwyd, Berwyn, Bryn Mawr, Devon, Gladwyne, Haverford, Malvern, Merion, Narberth, Paoli, Villanova, Wayne, Wynnewood.

f. The neighborhoods west of Rock Creek Park.

g. Potomac and the Maryland portions of Bethesda and Chevy Chase.

h. Evanston, Glencoe, Kenilworth, Wilmette, Winnetka.

i. Except for Beverly Hills, census tracts where the wealthy lived in Los Angeles have changed enough that reconstructing comparable neighborhoods for 1960 and 2000 was not possible.

j. Mill Valley, Sausalito, Tiburon.

k. Atherton, Los Altos, Menlo Park, Palo Alto, Portola Valley, Stanford.

How important are these relatively few elite towns and urban neighborhoods? Hugely so—precisely because they are so few, and yet home to so many in the broad elite and to an even higher proportion of the narrow elite.

Defining the SuperZips

The first step in making that point is to convey how radically elite neighborhoods differ from those in the rest of the country. To do so, I created a score combining education and income for each zip code in the country. The method for creating the scores may be found in appendix B.

These scores are expressed as centiles with the same interpretation as the percentile scores on standardized tests. If you were in the 80th percentile on the SAT, only twenty people out of a hundred who took the SAT got a score as high as you did. If you live in a zip code in the 80th centile, only twenty American adults out of a hundred live in a zip code that has as high a combination of education and income as yours does.

The SuperZips are zip codes in the 95th through 99th centiles. I chose that range in part because the top five centiles contain a population with education and income similar to that of the famous elite neighborhoods shown in table 3.1, with a mean of 63 percent of adults with college degrees and median family incomes of $141,400. Another consideration is that I want the population in the SuperZips to be big enough to catch a large proportion of the new upper class. The top five centiles have an aggregate population of 9.1 million people ages 25 and older—almost four times the 2.4 million people in my operational definition of the new upper class. In all, 882 zip codes qualify as SuperZips.

A Profile of the SuperZips

In appearance, the SuperZips vary widely. A few consist of old mansions in old neighborhoods. Some consist of developments that have been built since the 1980s, with huge houses, much larger than the traditional mansion, fitted out with every accoutrement that owners with unlimited budgets can think of. Many of these developments are gated or guarded by private security forces, visibly set off from the rest of the area. But a great many of the SuperZips are not visually imposing or set off. The housing stock in Chevy Chase mentioned in the prologue is typical of many. The housing stock mostly dates from the first half of the twentieth century. Many of these homes have recently been enlarged to the limits of their small lots, but others have an unchanged footprint and are no more imposing than homes in zip codes without nearly the wealth of a SuperZip. But even a modest Chevy Chase home can sell for several hundred thousand dollars— just because it is in Chevy Chase.

By definition, most of the people who live in SuperZips are affluent and well educated. They have other advantages as well. Previewing trends for the upper-middle class as a whole that I will present in detail in part 2, inhabitants of SuperZips are more likely to be married than elsewhere, less likely to have experienced divorce, and less likely to have children living in households with single mothers. The men in SuperZips are more likely to be in the labor force than other American men and less likely to be unemployed. They also work longer hours than other Americans. Crime in urban SuperZips is low, and crime in suburban SuperZips is rare.

One of the most distinctive aspects of the SuperZips is their ethnic profile. As of 2000, the 882 SuperZips were substantially whiter and more Asian than the rest of America. Inhabitants of SuperZips were 82 percent white compared to 68 percent of Americans who don't live in SuperZips. Asians constituted 8 percent of the population of SuperZips, compared to 3 percent of Americans who don't live in SuperZips. Meanwhile, blacks and Latinos each constituted just 3 percent of the SuperZip population, compared to 12 and 6 percent, respectively, in the rest of the zip codes.[14]

The 2010 census, which will be available when you read this, will provide a revealing update on how the SuperZips are evolving. Asian Americans have long been represented in elite colleges far beyond their proportion in the population, even though they suffer a systematic disadvantage in the admissions process, and in recent years they have been joined by growing numbers of top South Asian students.[15] Given the relationship between attendance at elite colleges and the likelihood of living in SuperZips to be described presently, there is every reason to think that Asian representation in the SuperZips grew significantly in the 2000s. But Asians have since the 1960s been seen by whites as "honorary whites," in sociologist Andrew Hacker's sardonic phrase, and an increase in the proportion of Asians in the SuperZips will not change the degree to which the composition of the SuperZips is strikingly at odds with what's going on everywhere else.[16] As I write, about one out of ten American counties has a majority of minorities. The early releases of 2010 census data revealed that Latinos now constitute 16 percent of the population and blacks 13 percent.[17] The year 2010 probably marked the point at which births to white women were a minority of all births. Whites will become a minority of the American population by midcentury if not sooner. But, as of 2000, these historic changes had not intruded upon the SuperZips.

If you want to do a quick check on how much things have changed since 2000, use the American FactFinder tool at the Bureau of the Census website to see what the 2010 racial composition was in these half-dozen SuperZips, all of which matched the average of 82 percent white in 2000: 02461 (Newton Highlands, MA), 10583 (Scarsdale, NY), 20007 (Georgetown, DC), 60657 (Downtown Chicago, IL), 90212 (Beverly Hills, CA), and 94301 (Palo Alto, CA).[18]

The Zip Codes Where the New Upper Class Lives

I have not yet established that the new upper class actually lives in the SuperZips. There are two main possibilities. The first is that I'm wrong to think that the new upper class congregates in such a narrow stratum of American neighborhoods. People in the new upper class look for neighborhoods that they like for idiosyncratic reasons. They want a neighborhood with nice houses and people in a roughly similar socioeconomic bracket, but they sort themselves into prosperous zip codes that are attractive to them for specific reasons such as the length of the commute to their job or the quality of the local schools.

They are willing to trade off being at the top of the income/education ladder in return for these other qualities. The second possibility is that members of the new upper class act as if they are attracted to a single overriding criterion, that the neighborhood be filled with people as rich and smart as possible. And, for the most part, that appears to be what is happening.

To make that point anecdotally, I will continue using the metropolitan area I know best, Washington, DC, and its environs, home to almost all of the nation's narrow elite in the political and policy-making worlds plus many of the narrow elite in the news media.

If you are invited to a dinner party at the home of a member of Washington's narrow elite, the address could conceivably be in Great Falls, Old Town Alexandria, a few neighborhoods in Arlington or Falls Church, or on Capitol Hill, but it would be a surprise if it were. Given only the knowledge that your host is a member of the narrow elite, you can lay big odds that the address will be in Georgetown, the rest of Northwest Washington, Bethesda, Chevy Chase, Potomac, or McLean.

Those communities contain thirteen zip codes.[19] All of them are SuperZips, but that's just the beginning. As of 2000, eleven of those zip codes were in the 99th centile. And not just any part of the 99th centile. Ten of the eleven were in the *top half* of the 99th centile— places with combinations of education and income shared by fewer than five out of every thousand Americans. The other three zip codes among the thirteen had centile scores of 99.4, 98.9, and 98.8.

The neighborhoods I named for the dinner party were not chosen on the basis of their zip codes' centiles. For someone who has been involved in the political or public policy worlds of Washington, those are just the obvious, everybody-knows-that places where the most influential people in Washington live—and those places turn out to be not just SuperZips, but usually in the top half of the top centile.

A more systematic way of identifying where the most successful members of the new upper class live is provided by the profiles of graduates of the Harvard Business School's class of 1979 published for the class's twenty-fifth reunion in 2004.

In 2004, members of the Harvard Business School's class of 1979 were almost all in their fifties and at the peak of their careers. The 547 graduates living in the United States whose zip codes could be determined included 51 CEOs, 107 presidents, 15 board chairs, and 96 others who were directors, partners, or owners of their businesses.[20] In addition, there were 115 who were CFOs, COOs, executive vice presidents, or managing directors. I will consider those 384 to represent people who are extremely likely to fit my operational definition of the broad elite. Figure 3.1 shows where they lived.

**FIGURE 3.1.   CENTILES OF ZIP CODES WHERE THE HARVARD BUSINESS
                 SCHOOL UPPER-CLASS SAMPLE LIVE**

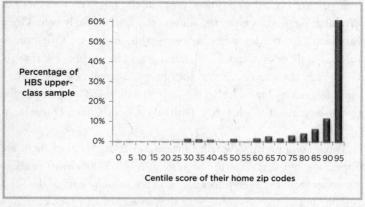

Source: Class of 1979 twenty-fifth reunion profile.

Sixty-one percent of them lived in SuperZips. Most of the ones who didn't live in the SuperZips lived in other places nearly as far out on the right-hand tail of the distribution. Eighty-three percent of the sample lived in zip codes with centiles of 80 or higher.

I chose alumni of the Harvard Business School class with positions that put them among the broad elite as a way of clarifying the discussion. But I needn't have bothered. The profile for their classmates who were merely borderline members of the new upper class was quite similar. Fifty-three percent of the rest of the class lived in Super-Zips and 80 percent lived in zip codes with centiles of 80 or higher.

We can combine the Harvard Business School subsamples to throw more light on the phenomenon I noted anecdotally for Washington: The SuperZips are not equal. Figure 3.2 shows the distribution *within*

FIGURE 3.2. **DISTRIBUTION OF CENTILES WITHIN THE SUPERZIPS**

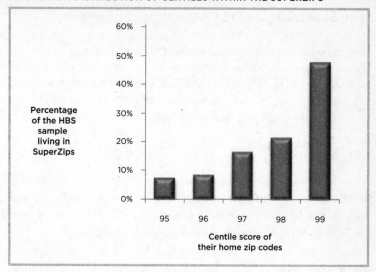

Source: Class of 1979 twenty-fifth reunion profile.

the top five centiles of the 61 percent of the Harvard Business School sample who lived in SuperZips.

Remember that the highly successful families buying homes in these elite zip codes didn't have a key matching neighborhoods with centiles that they could consult—it's not like rich people who can go into a wine store with the latest issue of *Wine Advocate* and buy only wines that Robert Parker scored 99 or 100. Rather, they were looking for something that was consistently satisfied by something that the centile score taps into. It was something other than the simple wealth of the zip code. Multivariate analysis reveals that the percentage of adults with BAs played at least as important a role as median income in discriminating between zip codes where the new upper class live and where they don't. That "something" was people like them—affluent, highly educated, and highly successful. They want to live in the very, very best neighborhoods. The evidence from both Washington's elite and the Harvard Business School sample reveals how clearly the new upper class can agree upon what the very, very best neighborhoods are.

The SuperZips Where Overeducated Elitist Snobs Live

On my former block in Washington DC were my next door neighbors (Princeton '57 and Radcliffe '66), the folks next to them (both Harvard '64) and the people across the street (Yale '71 and Yale Law '74), plus me (Harvard '66 and Yale Law '69). Just a typical American neighborhood, in other words.

Michael Barone

Email to the author

The culture of the new upper class carries with it an unmistakable whiff of a "we're better than the rabble" mentality. The daily yoga and jogging that keep them whippet-thin are not just healthy things for them to do; people who are overweight are less admirable as people. Deciding not to recycle does not reflect just an alternative opinion about whether recycling makes sense; it is inherently irresponsible. Smokers are not to be worried about, but to be held in contempt.

The people who suffer from this syndrome have been labeled by many other Americans as overeducated elitist snobs. The OES syndrome does not manifest itself like Margaret Dumont playing society lady to Groucho Marx. Overeducated elitist snobs may even be self-deprecating about their cultural preferences. They just quietly believe that they and their peers are superior to the rest of the population, intellectually and in their nuanced moral sensibility.

No external marker lets us define exactly who in the new upper class does and does not fit this indictment. Those who suffer from the OES syndrome tend to have high IQs, but lots of people with high IQs happily munch on double quarter-pounders with cheese and think that recycling is a farce. In my own experience, political ideology is not a reliable guide—I have found condescension toward the rabble among new-upper-class liberals and conservatives alike.

So we have to find a proxy measure: some population that is not defined by possessing the OES syndrome, but that is disproportionately dense with people suffering from it. I propose to use graduation from an elite college. To my fellow alumni of such schools, most of whom are fine people and who will understandably bridle at this, let me appeal to you: I'm not talking about all of us, or even most of us (I hope). I'm just saying that the OES syndrome is more densely found in the population of people who graduate from elite colleges than in the college-educated population at large.

Such a relationship is plausible for several reasons. First comes self-selection. Eighteen-year-olds do not end up at Duke or Yale by accident. They have to try hard to be there. In other words, most of them badly wanted as teenagers to be part of an elite institution, with all the implications that attraction to eliteness carries with it.

Second, they are only eighteen years old or thereabouts when they are admitted. They arrive on campus at an impressionable age, eager to fit in with whatever goes along with being a full-fledged member of that elite institution.

Third, the intense competition for admission to elite schools creates a powerful sense of validation. If you've gotten in, you're special, they say to themselves.

Fourth, as demonstrated in chapter 2, high proportions of those who get into elite schools have come from upper-middle-class backgrounds. They have already been socialized into the tastes and preferences of the upper-middle class, with little experience of any other realm of American life. They're more than halfway toward the OES syndrome when they arrive.

Fifth, the culture on elite campuses is intensely Bobo-like. David Brooks's discussion of what he called the "educated class" is saturated with examples associated with elite schools and their graduates, and rightly so.[21]

And so I am interested in seeing where the graduates of elite schools migrate as adults as an indirect measure of where the OES syndrome is most likely to be found.

The primary database I used for this exercise consists of the home zip codes of 14,317 graduates of Harvard, Princeton, and Yale (HPY, for convenience). The years to which the data apply range from 1989 to 2010, when almost all of the subjects were somewhere from ages 39 through 53.[22] The secondary database consists of 1,588 graduates of Wesleyan University, an elite school below the iconic level of HPY, who graduated during the 1970s and whose home zip codes were obtained as of 1996, when almost all of them ranged in age from 38 to 47. The sources of the data are alumni directories and class anniversary volumes borrowed from graduates of those schools.

As mature adults, fully a quarter of the HPY graduates were living in New York City or its surrounding suburbs. Another quarter lived in just three additional metropolitan areas: Boston (10 percent), Washington (8 percent), and San Francisco (7 percent). Relative to the size of their populations, the Los Angeles and Chicago areas got few HPY graduates—just 5 percent and 3 percent, respectively. Except for the Philadelphia and Seattle areas, no other metropolitan area got more than 1 percent.

Even though I didn't screen the sample for achieved success— just graduating from Harvard, Princeton, or Yale was enough—these alumni lived in zip codes nearly as exclusive as those of the Harvard Business School sample. Figure 3.3 replicates the graph I showed in figure 3.1, using the same scale for the vertical axis, but this time using the entire HPY sample.

FIGURE 3.3. CENTILES OF ZIP CODES WHERE GRADUATES OF HARVARD, PRINCETON, AND YALE LIVE

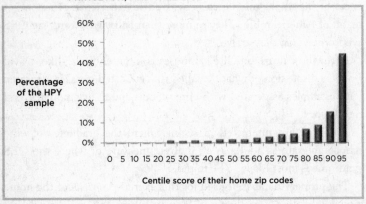

Sources: Various class directories.

The zip codes for all HPY graduates are not quite as exaggerated as those of the upper-class sample of the Harvard Business School, but almost. Forty-four percent of them lived in SuperZips; 74 percent of them lived in zip codes at the 80th centile or higher.

The data from the HPY sample are even more startling than those from the Harvard Business School sample. Everyone in figure 3.1 was a CEO, a CFO, or held some similarly elevated position that meant without doubt that they had enough money to live wherever they chose. But not everyone who enters Harvard, Princeton, or Yale at age 18 ends up a financial success. Many fail to accomplish much in life, and others choose to go into low-paying professions. Figure 3.3 includes all of them. That it is possible to select a sample exclusively on the basis of whether they were admitted to Harvard, Princeton, or Yale as a teenager, knowing nothing else whatsoever about what became of them, and produce the extreme concentration of those people in SuperZips when they were in their forties is remarkable on many counts.

If we were talking about only these three universities, these findings would be trivial. But there is no reason to think that the results are going to be much different for the other schools at the summit, such as Columbia, Stanford, or Duke. This brings us to the sample of Wesleyan graduates. In the most recent *U.S. News* college rankings, Wesleyan was ranked number 12 among liberal arts colleges—definitely elite, but, adding in the top national universities (a separate list from the liberal arts colleges), it is fair to say that Wesleyan is not at the summit. But look at figure 3.4, the third replication of the graph previously shown for the Harvard Business School upper-class sample and the HPY graduates, this time based on the Wesleyan graduates.

FIGURE 3.4. **CENTILES OF ZIP CODES WHERE GRADUATES OF WESLEYAN LIVE**

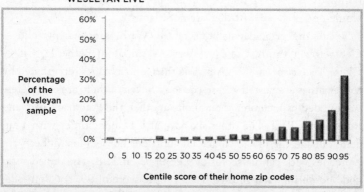

Source: Wesleyan University Alumni/ae Directory 1996.

Thirty-one percent of Wesleyan graduates were living in SuperZips, and 65 percent were living in zip codes at the 80th centile or higher. It would appear that the college sorting machine replicates itself with remarkable fidelity as a residential sorting machine. The hypothesis this suggests—testing it would push this exercise much further than appropriate for the purposes of this book—is that the rank order of colleges by mean SAT scores would be just about the same if ordered by the mean zip code centile of their graduates. If this is the case, then, ceteris paribus, the higher the centile of the SuperZip, the more densely it is populated by graduates of elite colleges and, by extension, the more densely it is populated by overeducated elitist snobs. I encourage others to explore this hypothesis empirically.

As for the phenomenon noted for the Washington elite and the Harvard Business School sample—within the SuperZips, the new upper class clusters at the highest possible centile—a graph based on the alumni from elite schools closely resembles figure 3.2. Among those alumni who lived in SuperZips, 9 percent were in zip codes at the 95th centile, 11 percent in the 96th, 15 percent in the 97th, 23 percent in the 98th, and 42 percent in the 99th.

The Elite Bubbles

If the SuperZips were islands bordered by reasonably ordinary neighborhoods, the segregation of the new upper class from everyone else would be mitigated. But they are not islands.

Recall the principal habitats of the Washington narrow elite—Georgetown, the rest of Northwest Washington, Bethesda, Chevy Chase, Potomac, and McLean. The thirteen zip codes represented by those names are nested within cocoons. Seven of them are completely surrounded by a combination of one another, the Potomac River, and Rock Creek Park. The other six have at least one border with a zip code outside the magic circle. The outsider borders for McLean are zip codes with centile scores of 99, 99, 93, and 98. The outsider zip code bordering Georgetown has a centile score of 99. For Bethesda, the bordering outsider zip codes have scores of 96, 99, and 97. The

outsider zip codes that border Potomac have scores of 96, 96, 97, plus
two other zip codes, both rural areas with centiles of merely 91 and
89, the far northwest nub of Potomac's zip code 20854, several miles
after leaving Potomac's residential areas behind.

The map in figure 3.5 shows the zip codes in and surrounding the
District of Columbia. The zip codes in black are SuperZips, in the top
five centiles. Dark gray indicates zip codes that just barely missed
qualifying as SuperZips, at the 90th–94th centiles. Light gray is for
zip codes that may not be elite by the rarefied standard I am using,
but are far above average for the nation as a whole, at the 80th–89th
centile. Unshaded zip codes are somewhere below the 80th centile.

FIGURE 3.5.   **SUPERZIP CLUSTERS AROUND WASHINGTON, DC**

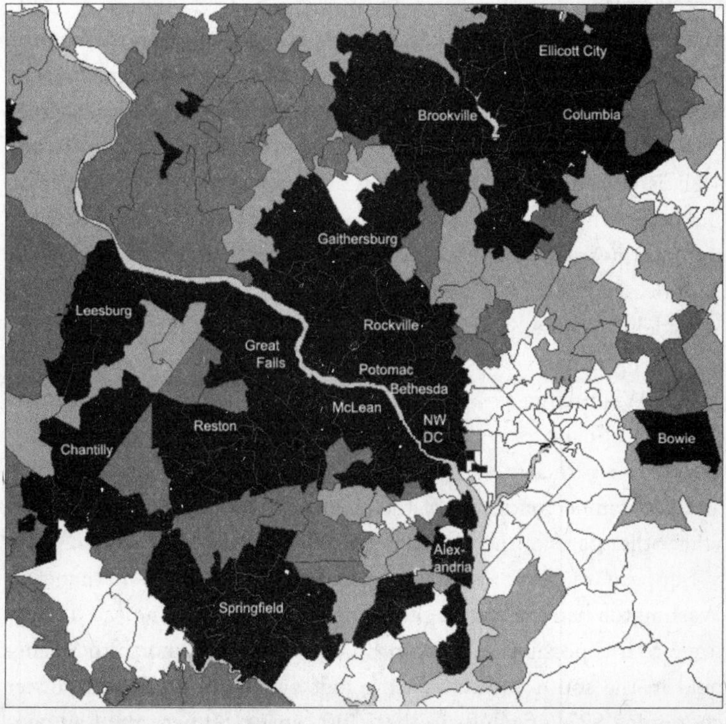

Black: SuperZips. Dark gray: zip codes in the 90th–94th centiles. Light gray: zip codes in the
80th–89th centiles. Unshaded: below the 80th centile.

The size of the SuperZip clusters around Washington is the most obvious feature of the map. In all, 931,512 adults ages 25 and older lived in those black zip codes in 2000. The clustering is even more important than the population. Notice how many of the black zip codes are contiguous.[23] Notice also how many of the zip codes bordering on the SuperZips are dark gray, meaning that they are nearly as affluent and well educated as the SuperZips—and conversely, how rarely are the SuperZips bordered by a white zip code that is below the 80th centile. The map seems to indicate that Northwest Washington is not so isolated in that regard, but that's an illusion. Along the border between the SuperZips in Northwest Washington and the nonelite bordering zip codes is Rock Creek Park, which separates the homes in the elite part of Northwest DC from everyone else with the broad, forested expanse through which Rock Creek runs.

The map's real shock for readers who are familiar with Washington will be some of the places that qualify as SuperZips. To someone who lives in the fashionable neighborhoods of Washington, communities such as Gaithersburg, Springfield, Chantilly, and Ellicott City are seen as unexceptional middle-class and upper-middle-class suburbs. But in fact the people in those zip codes have a combination of education and income higher than that enjoyed by all but 5 percent of other Americans. The main features of the new-upper-class culture prevail as widely in those SuperZips as they do in McLean or Georgetown, just on a less expensive scale.

The Washington area has the two critical conditions for the establishment of clusters in which the culture of the new upper class can flourish—a sufficiently large population of new-upper-class members and geographic contiguity of the neighborhoods where they live. Of what other parts of the United States may that be said?

Suppose we define a *cluster* as contiguous SuperZips.[24] In that case, Washington had the largest cluster in the country. As indicated in figure 3.5, it is possible to go from Ellicott City in the north to Springfield in the south without setting foot outside SuperZips, a cluster containing 827,746 adults in the 2000 census, 89 percent of all people in SuperZips in the Washington area.

The New York City area had the most people in SuperZips, though none of the individual clusters was as large as Washington's. Uptown Manhattan was by far the densest cluster, with 486,222 adults in SuperZips bordering the east, south, and west sides of Central Park. A triangle in north-central New Jersey bounded roughly by South Orange, Westfield, Annandale, Long Valley, and Mountain Lakes contained 314,189 adults. Another 246,709 adults lived in suburbs in Connecticut and New York roughly bounded by Greenwich, Granite Springs, Redding, and Westport. SuperZips along Long Island Sound had 194,725 adults. The Westchester area made up a cluster of 119,986 adults.

The third-largest aggregate population after New York and Washington is in the San Francisco area, which had four large SuperZip clusters. Downtown San Francisco had 118,555 adults in contiguous SuperZips plus other singletons. The area to the east of San Francisco, bounded roughly by Berkeley, Clayton, and Castro Valley, had 227,322 adults. Marin County had a cluster consisting of 75,583 adults. The biggest cluster in the greater San Francisco area is superimposed on Silicon Valley. It starts with Burlingame, a wealthy San Francisco suburb, and wends its way south through Palo Alto to Sunnyvale, enclosing SuperZips with 422,907 adults—the third-largest cluster in the country after Washington and Uptown Manhattan.

These clusters still don't completely capture the degree to which much of the new upper class lives in a world far removed from ordinary America. The clusters are defined by contiguous zip codes that are in the 95th centile. But a SuperZip usually borders several zip codes—four, on average—and only one of those need be another SuperZip to keep the cluster going. What is the average centile of *all* zip codes bordering the SuperZips? A very high 86. Even when a bordering zip code is not a SuperZip, it is likely to be nearly as affluent and highly educated.

Specifically, the average centile for people living in the zip codes bordering the SuperZips was at least 90 for 48 percent of them and 80 to 89 for another 30 percent. Another 13 percent had neighboring zip codes whose centiles averaged from 70 to 79, still well above the national average. Only 7 percent of the adults living in SuperZips bordered on zip codes averaging centiles of 50 to 69, and a minuscule 2 percent of them bordered on zip codes inhabited by Americans who averaged anywhere below the 50th centile.

The result is that people who live in small towns, apparently in the countryside, can actually be part of a large new-upper-class city—it just happens to be a city with a really, really low population density. Take, for example, zip code 01778, centile 99, which serves Wayland, Massachusetts, fifteen miles west of Boston. Wayland has a population of just 13,100. It is a pretty little town, and you drive through sparsely populated countryside to any of the adjacent towns. It doesn't look like an elite bubble worth worrying about. But bordering Wayland are the zip codes for Weston (centile 99), Sudbury (99), Natick (94), Lincoln (99), and the eastern zip code for Framingham (93). The *next* circle of zip codes beyond the adjacent ones include Wellesley (99), Wellesley Hills (99), Dover (99), Needham (99), Sherborn (99), Acton (99), Carlisle (99), Southborough (99), Concord (99), Lexington (99), North Sudbury (98), Bedford (97), Auburndale (98), and Newton Lower Falls (95). Add in this additional set, and Wayland is cocooned among 259,100 people with similarly exalted education and income—a population that would rank Greater Wayland as the sixty-ninth-largest city in the country.

These very large, very well-buffered SuperZip clusters are rare. Just how rare is quickly conveyed by the map in figure 3.6 showing the location of all the SuperZips.

The first thing to emphasize about the map in figure 3.6 is all the white space interspersed with a black dot or two. Of all the clusters of SuperZips, 64 percent consist of a single zip code surrounded by others that are not SuperZips. Furthermore, the neighboring zip codes are much closer to normal than the SuperZip in their midst. Among the 80 percent of the SuperZips that were in clusters of three or fewer, the average centile of the adjacent zip codes was 77—still in the top quartile of the American population, but representing neighborhoods with a lot of variety. In other words, about 80 percent of the SuperZips do not represent the kind of elite bubble, isolated from the rest of America, that I have been describing. The problem is that this 80 percent of

FIGURE 3.6. THE NATIONAL DISTRIBUTION OF PEOPLE WHO LIVE IN SUPERZIPS

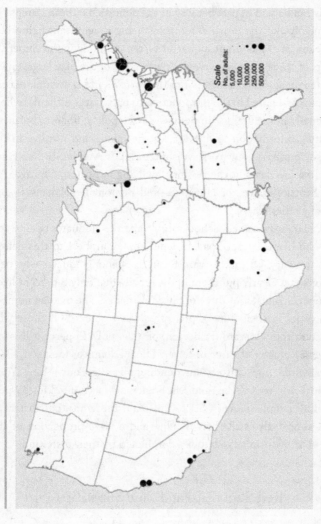

Source: 2000 census zip code data from American FactFinder on the Census Bureau website. "Adults" refers to persons age 25 and older. The smallest population visible on the scale used for the map is about 5,000 adults, meaning that about 41,000 adults (0.4 percent of all persons in SuperZips) lived in SuperZips not visible on the map.

SuperZips contains only 21 percent of the people who live in SuperZips. Furthermore, that 21 percent includes few of the people who qualify for the broad elite and almost no one who qualifies for the narrow elite.

This can be said in part because of the definition of both groups. To be a member of the broad elite means being a significant figure in a significant city, and about a quarter of the adults living in SuperZip clusters of three or fewer were not part of any of the fifty largest metropolitan areas. To be a member of the narrow elite is even more constraining. As I noted in the introduction to part 1, it is difficult to hold a nationally influential job in politics, public policy, finance, business, academia, information technology, or the media and not live in the areas surrounding New York, Washington, Los Angeles, or San Francisco. In a few cases, it can be done by living in Boston, Chicago, Atlanta, Seattle, Dallas, or Houston—and Bentonville, Arkansas—but not many other places.[25]

The Harvard Business School sample and the graduates of elite colleges who live in SuperZips let us put some numbers to this definitional necessity. Of the Harvard Business School graduates who held positions that clearly put them in the broad elite, only 8 percent lived in a SuperZip cluster of three or fewer zip codes. The median number of zip codes in their SuperZip clusters was eighteen. Of those who graduated from Harvard, Princeton, or Yale, only 13 percent lived in a SuperZip cluster of three or fewer. The median was fourteen.

Meanwhile, the clusters surrounding the Big Four—New York, Washington, Los Angeles, and San Francisco—accounted for 39 percent of all people living in SuperZips. And those are the clusters in which almost all of the narrow elite and a large proportion of the broad elite live—in large bubbles dominated by their own kind.

Red SuperZips and Blue SuperZips

I promised at the end of chapter 1 that I would eventually take up the political orientation of the new upper class. The SuperZips give us a way to do that.

It is widely accepted, with good reason, that the narrow elite is more liberal than the rest of the country. The dominance of liberal views among the faculties of elite universities is well documented.[26] So are the percentages of journalists in the elite media who are self-identified liberals.[27] The liberalism of the film industry is openly proclaimed by its top stars, producers, and directors.[28]

Furthermore, activist liberalism has become much more widespread in the business community over the last few decades, as documented by political scientist David Callahan in *Fortunes of Change*. It's not just the well-publicized cases such as George Soros. The new billionaires of the information technology industry are overwhelmingly liberal, and so are large proportions of the billionaires and centimillionaires in the financial community.

To some degree, this growth of activist liberals in the business community has happened everywhere. Callahan opens his book with the case of Preston Hollow, the exclusive Dallas neighborhood where George W. Bush moved after leaving office. In 2008, Barack Obama raised more money in Preston Hollow's zip code than John McCain did.[29] But while the increasing leftward dominance of American elites is a fact, it can easily be exaggerated.

The SuperZips and the 2004 Presidential Election

Consider the bitterly contested 2004 presidential election. Some places fitted the stereotype. The SuperZips in the San Francisco–Silicon Valley corridor gave John Kerry 70 to 80 percent of the vote.[30] Moving down the coast to Los Angeles, Kerry got a combined 71 percent of the vote in Beverly Hills, Santa Monica, and Malibu. The wealthy suburbs of Boston and the wealthy neighborhoods of Manhattan gave Kerry more than 70 percent of the vote.

But other places didn't fit the stereotype. Outside Beverly Hills, Santa Monica, and Malibu, Kerry didn't get even a majority in the other wealthy Los Angeles areas for which votes can be broken out. Moving farther south into the wealthy towns of Orange County, Kerry won Laguna Beach but nowhere else, getting a meager combined 35 percent of the vote in Newport Beach, Aliso Viejo, Tustin, and Yorba Linda.

On the East Coast, the towns of the new upper class in the Super-Zips surrounding New York City were not particularly blue. Kerry got huge margins in a few of the New Jersey suburbs—Montclair and South Orange gave Kerry larger margins than even the most liberal San Francisco suburbs. But thirty-three of the forty-six wealthy New Jersey towns for which votes could be broken out went for Bush, with Kerry getting just a combined 39 percent of the vote. In the wealthy Connecticut suburbs outside New York City, Kerry won only ten of the eighteen towns for which votes could be broken out. The combined vote across all eighteen was 49 percent for Kerry, barely more than his national percentage.

Moving away from the coasts, it becomes impossible to think of the new upper class as being predominantly liberal. For the most part, wealthy neighborhoods in the cities of the Midwest, South, and Southeast are about as conservative as the states in which they are located, and sometimes more so. The entire state of Kansas gave Bush 62 percent of the vote. The wealthy towns of Leawood, Lenexa, Shawnee, and Overland Park each gave more than 70 percent of their vote to Bush.

Austin, Texas, provides an object lesson in the perils of confusing the conspicuous exceptions with the underlying profile. Austin's liberal neighborhoods are so visible in the life of the city that Austin is known elsewhere in Texas as "the People's Republic of Austin." Judging from its description by journalist Bill Bishop (and he lives there), the most liberal zip code (78704) in Austin, Travis Heights, is almost a caricature of the doctrinaire, politically correct progressive neighborhood.[31] Travis Heights gave Kerry 82 percent of the vote in 2004. Its neighbor to the north, just west of the University of Texas campus, went for Kerry with 63 percent of the vote. But the zip code adjoining it to the west, with a higher median income and a higher percentage of college degrees than either of the two liberal zip codes I just mentioned, went for Bush with 61 percent of the vote. The wealthiest zip code in Austin, also with one of the top percentages of the college-educated, went for Bush with 62 percent of the vote. So it is true that the areas immediately to the south, west, and north of the campus and the Texas state capitol are bastions of intellectual liberalism, just as Austin's image has it. But that doesn't mean that all or perhaps even most members of the Austin new upper class are liberal.

Who Represents the SuperZips in Congress?

Presidential votes can be broken out for only some towns and urban neighborhoods. Elections to the House of Representatives offer a more systematic way to characterize the political orientation of the new upper class nationwide.

As the measure of the political orientation of a zip code I used the liberal quotient of its congressional representative. *Liberal quotient* is the term used by the Americans for Democratic Action (ADA) for the number it calculates for each congressperson in each congressional session. The liberal quotient represents the number of correct votes, in the ADA's view, on key legislation divided by the total number of votes cast by that representative. One hundred is therefore the perfect liberal score and 0 is the perfect conservative score. I averaged the liberal quotients for all representatives for the 108th through 111th Congresses (those elected in 2002, 2004, 2006, and 2008), which, serendipitously, consisted of two each with Republican and Democratic majorities.[32]

In the pie charts that follow, "doctrinaire liberal" means an average liberal quotient of 90 or more, "liberal" means 75–89, "mixed" means 25–74, "conservative" means 10–24, and "doctrinaire conservative" means 0–9.

First, consider the nation as a whole. From 2002 to 2008, the members of the House of Representatives had a mean liberal quotient of 51.5, just slightly to the left of center, but that may imply more centrism than actually existed. Fifty-seven percent of the representatives had liberal quotients at the doctrinaire extremes, either liberal or conservative, and a mere 21 percent had liberal quotients in the great middle range of scores from 25 to 74. Taking all the zip codes in the country, figure 3.7 shows how the balance looked when the ADA scores of the representatives are weighted by the adult population in the zip codes they represented.

FIGURE 3.7.   **ADA VOTING RECORDS OF PEOPLE REPRESENTING ZIP CODES THAT ARE NOT SUPERZIPS**

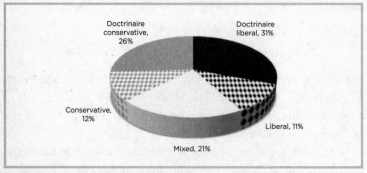

Source: Annual ADA reports and the zip code data base. Percentages are weighted by zip code population.

Outside the SuperZips, the nation was almost evenly split, with only a small edge for doctrinaire liberals.

The same balance between liberals and conservatives applies to most of the SuperZips. Figure 3.8 shows the representation for people who live in SuperZips—with one little caveat: It includes all the SuperZips except the ones surrounding the Big Four—New York, Washington, Los Angeles, and San Francisco.

FIGURE 3.8.   **ADA VOTING RECORDS OF PEOPLE REPRESENTING THE SUPERZIPS THAT ARE NOT NEAR THE BIG FOUR**

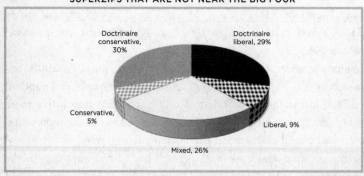

Sources: Annual ADA reports. Percentages refer to the aggregate population of the SuperZips.

The representatives of the SuperZips outside the Big Four are slightly more polarized than the entire House of Representatives, with 60 percent of the inhabitants being represented by doctrinaire liberals or conservatives. But the doctrinaire representation is equally balanced.

In figure 3.9 we look at who represents the people in the SuperZips surrounding the Big Four.

FIGURE 3.9.   ADA VOTING RECORDS OF PEOPLE REPRESENTING THE SUPERZIPS SURROUNDING THE BIG FOUR

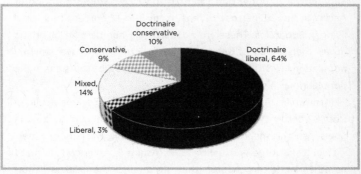

Sources: Annual ADA reports. Percentages refer to the aggregate population of the SuperZips.

Sixty-four percent of the people living in the SuperZips surrounding the Big Four are represented by doctrinaire liberals, compared to 19 percent who are represented by a conservative of any stripe. The reason figure 3.9 is significant is, of course, that the SuperZips surrounding New York, Washington, Los Angeles, and San Francisco are the home of almost all of the narrow elite whose decisions directly affect the economy, politics, and culture of the nation. These are also the SuperZips that are aggregated into the largest and most heavily buffered SuperZip clusters in the nation. The representatives they elect reflect a component of the new upper class that is just as liberal as its reputation.

What's Changed Since the 2000 Census?

I began the discussion of the SuperZips with a promise to update the results in later editions of *Coming Apart* after the 2010 census results became available.* Those results were published from December 2011 through the spring of 2012. This is the story they tell:

Ethnic Composition

My expectation that Asians would increase their presence in the SuperZips was borne out: From 2000 to 2010, the proportion of Asians in SuperZips rose by half, from 8 to 12 percent of people living in SuperZips. These are extraordinary numbers for an ethnic group that still constituted fewer than 5 percent of the national population in 2010. The ratio of Asians in SuperZips to Asians in the population as a whole is 2.6 to 1.

Meanwhile, the percentage of whites in the SuperZips declined from 82 percent in 2000 to 74 percent, a substantial reduction. In one sense, this means an increase in the ethnic diversity of America's elites. But the unusual status of Asians in American life that I noted earlier in this chapter—their status since the 1960s as "honorary whites"—clouds the situation. In terms of minorities considered to be disadvantaged, black representation in the SuperZips grew from 3 to 4 percent and Latino representation from 3 to 6 percent. Whites plus Asians constituted 90 percent of the SuperZips' population in 2000 and 86 percent in 2010.

Concentration of Overeducated Elitist Snobs in the SuperZips

In the original version of this chapter, I used the sample of 14,317 graduates of Harvard, Princeton, and Yale as my proxy for assessing the concentration of overeducated elitist snobs in the SuperZips.

---

*For convenience, I will refer to these results in terms of 2010, but it's more complicated than that. The ethnic figures are taken from the 2010 census, but the educational and income data used for computing the 2010 centile scores are taken from the American Community Survey (the Census Bureau's annual replacement for the long form of the decennial census). Its five-year file, from 2006 to 2010, provides data at the zip-code level, which can be roughly interpreted as where median family income and percentage of adults with college degrees stood as of 2008.

I did not address whether that concentration had increased over time. Here, I add a new analysis, based on the variation in the years in which the members graduated (from 1964 to 1991), the years in which we learned their home zip codes (from 1989 to 2010), and their ages at the time they reported those zip codes (from 40 to 52). The new question I am asking is: After statistically controlling for these variables, how did the probability that a graduate of those three schools lived in a SuperZip change from 1989 to 2010?*

It rose. The probability that someone in the Harvard-Princeton-Yale sample lived in a SuperZip at age 45 increased from 39 percent in 1989 to 47 percent in 2010. The SuperZips are distinguished not just by simple measures of income and college education, nor just by their historical attraction to graduates of elite schools, but by the *increasing* concentration of graduates of elite schools in those zip codes. It is a phenomenon that implies continuing increases in the cultural distance between the residents of SuperZips and mainstream America.

Concentration of SuperZips in the Big Four Metropolitan Areas

I noted earlier that an extremely high proportion of members of the narrow elite—people with national influence—live in what I have called the "Big Four" metropolitan areas, associated with New York, Los Angeles, San Francisco, and Washington, DC. It appears that the highest-status zip codes are becoming more concentrated in the Big Four as well. The percentage of all Americans who live in the Big Four fell by half a percentage point from 2000 to 2010 (to 15.1 percent). Over the same decade, the percentage of people who live in SuperZips who are also located in the Big Four grew from 43 to 47 percent. This too represents a longer-term trend. In 1980, just 40 percent of people who lived in SuperZips were located in the Big Four.

By far the biggest gainer of SuperZip residents was the Wash-

---

*I conducted a logistic regression analysis in which the dependent variable was scored "1" if the person lived in a SuperZip, "0" otherwise, and the independent variables were the year in which the information about home zip code was valid and the age of the person in that year. This and subsequent statistical results reported in the text were all statistically significant beyond the .001 level.

ington metropolitan area, followed by New York. Los Angeles had a modest increase in its proportion of SuperZip residents. San Francisco and the Silicon Valley corridor did not increase their percentage of SuperZip residents during the decade.

The Elite Bubbles

The elite bubbles—clusters of contiguous SuperZips—have continued to grow. On page 89, I show a map of the SuperZips clustered around Washington, DC, based on the 2000 census. If that map were redrawn based on the 2010 census, there would be a lot more black on it—in some of the downtown DC zip codes, filling some of the previous gaps to the north and northeast of the District of Columbia, and especially filling gaps to the west. Just about all of the gray-shaded zip codes to the west of the District of Columbia have turned black, and newly black zip codes continue westward off the edge of the map. In all, the DC cluster added more than half a million people from 2000 to 2010. This single SuperZip bubble now consists of 93 zip codes and a population of 1.7 million people.

In Manhattan, the number of SuperZips grew from 19 in 2000 to 28 in 2010. All of Manhattan south of Ninety-Sixth Street is a mass of SuperZips with a few exceptions, such as the theater district, near the Brooklyn Bridge, and the Tribeca area (which barely missed at centile 94). A separate small bubble of SuperZips formed in fashionable parts of Brooklyn.

The suburban bubbles surrounding New York City have expanded so that they are nearly joined, with only minor gaps in a semi-circle that runs from Fairfield, Connecticut, through Westchester County and across the Hudson, extending south to Princeton, New Jersey, plus more isolated bubbles on the north shore of Long Island and, of all places, Hoboken, New Jersey. In all, the bubbles in the New York metropolitan area contain 202 zip codes, with a population of 2.7 million, up from 169 zip codes and 2.4 million in 2000.

Other elite bubbles that saw significant growth during the decade, defined as an increase of more than 40,000 people living in contiguous SuperZips, were in the San Diego area, separate clusters in downtown Seattle and nearby Bellevue, suburbs to the west of Boston, suburbs to the west of Houston, and suburbs to the west and north of Columbus, Ohio. The bubbles that lost more than 40,000 in population during the decade were Ann Arbor, Michigan, the North Shore of Chicago, suburbs to the west of Chicago, and suburbs south of Denver. The unrivaled leader among shrinking bubbles was the cluster of suburbs in the Bloomfield area to the northwest and north of Detroit, which saw a loss of more than 91,000 people living in SuperZips.

So that's the update from 2000 to 2010. Nothing surprising happened. All of the trends that were established by 2000 continued unabated. America's elites continued to sort themselves into enclaves, with graduates of the elite schools increasingly congregating in SuperZips. The enclaves surrounding the two most powerful cities in the nation, Washington and New York, already the largest in 2000, grew the most.

Charles Murray
August 2012

4

How Thick Is Your Bubble?

*A new upper class that makes decisions affecting the lives of
everyone else but increasingly doesn't know much about how
everybody else lives is vulnerable to making mistakes.
How vulnerable are you?*

N O VICE OF the human heart is so acceptable to [a despot]
as egotism," wrote Alexis de Tocqueville. "A despot easily
forgives his subjects for not loving him, provided they
do not love each other." That couldn't happen in the United States,
Tocqueville argued, because of the genius of the founders in devolv-
ing power:

> Local freedom . . . perpetually brings men together, and forces
> them to help one another, in spite of the propensities which
> sever them. In the United States, the more opulent citizens take
> great care not to stand aloof from the people. On the contrary,
> they constantly keep on easy terms with the lower classes: they
> listen to them, they speak to them every day.[1]

That's not true anymore. As the new upper class increasingly consists of people who were born into upper-middle-class families and
have never lived outside the upper-middle-class bubble, the danger
increases that the people who have so much influence on the course
of the nation have little direct experience with the lives of ordinary

Americans, and make their judgments about what's good for other people based on their own highly atypical lives.

In one sense, there is no such thing as an "ordinary American." The United States comprises a patchwork of many subcultures, and the members of any one of them is ignorant about and isolated from the others to some degree. The white fifth-grade teacher from South Boston doesn't understand many things about the life of the black insurance agent in Los Angeles, who in turn doesn't understand many things about the life of the Latino truck driver in Oklahoma City. But there are a variety of things that all three *do* understand about the commonalities in their lives—simple things that you have no choice but to understand if you have to send your kids to the local public school, you live in a part of town where people make their living in a hundred different ways instead of a dozen, and you always eat out at places where you and your companion won't spend more than $50 tops, including tip.

Those specifications embrace an extremely large part of the American population. Tack on a few other specifications—that you watch at least twenty-four hours of commercial television a week (still well below the national average of thirty-five hours) and that you see most of the most popular new movies, either in theaters or on DVDs—and you have guaranteed a substantial degree of common familiarity about the culture as well. So while there is no such thing as an ordinary American, it is not the case that most Americans are balkanized into enclaves where they know little of what life is like for most other Americans. "The American mainstream" may be hard to specify in detail, but it exists.

Many of the members of the new upper class *are* balkanized. Furthermore, their ignorance about other Americans is more problematic than the ignorance of other Americans about them. It is not a problem if truck drivers cannot empathize with the priorities of Yale professors. It is a problem if Yale professors, or producers of network news programs, or CEOs of great corporations, or presidential advisers cannot empathize with the priorities of truck drivers. It is inevitable that people have large areas of ignorance about how others live, but that makes it all the more important that the members of the new upper class be aware of the breadth and depth of their ignorance.

To my knowledge, sociologists haven't gotten around to asking upper-middle-class Americans how much they know about their fellow citizens, so once again I must ask you to serve as a source of evidence by comparing your own experience to my generalizations. This time, I have a twenty-five-question quiz for you to take.[2] I hope it will serve two purposes: first, to calibrate the extent of your own ignorance (if any); second, to give you a framework for thinking about the ignorance that may be common in your professional or personal circles, even if it doesn't apply to you.

The questions you should take most seriously are the opening ones that ask about the places you have lived and the variation in conditions of life that you have experienced. The ignorance they imply is certain. If you have never lived or worked in a small town, you *must* be ignorant about day-to-day life in a small town, no matter how many movies set in rural Georgia you've seen. If you have never held a job that caused a body part to hurt by the end of the day, you don't know what that's like—period.

When I move to informational questions about sports, popular culture, and some American institutions, you are free to complain that some of them aren't fair. Some questions have a gender bias (though I've tried to balance those). Some are sneaky and several poke fun. In no case does an inability to answer reflect on your intelligence, character, or all-around goodness of heart.

Some of the questions are ones that whites will get right more often than minorities, and that people who do not live in metropolises will get right more often than people who do. That's because I am writing about the problems of the new upper class, the new upper class is overwhelmingly white and urban, and the readers of this book are overwhelmingly white and urban. Note, however, that had I included questions that would be more easily answered by minorities in working-class urban neighborhoods, your score would probably be even worse.

Unless I specify an age range, the questions apply to experiences that occurred at any point in your life.

Please take out your no. 2 pencil and begin.

The Questions

Life History

1. Have you ever lived for at least a year in an American neighborhood in which the majority of your fifty nearest neighbors probably did not have college degrees?

2. Did you grow up in a family in which the chief breadwinner was *not* in a managerial job or a high-prestige profession (defined as attorney, physician, dentist, architect, engineer, scientist, or college professor)?

3. Have you ever lived for at least a year in an American community under 50,000 population that is not part of a metropolitan area and is not where you went to college?

4. Have you ever lived for at least a year in the United States at a family income that was close to or below the poverty line? You may answer "yes" if your family income then was below $30,000 in 2010 dollars. Graduate school doesn't count. Living unemployed with your family after college doesn't count.

   Take your best guess. For estimating your family's past income, you should multiply what you or your parents used to make by the inflator appropriate to that time. For example, if your dad made $7,000 a year when you were growing up in 1970, you should multiply that by 5.61. He made about $39,270 in 2010 dollars. You may estimate the inflator for any particular year from these: 1940, 15.66; 1950, 9.12; 1960, 7.41; 1970, 5.61; 1980, 2.64; 1990, 1.67; 2000, 1.26.

5. Have you ever walked on a factory floor?

6. Have you ever held a job that caused something to hurt at the end of the day?

People Who Have Been Part of Your Life

7. Have you ever had a close friend who was an evangelical Christian?

8. Do you now have a close friend with whom you have strong and wide-ranging political disagreements?

9. Have you ever had a close friend who could seldom get better than Cs in high school even if he or she tried hard?

10. During the last month, have you voluntarily hung out with people who were smoking cigarettes?

11. What military ranks do these five insignia represent?

Sports, Pastimes, and Consumer Preferences

12. Choose one. Who is Jimmie Johnson? Or: Have you ever purchased Avon products?

13. Have you or your spouse ever bought a pickup truck?

14. During the last year, have you ever purchased domestic mass-market beer to stock your own fridge?

15. During the last five years, have you or your spouse gone fishing?

16. How many times in the last year have you eaten at one of the following restaurant chains? Applebee's, Waffle House, Denny's, IHOP, Chili's, Outback Steakhouse, Ruby Tuesday, T.G.I. Friday's, Ponderosa Steakhouse

Some American Institutions

17. In secondary school, did you letter in anything?

18. Have you ever attended a meeting of a Kiwanis Club or Rotary Club, or a meeting at a union local?

19. Have you ever participated in a parade not involving a war, a political campaign, abortion rights (pro or con), or gay rights (pro or con)?

20. Since leaving school, have you ever worn a uniform?

21. Have you ever ridden on a long-distance bus (e.g., Greyhound, Trailways) or hitchhiked for a trip of fifty miles or more?

Media and Popular Culture

22. Which of the following movies have you seen (at a theater or on a DVD)? *Iron Man 2, Inception, Despicable Me, Tron Legacy, True Grit, Clash of the Titans, Grown Ups, Little Fockers, The King's Speech, Shutter Island*

23. During the 2009–10 television season, how many of the following series did you watch regularly? *American Idol, Undercover Boss, The Big Bang Theory, Grey's Anatomy, Lost, House, Desperate Housewives, Two and a Half Men, The Office, Survivor*

24. Have you ever watched an *Oprah, Dr. Phil,* or *Judge Judy* show all the way through?

25. What does the word *Branson* mean to you?

Scoring Your Access to the Rest of America

1. *Have you ever lived for at least a year in an American neighborhood in which the majority of your fifty nearest neighbors did not have college degrees?* Seven points maximum. Score 4 points if you answered "yes" plus a bonus point for every five years you have lived in such a place up to fifteen years. Zero points if you are thinking of a gentrifying neighborhood in which you were one of the gentrifiers.

   In the 2000 census, 92 percent of Americans lived in zip codes in which the majority of adults ages 25 and older did not have college degrees. Seventy-seven percent lived in zip codes where fewer than a third of those adults had degrees. You should make your judgment with regard to your neighborhood, not your zip code.

2. *Did you grow up in a family in which the chief breadwinner was not in a managerial job or a high-prestige profession (defined as attorney, physician, dentist, architect, engineer, scientist, or college professor)?* Seven points maximum. Score 4 points if you answered "yes" and 3 bonus points if the chief breadwinner for most or all of your childhood was in what you consider to be a blue-collar job.

   The percentages of households in which the chief breadwinner was not in a managerial job or a high-prestige profession ranged from 85 percent in 1960 to 75 percent in 2010.[3]

3. *Have you ever lived for at least a year in an American community under 50,000 population that is not part of a metropolitan area and is not where you went to college?* Seven points maximum. Score 5 points if you answered "yes," 6 points if the place was under 25,000, and 7 points if you lived in a town of fewer than 10,000 people or in a rural area.

    The percentage of Americans fitting the description in the question was 58 percent in the 1960 census and 48 percent in the 2000 census. You may find it surprising, as I did, that 21 percent of Americans still lived in rural areas as of the 2000 census and another 10 percent lived in towns of fewer than 10,000 people—in total, almost a third of the population. That figure is not completely cleansed of bedroom communities, but it's close.

4. *Have you ever lived for at least a year in the United States at a family income that was close to or below the poverty line? You may answer "yes" if your family income then was below $30,000 in 2010 dollars. Graduate school doesn't count. Living unemployed with your family after college doesn't count.* Seven points maximum. Score 5 points if you answered "yes" and two bonus points if you experienced poverty both as a child and as an adult.

    A majority of Americans in their forties have been below the poverty line for a year at least once since their teens—56 percent for the 1979 cohort of the NLSY.[4]

5. *Have you ever walked on a factory floor?* Six points maximum. Score 2 points for "yes," 4 points if you have ever had a job that entailed routine visits to factory floors, and 6 points if you have worked on a factory floor.

    I was prompted to use this question because of a personal experience. In the mid-1980s, my sponsor for a speech at a local college in Wichita was the owner of a factory that made cardboard boxes, and my host took me to see it. It was fascinating— the ingenious machines, the noise, the speed, the organization. Then it struck me that every product I used was made in such a place—in the aggregate, thousands of them, constituting the world that made my life possible—and until then I had never seen even a glimpse of it except as a small child on a single visit to Maytag Company's assembly line. My visit to the box factory was a quarter of a century ago, and I haven't been on another factory floor since.

6. *Have you ever held a job that caused something to hurt at the end of the day?* Six points maximum. Score 3 points if you answered "yes," add 2 bonus points if the job lasted longer than a summer, and a bonus point if you're talking about a job that made you ache all over.

The question applies to any part of the body that hurts because of physical labor using the large muscles. Headaches don't count, and neither does carpal tunnel syndrome. Sore feet from having to stand up for long periods of time does count.

If you answered "no" to this one, your bubble is thick indeed. John Kenneth Galbraith, who grew up on a farm, once said that after you've worked on a farm, nothing else you ever do is work. One might also say that if you've never had a job where something hurts at the end of the day, you don't know what work is. You certainly don't know what work is like for the large proportion of the American population who do hold jobs that cause something to hurt at the end of the day.

7. *Have you ever had a close friend who was an evangelical Christian?* Four points maximum. Score 2 points if you answered "yes," and 4 points if you are an evangelical Christian yourself.

The distinguishing characteristics of evangelical Christians are belief in the historical accuracy of both the Hebrew Bible and the New Testament, including especially the divinity and resurrection of Christ, and belief in the necessity of personal conversion—being "born again"—as a condition for salvation. In the Pew Forum's survey of the U.S. religious landscape in 2004, with a sample of more than 35,000, 26.3 percent of the respondents said they were affiliated with evangelical Protestant churches, the single largest category. Catholics came in second at 23.9 percent, mainline Protestant churches third at 18.1 percent, and "unaffiliated" fourth at 16.1 percent.[5]

8. *Do you now have a close friend with whom you have strong and wide-ranging political disagreements?* Four points maximum. Score 2 points if you have one such close friend, 4 points if you have more than one, but *not* if they are disagreements within the same side of the political spectrum (no points if you are a liberal who has an ultraliberal friend or a conservative with an ultraconservative friend).

The reason for this question is obvious from the discussion of red and blue SuperZips in chapter 3. See Bill Bishop's *The Big Sort* for a comprehensive analysis of this issue.[6]

9. *Have you ever had a close friend who could seldom get better than Cs in high school even if he or she tried hard?* Score 4 points for "yes."

I use this question as a way of getting at the question I would like to ask, "Have you ever had a close friend who would have scored below the national average on an IQ test?" I can't ask that question, because readers who grew up in an upper-middle-class neighborhood or went to school with the children of the upper-middle class have no way of knowing what *average* means. The empirical case for that statement is given in detail elsewhere, but it may be summarized quickly.[7] The typical mean IQ for students in schools that the children of the upper-middle class attend is around 115, compared to the national mean of 100. In such a school, almost all of the below-average students, the ones you thought of as the school's dummies, actually were above the national average. Even if the students were arranged in a normal distribution around a mean of 115, only 11 percent of the students could be expected to have IQs under 100.[8] But they probably weren't normally distributed, especially at a private school that uses a floor of academic ability in its admission decisions. So if you went to upper-middle-class schools and think you had a good friend who was below the national IQ mean, and are right, it had to have been one of the students who was at the absolute bottom of academic ability.

If you answered "yes" to this question as stated, you need to ask yourself if you fudged about the definition of "close friend." We hate to think we're such snobs that we have consorted only with people as smart as we are, and the temptation is strong to define as a "close friend" a classmate in K–12 who didn't seem very smart but with whom we exchanged friendly greetings in the lunchroom.

10. *During the last month have you voluntarily hung out with people who were smoking cigarettes?* Score 3 points for "yes."

In the Centers for Disease Control's Behavioral Risk Factor Surveillance System for 2009, 35 percent of the respondents said that they smoked some days or every day.[9] Rates of smoking have a strong socioeconomic gradient, but the wording of the question is designed to get at something else. Open smoking in the world of the new upper class has become so rare that it is nearly invisible. Cigars and pipes appear occasionally, but it is possible to go for weeks in the new-upper-class milieu without smelling a whiff of cigarette smoke anywhere except on a public street. Elsewhere in America, there are still lots of homes, bars, and work sites where smoking goes on openly, and nonsmokers in those settings accept it as a fact of life. The question asks to what extent you have any voluntary participation in that part of America.

11. *What military ranks are denoted by these five insignia?* From left to right, the five stand for colonel (or navy captain), major general (or navy rear admiral, upper half), corporal, master sergeant, and captain (or navy lieutenant). Five points maximum. Score 1 point if you got at least one correct, 3 points if you identified all of them, and 5 points if you ever served in the armed forces.

In 2007, 1.4 million Americans were on active duty in the armed forces, another 1.3 million were in the reserve, and 805,000 civilians worked directly for the Department of Defense. People who live in counties where a large military base is located account for another 8.4 million.[10] In the 2000 census, 26.4 million Americans were veterans of the armed forces. In mainstream America, just about every neighborhood is peppered with numerous veterans, and the local chapter of the VFW or American Legion is still a significant civic force in much of America.

12. *Option 1: Who is Jimmie Johnson?* Three points maximum. Score 3 points if you identified Jimmie Johnson as the NASCAR driver.

Score 1 point (consolation prize) if you identified him as the former coach of the Dallas Cowboys (the coach spells it *Jimmy*, not *Jimmie*).

For tens of millions of Americans, Jimmie Johnson is the most important figure in sports. He was the NASCAR Sprint Cup Series champion for five consecutive years from 2006 to 2010, a feat as unlikely as pulling off the Grand Slam in golf or tennis. NASCAR itself rivals the NFL, NBA, and Major League Baseball by several measures of attendance, economic clout, and size of fan base.

Option 2: Have you ever purchased Avon products? Score 3 points for "yes."

Avon is one of the largest companies selling cosmetics and perfume door-to-door, with sales of $9.9 billion in 2007.

13. *Have you or your spouse ever bought a pickup truck?* Score 2 points for "yes."

In 2010, Americans bought about 1.6 million new pickup trucks.[11] Occasionally members of the new upper class buy one for fun or because they need one at their summer place in Montana. But it remains true that people who have a need for the things that a pickup truck can do are usually engaged in activities that people in the new upper class often don't do at all, or things that the new upper class hires other people to do for them.

14. *During the last year, have you ever purchased domestic mass-market beer to stock your own fridge?* Score 2 points for "yes."

The leading qualifying beers are Budweiser, Coors, Miller, or Busch, light or regular. The disdain of the new upper class for domestic mass-market beer is nearly as intense as its disdain for people who smoke cigarettes.

15. *During the last five years, have you or your spouse gone fishing?* Two points maximum. Score 1 point for "yes" and 2 points if you or your spouse go fishing more than once a year.

Fishing is a regular pastime for about 40 million Americans, and at the center of the annual vacation for millions more who don't fish regularly.[12] It is so popular that it supports not just one but two professional bass-fishing tournament circuits, the Bassmaster Tournament Trail and the Walmart FLW Tour, plus several regional tours. Top prize for the Bassmaster Classic is $500,000. Win the Forrest Wood Cup, and you get $1 million. Both major tours are nationally televised.

16. *How many times in the last year have you eaten at one of the following restaurant chains? Applebee's, Waffle House, Denny's, IHOP, Chili's, Outback Steakhouse, Ruby Tuesday, T.G.I. Friday's, Ponderosa Steakhouse.* Four points maximum. Score a point for each time you ate at one of them up to 4.

However much they disapprove of fast food in theory and restrict their visits, almost all members of the new upper class at least know what the inside of a McDonald's looks like. But how about the chains of sit-down restaurants that form such an integral part of life in most of America? The nine I listed are the ones with the most outlets in the United States.[13] I could not get statistics on meals served by them, but given that these nine chains had revenues of more than $12 billion in 2009 (probably much more), and all of that comes from dinner checks that ran around $5 to $25 per person, the aggregate number of meals served by just the top nine chains has to be in the high hundreds of millions, at least.[14] Why a list of nine chains instead of the more natural top ten? Because one of the top ten is Chipotle Mexican Grill, which is to the casual-dining genre of restaurants as Whole Foods is to grocery stores.

17. *In secondary school, did you letter in anything?* Two points maximum. Score 2 points if you got any high school varsity letter *except* for the debating team or chess club. Score 2 points if you were a cheerleader or in the marching band.

The stereotype of the overeducated elitest snob as a teenager is someone who either went to a private school where team sports were not a big deal or went to a public school where he held himself aloof from the team sports and collateral activities that are such an important part of the culture of public high schools. Does the stereotype fit you?

18. *Have you ever attended a meeting of a Kiwanis Club or Rotary Club, or a meeting at a union local?* Score 2 points for "yes."

Kiwanis and Rotary Clubs have for several decades been a primary networking organization for local businessmen. They are more influential in small cities than in large ones, but their reach extends everywhere. They are a significant source of secular social capital as well, playing an active role in a variety of civic activities. Unions usually do not play a large role in generating social capital for the community at large, but they are often centrally important to the work life of members of the union.

19. *Have you ever participated in a parade not involving a war, a political campaign, abortion rights (pro or con), or gay rights (pro or con)?* Score 2 points for "yes." Helping to decorate a float counts even if you didn't get to ride on it.

    Celebratory parades, as opposed to parades on behalf of causes, occur everywhere in America, from small towns to ethnic neighborhoods in the largest cities, but not so often in the enclaves of the new upper class. This question asks if you have ever been part of one.

20. *Since leaving school, have you ever worn a uniform?* Three points maximum. Score 1 for "yes," a bonus point if you did so as part of your job, and a third point if it was while you served in the armed forces.

    A uniform can consist of as little as a shirt with your employer's logo that you are required to wear on the job. It gives you a chance to score a point or two if you are a member of a social club that occasionally has rituals involving uniforms, if you are a Civil War reenactor, or if you participate in an adult athletic league. Wearing a uniform in a dramatic production or on Halloween does not count.

21. *Have you ever ridden on a long-distance bus (e.g., Greyhound, Trailways) or hitchhiked for a trip of fifty miles or more?* Two points maximum. Score 1 point for having used each form of transportation.

    About 25 million people rode on a Greyhound Bus in 2008 alone. There are no statistics on hitchhiking.

22. *Which of the following movies have you seen (at a theater or on a DVD)? Iron Man 2, Inception, Despicable Me, Tron Legacy, True*

Grit, Clash of the Titans, Grown Ups, Little Fockers, The King's Speech, Shutter Island. Four points maximum. Score a point for each movie seen up to 4.

These represent the ten top-grossing films of 2010 that were not principally directed at children or teens.[15]

23. *During the 2009–10 television season, how many of the following series did you watch regularly? American Idol, Undercover Boss, The Big Bang Theory, Grey's Anatomy, Lost, House, Desperate Housewives, Two and a Half Men, The Office, Survivor.* Four points maximum. Score a point for each series up to 4.

These were the ten television series (omitting a sports series, NBC *Sunday Night Football*) with the highest Nielsen ratings for the 2009–10 television season. Number 1, *American Idol*, had a rating of 9.1 and an audience share of 24 percent. Number 10, *Survivor* (the "Heroes and Villains" sequence), had a rating of 4.5 and an audience share of 13 percent.[16]

24. *Have you ever watched an* Oprah, Dr. Phil, *or* Judge Judy *show all the way through?* Four points maximum. Score 1 point for each of the three for which you have watched an entire episode and a bonus point if you watch any of them regularly.

The Oprah Winfrey Show is, of course, the highest-rated talk show in American history, in its twenty-fifth and last year as I write. *Dr. Phil* is in its ninth year, and is rated second only to *Oprah. Judge Judy* is now in its fifteenth year and is said to be watched by about 10 million people on a typical day. References to them have become a common part of the popular culture.

25. *What does the word* Branson *mean to you?* Four points maximum. Score 2 points if you knew that Branson is a big entertainment center in the Midwest, and 4 points if you've gone to Branson yourself. No points for thinking of Richard Branson.

Branson, Missouri, is one of the leading tourist destinations in America. With a permanent population of only 6,050 in the 2000 census, it has more than fifty different theaters offering daily live performances, almost all of them devoted to country music and its derivatives. In 2009, during the worst year of the recession, it still attracted more than 7 million visitors.[17]

Interpreting Your Score

Here are the scores that you could expect to get if you fit the following descriptions.

- *A lifelong resident of a working-class neighborhood with average television and moviegoing habits.* Range: 48–99. Typical: 77.
- *A first-generation middle-class person with working-class parents and average television and moviegoing habits.* Range: 42–100. Typical: 66.
- *A first-generation upper-middle-class person with middle-class parents.* Range: 11–80. Typical: 33.
- *A second-generation (or more) upper-middle-class person who has made a point of getting out a lot.* Range: 0–43. Typical: 9.
- *A second-generation (or more) upper-middle-class person with the television and moviegoing habits of the upper-middle class.* Range: 0–20. Typical: 2.

The scoring of the archetypes reflects a few realities about socioeconomic background and the bubble.

If you grew up in a working-class neighborhood, you are going to have a high score even if you are now an investment banker living on Park Avenue. Your present life may be completely encased in the bubble, but you brought a lot of experience into the bubble that will always be part of your understanding of America.

Growing up in a middle-class neighborhood also scores points for you on several questions, and this, too, is reflected in the real-world experiences that people bring to their adult lives in the new upper class. But *middle class* covers a wide variety of environments, and the degree to which people who grew up in the middle class seal themselves off from that world after they reach the new upper class also varies widely, which is reflected in the wide range of possible scores.

Having grown up in an upper-middle-class neighborhood inevitably means some restriction to your exposure to average American life. If you grew up in an exclusive part of town such as Chicago's North Shore or Northwest Washington, you or your parents had to take proactive steps to force you out of the bubble. That sort of thing happens, but even then it is often artificial—your parents made you help out in a soup kitchen during high school and you volunteered for Habitat for Humanity during college, so you have had brief exposure to some of the most downtrodden people and disorganized neighborhoods. The truth is, such experiences still leave people with little idea of what life in an ordinary working-class or middle-class neighborhood is like.

5

The Bright Side of the New Upper Class

In which it is argued that even if living with the new upper class has its problems, living without it is neither a good idea nor an option.

AFTER ALL THE complaints I have lodged against the isolation and ignorance of the new upper class, it is time to give these Americans their due. As individuals, the members of the new upper class are usually just fine—engaging, well mannered, good parents, and good neighbors. Some good things can also be said for the new upper class as a class.

Starting with the prologue, I have described the America of 1960 in ways that have sometimes sounded nostalgic. But if a time machine could transport me back to 1960, I would have to be dragged into it kicking and screaming. In many aspects of day-to-day life, America today is incomparably superior to the America of 1960. The coalescence of the new upper class must get some credit for the good things that have happened, especially those having to do with economic growth and improvements in the standard of living.

When America got serious about identifying cognitive talent, shipping the talented to colleges and the most talented to the best colleges, it also augmented the nation's efficiency in tapping its human capital by some unknowable but large amount. The result over the long term was that cognitive talent that in an earlier era would have been employed in keeping a store or repairing broken-down engines was employed instead in running large corporations and inventing new kinds of engines.

How much difference did that make? The effects of upgrading cognitive talent in an organization are less obvious now, long after the revolutions in higher education and the college sorting machine have upgraded the cognitive talent in the upper levels of almost all organizations. But a natural experiment of sorts was undertaken back in 1940 by the New York City Police Department that allows us to look at an episode in isolation.[1]

In 1939, a decade into the Great Depression and with unemployment still at 17 percent, the NYPD had just three hundred new slots to offer its next class and a vast pool of applicants—thirty-three thousand men. The NYPD decided to select exclusively on the basis of test scores, with no edge given to nephews of influential politicians and no edge for a favorable impression in a job interview. The applicants took two tests, one of cognitive ability (an IQ test similar to the one used by the federal civil service) and a test of physical ability. The composite score gave a 7:3 weight to the IQ score.

The applicants with the top composite scores were offered entrance to the police academy. In an age when few of the men had more attractive job alternatives, the three hundred slots ended up being filled by men who earned among the top 350 scores. The best estimate is that they had a mean IQ of around 130—near the mean IQ of incoming freshmen at elite schools today. They graduated from the police training academy in June 1940.

When the NYPD's class of '40 gathered for its fortieth anniversary in 1980, the results had been spectacular. Its three hundred members achieved far higher average rank and suffered far fewer disciplinary penalties than the typical class of recruits. Some of them made important contributions to police training. Many had successful careers as lawyers, businessmen, and academics after leaving the police department. Within the department, the class produced four police chiefs, four deputy commissioners, two chiefs of personnel, one chief inspector, and one commissioner of the New York City Police Department.

That's what can happen when an organization gets an infusion of cognitive talent, and there is reason to think that similar effects occurred throughout the American economy as cognitive sorting occurred. I cannot make an ironclad case for it, but the timing of various events in America's economic history during the last half century is worth thinking about.

The conditions for the formation of the new upper class that I described in chapter 2 began in the aftermath of World War II. As of 1960, the root cause of the new upper class—the increasing value of brains in the marketplace—had been growing in strength for years. College enrollment of the top IQ quartile of high school students had gone from 55 percent to more than 70 percent in just the preceding ten years.[2] The college sorting machine had spread from the elite schools of the Northeast and was shifting into high gear throughout the nation.

Without knowing anything else about what would happen next, a knowledgeable observer of colleges in 1960 would have known that the campuses of the nation's leading schools were more dense with talent than they had ever been, that they were getting denser with talent each year, and that there would be implications down the road. The point is not just that more people who could benefit from college were getting the chance to go to college, but that young people with the most potential were systematically being identified and put in situations where it was easier than in earlier decades for them to realize their potential. When those cohorts of young people reached professional maturity, this knowledgeable observer could have predicted, they were going to inject a massive jolt of human capital into the American economy.

That brings us to the timing of changes in the American standard of living. From the early 1960s to the late 1970s, not much changed in the technology of daily life. Televisions that had been black and white in 1960 were color. Copying machines had improved and were in wide use. The mainframe computer had taken its place in many offices, tended by a staff of acolytes. But daily life was about the same.

Automobiles, restaurants, hotels, merchandising, radios, hi-fidelity systems, shopping centers, telephones, the transportation of mail and packages, bank services, brokerage services, the equipment in a physician's office, typewriters, kitchen equipment, lighting, and the chair at your work desk were all similar to the way they had been in 1960.

Then things took off. Beginning around the mid-1970s—the appearance of the Apple II in 1977 is a good symbolic opening—the cascade of changes has been unending. They range from the trivial (it was still difficult to get a really good cup of coffee or loaf of bread in most parts of America in the late 1970s) to the momentous (the Information Revolution is rightly classified alongside the Industrial Revolution as an epochal event). The design, functionality, and durability of almost any consumer product today are far better than they were in 1960. Merchandisers have made it easy for customers in even the most remote parts of the country to get what they want when they want it at rock-bottom prices. For millions of people—me among them—taken-for-granted medications make the difference between debilitated lives of chronic discomfort and the active, comfortable lives they actually lead. Go back to 1960? I wouldn't dream of it.

Many explanations for this explosion of innovation compete for recognition. The coming of age of the microchip and laser technology in the late 1970s. The end of stagflation and the beginning of an economic boom in the early 1980s. Globalization. A dozen other factors. But among all the other things that were going on, it remains the case that at about the time the new infusion of talent hit the American economy, a great many good things started to happen within the private sector.

So are we sorry that we have this new kind of upper class? The question has to be put in that way, because we don't have the option of getting all the benefits of an energized, productive new upper class, one that makes all of our lives better in so many important ways, without the conditions that also tend toward a wealthy and detached new upper class.

How might we go about fixing the problems with the new upper class by changing laws? Would you like to roll back rising income inequality? How? Hike taxes back to the 91 percent top marginal rate that prevailed in 1960? If you actually succeed in substantially lowering compensation in all forms, you will also get reduced productivity from those who remain in the United States and a major brain drain among those who accept the opportunities that they will find elsewhere—the same responses among the most entrepreneurial and most able that have already beset European countries that have made it difficult for talent and hard work to be rewarded.

Apart from that, rolling back income inequality won't make any difference in the isolation of the new upper class from the rest of America. The new-upper-class culture is not the product of great wealth. It is *enabled* by affluence—people with common tastes and preferences need enough money to be able to congregate—but it is not *driven* by affluence. It is driven by the distinctive tastes and preferences that emerge when large numbers of cognitively talented people are enabled to live together in their own communities. You can whack the top income centile back to where it was in the 1980s, and it will have no effect whatsoever on the new-upper-class culture that had already emerged by that time. Places like Marin County are not fodder for cultural caricature because they are so wealthy.

Those are theoretical observations. Realistically, rolling back the disposable income of the new upper class in a major way is not an option. The American political culture doesn't work that way. The same Congress that passes higher marginal tax rates in this session will quietly pass a host of ways in which income can be sheltered and companies can substitute benefits for cash income in the next session. The new upper class will remain wealthy, and probably continue to get wealthier, no matter what.

If the most talented remain wealthy, they will congregate in the nicest places to live, with *nicest* defined as places where they can be around other talented, wealthy people like them, living in the most desirable parts of town, isolated from everyone else. It is human nature that they should do so. How is one to fight that with public policy? Restrict people's right to live where they choose?

Congregations of talented people will create a culture that differs in important ways from the mainstream culture and that consequently leaves them ignorant about how much of the rest of the population lives. How shall we prevent that?

Changing the new upper class by force majeure won't work and isn't a good idea in any case. The new upper class will change only if its members decide that it is in the interest of themselves and of their families to change. And possibly also because they decide it is in the interest of the country they love.

Part II

The Formation of a
New Lower Class

I F PART 1 succeeded in realizing my intent, you now have a sense of the degree to which a new upper class has formed that is composed of people who are more and more removed from the lives of everybody else. It is in that context that we start to explore what's been happening to everybody else, focusing on the working class.

Far from the life of the SuperZips is working-class America. For most of its history, working-class America *was* America, for practical purposes. In 1900, 90 percent of American workers were employed in low-level white-collar or technical jobs, manual and service jobs, or worked on farms. Even when our time horizon opens in 1960, 81 percent of workers were still employed in those jobs.[1] Within that mass of the working population, there were racial and ethnic distinctions, but not many others. Skilled craftsmen considered themselves to be a cut above manual laborers, and clerks in offices considered themselves to be a cut above people who had to work with their hands (even if being a clerk didn't pay any more than being a carpenter), but they all considered themselves to be working stiffs.

Michael Harrington's *The Other America* created a stir when it was published in 1962 partly because Harrington said America's poor constituted a class separate from the working class—a daring proposition. At that time, the poor were not seen as a class, either by other Americans or in their own eyes. The poor were working-class people who didn't make much money. They were expected to participate in the institutions of American life just as everybody else did. When white Americans thought about the lower class, a lot of them thought in terms of race—that's one of the bad realities of 1960. Insofar as they thought of a lower class among whites, they had in mind people at the fringes of American life—the broken-down denizens of the Bowery and Skid Row, or the people known as white trash. In the years after 1960, America developed something new: a white lower class that did not consist of a fringe, but of a substantial part of what was formerly the working-class population. Part 2 describes the trajectory of its formation.

The new lower class grew under the radar for a long time. In the 1960s and 1970s, two groups of Americans at opposite ends of the socioeconomic spectrum notoriously defied the traditional American expectations of respectable behavior. One consisted of white youths who came of age in the 1960s, mostly from middle-class and upper-middle-class families, who formed the counterculture that blossomed in Haight-Ashbury in the mid-1960s, gathered strength nationally during the years of the Vietnam War, and died away during the 1970s. The other was black and urban, a small minority of the black population that became so socially disorganized that by the early 1980s it had acquired the label of underclass.

The counterculture got most of the nation's attention during the 1970s and the underclass got most of the attention during the 1980s. But during those decades—quietly, gradually, without creating obvious social problems for America as a whole—the population of white Americans who defied traditional American expectations grew in size. By the 1990s and 2000s, the new lower class was a shaping force in the life of working-class America.

The separation of the new lower class from the norms of traditional America would be interesting but not alarming if it represented nothing more than alternative ways of living that work equally as well as the old ways of living. The nation is not going to the dogs because people wear jeans to church, smoke marijuana, or pierce a wider variety of body parts than their parents did. But the separation of the classes described in part 2 does not consist of these kinds of differences. Rather, it comprises differences that affect the ability of people to live satisfying lives, the ability of communities to function as communities, and the ability of America to survive as America.

6

The Founding Virtues

*In which it is argued that the feasibility of the American
project has historically been based on industriousness, honesty,
marriage, and religiosity; and that these aspects of American life
can be used to frame the analysis of changes in white America
from 1960 to 2010.*

I N 1825, FRANCIS Grund, seventh son of a German baron, educated in Vienna, decided to seek his fortune in the New World.
After spending a year as a professor of mathematics at the Brazil-
ian military academy, he moved on to the United States and settled in
Philadelphia. A decade later, he published a two-volume appraisal of
the American experiment from a European's perspective titled *The
Americans, in Their Moral, Social, and Political Relations.* Midway
through the first volume, he observed that "no government could be
established on the same principle as that of the United States, with a
different code of morals."

> The American Constitution is remarkable for its simplicity; but
> it can only suffice a people habitually correct in their actions,
> and would be utterly inadequate to the wants of a different na-
> tion. Change the domestic habits of the Americans, their reli-
> gious devotion, and their high respect for morality, and it will
> not be necessary to change a single letter of the Constitution in
> order to vary the whole form of their government.[1]

The idea that Americans were "habitually correct in their actions" was not one shared by all European observers. On the contrary, many visitors to the United States at about the same time were appalled by American behavior.

There was American hygiene, as noted by the Duc de Liancourt, who found that Americans were "astonished that one should object to sleeping two or three in the same bed and in dirty sheets, or to drink from the same dirty glass after half a score of others."[2] All foreign observers agreed that the amount of spitting, everywhere, indoors and out, was disgusting.

There was the American diet. "I will venture to say," declared one European visitor, "that if a prize were proposed for the scheme of a regimen most calculated to injure the stomach, the teeth, and the health in general, no better could be invented than that of the Americans," who "swallow, almost without chewing, hot bread, half baked, toast soaked in butter, cheese of the fattest kind, slices of salt or hung beef, ham, etc., all which are nearly insoluble."[3]

There was the prodigious drinking. Americans from adolescence onward drank at every meal—not the wine or beer of Europe, but the fiery rye whiskey of the New World. William Cobbett saw alcohol as the national disease. Young men, "even little boys, at or under twelve years of age, go into stores and tip off their drams" at all hours, he wrote.[4]

Not even the society to be found in the town houses of Philadelphia was really up to standard, Europeans sniffed. In his history of the period, Henry Adams quoted one foreign observer who was offended to discover that both married women and maidens at Philadelphia tea parties "were given to indecent allusions, indelicate expressions, and even at times immoral innuendoes. A loud laugh or a coarse exclamation followed each of these."[5]

And yet Grund's observation about the United States at the end of its first half century would not have surprised the founders. Everyone involved in the creation of the United States knew that its success depended on virtue in its citizenry—not gentility, but virtue. "No theoretical checks, no form of government can render us secure,"

James Madison famously observed at the Virginia ratifying convention. "To suppose that any form of government will secure liberty or happiness without any virtue in the people is a chimerical idea."[6]

It was chimerical because of the nearly unbridled freedom that the American Constitution allowed the citizens of the new nation. Americans were subject to criminal law, which forbade the usual crimes against person and property, and to tort law, which regulated civil disputes. But otherwise, Americans faced few legal restrictions on their freedom of action and no legal obligations to their neighbors except to refrain from harming them. The guides to their behavior at any more subtle level had to come from within.

For Benjamin Franklin, this meant that "only a virtuous people are capable of freedom. As nations become more corrupt and vicious, they have more need of masters." On the other hand, virtue makes government easy to sustain: "The expense of our civil government we have always borne, and can easily bear, because it is small. A virtuous and laborious people may be cheaply governed."[7]

For Patrick Henry, it seemed a truism that "bad men cannot make good citizens. . . . No free government, or the blessings of liberty, can be preserved to any people but by a firm adherence to justice, moderation, temperance, frugality, and virtue." George Washington said much the same thing in the undelivered version of his first inaugural address, asserting that "no Wall of words, no mound of parchment can be formed as to stand against the sweeping torrent of boundless ambition on the one side, aided by the sapping current of corrupted morals on the other."[8] Or as he put it most simply in his Farewell Address: "Virtue or morality is a necessary spring of popular government." In their various ways, the founders recognized that if a society is to remain free, *self-government* refers first of all to individual citizens governing their own behavior.

The Americans may not have been genteel, but, as a people, they met the requirements of virtue. The European traveler who was offended by American women at Philadelphia tea parties failed to understand the distinction between American manners and American morals, Henry Adams wrote:

Yet public and private records might be searched long, before
they revealed evidence of misconduct [of American women]
such as filled the press and formed one of the commonest topics
of conversation in the society of England and France. . . . The
society of 1800 was often coarse and sometimes brutal, but, except for intemperance, was moral.[9]

Adams was not being chauvinistic. "Although the travelers who
have visited North America differ on a great number of points,"
Tocqueville wrote, "they all agree in remarking that morals are far
more strict there than elsewhere."[10]

WHAT DID ADAMS, writing in the 1880s; Grund and Tocqueville,
writing a half century earlier; and the founders, writing a half century
before that, have in mind when they spoke of virtue in the people?

Different writers stressed different aspects of the topic, and they
could be parsed in several ways. But if there is no canonical list, four
aspects of American life were so completely accepted as essential that,
for practical purposes, you would be hard put to find an eighteenth-
century founder or a nineteenth-century commentator who dissented
from any of them. Two of them are virtues in themselves—industriousness and honesty—and two of them refer to institutions through
which right behavior is nurtured—marriage and religion. For convenience, I will refer to all four as the *founding virtues*.

Some of the founders would say my list is incomplete, with frugality being one candidate for addition, and philanthropy (or benevo-
lence) another. American conservatives today might chide me for
omitting self-reliance, a concept that overlaps with industriousness
but was not prominent on its own until well into the nineteenth century. The four I have decided upon meet this test: Would any of those
who shaped the American project and observed it in its first century
say that it could succeed *without* industriousness, honesty, marriage,
and religiosity in the people? For these four, there is no doubt about
the answer. No.

Industriousness

The founders talked about this virtue constantly, using the eighteenth-century construction, *industry*. To them, industry signified a cluster of qualities that had motivated the Revolution in the first place—a desire not just to be free to speak one's mind, to practice religion as one saw fit, and to be taxed only with representation, but the bone-deep American assumption that life is to be spent getting ahead through hard work, making a better life for oneself and one's children. I will use the more familiar modern term *industriousness* instead of *industry*, but I have the same broad sense of the word in mind.

American industriousness fascinated the rest of the world. No other American quality was so consistently seen as exceptional. Francis Grund made it the subject of the opening paragraph of his book:

> Active occupation is not only the principal source of [the Americans'] happiness, and the foundation of their natural greatness, but they are absolutely wretched without it. . . . [It] is the very soul of an American; he pursues it, not as a means of procuring for himself and his family the necessary comforts of life, but as the fountain of all human felicity.[11]

Underlying the willingness to do the work was the abundance of opportunity that America offered as a lure, and it affected people in every class. Henry Adams pointed out that it affected those on the bottom of American society more powerfully than those on the top.

> Reversing the old-world system, the American stimulant increased in energy as it reached the lowest and most ignorant class, dragging and whirling them upward as in the blast of a furnace. The penniless and homeless Scotch or Irish immigrant was caught and consumed by it; for every stroke of the axe and the hoe made him a capitalist, and made gentlemen of his

children. . . . The instinct of activity, once created, seemed heritable and permanent in the race.[12]

Not all visitors thought this American industriousness so very admirable, because it was closely linked with what they saw as an undesirable obsession with money. "An English shop-keeper is a tradesman all morning, but a gentleman in the evening," wrote one English visitor approvingly, whereas the Americans—New Englanders were especially egregious offenders—never put aside business. "Mammon has no more zealous worshipper than your true Yankee," he continued. "His homage is not merely that of the lip, or of the knee; it is an entire prostration of the heart; the devotion of all powers, bodily and mental, to the service of the idol."[13]

A side effect of this passion for industriousness was embarrassment at being thought a failure. Francis Grund wrote that during a decade of life in the United States, "I have never known a native American to ask for charity. No country in the world has such a small number of persons supported at the public expense. . . . An American, embarrassed by his pecuniary circumstances, can hardly be prevailed upon to ask or accept the assistance of his own relations; and will, in many instances, scorn to have recourse to his own parents."[14]

If just one American virtue may be said to be defining, industriousness is probably it.

Honesty

The importance of honesty in making a limited government work is self-evident—nothing short of a police state will force people to refrain from crime if they are predisposed otherwise, and an assumption that people will follow the rules is indispensable for making a free market work. The founders could see that as easily as we. For Thomas Jefferson, "honesty is the first chapter in the book of wisdom."[15] George Washington was himself legendarily honest (as in the cherry tree tale), and twice he included honesty in lists of virtues necessary in the American people.[16] Along with the importance of honesty went the belief that Americans were more honest than the Europeans, who were believed to be corrupt. Thus John Adams would look glumly upon the prospects for republicanism in the Netherlands or France. What was the difference between their revolutions and the American one? "It is a want of honesty; and if the common people in America lose their integrity, they will soon set up tyrants of their own."[17] Conversely, Jefferson was optimistic about assimilating European immigrants to the United States because, while they would bring their European vices with them, "these, I think, will soon be diluted and evaporated in a country of plain honesty."[18]

There is reason to think that Americans were in fact unusually law-abiding.[19] One of the rare quantitative analyses of crime in the early years of the new nation examined all the court cases in Massachusetts's Middlesex County, which embraced the most populous part of Massachusetts outside Boston. Over the period 1760–1810, the annual number of prosecutions for theft averaged 2.7 per 10,000 population.[20] Even considering that the number represents prosecutions, not the occurrence of thefts, it seems safe to conclude that the crime rate was extraordinarily low.[21]

The exception to America's low levels of crime was probably the crime now known as aggravated assault. European visitors were fascinated and horrified by the streak of violence in American frontier life, filling pages of their letters home and their published accounts with descriptions of the spontaneous street fights in which gouging, biting, and kicking were all permitted, and which the spectators treated as a diverting pastime. But while these fights technically constituted aggravated assault, they were seldom the result of one citizen gratuitously attacking a peaceable stranger. Much of frontier violence seems to have been consensual.[22]

We have no more glimpses of crime rates until the middle of the nineteenth century, but the stance of Americans toward crime remained as hostile as any of the founders could have wished. When Tocqueville was traveling around America to observe our prisons (the original reason for his visit), he commented on how few magistrates and public officers America employed for apprehending crime, "yet I believe that in no country does crime more rarely elude punishment.

The reason is that every one conceives himself to be interested in furnishing evidence of the crime and in seizing the delinquent. . . . In America, [the criminal] is looked upon as an enemy of the human race, and the whole of mankind is against him."[23]

Americans certainly saw themselves that way—to the point of tedium, in a Scottish writer's view, so often was the European visitor asked "whether he does not admire the extraordinary respect which the people pay to the law."[24] Francis Grund thought the pride was justified. Americans have an "unbounded respect for the law," he wrote. "There exists in the United States an universal submission to the law, and a prompt obedience to the magistrates, which, with the exception of Great Britain, is not to be found in any other country."[25]

Marriage

The founders took for granted that marriage was the bedrock institution of society. One of the few explicit discussions during the Revolutionary era is found in James Wilson's *Lectures on Law*:

> Whether we consult the soundest deductions of reason, or resort to the best information conveyed to us by history, or listen to the undoubted intelligence communicated in holy writ, we shall find, that to the institution of marriage the true origin of society must be traced. . . . To that institution, more than to any other, have mankind been indebted for the share of peace and harmony which has been distributed among them. *"Prima societas in ipso conjugio est,"* ["The first bond of society is marriage"] says Cicero in his book of offices; a work which does honor to the human understanding and the human heart.[26]

The question for the founders and for commentators in the nineteenth century was not whether marriage itself was essential to the functioning of society—of course it was—but about behavior within marriage. You may have noticed in this chapter's opening quotations how often the word *morality* was used. Typically, morality referred simply to fidelity within marriage and to the permanence of marriage. John Adams, whose fifty-four years with Abigail Adams constitute one of America's historic marriages, confided to his diary, "The foundation of national morality must be laid in private families. . . . How is it possible that children can have any just sense of the sacred obligations of morality or religion if, from their earliest Infancy, they learn their mothers live in habitual Infidelity to their fathers, and their fathers in as constant Infidelity to their mothers?"[27] On another occasion, he was alluding to the French liberal divorce law of 1792 when he referred to the "sacred bands of marriage" and called on young people to "beware of contaminating your country with the foul abominations of the French revolution."[28]

Were the Americans in fact more faithful to the marriage vows than the Europeans? Everyone thought so, Americans and foreigners alike. Even Harriet Martineau, an Englishwoman who resided in Cincinnati for several years and was a radical feminist long before the phrase was invented, thought that "marriage is in America more nearly universal, more safe, more tranquil, more fortunate than in England," and that "the outward requisites to happiness are nearly complete, and the institution is purified from the grossest of the scandals which degrade it in the Old World."[29] She wasn't happy with the situation in the United States, and grumbled that it was deteriorating, but she conceded that Americans did give women a better break than the Europeans did.

Practicing What They Preached, Mostly

Historians can never know for certain about these things, but the core group of founders appears to have been good husbands, with a caveat for one, plus one notorious exception.

George Washington enjoyed flirting with handsome women and presumably had abundant opportunities to carry things further, but none of the scholars of his exhaustively examined life have found evidence of infidelity, and his correspondence with Martha indicates a close bond. John and Abigail Adams were one of the most celebrated husband-wife pairs in American history. The debate about Thomas Jefferson and Sally Hemings goes on, but no one alleges that he strayed while his wife was alive. James and Dolley Madison were such a devoted couple that historians have only a handful of letters between them—they arranged their lives so that they spent very little time apart. John Jay and Sarah Jay did leave an extensive correspondence (along with six children) documenting an enduring and loving marriage.

The caveat is required for Alexander Hamilton. He had eight children with his wife, Elizabeth, and they remained a loving couple until his death, but he did have a known affair with a con man's wife.

And then there's Benjamin Franklin. He had a common-law marriage of forty-four years with Deborah (they couldn't have a civil ceremony because her first husband had disappeared and they couldn't prove that he was dead). The Franklins established a modus vivendi that left her, as she sometimes signed herself, "your A Feck SHONET Wife," but he began their cohabitation by bringing his illegitimate son from a previous liaison into the family circle, and he had dalliances throughout his life. Most of them were the unconsummated flirtation that the French call *amitié amoureuse*, but by no means all of them.

American exceptionalism with regard to marriage went beyond simple fidelity, however. Marriage in the United States was seen as a different kind of union than marriage in Europe. Part of the difference consisted of America's rejection of arranged marriages. But the ramifications went further than that. Men courted, but the women accepted or rejected, and the knowledge that a little girl would eventually have the responsibility for evaluating prospective mates affected her upbringing. "If democratic nations leave a woman at liberty to choose her husband," Tocqueville wrote,

> . . . they take care to give her mind sufficient knowledge, and her will sufficient strength, to make so important a choice. As in America paternal discipline is very relaxed and the conjugal tie very strict, a young woman does not contract the latter without considerable circumspection and apprehension. Precocious marriages are rare. Thus American women do not marry until

their understandings are exercised and ripened; whereas in other countries most women generally only begin to exercise and to ripen their understandings after marriage.[30]

American marriages were different from European ones (or so both Americans and foreign observers seemed to agree) in the solemnity of the marital bond. Americans "consider marriage as a covenant which is often onerous, but every condition of which the parties are strictly bound to fulfill, because they knew all those conditions beforehand, and were perfectly free not to have contracted them."[31]

To Tocqueville, the effects on American culture were profound, and had largely to do with the role that American marriage gave to America's women. Near the end of *Democracy in America*, he summarized his position with a remarkable passage. "If I were asked, now that I am drawing to the close of this work, in which I have spoken of so many important things done by the Americans, to what the singular prosperity and growing strength of that people ought mainly to be attributed, I should reply—to the superiority of their women."[32]

Francis Grund presented a similar analysis, and then summarized the effects of strong marriages on American life:

> I consider the domestic virtue of the Americans as the principal source of all their other qualities. It acts as a promoter of industry, as a stimulus to enterprise, and as the most powerful restrainer of public vice. It reduces life to its simplest elements, and makes happiness less dependent on precarious circumstances; it ensures the proper education of children, and acts, by the force of example, on the morals of the rising generation; in short, it does more for the preservation of peace and good order, than all the laws enacted for that purpose; and is a better guarantee for the permanency of the American government, than any written instrument, the Constitution itself not excepted.[33]

The American concept of marriage demanded a lot of both parties, but it was seen as the fundamental institution of civil society in a free nation.

Religiosity

The founders were products of the Enlightenment, if more of the Scottish variety than of the French, and many of them held a view of Christianity that would have been unthinkable a century earlier. Jefferson was openly a Deist. Benjamin Franklin frequently invoked the language of religion, but rarely attended church and did not believe in the divinity of Christ, nor did John Adams, a practicing Unitarian. Washington was evasive about his views on traditional Christian doctrine. Hamilton and Madison were Anglicans who were also suspected to be less than orthodox about the details. And yet all were united in this: Religion was essential to the health of the new nation. They made the case in similar terms, which Catholic philosopher Michael Novak summarized this way:

> Liberty is the object of the Republic.
> Liberty needs virtue.
> Virtue among the people is impossible without religion.[34]

George Washington put it explicitly in his Farewell Address: "Of all the dispositions and habits which lead to political prosperity, religion and morality are indispensable. . . . Whatever may be conceded to the influence of refined education on minds of peculiar structure, reason and experience both forbid us to expect that national morality can prevail in exclusion of religious principle."[35]

It is a nuanced statement, with Washington accepting that it is possible to be moral without believing in a personal God (he probably had Jefferson in mind with that wonderful clause "Whatever may be conceded to the influence of refined education on minds of peculiar structure"), but also saying that you cannot expect a whole nation of people to be that way. John Adams made the same argument less elliptically:

> We have no government armed with power capable of contending with human passions unbridled by morality and religion.

Avarice, ambition, revenge, or gallantry, would break the strongest cords of our Constitution as a whale goes through a net. Our Constitution was made only for a moral and religious people. It is wholly inadequate to the government of any other.[36]

For Adams, the essence of politically useful religion was the Judaic monotheistic God. "I will insist that the Hebrews have done more to civilize men than any other nation," he wrote, by propagating "to all mankind the doctrine of a supreme, intelligent, wise, almighty sovereign of the universe, which I believe to be the great essential principle of all morality, and consequently of all civilization."[37] James Madison echoed the sentiment when he wrote that "the belief in a God All Powerful, wise, and good, is so essential to the moral order of the World and to the happiness of man, that arguments which enforce it cannot be drawn from too many sources."[38]

Jefferson agreed. Writing in *Notes on the State of Virginia*, he asked, "Can the liberties of a nation be thought secure when we have removed their only firm basis, a conviction in the minds of the people that these liberties are the gift of God? That they are not violated but with his wrath?"[39] This appreciation of the role of religious belief, and specifically Christianity, is consistent with Jefferson's church attendance during his presidency. A diary of the era records an encounter in which Jefferson is chided for hypocrisy as he walks to church one Sunday "with a large red prayer book under his arm." Jefferson reportedly responded that "no nation has ever yet existed or been governed without religion. Nor can be. The Christian religion is the best religion that has ever been given to man and I as chief Magistrate of this nation am bound to give it the sanction of my example. Good day sir." It is a secondhand account and may have been embroidered in the retelling, but the sentiment is consistent with Jefferson's well-documented admiration for the moral code expressed in Jesus's teachings.[40] "Of all the systems of morality, ancient or modern, which have come under my observation, none appear to me so pure as that of Jesus," he wrote, and invested great effort in compiling what became known as the "Jefferson Bible," the teachings of Jesus stripped of miracles and theology.[41] Benjamin Franklin took the same position.

"As to Jesus of Nazareth," he wrote to Ezra Stiles, president of Yale, "I think his system of morals and his religion, as he left them to us, the best the world ever saw or is likely to see." He thought that belief in Jesus's divinity did no harm "if that belief has the good consequences, as probably it has, of making his doctrines more respected and observed."[42] Many others saw the Christian Bible's teachings of humility, self-denial, brotherly kindness, and the golden rule as precisely what a self-governing democracy needed—"It is the most republican book in the world," in John Adams's words.[43]

The same relationship between religiosity and a functioning limited government was asserted by observers of American life, including secular ones, for the next century. As on so many other topics, Tocqueville summed it up best of all, and I have nothing to add to his appraisal:

> Thus, while the law permits the Americans to do what they please, religion prevents them from conceiving, and forbids them to commit, what is rash or unjust. Religion in America takes no direct part in the government of society, but it must be regarded as the first of their political institutions; for if it does not impart a taste for freedom, it facilitates the use of it. Indeed, it is in this same point of view that the inhabitants of the United States themselves look upon religious belief. I do not know whether all Americans have a sincere faith in their religion—for who can search the human heart?—but I am certain that they hold it to be indispensable to the maintenance of republican institutions. This opinion is not peculiar to a class of citizens or to a party, but it belongs to the whole nation and to every rank of society. . . . The Americans combine the notions of Christianity and of liberty so intimately in their minds that it is impossible to make them conceive the one without the other.[44]

Since the 1830s

Until well into the twentieth century, all four of the founding virtues were seen much as they were in the first half century of the nation's existence. They were accepted as well by the children of immigrants within a few years of getting off the boat. Describing in detail how this feat was accomplished would take a book of its own, but a major part of the answer is that America used the schoolhouse to relentlessly socialize its children. In effect, American children were taught a national civil religion consisting largely of the virtues I just described.

The main vehicle for nineteenth-century socialization was the reading textbook used in elementary school, the variants of which were modeled on the overwhelmingly most popular series, the McGuffey Readers. They were so widely used that selections in them became part of the national language. When Theodore Roosevelt once told a newspaper reporter that he had "no intention of becoming an international Meddlesome Mattie" by injecting himself into some foreign dispute,[45] he could assume everybody would know what he meant because the story about Meddlesome Mattie had been part of McGuffey's Fourth Reader in all its editions since 1853. Theodore Roosevelt, scion of an elite New York family, schooled by private tutors, had been raised on the same textbooks as the children of Ohio farmers, Chicago tradesmen, and New England fishermen. If you want to know what constituted being a good American from the mid-nineteenth century to World War I, spend a few hours browsing through the selections in the McGuffey Readers (the full texts are available at Google Books). They are filled with readings that touch on the founding virtues.

Stereotype and Reality About the McGuffey Readers

When people today think of the McGuffey Readers at all, it is likely to be with condescension, looking upon them as collections of stories that were perhaps suitable for a less enlightened time but that would be unacceptable today. If you browse the Readers, you may find yourself surprised. You will have a hard time finding references to women as the weaker sex or to women as inferior to men in any way, and many cases in which women are exemplars of courage and fortitude. The Readers do not celebrate macho virtues but emphasize the *gentle* in *gentleman*. American Indians are not portrayed as savages, but as humans displaying the same virtues that are extolled for everyone. Similarly, there are many stories set in foreign countries, but no invidious comparisons of foreigners with Americans. The religious teachings in the Readers after mid-century were religiously ecumenical, including, for example, both the twenty-third psalm from the Hebrew Bible and the Sermon on the Mount from the New Testament, but with no passages (that I found) that explicitly presented Christian doctrine.

The most obvious lacuna in the Readers is race. In the Readers I reviewed, I found no reference to African Americans at all, positive or negative—perhaps because the people who chose the selections realized that if the Readers addressed race in the same tolerant and egalitarian tone they applied to everything else, many Southern schools would stop using them.

By the mid-twentieth century, the idea that school was a place to instill a particular set of virtues through systematic socialization had been rejected, the McGuffey Readers had disappeared, and so had some of the coherence in the idea of what it meant to be a good American. This is not to say that the practice of the virtues had decayed, but that the American civic religion had evolved. The idea of America as the land of opportunity was still prevalent. The Constitution was still seen as the bedrock on which the nation stood. Americans still saw their country as the freest, most prosperous, and best country in the world. The idea of "one nation, under God, indivisible, with liberty and justice for all" was drummed into the heads of schoolchildren every morning with the Pledge of Allegiance. But the belief that being a good American involved behaving in certain kinds of ways, and that the nation itself relied upon a certain kind of people in order to succeed, had begun to fade and has not revived. It came to be tacitly assumed that the American system itself would work under any circumstances as long as we got the laws right.

To people who share that assumption, the reasonable response to my account of the founding virtues is to ask "So what?" So what if Americans began the nation with a romanticized view of their own virtue, and managed to transmit that romanticized view for the next century and a half? America at the founding was a small, sparsely populated country of farmers, with half the nation operating a system of chattel slavery. The virtues were never as universally observed as Americans wanted to think, and in any case they are not relevant today. None of the great political, economic, or social issues that face the nation in the twenty-first century are going to be informed by seeing where America stands today on the founding virtues.

I take another view: The founders were right. The success of America depended on virtue in the people when the country began and it still does in the twenty-first century. America will remain exceptional only to the extent that its people embody the same qualities that made it work for the first two centuries of its existence. The founding virtues are central to that kind of citizenry. That's why the following chapters use them as a framework for describing the formation of the new lower class.

7

Belmont and Fishtown

*In which I describe two fictional neighborhoods called Belmont
and Fishtown, and explain how I will use these neighborhoods to
track the founding virtues from 1960 to 2010.*

THE NEW UPPER class is a subset of the upper-middle class
and the new lower class is a subset of the working class. I
have devised what I hope you will find an intuitively under-
standable way to think about the trends in the larger classes from
which they are drawn by creating two fictional neighborhoods named
Belmont and Fishtown. The details are given in appendix C, but the
following will give you the essentials.

Two Neighborhoods

Belmont

The real Belmont, zip code 02478, centile 97, is a suburb of Boston and
the home of people who are mostly in the upper-middle class. Many
people in the professions live in Belmont—physicians, attorneys, engineers, scientists, university professors—alongside business executives
and managers of nonprofits and government agencies. The people of
Belmont are highly educated—63 percent of the adults had BAs in
2000. It is affluent, with a median family income of $124,200 in 2000.

The fictional Belmont that I will be using in part 2 differs from the real Belmont in that there are no exceptions. For whatever database I am using, I assign unmarried persons to Belmont if and only if they have at least a bachelor's degree and are managers, physicians, attorneys, engineers, architects, scientists, college faculty members, or in content-production jobs in the media (e.g., journalists, writers, editors, directors, producers). I assign married persons to Belmont if either they or their spouse has at least a college degree and is in one of those occupations.

Fishtown

The real Fishtown, zip code 19125, centile 8, is located in the northeastern part of Philadelphia. It has been a white working-class neighborhood since the eighteenth century. In the real Fishtown, some people still don't finish high school, but most get their diploma and go straight to work. Some have gotten technical training after high school. Some have attended community college or given a four-year college a try for a year or two. Some have been in the military, where they have received technical training. But completed college educations are rare in Fishtown—only 8 percent of the adults had college degrees in 2000.

Fishtown has many highly skilled blue-collar workers, such as electricians, plumbers, machinists, and tool and die makers, but also many people in midskill occupations—drywall installers or heavy-equipment operators, for example. Low-skill jobs are also heavily represented among the breadwinners in Fishtown—assembly-line workers, construction laborers, security guards, delivery truck drivers, or people who work on loading docks. Most families in Fishtown have incomes somewhere in the bottom half of the national income distribution—the median family income in 2000 was only $41,900—and almost all the people who are below the poverty line live in a place like Fishtown.

In my fictional Fishtown, I once again lop off the exceptions. To be assigned to Fishtown, the basic criteria are a blue-collar, service, or low-level white-collar occupation, and no academic degree more advanced than a high school diploma. The detailed rules for assigning married couples with various permutations of occupation and education to Fishtown are spelled out in appendix C.

What About Everybody Else?

The occupations that qualify people for the two neighborhoods leave out a lot of others—owners of small businesses, mid-level white-collar workers, K–12 teachers, police officers, insurance agents, salesmen, social workers, technicians, real estate brokers, nurses, and occupational therapists, to name a few. It leaves out people without a college degree who succeeded in becoming managers. I omit them not because they are unimportant, but because of what I discovered when I worked through the topics we will be covering in the next four chapters. On every indicator, this group was in the middle. It made no difference whether the indicator was about marriage, industriousness, honesty, or religiosity, their results were somewhere between the results for Belmont and Fishtown. Moreover, there were no themes in the degree of their in-between-ness. Occasionally the people in the middle became more like either Belmont or Fishtown as the decades went on, but not consistently. Concentrating on Belmont and Fishtown allows a presentation that is easier to follow and that can focus more efficiently on the important trends.

A Quick Way to Think About the Neighborhoods

Belmont: Everybody has a bachelor's or graduate degree and works in the high-prestige professions or management, or is married to such a person.

Fishtown: Nobody has more than a high school diploma. Everybody who has an occupation is in a blue-collar job, mid- or low-level service job, or a low-level white-collar job.

Everybody Else: A wide range of occupations and education, but a strong central tendency toward mid-level white-collar and technical occupations and thirteen to fifteen years of education.

Adults in the Prime of Life

There is an additional oddity about my two fictional neighbor-hoods. Except for a few instances that I will clearly specify, the numbers and graphs you will see in the following chapters are based on people who are no younger than thirty and no older than forty-nine. I want to focus on adults in the prime of life, with their educations usually completed, engaged in their careers and raising families. People in their twenties and fifties are in decades of transition—people who end up in Belmont are often still in school in their twenties, and people in Fishtown are increasingly likely to be physically disabled or to have taken early retirement in their fifties. I eliminate them altogether to simplify the interpretation of the results. I often use the term *prime-age adults* to refer to persons ages 30 through 49.

The Top 20 Percent and the Bottom 30 Percent

Throughout part 2, I present trendlines showing the percentages of people in Belmont and Fishtown who behaved in certain ways or held certain opinions. These trends are interpretable as changes in the way that an upper-middle-class and a working-class neighborhood look and feel. But the proportions of white Americans living in those neighborhoods changed. In 1960, 64 percent of prime-age white Americans qualified for Fishtown and only 6 percent of prime-age white Americans qualified for Belmont. By 2010, only 30 percent qualified for Fishtown and 21 percent qualified for Belmont.

This raises a problem of interpretation. Perhaps things changed in Fishtown because the most able people in the Fishtowns of the 1960s had moved up into the middle class by the 2000s—what is known in the jargon as a creaming effect. Perhaps things changed in Belmont as the college-educated population expanded. We need to have an idea of what the trends would have looked like if Fishtown had consisted of 30 percent of the white prime-age population in 1960 instead of 64 percent, and what Belmont would have looked like in 1960 if (using a round number) it had consisted of 20 percent of the white prime-age population instead of 6 percent.

I therefore created an index combining educational attainment and the cognitive demands of occupations that enables everyone to be rank-ordered from top to bottom. Appendix C describes what "cognitive demands of an occupation" means and how the index was constructed. Every graph includes a marker showing the percentages for the people who ranked in the top 20 percent and bottom 30 percent on this index for whatever year marks the beginning of the trendline and whatever year marks the end of the trendline. I also occasionally add markers for the top 20 percent and bottom 30 percent when a trend changed direction. You should look upon these markers as a way of judging how much of the change in the trendline is owed to changes in working-class behavior and how much to a creaming effect. In most cases, changes in the composition of the neighborhood make remarkably little difference, for reasons that are discussed in appendix C.

The Rest of the Underpinnings

You now know enough to read the rest of part 2. There are many details about the analyses that I have put in appendix C, trying to keep the main text as uncluttered as possible. I recommend that you begin with the main text, and then use the technical material in the appendix to explore whatever questions you might have.

8

Marriage

*In which I describe a decline of marriage in white America
that took different courses for Belmont and Fishtown during
the 1980s, and an unprecedented increase in white nonmarital
births that has been concentrated in Fishtown and scarcely
touched Belmont.*

I HAVE CHOSEN TO present class divergence in marriage first because it is so elemental. Over the last half century, marriage has
become the fault line dividing American classes.[1]

What Whites Said About Marriage

In 1962, the *Saturday Evening Post*—the magazine with the Norman
Rockwell covers—commissioned the Gallup Organization to conduct
a survey of the attitudes of American women. For the ever-married
sample whose opinions are reported here, Gallup interviewed 1,813
women ages 21–60.

"In general, who do you think is happier," the Gallup interviewer
asked, "the girl who is married and has a family to raise, or the unmarried career girl?" Ninety-six percent of the wives said the married
girl with a family was happier. Ninety-three percent said that they
did not, in retrospect, wish they had pursued a career instead of getting married.

More than half the ever-married women thought that the ideal age for a woman to be married was 20 through 23, with 21 being the most commonly named year. Only 18 percent thought a woman should wait until age 25 or older.

More than a third of the ever-married women knew a woman who had engaged in an affair after she married, but they didn't approve. Eighty-four percent said there was never any justification for women having sexual affairs with men other than their husbands.

A Different World

To get a sense of just how different attitudes were in the early 1960s, perhaps this will do it. These ever-married women were asked, "In your opinion, do you think it is all right for a woman to have sexual relations before marriage with a man she knows she is going to marry?" Note the wording. Not sex with someone a woman is dating, nor with someone a woman loves, but with a man she knows she is going to marry. Eighty-six percent said no.[2]

Gallup's survey for the *Saturday Evening Post* didn't ask under what circumstances divorce was justified, but we have another poll conducted in 1960 that asked whether divorce should be made more difficult or easier to obtain. In 1960, no-fault divorce did not exist and a speedy divorce was possible only in Nevada. In many states, the only legal grounds for divorce were adultery or cruelty. Even so, 56 percent of the respondents said that divorce should be made more difficult, compared to only 9 percent who thought it should be made easier.[3]

The General Social Survey, abbreviated GSS and conducted since 1972 by the National Opinion Research Center at the University of Chicago, is the most widely used database for tracking American social trends. By the time the GSS began to ask questions about attitudes toward marriage, things had already changed, and then continued to change even more in the next decades. For example, the GSS began asking in 1977 whether their respondents agreed with this statement: "It is much better for everyone involved if the man is the achiever outside the home and the woman takes care of the home and family." We cannot know exactly what the 1960s answers to that question would have been, but if 96 percent of wives in the 1962 Gallup survey thought women were generally happier with a family than with a career, we have to assume that the "agree" responses for the GSS item would have been at least somewhere above 90 in the early 1960s. Appendix D describes how I reached my estimate of 95 percent, designated by the unattached X you see in figure 8.1. It represents an estimate for the first half of the 1960s, not the entire decade.

FIGURE 8.1. THE WOMAN'S ROLE IN MARRIAGE

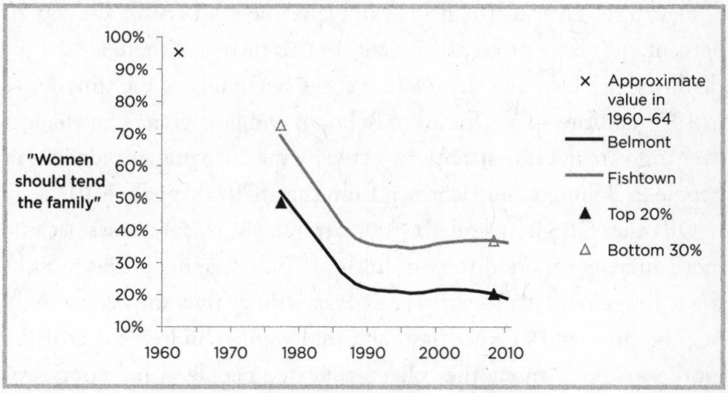

Source: GSS. Sample limited to whites ages 30–49. Data smoothed using locally estimated regression (LOESS). See appendix A for a description of LOESS.

The main effect applied across all classes, and comes as no surprise: The traditional conception of marital roles took a big hit from the 1960s through the 1980s. A substantial class difference remained, however. As of the 2000s, almost 40 percent of Fishtown still took a traditional view of the woman's role, compared to less than 20 percent of Belmont.

About the Graphs

Almost all of the graphs in part 2 go from 1960 through 2010 on the horizontal axis, even when data for the end points are not available, and show percentages on the vertical axis. This raises a perennial problem in presenting such data: How big a range should the vertical axis show? If the range goes all the way from zero to 100 percent, the shape and importance of trends can be obscured.

Make the range too narrow, and a small change can be visually exaggerated. There's no pat answer, because sometimes a small percentage change over fifty years is important and sometimes it isn't. I have included only graphs with changes that I judge to be important, gearing the range to the minimum and maximum values of the variables being plotted, but with a minimum range of twenty percentage points.

Figure 8.1 gives us the first example of the markers for the top 20 percent and the bottom 30 percent. In this instance, there is very little difference between their values at the beginning of the time series in 1977 and the values for all of Belmont and Fishtown. The changes over time are not importantly affected by the changing proportions of people in Belmont and Fishtown from the 1970s through 2010.

On other GSS items relating to marriage, the social classes became more alike, not more different. In the 1970s, large majorities in Fishtown thought that premarital sex was wrong, that the wife should help her husband's career first, and that young children suffer if the mother works. Among the college-educated people of Belmont, support for all these propositions was much lower. By the 2000s, support had dropped everywhere, but most of all in Fishtown, so that there was little remaining difference between Belmont and Fishtown on most of them.

In two respects, Belmont did most of the moving, approaching Fishtown's position. The first involved attitudes toward divorce. Over the decades, growing numbers of people in Belmont agreed that divorce law should make divorce more difficult, almost erasing the gap with Fishtown that had existed in the 1970s. The second and the most striking change was that Belmont became more traditional in its attitude toward married people having sex with someone other than their spouses, as shown in figure 8.2. I put the estimate for the first half of the 1960s at 80 percent overall, for reasons explained in appendix D.

Before getting to the convergence, take a close look at the huge class differences that had emerged on this issue by the 1970s. Based

FIGURE 8.2.   IS EXTRAMARITAL SEX WRONG?

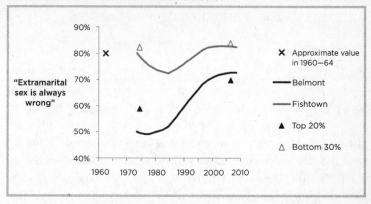

Source: GSS. Sample limited to whites ages 30–49. Data smoothed using locally estimated regression (LOESS).

on collateral evidence such as the Gallup survey of American women, we have to assume that in the early 1960s Belmont was about as strict in its attitudes as Fishtown. Within just a few years, white college-educated men and women became enthusiastic recruits to the sexual revolution. It is one of the most dramatic and rapid examples of divergence of elite norm and mainstream norms. It is also clearly concentrated among the college educated—note the difference between acceptance of extramarital sex among the college educated people of Belmont compared to the people in the top 20 percent, who in the 1970s still included many who were not college educated.

During the 1980s, the percentage of Belmonters who said that extramarital sex was always wrong began to rise and continued to do so. By the 2000s, Belmont still was not quite as strict on this point as Fishtown, but college-educated professionals had clearly returned to a more traditional attitude than they had held in the 1970s. While class differences remained in attitudes toward marriage, many of these differences were smaller in 2010 than they had been in the 1970s. And yet actual behavior regarding marriage diverged sharply. It is time to tell that story.

What Whites Did About Marriage

The Decline of Marriage

Starting around 1970, marriage took a nosedive that lasted for nearly twenty years. Among all whites ages 30–49, only 13 percent were not living with spouses as of 1970. Twenty years later, that proportion had more than doubled, to 27 percent—a change in a core social institution that has few precedents for magnitude and speed. Figure 8.3 uses the 1960 decennial census and the Current Population Survey for 1968–2010 (hereafter referred to as the CPS database) to show how the prevalence of marriage changed among the people of Belmont and Fishtown.

FIGURE 8.3. **MARRIAGE**

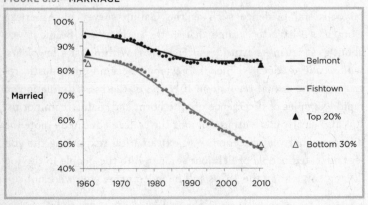

Source: IPUMS. Sample limited to whites ages 30–49. "Married" refers to persons married and not separated.

In 1960, the proportions of married couples in Belmont and Fishtown were separated by about 10 percentage points, but both were high—94 percent in Belmont and 84 percent in Fishtown. Nothing much changed in the 1960s. A sexual revolution may have been under way among the twentysomethings, but the proportions of whites in their thirties and forties who were married in 1970 were within a percentage point of their 1960 levels. Then, beginning during the last half of the 1970s, the neighborhoods started to diverge. By the mid-

1980s, the decline had stopped in Belmont, and the trendline remained flat thereafter. Marriage in Fishtown kept falling.

The net result: The two neighborhoods, which had been only 11 percentage points apart as late as 1978, were separated by 35 percentage points as of 2010, when only 48 percent of prime-age whites in Fishtown were married, compared to 84 percent in 1960. Furthermore, the slope of the decline in Fishtown after the early 1990s had yet to flatten.

The Rise of the Never-Marrieds

People ages 30–49 are unmarried for two main reasons: They are divorced or they never got married in the first place (widowhood at that age is rare). I begin with the never-marrieds.

The percentage of whites ages 30–49 who had not yet married started going up in the early 1970s, doubling from 1977 to 1991. Figure 8.4 shows how differently those increases played out in Belmont and Fishtown.

FIGURE 8.4.   **REMAINING SINGLE**

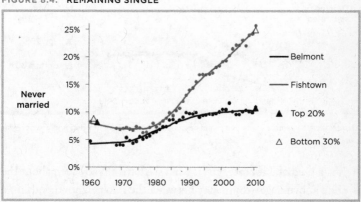

Source: IPUMS. Sample limited to whites ages 30–49.

The stereotypes of the 1970s and 1980s, of yuppies and feminists remaining single into their thirties or forties, had some basis in fact—the percentage of never-married whites in Belmont doubled from 1970 to 1984. But after 1984, that percentage barely rose at all, from

9 percent to 11 percent. The big news is the relentless increase in Fishtown of people who had never married. It showed no signs of decreasing through 2010, when more than one out of four Fishtown whites ages 30–49 had not yet married. That increase was driven mostly by the retreat of men from the marriage market. As of 2010, almost one out of three Fishtown males ages 30–49 had not yet married.

The Rise of Divorce

Divorce played about an equal role with the never-marrieds in explaining the overall class divergence in marriage. The story is shown in figure 8.5 for people who have ever married (excluding those who are widowed).

FIGURE 8.5.   **DIVORCE**

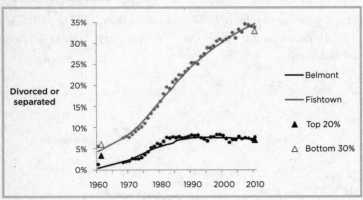

Source: IPUMS. Sample limited to whites ages 30–49 who have married and are not widowed.

It is a predictable story, given what we have already seen about the decline in marriage—similarity between the two neighborhoods for a while, then divergence. In the case of divorce, the trends were similar into the early 1980s. The trendline in Belmont flattened in the early 1980s. In Fishtown, the trendline continued steeply upward, with the slope shallowing only a little in the 2000s. As of 2010, one-third of Fishtown whites ages 30–49 had been divorced.

Happy and Not So Happy Marriages

One other divergence among the classes with regard to marriage needs to be mentioned before moving on. Not only did marriage become much rarer in Fishtown over the half century ending in 2010, the quality of marriages that did exist apparently deteriorated. Since 1973, the GSS has asked, "Taking all things together, how would you describe your marriage?" and given the respondent the choice of answering "very happy," "pretty happy," or "not too happy." The results by decade are shown in figure 8.6. Based on the 1962 Gallup survey for the *Saturday Evening Post,* I put the estimate of people saying they had very happy marriages in the first half of the 1960s at 63 percent.

FIGURE 8.6.   **SELF-REPORTED "VERY HAPPY" MARRIAGES AMONG THOSE MARRIED AND NOT SEPARATED**

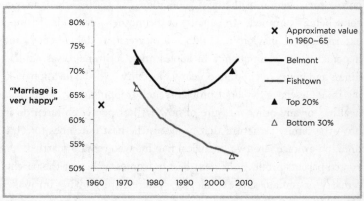

Source: GSS. Sample limited to married whites ages 30–49. Data smoothed using locally estimated regression (LOESS).[4]

If the estimate for the first half of the 1960s is correct, the implication is that the proportion of happy marriages increased during the late 1960s and early 1970s. It may well be true—the introduction of no-fault divorce in the late 1960s and the surge in divorces that followed ended a lot of unhappy marriages. But perhaps the wording of the 1962 Gallup question, which asked if people were *extremely* happily married, compared to the GSS's milder *very* happily married, means that I have substantially underestimated the proportion of happy marriages in the early 1960s (see appendix D for a discussion of that issue).

In any case, the story from the 1970s onward is reasonably clear. In Belmont, the percentage of people saying their marriages were very happy was on an upward trend after the 1980s. Self-reported happy marriages in Fishtown declined. For the surveys in the 2000s, the gap with Belmont had reached about 20 percentage points.

Children and Marriage

Trends in marriage are important not just with regard to the organization of communities, but because they are associated with large effects on the socialization of the next generation. No matter what the outcome being examined—the quality of the mother-infant relationship,[5] externalizing behavior in childhood (aggression, delinquency, and hyperactivity),[6] delinquency in adolescence,[7] criminality as adults,[8] illness and injury in childhood,[9] early mortality,[10] sexual decision making in adolescence,[11] school problems and dropping out,[12] emotional health,[13] or any other measure of how well or poorly children do in life—the family structure that produces the best outcomes for children, on average, are two biological parents who remain married. Divorced parents produce the next-best outcomes. Whether the parents remarry or remain single while the children are growing up makes little difference. Never-married women produce the worst outcomes. All of these statements apply after controlling for the family's socioeconomic status.[14] I know of no other set of important findings that are as broadly accepted by social scientists who follow the technical literature, liberal as well as conservative, and yet are so resolutely ignored by network news programs, editorial writers for the major newspapers, and politicians of both major political parties. In any case, the change in the family structure in which the children of Fishtown grow up has been huge.

Children Living with a Single Divorced or Separated Parent

Figure 8.7 shows the trends for children living in single-parent homes consisting of a divorced or separated parent.[15]

The trends roughly correspond to the trends in divorce shown earlier. The divergence between Belmont and Fishtown is substantial, with 22 percent of Fishtown children living with a lone divorced or separated parent as of 2010, compared to just 3 percent of Belmont children. Divorce isn't the biggest problem that the children of Fishtown face, however. The problem is never-married mothers.

FIGURE 8.7.   **CHILDREN OF BROKEN MARRIAGES LIVING WITH A SINGLE PARENT**

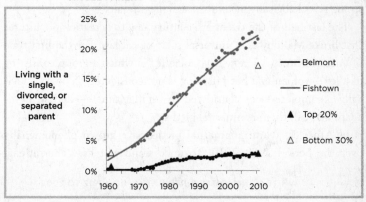

Source: IPUMS. Sample limited to married whites ages 30–49.

Nonmarital Births

From the founding until well into the twentieth century, it was unquestioned that children should be born only within marriage and that failure to maintain that state of affairs would produce catastrophic consequences for society. That universal understanding explains why children born out of marriage were called by an invidious name, *bastards;* had diminished legal standing; and were so relentlessly stigmatized that even children of unmarried women who rose to eminence (Alexander Hamilton, for example) felt the sting of that stigma all their lives.

In the twentieth century, *illegitimate* supplanted *bastard* as the favored label for children born out of wedlock, helped along by the imprimatur of one of the first great anthropologists, Bronisław Malinowski. In his 1930 book, *Sex, Culture, and Myth*, Malinowski concluded that the "principle of legitimacy" amounted to a "universal sociological law." *Every* culture, he concluded, had a norm that "no child should be brought into the world without a man—and one man at that—assuming the role of sociological father, that is, guardian and protector, the male link between the child and the rest of the community." Without that man, Malinowski wrote, "the group consisting of a woman and her offspring is sociologically incomplete and illegitimate."[16]

The last half of the twentieth century saw the creation of cultures that broke Malinowski's universal sociological law. For the first time in human history, we now have societies in which a group consisting of a lone woman and her offspring is not considered to be sociologically incomplete—not considered to be illegitimate—and so I will adapt and call them nonmarital births.

In America, white nonmarital births have grown phenomenally over the period 1960–2010. To understand just how aberrational

FIGURE 8.8.   WHITE NONMARITAL BIRTH RATIO FROM 1917 TO 2008

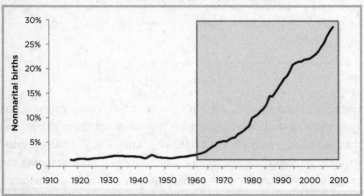

Source: For 1917–39, National Center for Health Statistics, 1941, table Q. For 1940–60, Grove, 1968, table 29. For 1960–2008, annual Vital Statistics reports of the National Center for Health Statistics.

1960–2010 was, you have to see it in the context of the last century, shown in figure 8.8.

The shaded area contains the decades we are studying, 1960–2010, when the percentage of nonmarital births rose steeply throughout. But before that, hardly anything had changed since the first numbers were collected in 1917. Studies of the white family in earlier eras indicate that the line hugging the bottom of the graph from 1917 to 1960 would have been flat all the way back to the Revolution.[17] White children were conceived outside marriage at varying rates in different social classes, but hardly ever born outside marriage in any class.

To see which white women were having those babies, I turn to the national birth records assembled by the National Center for Health Statistics (NCHS). Since 1970, the NCHS has included information on the mother's years of education at the time of birth. The breakdown of nonmarital births by education is shown in figure 8.9.

FIGURE 8.9. **WHITE NONMARITAL BIRTH RATIO BY MOTHER'S EDUCATION**

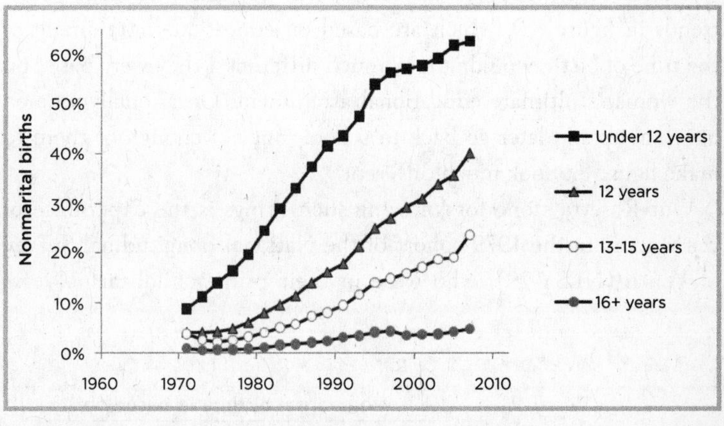

Source: Author's analysis of alternate years of the Natality Public Use Files of the Centers for Disease Control, beginning with 1970. Sample limited to white women.

That information reveals an extraordinarily strong relationship between the mother's education and the likelihood that she gives birth as an unmarried woman. If she has a college education, she almost never does. Whether she has a graduate degree makes no difference— the trendlines for women with bachelor's degrees and graduate degrees are indistinguishable. Even in the most recent data from 2008, fewer than 5 percent of babies born to women with sixteen or more years of education were nonmarital. But anywhere below sixteen years of education, the increase in the likelihood of a nonmarital birth was substantial. For women who did not finish high school, the percentage was closing in on levels in excess of 60 percent of live births that previously have been associated with the black underclass.

There is no way to translate these data into precise breakdowns for Belmont and Fishtown, partly because we lack any occupational data and partly because of a major interpretive problem. Women with high school educations can be assigned to Belmont because they are married to men with college educations and a Belmont occupation. It seems highly unlikely that this population of women has the same probability of having experienced a nonmarital birth as women with high school educations who remain unmarried or who marry a man with a high school education and a Fishtown occupation.

Despite this interpretive problem, we know that the shape of the trends in figure 8.9, which are based on educational attainment at the time of birth, wouldn't look much different if they were based on the woman's ultimate educational attainment. Occasionally women have babies and later go back to school, but not enough of them to make figure 8.9 look much different.

Our Rosetta stone for knowing such things is the experience of the women in the 1979 cohort of the National Longitudinal Survey of Youth (NLSY-79), who were in their prime childbearing years

TABLE 8.1.   NONMARITAL BIRTH RATIO BY MOTHER'S EDUCATION

	Nonmarital birth ratio based on . . .	
Highest grade completed	Mother's years of education at the child's birth	Mother's years of education by age 40
16 years and more	2.9%	3.5%
13–15 years	5.9%	9.1%
12 years	12.1%	12.8%
Fewer than 12 years	21.2%	18.8%

Source: NLSY-79. Sample limited to children of white mothers.

from the late 1970s to the mid-1990s. As shown in table 8.1, their nonmarital birth ratios based on education when their children were born and based on their education when they had reached age 40 are quite close.

So whereas I cannot calculate precise numbers for the trends in Belmont and Fishtown, you can get a good idea of what they would look like by imagining a line for Belmont that is close to the line for women with sixteen or more years of education, but slightly higher, and a line for Fishtown that is moderately higher than the line for women with twelve years of education. My best estimate is that nonmarital births in Belmont as of 2008 were around 6 to 8 percent of all births, whereas in Fishtown they were around 43 to 48 percent of all births.

Maybe It Isn't as Bad as It Looks

There are two reasons why this portrait of the breakdown of the family in working-class white America might not be the disaster that I have inferred. One is statistical. People with lower levels of education marry at younger ages and have babies at younger ages than people who are busy with school through most of their twenties. If we control for these differences, how different would the results in this chapter look? The answer (not much) is discussed in appendix D. The other is a hot topic in today's America: cohabitation. The old-fashioned dichotomy between *married* and *unmarried* is unrealistic in today's world, the argument goes. People may cohabit rather than formally marry, but the children are still being raised in a two-parent family, with the advantages of a two-parent family.

The increase in cohabitation has been rapid and large. For the last two decades, a majority of people in their twenties and thirties have cohabited.[18] In the 1990s, about 40 percent of all births to single women actually occurred to women who were cohabiting with the biological father of the baby, and presumably that percentage grew during the 2000s.[19] Statistically, almost all of the increase in nonmarital childbearing in the last few decades is explained by an increase in children born to cohabiting parents.[20]

The question then becomes: How do the children of cohabiting parents fare? The answer: About the same as the children of the old-fashioned form of single parenthood, women who are unmarried and not cohabiting.

The differences begin in infancy, when most of the cohabiting couples are still living together and the child has a two-parent family. Stacey Aronson and Aletha Huston used data from a study of early child care conducted by the National Institute of Child Health and Human Development to assess the mother-infant relationship and the home environment for children at ages 6 months and 15 months.[21] On both measures and at both ages, the children of married couples did significantly better than the children of cohabiting parents, who in turn had scores that were only fractionally higher than the children of single mothers. The differences could only be attenuated, not explained away, when other demographic variables were entered into the analysis.[22] But the demographic variables made a difference, too. The mothers in cohabiting couples tended to have lower education, to be younger, to have poorer psychological adjustment, less social support, and less money than the married mothers. Those factors statistically explain some of the difference—but they make no difference at all to the divergence of the social classes. Cohabiting mothers come disproportionately from the lower socioeconomic classes and they tend to provide worse environments for raising children than married mothers. That's not only the reality on the ground, shaping the environments in the neighborhoods where they live, it is a reality that is likely to accelerate the deterioration of those neighborhoods as the children reach adulthood. Examples will be found when it comes time to discuss life in the real Fishtown in chapter 12.

The disadvantages of being born to cohabiting parents extend into childhood and adolescence, even when the cohabiting couple still consists of the two biological parents. Susan Brown used the 1999 cohort for the National Survey of America's Families to examine behavioral and emotional problems and school engagement among six- to eleven-year-olds and twelve- to seventeen-year-olds. Same story: Having two unmarried biological parents was associated with worse outcomes than having two married biological parents, and the outcomes were rarely better than those for children living with a single parent or in a "cohabiting stepparent" family.[23] Once again, entering additional variables explained some but not all of the difference, but those additional variables revealed the same story that others have found—there is a strong inverse relationship between socioeconomic status and the likelihood that children are born to cohabiting women. Cohabitation with children occurs overwhelmingly in Fishtown.

Cohabitation has been a common feature in American life for more than two decades, and it may be asked whether there are signs that cohabitation itself will evolve for the better. Not so far. The two studies I cited were the most recent available as I write, but there is also a literature from studies conducted in the 1990s and 1980s.[24] The story seems to be consistent. If you are interested in the welfare of children, knowing that the child was born to a cohabiting woman instead of a lone unmarried woman should have little effect on your appraisal of the child's chances in life. That's the common theme of the systematic studies of this issue for more than twenty years.

It's Even Worse Than It Looks

The pessimistic title of this section springs from my belief that families with children are the core around which American communities must be organized—*must*, because families with children have always been, and still are, the engine that makes American communities work—and from my conclusion that the family in Fishtown is approaching a point of no return. The extent of the collapse of the Fishtown family may not be evident from the separate pieces that I have presented, so let me conclude this chapter with two summary measures.

The first, figure 8.10, is based on whites ages 30–49 who are in happy marriages, expressed as a percentage of all whites ages 30–49 (not just married whites, as shown in figure 8.6).

If the issue were happiness, the steep decline in Fishtown would not be as bad as it looks. Many people who are not married are happy, including people who are divorced. Instead of thinking about percent-

FIGURE 8.10. **PROPORTION OF ALL WHITES AGES 30–49 WHO
SELF-REPORT BEING IN VERY HAPPY MARRIAGES**

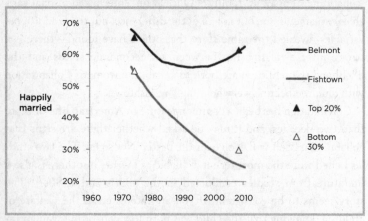

Source: GSS. Sample limited to whites ages 30–49. Data smoothed using locally estimated regression (LOESS).

ages of happy and unhappy people, think about the role of marriage as the bedrock institution around which communities are organized and, writ large, around which the nation is organized. A neighborhood in which that function is being performed will be characterized by a large core of happy marriages.

When we get our first look at the situation by social class in the 1970s, over half of both neighborhoods consisted of people in happy marriages. In the 2000s, such people still constituted almost 60 percent of the prime-age whites of Belmont. But the percentage in Fishtown had been halved, from 52 percent in the GSS surveys of the 1970s to 26 percent in the surveys of the 2000s. Twenty-six percent is arguably no longer a large enough group to set norms or to serve as a core around which the community functions. Fishtown in 2010 was rudderless in a way that it had not been in the 1970s and earlier.

My second summary measure is the percentage of all children who are raised with both biological parents. We cannot obtain that measure from CPS data because the CPS does not discriminate between families consisting of married and remarried couples. Instead, I turn to three National Longitudinal Surveys to reconstruct the trendline for children living with both biological parents: the Mature Women

Survey, whose subjects turned age 40 from 1964 to 1977, the Young Women Survey, whose subjects turned 40 from 1982 to 1993, and the 1979 National Longitudinal Survey of Youth, whose subjects turned 40 from 1997 to 2004. Figure 8.11 shows the trendlines for Belmont and Fishtown.

FIGURE 8.11. **PERCENTAGE OF CHILDREN LIVING WITH BOTH BIOLOGICAL PARENTS WHEN THE MOTHER WAS AGE 40**

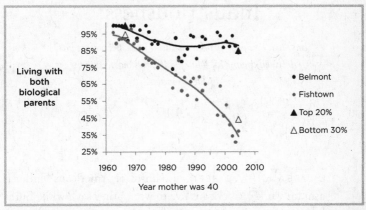

Sources: NLS Mature Women, NLS Young Women, NLSY-79. Top 20 percent and bottom 30 percent are based on women who were age 40 in 1963 and 2004.

Fishtown's higher divorce rate and much higher nonmarital-birth ratio combined to produce wide divergence from Belmont; this divergence continued to widen at the end of these observations. For the NLSY-79 cohort, whose mothers turned age 40 between 1997 and 2004, the percentage of children living with both biological parents when the mother was 40 was sinking below the 30 percent level, compared to 90 percent of Belmont children who were still living with both biological parents. The divergence is so large that it puts the women of Belmont and Fishtown into different family cultures. The absolute level in Fishtown is so low that it calls into question the viability of white working-class communities as a place for socializing the next generation.

9

Industriousness

*In which evidence is presented that industriousness has
declined among all white males, but mostly among
Fishtown males.*

EUROPEANS HAVE BEEN disdainful of Americans' enthusiasm for work. "Americans live to work," they say, "while Europeans work to live." Many Americans have agreed, me among them, and felt sorry for Europeans.

Yes, you can overdo it. There is more to life than work, and a life without ample space for family and friends is incomplete. But this much should not be controversial: Vocation—one's calling in life—plays a large role in defining the meaning of that life. For some, the nurturing of children is the vocation. For some, an avocation or a cause can become an all-absorbing source of satisfaction, with the job a means of paying the bills and nothing more. But for many others, vocation takes the form of the work one does for a living. Working hard, seeking to get ahead, and striving to excel at one's craft are not only quintessential features of traditional American culture but also some of its best features. Industriousness is a resource for living a fulfilling human life instead of a life that is merely entertaining.

What Whites Said About Work

Beginning in 1973, the GSS showed a card to the person being interviewed and asked, "Would you please look at this card and tell me which one thing on this list you would most prefer in a job?" The card had these choices:

- High income
- No danger of being fired
- Chances for advancement
- Working hours are short; lots of free time
- Work important and gives a feeling of accomplishment

After the subject gave his first priority, the interviewer ascertained which were his second, third, fourth, and last priorities. The item was given in almost every survey from 1973 through 1994. Then the GSS dropped it for the next twelve years, perhaps because the answers had been so consistent. Among prime-age whites, the most popular first choice was always work that "gives a feeling of accomplishment," getting an average of 58 percent of the votes in each decade. The two least-chosen first choices were always short work hours (averaging 4 percent) and no danger of being fired (6 percent).

In 2006, the GSS resurrected the question, and the results were startling. The 58 percent that had always voted first place to work that "gives a feeling of accomplishment" was down to 43 percent. First-place votes for short working hours more than doubled to 9 percent. "No danger of being fired" doubled to 12 percent, with another 13 percent ranking it in second place.

There is no reason to think that the 2006 results were a fluke. Unusual economic troubles don't explain them—the national unemployment rate stood at a low 4.6 percent and GDP growth was a healthy 6.1 percent. The results are not a function of something peculiar about the 30–49 age group; they persisted when I looked at older and younger respondents. Still, it's just one survey, and I wish we had corroborating evidence of such large changes in other recent GSS surveys. So I will leave it at this: We can't be sure, but it looks as if during the last half of the 1990s and the first half of the 2000s, whites by their own testimony became less interested in meaningful work and more interested in secure jobs with short working hours. Furthermore, these trends applied to both Belmont and Fishtown. This is not the way Tocqueville or Grund described the American attitude toward work. In fact, the responses in 2006 looked downright European.

That's what white Americans have been saying about work over the years. What have they actually been doing? It makes a big difference whether you are asking about men or women.

What Whites Did About Work: Men

Until recently, healthy men in the prime of life who did not work were scorned as bums. Even when the man was jobless through no fault of his own, America's deeply rooted stigma against idleness persisted—witness the sense of guilt that gripped many men who were unemployed during the Great Depression even though they knew it wasn't their fault they were unemployed.

The Unbelievable Rise in Physical Disability

That norm has softened. Consider first the strange case of workers who have convinced the government that they are unable to work. The percentage of workers who *actually* are physically or emotionally unable to work for reasons beyond their control has necessarily gone down since 1960. Medical care now cures or alleviates many ailments that would have prevented a person from working in 1960. Technology has produced compensations for physical handicaps and intellectual limitations. Many backbreaking manual jobs in 1960 are now done by sitting at the controls of a Bobcat. Yet the percentage of people qualifying for federal disability benefits because they are unable to work rose from 0.7 percent of the size of the labor force in 1960 to

5.3 percent in 2010. Figure 9.1 shows the trendline in proportional terms, using 1960 as the baseline.

FIGURE 9.1.   **PROPORTIONAL CHANGES IN THE PEOPLE DEEMED DISABLED FOR WORK**

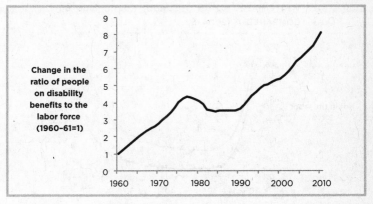

Source: Social Security Administration, *Annual Statistical Report on the Social Security Disability Insurance Program, 2010*, Table 1.

This rising trendline is not produced by changes in the legal definition of physical disability or the pool of people who qualify for benefits. Both have been tweaked but not substantially changed since 1960. Increases in substance abuse don't explain it (substance abuse is not a qualifying disability). Maybe some of the growth in the 1960s can be explained by disabled people first learning about the program. But the rest of the trendline reflects in part an increase in the number of people seeking to get benefits who aren't really unable to work—an increase in Americans for whom the founding virtue of industriousness is not a big deal anymore.

Labor Force Participation

More evidence for the weakening of the work ethic among males comes from the data on *labor force participation*—the economist's term for being available for work if anyone offers you a job. When the average labor force participation rate in 1960–64 is compared with the rate from 2004 through 2008 (before the recession began), as shown in figure 9.2, white male labor-force participation fell across the entire age range.[1]

FIGURE 9.2.   **WHITE MALES NOT IN THE LABOR FORCE: 1960–64 COMPARED TO 2004–8**

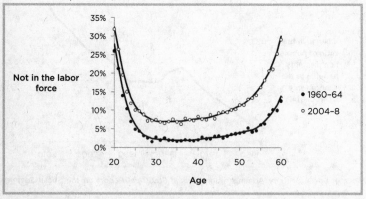

Source: IPUMS. Sample limited to civilian white males ages 20–60.

The differences weren't large for men in their early twenties, and even those small differences are largely explained by increases in post– high school education that delay entry into the labor force. The differences were much larger for white males in their late fifties, but that's not necessarily worrisome either. More men had pensions or savings that enabled them to take early retirement in the 2000s than in the early 1960s.

Why the Trendlines in This Chapter Stop in 2008

In the fall of 2008, the American economy went into a tailspin. Unemployment at the close of 2010 remained close to double digits. This has produced a spike in some of the indicators I discuss in this chapter, widening the gaps between Belmont and Fishtown. To simplify the interpretation of long-term trends, the trendlines are based only on data from 1960 through the March 2008 CPS data (collected before the downturn later in the year). I show the raw

percentages for 2009 and 2010 so you can see the magnitude of
the spike, if any, since 2008.

But what's going on with the men at the center of our interest,
white males ages 30–49? They're supposed to be working. Most of
them were—only 8 percent of them were out of the labor force in
2004–8. But that's still more than three times the percentage of
prime-age men who were out of the labor force in 1960–64.

If you believe in the importance of industriousness among prime-age
males, there's no benign explanation for the gap. I have already pointed
out that disability and illness should have made the line go the other
way. Nor can we blame increased unemployment that created discouraged workers—the average white unemployment rate in 2004–8 was
actually a bit lower (4.5 percent) than it had been in 1960–64 (5.1
percent). A substantial number of prime-age white working-age men
dropped out of the labor force for no obvious reason.

Whatever that reason may have been, it affected men with low
education much more than men with high education. We cannot divide white males by combinations of occupation and education in this
instance, because almost all of the people not in the labor force gave
no occupation to the CPS interviewer. But we can divide males by the

FIGURE 9.3. **PRIME-AGE MALES WHO ARE NOT IN THE LABOR FORCE,
BY EDUCATION**

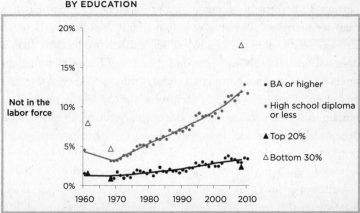

Source: IPUMS. Sample limited to white males ages 30–49.

educational levels that qualify people for Belmont and Fishtown—
a college degree for Belmont, twelve or fewer years of education for
Fishtown. I also define the educational bottom 30 percent as of 1960,
which consisted of everyone with nine or fewer years of education,
and the educational top 20 percent as of 1960, which consisted of
everybody with more than twelve years of education. The results are
shown in figure 9.3.

Throughout the 1960s, American white males of all educational
levels inhabited the same world. Participation in the labor force was
close to universal among the 30–49 age group.[2] Four and a half percent of males in Fishtown with no more than a high school education
were out of the labor force in 1960, compared to about 1 percent of
those with sixteen or more years of education—a large proportional
difference, but a small absolute one. By 1968, that difference had
shrunk to 3 percentage points.

Starting in the 1970s and continuing up to 2008, white males with
only a high school education started leaving the labor force. As of
March 2008, 12 percent of prime-age white males with no more than
a high school diploma were not in the labor force compared to 3 percent of college graduates.[3] The bottom 30 percent tracked with the
trendline of Fishtown, but at somewhat higher levels of labor force
absence.

Why should the difference between Fishtown as a whole and the
bottom 30 percent be so much greater for labor force participation
than for marriage? The answer is that cognitive ability has a much
stronger relationship with employability and job productivity than it
does with marriageability.[4] Fifty-nine percent of Fishtown prime-age
males in 1960 had not gotten past eighth grade, even though they had
grown up at a time when children were already legally required to
remain in school until age 16. In the ordinary course of events, children finish eighth grade when they are age 14. Some extremely high
proportion of those with no more than eight years of education had
repeated a grade in elementary school or junior high, which is a strong
indicator of serious learning difficulties. A society can have social and
legal norms that lead almost everyone, at all levels of cognitive ability,
to get married and stay married. But when men are competing for

jobs, low cognitive ability carries a big disadvantage at all times, extending deep into the unskilled occupations.

Unemployment

Now we're talking about men who are in the labor force but who report that they cannot find work. Mathematically, trends in unemployment are unrelated to trends in labor force participation.

Underlying trends in unemployment are obscured by year-to-year changes in the state of the economy. Figure 9.4 takes the state of the economy into account by expressing the unemployment rate for white males ages 30–49 in Belmont and Fishtown in any given year as a percentage of the national unemployment rate that year.[5]

FIGURE 9.4.   MALE UNEMPLOYMENT AS A RATIO OF THE NATIONAL
               UNEMPLOYMENT RATE

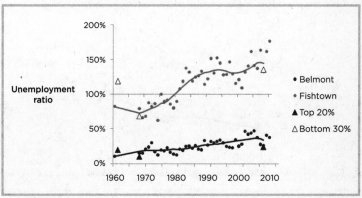

Sources: IPUMS and Bureau of Labor Statistics. Sample limited to white males ages 30–49 in the labor force.

To interpret the graph, think of 100 percent as the success rate of the average person, of any age, race, or sex, who was looking for work in a given year. Anything below 100 on the graph indicates better than average success in finding work, while anything over 100 indicates worse than average success. Through the 1960s and into the 1970s, Fishtown men did a little better than the average person who was looking for work. That changed in the 1980s. For the most recent two decades, Fishtown men have done worse than the average person looking for work, and the overall trend has been up. Multivariate analysis yields results consistent with the portrait in the graph.[6]

Note that the unemployment ratio for the bottom 30 percent was far above that of Fishtown in 1960, but by 1968 was almost identical with Fishtown. Thereafter, the rise for the bottom 30 percent paralleled the rise in Fishtown as a whole.

Hours of Work

The virtue called *industriousness* means working hard as well as holding a job. "Hours worked per week" is our available quantitative indicator of working hard.

FIGURE 9.5. MALES WITH JOBS WHO WORKED FEWER THAN 40 HOURS IN THE PRECEDING WEEK

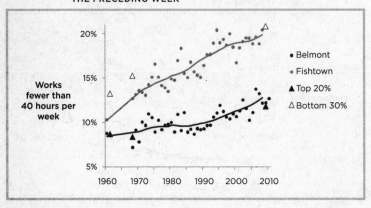

Source: IPUMS. Sample limited to employed white males ages 30–49.

As a group, prime-age white males continued to work long hours throughout the half century, averaging around forty-five hours per week throughout.[7] But a growing minority of them weren't working a forty-hour week, as shown in figure 9.5.

The increase in less-than-full-time work in Fishtown is notable, doubling from 10 percent in 1960 to 20 percent in 2008. Since the rise continued throughout the hottest boom years of the 1990s, it is difficult to attribute the rise to an ailing economy in which men couldn't find as many hours of work as they wanted.

A very different picture emerges for men who worked unusually long hours, as shown in figure 9.6.

FIGURE 9.6.   **MALES WITH JOBS WHO WORKED MORE THAN 48 HOURS IN THE PRECEDING WEEK**

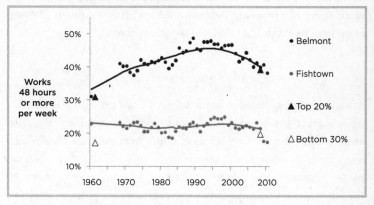

Source: IPUMS. Sample limited to employed white males ages 30–49.

In 1960, about a third of Belmont men reported working more than forty-eight hours in the week before the interviewer talked to them. But 23 percent of Fishtown men also worked long hours.

This is one of the rare measures on which nothing much changed in Fishtown over the next half century. Note the contrast between the stories for labor force participation, unemployment, and less-than-full-time work, all of which showed marked deterioration in Fishtown. Recall further that we are talking only about prime-age men who were employed and at work in the week preceding the interview—these trends are independent of the trends in labor force participation and unemployment. Despite the other indications of decay, the proportion of Fishtown men who worked long hours was still 23 percent in 2008, exactly what it had been in 1960, and 5 percentage points higher than the proportion of men in the bottom quartile who had worked more than forty-eight hours in 1960. Alongside diminished industriousness among some Fishtown men is another set of Fishtown men who were working as hard as ever in the 2000s.

Meanwhile, Belmont left Fishtown in the dust.[8] By the end of the 1980s, almost half of Belmont men reported that they worked more than forty-eight hours in the preceding week. The percentage of hardworking Belmont men began to slack off in the 2000s, drifting down to 40 percent by 2008. But that still left a gap between the work effort of prime-age Belmont men and Fishtown men that was more than twice the gap that had separated them in 1960.

"It's the Labor Market's Fault"

A natural explanation for the numbers I have presented is that the labor market got worse for low-skill workers from 1960 to 2008. More Fishtown men worked short hours because they couldn't get work for as many hours as they wanted; more of them were unemployed because it was harder for them to get jobs; more of them left the labor market because they were discouraged by the difficulty of finding jobs.

"Jobs didn't pay a living wage." In one respect, the labor market did indeed get worse for Fishtown men: pay. Recall figure 2.1 at the beginning of the book, showing stagnant incomes for people below the 50th income percentile. High-paying unionized jobs have become scarce and real wages for all kinds of blue-collar jobs have been stagnant or falling since the 1970s. But these trends don't explain why Fishtown men in the 2000s worked fewer hours, found it harder to get jobs than other Americans did, and more often dropped out of the labor market than they had in the 1960s. On the contrary: Insofar as men *need to work to survive*—an important proviso—falling hourly income does not discourage work.

Put yourself in the place of a Fishtown man who is at the bottom of the labor market, qualified only for low-skill jobs. You may wish you could make as much as your grandfather made working on a General Motors assembly line in the 1970s. You may be depressed because you've been trying to find a job and failed. But if a job driving a delivery truck, or being a carpenter's helper, or working on a cleaning crew for an office building opens up, why would a bad labor market for blue-collar jobs keep you from taking it? As of 2009, a very bad year economically, the median hourly wage for drivers of delivery trucks was $13.84; for carpenter's helpers, $12.63; for building cleaners, $13.37.[9] That means $505 to $554 for a forty-hour week, or $25,260 to $27,680 for a fifty-week year. Those are not great incomes, but they are enough to be able to live a decent existence—almost twice the poverty level even if you are married and your wife doesn't work. So why would you *not* work if a job opening landed in your lap? Why would you not work a full forty hours if the hours were available? Why not work more than forty hours?

"There weren't any jobs." So far, I have put the scenario in terms of 2009 wages. What about all the previous years when dropout from the labor force was rising in Fishtown but jobs were plentiful? The last twenty-six years we are examining coincided with one of the longest employment booms in American history, as shown in figure 9.7.

FIGURE 9.7.   NATIONAL UNEMPLOYMENT RATE AND DROPOUT FROM THE LABOR FORCE AMONG MALES WITH A FISHTOWN EDUCATION

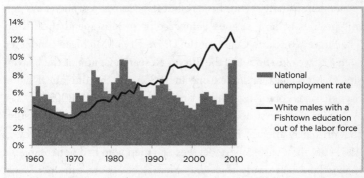

Source: IPUMS, Bureau of Labor Statistics. Labor force sample limited to white males ages 30–49 with no more than a high school diploma.

From 1960 through the early 1980s, changes in Fishtown male dropout from the labor force moved roughly in tandem with the national unemployment rate. But after the mid-1980s, the argument that "there weren't any jobs" loses force. Unemployment went down, but dropout from the labor force among white males with a Fishtown education continued to increase. During the fourteen years from

1995 through 2008, no year had higher than 6.0 percent unemployment, and the median was 5.0 percent. For mature economies, these are exceptionally low unemployment rates. But those who remember these years don't need the numbers. "Help wanted" signs were everywhere, including for low-skill jobs, and the massive illegal immigration that occurred during those years was underwritten by a reality that everyone recognized: America had jobs for everyone who wanted to work.

Inside the black box. Citing macroeconomic conditions leaves us outside the black box. What was going on with these men who were no longer employed or were not even looking for work? You will get some vivid examples of what was happening in the real Fishtown in chapter 12. Economists Mark Aguiar and Erik Hurst gave us another kind of look inside that black box with their analysis of American time-use surveys from 1965 through 2005. "Time-use surveys" ask respondents what they did on the previous day, separated into fifteen-minute increments. At the end, the entire day is accounted for. The answers for any one respondent might be atypical of how that respondent usually spends his day, but large samples of such days permit profiles of how various demographic groups spend their time. The Survey Research Center at the University of Michigan conducted such a survey in 1965–66, the Survey Research Center at the University of Maryland conducted one in 1985, and the Bureau of Labor Statistics has conducted annual time-use surveys since 2003.[10]

Aguiar and Hurst document what they call an increase in "leisure" that primarily affected men with low education. In the first survey, in 1965–66, men with college degrees and men who had not completed high school had nearly the same amount of leisure time per week, with just a two-hour difference.[11] They were only an hour apart in 1985. Then something changed. "Between 1985 and 2005," Aguiar and Hurst write, "men who had not completed high school increased their leisure time by eight hours per week, while men who had completed college decreased their leisure time by six hours per week."[12]

When Aguiar and Hurst decomposed the ways that men spent their time, the overall pattern for men with no more than a high school diploma is clear. The men of Fishtown spent more time goofing off. Furthermore, the worst results were found among men without jobs. In 2003–5, men who were not employed spent less time on job search, education, and training, and doing useful things around the house than they had in 1985.[13] They spent less time on civic and religious activities. They didn't even spend their leisure time on active pastimes such as exercise, sports, hobbies, or reading. All of those figures were lower in 2003–5 than they had been in 1985. How did they spend that extra leisure time? Sleeping and watching television. The increase in television viewing was especially large—from 27.7 hours per week in 1985 to 36.7 hours in 2003–5. Employed men with no more than high school diplomas also goofed off more in 2003–5 than in 1985, but less consistently and with smaller differentials.[14]

To sum up: There is no evidence that men without jobs in the 2000s before the 2008 recession hit were trying hard to find work but failing. It was undoubtedly true of some, but not true of the average jobless man. The simpler explanation is that white males of the 2000s were less industrious than they had been twenty, thirty, or fifty years ago, and that the decay in industriousness occurred overwhelmingly in Fishtown.

"It's Because They Didn't Marry"

It makes sense that women would choose mates who have already exhibited evidence that they will be successful economically, and social scientists have demonstrated that this is in fact a statistical tendency: Men with high earnings are more likely to get married and less likely to get divorced.[15] But there's another possibility: Married men become more productive after they are married *because* they are married. Economist Gary Becker predicted this outcome in *A Treatise on the Family* because of the advantages of role specialization in marriage.[16] George Gilder predicted it even earlier, in *Sexual Suicide*, through a more inflammatory argument: Unmarried males arriving at adulthood are barbarians who are then civilized by women through marriage. The inflammatory part was that Gilder saw disaster looming as women stopped performing this function, a position derided as the worst kind of patriarchal sexism.[17] But, put in less vivid language, the argument is neither implausible nor inflammatory: The responsibilities of marriage induce young men to settle down, focus, and get to work.

Then, in the late 1980s, economists began to identify what became known as the "marriage premium," whereby married men make 10 to 20 percent more money than unmarried men, even after controlling for the usual socioeconomic and demographic factors. The puzzling thing about the marriage premium (if you do not agree with either Becker's or Gilder's argument) is that it cannot be a simple case of women choosing to marry men who are already more productive—the marriage premium occurs *after* the wedding vows have been taken. And so the technical literature has been filled with debates about why this marriage premium comes about—is it something about being married that produces the effect, or is the marriage premium the result of women seeing potential in men that they are going to fulfill, even if they haven't already done so while they are single?

The note on page 375 gives you some of the most important sources for following the debate.[18] What we can say for certain is that married men in the CPS behave far differently with regard to the labor force than unmarried men. Put plainly, single prime-age males are much less industrious than married ones. Both the decline in marriage and the increased detachment from the labor force in Fishtown cannot be understood without knowing that the interaction exists.

Participation in the labor force. Prime-age men are much more than three times as likely to be out of the labor force if they are unmarried, and this was true throughout the entire half century from 1960 to 2010 for both Belmont and Fishtown males. Using an analysis that controls for the year and the unemployment rate, unmarried white males ages 30–49 with a college education were 3.6 times more likely to be out of the labor force than their married counterparts in 1960 and 3.5 times more likely in 2010.[19] Among those with no more than a high school diploma, the comparable ratios were 3.9:1 in 1960 and 3.7:1 in 2010.

Unemployment. The unmarried-to-married unemployment ratio

for men was close to identical in 1960 and 2010. Among those with a college education, 2.9 times as many unmarried men were unemployed in both 1960 and 2010. Among those with no more than a high school diploma, the comparable ratio was 2.3:1 in both years.

Men who worked fewer than forty hours per week. Limiting the analysis to men who held jobs—an important change in the sample—unmarried college-educated men were 1.5 times as likely as married college-educated men to work fewer than forty hours per week in both 1960 and 2010. For men with just a high school diploma, unmarried men were 1.7 times more likely to work fewer than forty hours a week in 1960 and 1.6 times more likely to do so in 2010.

The meaning of all this is that the labor force problems that grew in Fishtown from 1960 to 2010 are intimately connected with the increase in the number of unmarried men in Fishtown. The balance of the literature suggests that the causal arrow for the marriage premium goes mostly from marriage to labor force behavior—in other words, George Gilder was probably mostly right. But some causation goes the other way as well. In the 2000s Fishtown had a lot fewer men who were indicating that they would be good providers if the woman took a chance and married one of them than it had in 1960.

What Whites Did About Work: Women

Detecting changes in industriousness among American women is impossible unless you assume that a woman working at a paid job is more industrious than a full-time mother, which is not an assumption that I am willing to make. But the story of the deterioration in male industriousness in Fishtown would be incomplete without knowing what happened to women as well.

America experienced a social and economic revolution from the early 1970s to the early 1990s. The percentage of white women in the labor force rose from 40 percent in 1960 to 74 percent by 1995. In the fifteen years after 1995, little changed, with the percentage hitting its high of 75 percent in 2000 and standing at 70 percent in 2008.[20]

Who Joined the Revolution and When?

The revolution occurred similarly for many different kinds of women. Once again, I must divide whites ages 30–49 by educational level instead of dividing the sample into Belmont and Fishtown, for the same reason that applied to males out of the labor force. I begin with married women, shown in figure 9.8.

FIGURE 9.8. LABOR FORCE PARTICIPATION AMONG MARRIED WOMEN BY EDUCATION

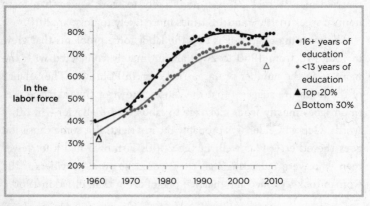

Source: IPUMS. Sample limited to married white women ages 30–49.

The short story is that married women in Belmont and Fishtown behaved similarly, starting out within 6 percentage points of each other in 1960 and ending up within 7 percentage points of each other in 2008. Married women in both neighborhoods roughly doubled their labor force participation. It was a revolution indeed, transforming the labor force participation of married women. Creaming had a trivial effect.

Now turn to single women, who exhibit the different pattern shown in figure 9.9.

The gap between Belmont and Fishtown unmarried women was already wide in 1960, and the feminist revolution made little difference subsequently. This is not surprising in the case of college-educated unmarried women, more than 90 percent of whom were

FIGURE 9.9. LABOR FORCE PARTICIPATION AMONG UNMARRIED WOMEN BY EDUCATION

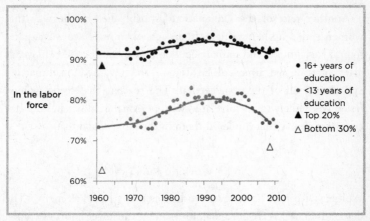

Source: Author's analysis of IPUMS CPS.[21] Sample limited to unmarried white women ages 30–49.

already in the labor force in 1960. For unmarried women with no more than a high school education, labor force participation never got higher than 83 percent. After its peak in 1986, the rate in Fishtown declined, dropping to 74 percent in 2008, slightly lower than it was in 1960.

Whereas there was little creaming effect among married Fishtown women, there was a big one for unmarried ones—that is, the bottom 30 percent of unmarried women were much less likely to be in the labor force in 1960 than unmarried Fishtown women as a whole. Why the difference? Part of the explanation lies in the very different expectations that married and unmarried women had to meet. In 1960, a married Fishtown woman wasn't expected to work outside the home if she didn't have to, and two-thirds of them weren't trying to do so. Married Fishtown women with no more than eight years of education could be in the labor force at about the same rate as their better-educated married neighbors and still have a low rate of labor force participation. The labor force participation rate of unmarried women in the bottom 30 percent was 62 percent, much higher than the 31 percent rate for married women in the bottom 30 percent. It just didn't look good in comparison with better-educated unmarried Fishtown women.

Another part of the explanation probably lies in the way that women ended up being single. In an age when marriage was a paramount social norm and unmarried women were still called old maids after a certain age, almost all Fishtown women wanted to get married and almost all of them succeeded. The reasons that some women failed were likely to be correlated with personal qualities besides low cognitive ability that hindered them in the labor market.

Women Working Full Time

Women with jobs have never worked as many hours as men.[22] The demands of child care are a major reason for the lower hours—women with children under age 5 worked an average of thirty-three hours. But they don't explain everything. Even women with no children of any age worked an average of forty hours in the week preceding the CPS interview, compared to the male average of forty-five.

The trends in hours worked showed clear differences and divergences among classes. For women working more than forty-eight

FIGURE 9.10.   **WORKING WOMEN AGES 30–49 WHO WORKED 40 OR MORE HOURS IN THE PRECEDING WEEK**

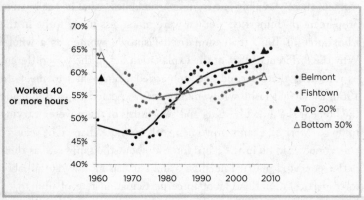

Source: Author's analysis of IPUMS CPS. Sample limited to women with jobs who worked in the week preceding the interview.

hours, the pattern looked almost exactly the same as the one for men: increases for Belmont, flattening in the 1990s and then dropping slightly in the 2000s, with a nearly flat trendline for Fishtown. But a better way to get a sense of the change in working hours among women is to use the forty-hour standard. Over the period 1960–2008, what proportions of working women were employed full time by the traditional definition of a forty-hour week? The answer is shown in figure 9.10.

In 1960, 64 percent of Fishtown working women worked at least a forty-hour week, conspicuously more than the 50 percent of Belmont women. By 1983, that gap had completely closed. Thereafter, a working woman in Belmont has been modestly more likely to work forty-hour weeks than a working Fishtown woman. One telling feature of the graph: In 1960, the top 20 percent included many women who weren't college graduates, which probably accounts for the gap between the working women of Belmont (all of whom were college graduates in 1960 or married to college graduates) and the working women of the top 20 percent.

Adding Up the Pieces

In 1960, a normally industrious American family had at least one adult working at least a forty-hour week. If that wasn't the case, and the family wasn't wealthy, something was probably wrong—someone had been laid off, was sick, or was injured. Figure 9.11 summarizes how that norm changed from 1960 to 2010.[23]

FIGURE 9.11.   FAMILIES IN WHICH THE HEAD OF HOUSEHOLD OR SPOUSE
WORKED 40 OR MORE HOURS IN THE PRECEDING WEEK

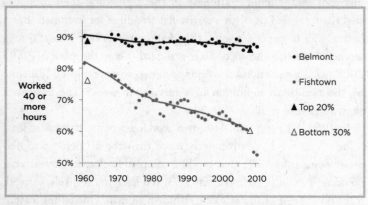

Source: IPUMS. Sample limited to unmarried persons designated as the head of household
and married couples, and to whites ages 30–49. In the case of married couples, the household was scored as "yes" if either the husband or wife worked 40 or more hours in the preceding week.

In effect, the graph adds up the separate divergences among both
men and women on labor force participation, unemployment, and
hours worked. It portrays a divergence between Belmont and Fishtown
nearly as great in aggregate as the change in marriage. In 1960, 81 percent of Fishtown households had someone working at least forty hours
a week, with Belmont at 90 percent. By 2008, Belmont had barely
changed at all, at 87 percent, while Fishtown had dropped to 60 percent. And that was before the 2008 recession began. As of March 2010,
Belmont was still at 87 percent. Fishtown was down to 53 percent.

10

Honesty

*In which evidence is presented that Belmont has never had a
crime problem worth worrying about; that Fishtown has suffered
from a transforming growth in crime; and that it is difficult to
tell whether other kinds of honesty have deteriorated.*

T RENDS IN HONESTY are most concretely reflected in trends
in crime, so I begin with them. I then turn to broader questions of honesty not measured by crime data.

Crime and Class

Ever since criminology became a discipline, scholars have found that
criminals are overwhelmingly drawn from working-class and lower-
class neighborhoods. This remains true for incarcerated felons today,
as shown in figure 10.1. Because young males commit most of the
crimes, the samples for the discussion of crime are limited to males
and the age range is broadened from 30 to 49 to include ages 20 to 49.

In inmate surveys conducted periodically by the federal government from 1974 to 2004, about 80 percent of whites in state and
federal prisons consistently came from Fishtown and fewer than
2 percent from Belmont. It is probably even worse than that. As discussed in appendix E, the imprisonment data are more likely to

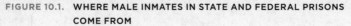

FIGURE 10.1. **WHERE MALE INMATES IN STATE AND FEDERAL PRISONS COME FROM**

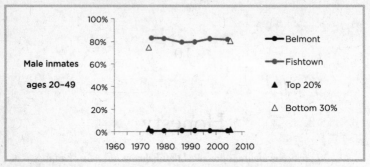

Sources: Federal surveys of state and federal inmate populations. Sample limited to white males ages 20–49.[1]

understate than overstate the proportion of serious crimes committed by people from Fishtown.

Neighborhood Trends Over Time

Imprisoned Neighbors

Figure 10.2 shows the ratio of white prisoners of any age to white adults ages 18–65 in Belmont and Fishtown from the first inmate survey in 1974 through 2004.

The inhabitants of Fishtown were battered by three national trends. The first was the increase in crime from the mid-1960s to the early 1990s, the second was the increase in imprisonment from the early 1970s through 2009, and the third was the outmigration from Fishtown. The net result: Most of the national growth in white crime and imprisonment was concentrated into a shrinking part of the white population, the working class of Fishtown. For every 100,000 Fishtowners ages 18–65 in 1974, 213 were imprisoned. By the time of the 2004 survey, that number was up to 957. And those numbers are based on just state and federal prisoners. They don't count people in jails, who amounted to around 100,000 whites in 1974 and 317,000 whites in 2004.

FIGURE 10.2. WHITE PRISONERS

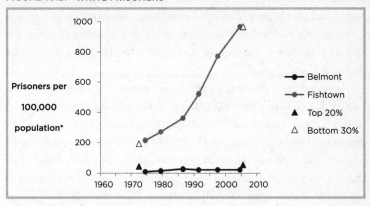

Sources: IPUMS and the six federal inmate surveys (appendix A).

*The numerator is based on white male state and federal prisoners of all ages. The denominator is based on whites ages 18–65.

Interpreting the Ratios

There is no natural denominator for computing ratios of crime indicators to population. I use whites ages 18–65 as a way to think about the numbers relative to the working-age population.

In contrast, the environment in Belmont changed hardly at all. The parallel numbers for Belmont were 13 in the 1974 survey and 27 in the 2004 survey. It is statistically unlikely that someone living in Belmont knew of a family with one of its men in prison even in 2004. Someone living in Fishtown was likely to know of at least one such family, and perhaps several.

Neighbors on Probation and Parole

While imprisonment is likely to be a misfortune for the prisoners' families, at least it has one positive effect on neighborhood life: It locks up people who otherwise would still be making trouble. The same cannot be said for persons on probation or parole. Some of them are getting their lives in order, but others are not. The size of the probation and parole population in a neighborhood is an indicator of ongoing risk for the rest of the people in the neighborhood. Alongside that direct effect is a cascade of damaging secondary effects on social capital and social trust.

The number of parolees increased in tandem with the increase in incarceration. When the first national data on parolees were released in 1980, there were about 79,000 whites on parole. That number had grown to 191,000 by 1990, to 275,000 by 2000, and stood at 337,000 in 2008. The government figures do not include background data, but there is no reason to assume that the educational and occupational profiles of parolees are radically different from those of the general prison population (although the offense histories may be different). Figure 10.2 for prisoners would apply in its broad outlines to a graph for parolees.

Probation, which often serves as a substitute for incarceration, represents a potentially different population. It is different first in its mammoth size. In 1980, there were about 581,000 whites on probation. Those numbers grew to 1,389,000 by 1990, 2,066,000 by 2000, and 2,392,000 by 2008. There has been only one federal survey of adults on probation, conducted in 1995, that includes information on the educational and occupational distributions of probationers. At that time, 38 percent of white males ages 20–49 who were on probation had not completed high school, more than four and a half times the overall dropout rate. Only 6 percent of the white male probationers of that age range had completed college or an advanced degree, compared to 29 percent for all white males ages 20–49.[2]

Overall, the population of probationers is less extremely concentrated at the bottom of the educational and occupational ladders than prisoners, but they are nonetheless extremely concentrated at the bottom in comparison to the general population. I cannot construct trendlines for probationers (the necessary data don't exist), but go back to figure 10.2 and envision a growth trend for Fishtown that is close to, but not quite as steep as, that for prisoners.

The Neighborhood Crime Rate

Optimistic readers may be thinking about a glimmer of better news. America's increase in persons under correctional supervision in the last quarter century is well known, but so is the reduction in crime that began in the early 1990s and continued into the 2000s. These reductions were substantial. As of 2009, the FBI's overall crime index

FIGURE 10.3. **WHITE ARRESTS FOR INDEX CRIMES**

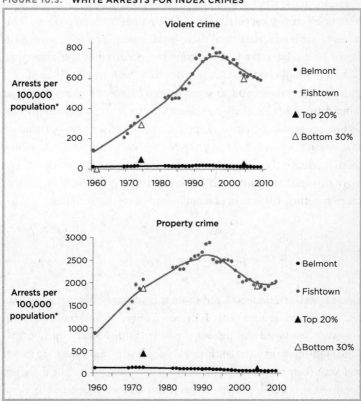

Sources: IPUMS, the FBI Uniform Crime Reports, the Bureau of Justice Statistics annual prison reports, and the six inmate surveys.

*The numerator is based on white prisoners of all ages. The denominator is based on whites ages 18–65. The top 20 percent and bottom 30 percent are shown for 1974 and 2004 because they depend on information about inmates not available earlier or later than those years.

was 40 percent below its peak in 1991. Figure 10.3 shows how arrest rates changed in Belmont and Fishtown.

In appendix E, I discuss the reasons for concluding that changes in arrest rates among whites reflect changes in the crime rate among whites. Perhaps the most interesting feature of figure 10.3 is how few arrests occurred in Belmont at any point in the half century from 1960 to 2010. The American crime problem had been overwhelmingly borne by people who are not part of Belmont.

Fishtown has shared in the reduction in crime, but the levels of arrests in Fishtown, especially for violent crime, remain far above their levels of earlier decades. And there is the sobering reality conveyed in figure 10.2: The reduction in crime has occurred at the same time that large numbers of Fishtown males have been taken off the streets and put into prison, and to some degree *because* they are no longer around to victimize their neighbors. There is no natural metric for adding up prisoners, parolees, probationers, and arrests in Fishtown that doesn't double-count in unknowable ways, but we can combine them qualitatively. Lots more prisoners, lots more probationers, lots more parolees, and somewhat diminished arrests probably mean that, taken together, the rise in *criminality* in Fishtown continues.

Honesty as Integrity

Honesty as the founders talked about it encompassed much more than refraining from crime. What Jefferson referred to as American "plain honesty" developed throughout the nineteenth century into our national self-image of a straightforward people who said what they meant and kept their word. The topic is integrity—doing the right thing not because the law will put you in jail if you don't, but because of moral principles that you follow regardless of consequences.

Integrity in the Business World

As I noted in chapter 6, American honesty existed side by side with the sharp American business practices that offended some foreign observers. It was an odd mix. To take advantage of another person in a business deal was not considered dishonorable, but there was a distinction between taking advantage and taking unfair advantage. If the other person signed a contract he hadn't read or he failed to appreciate the real value of his property, an honest American businessman was not expected to protect the other person from himself. But to lie about the terms of a contract, to defraud someone, or to cheat one's partners or stockholders were considered both dishonest and dishonorable. An American accolade was to say of a man that you could do business with him with a handshake.

Since the 1980s, one strain of thought has argued that the American business community has become more corrupt than it used to be. People who hold this view labeled the 1980s "The Decade of Greed," with Mike Milken as the exemplar of the villain. Then in the early 2000s came a series of spectacular cases of corporate malfeasance, most conspicuously at Enron, Tyco, and WorldCom, and they prompted the Sarbanes-Oxley Act of 2002, intended to tighten corporate governance.

The most damning evidence of systemic wrongdoing has come out of Wall Street in the aftermath of the financial meltdown of 2008. Describing *Inside Job*, a documentary film about the behaviors on Wall Street leading up to the crisis, the *New York Times*' Joe Nocera writes,

> Here is Wall Street actively encouraging subprime lenders to lower their already low standards—and then buying those loans knowing they are likely to default, but not caring. Here are traders up and down Wall Street making millions in bonuses selling products that are . . . "ticking time bombs." Here is Moody's, one of the three big credit ratings agencies, quadrupling its profits in seven years by handing out triple-A ratings like candy. Here are the regulators, ignoring impassioned entreaties to investigate fraudulent lending practices and excessive leverage. These were not anomalies. This was standard operating procedure in the years before the crisis.[3]

Evidence for those behaviors gathered in Senate and House hearings led to the Dodd-Frank bill for regulating the financial markets, signed into law by President Obama in July 2010. To what extent is the subprime mortgage story indicative of broader rot within the American business community, or broader rot in the parts of the financial industry that did not get caught up in the subprime story? It is a question for which I have been unable to find good answers. In appendix E, I lay out data from investigations conducted by the Securities and Exchange Commission and the Internal Revenue Service. Neither provides quantitative evidence for a broad decline in corporate integrity. The IRS evidence on tax fraud actually points in the other direction, though inconclusively. The famous examples of corporate and financial wrongdoing are real, but it is not clear whether they reflect a growing loss of integrity within the business community as a whole.

Integrity in Personal Finances

The state of personal integrity is almost as hard to track as the state of corporate integrity. It would be nice to know if there have been trends over time in the consistency with which people keep their word, insist on taking responsibility for their mistakes, and tell the cashier when they have been given too much change, but I have been unable to find databases that would tell us what those trends have been, with one exception: use of the bankruptcy laws.

Personal bankruptcies have always been legal in the United States as a way of giving people a second chance. Some famous Americans have availed themselves of that remedy, notably Mark Twain. But Americans have also seen the act of reneging on a debt as dishonorable. Twain was part of this tradition, too, eventually repaying all his debts despite having no legal obligation to do so.

The quantitative indicator I use is a particular kind of bankruptcy, now known as Chapter 7 bankruptcy, in which the bankrupt walks away without any further attempt to repay debts.[4] I restrict it to personal bankruptcies, to avoid conflating some important differences between personal and corporate bankruptcies. Persons declaring bankruptcy under Chapter 7 are required to sell most or all of their assets (the states have varying requirements) to pay off as much of their debt as possible, and are legally free to ignore the unpaid remainder. Figure 10.4 shows the overall trend in individual filings for bankruptcy from 1960 to 2008.

FIGURE 10.4. **FILINGS FOR CHAPTER 7 PERSONAL BANKRUPTCIES**

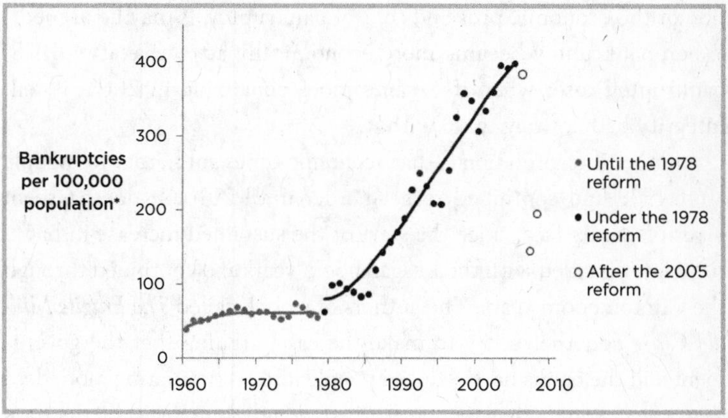

Source: Statistical Abstract of the United States 2010, table 752, and comparable tables in earlier editions.[5] Nonbusiness filings under Chapter 11 are not shown because they represented less than a percentage point of all nonbusiness filings throughout.

From 1960 to 1978, bankruptcies increased on a shallow slope. Then in 1978, the bankruptcy law was changed in several ways that made bankruptcy more attractive.[6] The big jump in bankruptcies in 1979–80 looks suspiciously like a result of the law, but bankruptcies leveled off again through the mid-1980s.[7] In 1984, modifications to the Bankruptcy Code even weakened some of the prodebtor provisions of the 1978 act. But in 1986, bankruptcies began a sustained, steep increase that lasted until 2005, when the rate reached 7.2 times its 1978 level.

Then the rate plunged from 2006 to 2007, and from an easily identified cause. Another major reform of the Bankruptcy Code was passed in 2005, making it much more difficult for people with good incomes to declare bankruptcy under Chapter 7, forcing them instead to use Chapter 13—in effect, requiring them to establish a repayment plan instead of being legally forgiven their debt. Nonbusiness filings of bankruptcy subsequently plunged—not just for Chapter 7, but for Chapter 13 as well. They started to rise again in 2008.

How are we to interpret this history? One possibility is that I am wrong to think bankruptcy has any relationship to integrity. The propensity of Americans to declare bankruptcy has always been a function of the economic pros and cons of bankruptcy, it may be argued.[8] When bankruptcy became more economically attractive after 1978, bankruptcy rose; when it became more penalizing in 2005, it fell. Integrity had nothing to do with it.

Another interpretation is that economic times got harder for people after 1978 and continued to get harder until 2010. It doesn't seem plausible on its face, since the start of the sustained increase in bankruptcies coincided with the Reagan boom years and continued through the Clinton boom years. The authors of a book called *The Fragile Middle Class* nonetheless try to make the case, arguing that the government and the banks have seduced people into accumulating more debt than they should, that increased divorce and nonmarital births have created millions of financially vulnerable households, and that the incidence of ruinous medical costs has increased.[9] But an examination of all personal bankruptcy filings in Delaware for 2003 casts doubt on the proposition that the increased bankruptcies can be blamed on events beyond people's control. Divorce and unemployment were seldom implicated. Medical costs played a secondary role. The main cause of bankruptcy was imprudent expenditures on durable consumer goods such as houses and automobiles.[10]

A third interpretation is that the propensity to declare bankruptcy *has* changed and that integrity has deteriorated. Have the bankruptcy laws become more lenient? To respond to the increased leniency by declaring bankruptcy more readily is akin to deciding to shoplift if the criminal justice system becomes more lenient. Are the banks offering credit too easily? Someone for whom integrity is paramount is scared of incurring debts that can't be repaid, and doesn't take out the loan. Is a woman facing a divorce? Someone for whom integrity is paramount changes her lifestyle, drastically if necessary, to avoid the shame of being unable to repay her debts.

I am not arguing that people of integrity never declare bankruptcy. Rather, I am arguing that there are always temptations to get into debt and always patches in life where finances become dicey. In a nation where integrity is strong, the effects of temptations and of rough patches are damped down. That trendline in figure 10.4, showing a quadrupling of personal bankruptcies over a period that included one of the most prosperous decades in American history, looks suspiciously like a decline in personal integrity. The data do not permit us to assess whether the decline has been more serious in Belmont or in Fishtown.

11

Religiosity

In which evidence is presented that white America as a whole became more secular between 1960 and 2010, especially from the beginning of the 1990s. Despite the common belief that the working class is the most religious group in white American society, the drift from religiosity was far greater in Fishtown than in Belmont.

THE IMPORTANCE THAT the founders attached to religion bordered on hypocrisy. They went to church, but few of them were devout. Today, there is less hypocrisy, but also little reflection on the issue. Was George Washington correct when he said, "Reason and experience both forbid us to expect that national morality can prevail in exclusion of religious principle"? It is not a philosophical question, but a political question with concrete consequences.

The jury is still out on the metaquestion of whether secular democracies can long survive. But the last few decades have brought forth a large technical literature about the role of religion in maintaining civic life and the effects of religion on human functioning.

Religion's role as a source of social capital is huge. "As a rough rule of thumb," Robert Putnam wrote in *Bowling Alone*, "our evidence shows [that] nearly half of all associational memberships are church-related, half of all personal philanthropy is religious in character, and half of all volunteering occurs in a religious context."[1] But it's not just the contributions of Americans in religious settings that make religion so important to social capital. People who are religious also account for a large proportion of the secular forms of social capital. Robert Putnam again:

> Religious worshippers and people who say religion is very important to them are much more likely than other persons to visit friends, to entertain at home, to attend club meetings, and to belong to sports groups; professional and academic societies; school service groups; youth groups; service clubs; hobby or garden clubs; literary, art, discussion, and study groups; school fraternities and sororities; farm organizations; political clubs; nationality groups; and other miscellaneous groups.[2]

Apart from augmenting social capital in general, churches serve specifically as a resource for sustaining a democratic citizenry. Various studies have found that active involvement in church serves as a kind of training center for important civic skills.[3] All of these relationships hold true even after controlling for demographic and socioeconomic variables.

Beyond these benefits for the civic culture, claims began surfacing in the 1970s and 1980s that religious faith is empirically associated with good things such as better physical health, mental health, and longevity. Many of the early claims were advanced by religiously committed people, and were regarded suspiciously. But over the last few decades, social scientists who have no personal interest in vindicating religion have been building a rigorous literature on these issues, and it turns out that most of the claims are true.[4] People who attend church regularly and report that religion is an important part of their lives have longer life expectancies,[5] less disability in old age,[6] and more stable marriages.[7] A review of the literature as of 2001 concluded there is strong evidence for the relationship of religiosity to happiness and satisfaction with life, self-esteem, less depression, and less substance abuse.[8] The list goes on, including many positive outcomes for children raised by religious parents.[9]

All of these effects of religion make it important to inquire, as we do in this chapter, about the trajectory of American religiosity from 1960 to 2010.

Secularization

The central fact about American whites and religion since 1960 is that whites have become more secular across the board, in every socioeconomic class. But the whole story is more complicated and interesting than that.

From the beginning of the twentieth century through the eve of World War II, American church membership and attendance did no more than keep pace with population growth. Maybe not even that. After piecing together the elusive data on such questions for the first decades of the century, historian William Hutchinson concluded that attendance actually eroded over that period.[10] Nominal membership remained high, with three-quarters of Americans claiming membership in a church or synagogue when asked by pollsters, but weekly attendance was much lower. In the prewar Gallup polls, the low point occurred in 1940, when only 37 percent of the respondents said they attended worship services in the preceding week.[11]

Then, suddenly and for no obvious reason, membership and attendance both started to rise and continued to rise during the 1950s, reaching historic highs. The membership apogee occurred in the mid-1960s.[12] The attendance apogee occurred around 1963, according to the Gallup data.[13] So when the General Social Survey (GSS) took its first reading of religiosity in 1972, America was already several years into a decline. With that in mind, here's the story that the GSS documents.

Secularization Version 1: Nonbelievers

The hard-core definition of secular is represented by people who, when asked about their religious preference, forthrightly answer "none." Among whites ages 30–49 in 1972, when the GSS first asked the question, only 4 percent met that definition. It was so low that it couldn't have been much lower in the 1960s. But it rose rapidly thereafter. By 1980, 10 percent of GSS subjects were willing to say they had no religious preference. The trend flattened and even dipped a bit through the 1980s. Then the trendline shot upward, and by 2010 stood at 21 percent of all whites ages 30–49. That figure represents a quintupling of the hard-core secular white population since 1972 and a doubling since the early 1990s. Figure 11.1 shows how the hard-core secularization broke out by neighborhood.

FIGURE 11.1. **NONBELIEVERS**

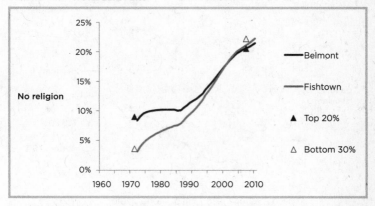

Source: GSS. Sample limited to whites ages 30–49. Data smoothed using locally estimated regression (LOESS).

Figure 11.1 shows a rare instance of convergence between Fishtown and Belmont. But the main message of the graph is not the difference between the two neighborhoods; it is the steep rise in the percentage of whites in both neighborhoods who said they had no religion. The increase was especially pronounced from the mid-1980s onward.

Secularization Version 2: De Facto Seculars

Many Americans still feel that they are supposed to be religious, and so they tend to tell interviewers that they profess a religion even if they haven't attended a worship service for years. They also tend to tell interviewers that they attend worship services more often than they actually do.[14] In the GSS, about a third of all whites who say they profess a religion also acknowledge that they attend no more than once a year. It seems reasonable to assume that, for practical purposes, these people are as little involved in religious activity as those who profess no religion. Let us look at the trends using a broader definition of *secular*, adding everyone who professes a religion but attends worship services no more than once a year to those who say they profess no religion. Figure 11.2 shows how the neighborhoods break out under the broader definition.

FIGURE 11.2.   THE DE FACTO SECULARS

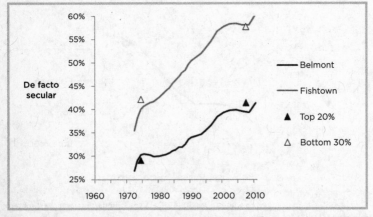

Source: GSS. Sample limited to whites ages 30–49. Data smoothed using locally estimated regression (LOESS).

Changing the definition transforms the picture. If we think in terms of disengagement from religion, Fishtown led the way, and the divergence was significant. In the first half of the 1970s, about 10 percentage points separated Belmont from Fishtown. Over the next three decades, disengagement increased in Belmont to 41 percent in the last half of the 2000s. In Fishtown, the religiously disengaged became a majority amounting to 59 percent.

Before leaving the topic of secularization, I should point out that, even after the decline, the percentage of white Americans who are actively religious is still higher in both neighborhoods than in other advanced countries. In an international survey of religious attendance conducted in 1998–99, the percentages attending church regularly in Scandinavia, Germany, the Netherlands, France, and Great Britain ranged from 2 percent in Denmark to 14 percent in

Great Britain, compared to 32 percent for the United States.[15] America is still exceptional in this regard; it is just less religious than it used to be.

Religious Involvement Among Believers

Among whites who do profess a religion, how strong is their religious affiliation? How observant are they? Now I am limiting the sample to those who profess a religion and attend a worship service more than once a year—*believers* is the label I will use for this group.

Little changed from the 1970s to the 2000s in strength of affiliation. About half of the believers in the GSS said their affiliation was strong throughout the surveys, and Belmont and Fishtown were within a few percentage points of each other throughout. But observance did change. Figure 11.3 shows the percentages who said they attended a worship service nearly every week, every week, or more than once a week.

FIGURE 11.3. **REGULAR ATTENDANCE AT WORSHIP SERVICES BY BELIEVERS**

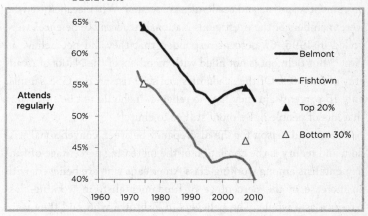

Source: Author's analysis of the GSS. Sample limited to whites ages 30–49 who profess a religion and attend worship services more than once a year. "Attends church regularly" includes all who respond "Nearly every week" or more. Data smoothed using locally estimated regression (LOESS).

Religious attendance among believers has dropped in both neighborhoods. The reduction is not huge—note that the scale on the graph goes only from 40 percent to 65 percent.

Why the Discrepancy Between Conventional Wisdom and Reality?

None of the graphs I have just shown you fit the conventional wisdom that working-class white America is still staunchly religious while white American elites are dominated by secular humanists. There are two explanations for the discrepancy between those popular images and the data from the GSS.

The first is that Belmont is not synonymous with either the broad or narrow elite. It represents the upper-middle class, but that takes in a far wider range of neighborhoods than the SuperZips and a far wider range of people than make it to the top 5 percent of people in Belmont occupations—the definition of the broad elite. Consider, for example, academics and scientists, who according to popular impressions are overwhelmingly secular. There is indeed evidence that the most prominent scientists and academics are secular. When academics who were members of the prestigious National Academy of Sciences were polled in 1996, 65 percent responded that they did not believe in God.[16] But Belmont is not filled with members of the National Academy of Sciences. Of the academics and scientists in the GSS sample, only 16 percent said they had no religion. It should not be surprising that lots of people in Belmont still go to church.

The second reason for the discrepancy between conventional wisdom and reality is the conflation of the increasing percentage of fundamentalists among working-class Americans who are believers with an increase in the percentage of fundamentalists in working-class America as a whole. The believers in Fishtown who said they were fundamentalist grew from 34 percent in the 1970s to 46 percent in the 2000s. The political fallout of that fundamentalism—for example, opposition to the teaching of evolution in the public schools—gives the impression of growing fundamentalism in working-class

America. But that is mostly an illusion. When we include all of the population in the calculation (not just believers), 32 percent of Fishtown was fundamentalist in the 1970s, and 34 percent was in the 2000s—in effect, no change. Two-thirds of Fishtown is *not* fundamentalist, and it has apparently been that way for almost forty years.

Even the rise in fundamentalism among believers does not necessarily mean that fundamentalism is becoming more popular in Fishtown. Winnowing out is the simpler explanation. As people in Fishtown dropped away from religion, the ones who were least susceptible to secularizing influences were the most deeply religious, and it seems plausible that they in turn were often fundamentalists.

The Religious Core

To pull these strands together, consider religion as one of the key sources of social capital in a community. The people who generate that social capital through their churches and synagogues are not necessarily people who believe fervently in every theological doctrine of their faith. They may or may not. But the people who, when asked by the GSS interviewer, report that they attend worship services regularly and have a strong affiliation with their religion are the people who teach in the Sunday school, staff the booths at the charity fund drives, take the synagogue's youth group on outings, arrange help for bereaved families, and serve as deacons. Figure 11.4 shows the prevalence of these people in Belmont and Fishtown.

FIGURE 11.4.　**THE RELIGIOUS CORE**

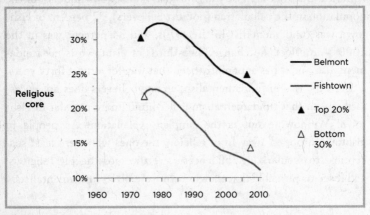

Source: GSS. Sample limited to whites ages 30–49. Data smoothed using locally estimated regression (LOESS).

What is the critical mass for generating the social capital that religion has historically contributed to American communities? On the face of it, having 25 to 30 percent of the entire population actively engaged in their church or synagogue plus most of the rest of the community paying lip service—the situation that existed in the first half of the 1970s—would seem to be plenty. I cannot judge whether the reduction in Belmont to 23 percent in the last half of the 2000s made a big difference. But Fishtown's reduction from 22 percent in the first half of the 1970s to 12 percent in the last half of the 2000s does seem significant from any perspective. Such a small figure leaves the religious core not as a substantial minority that is still large enough to be a major force in the community, but as a one-out-of-eight group of people who are increasingly seen as oddballs.

12

The Real Fishtown

*In which the people who lie behind the numbers describe what
has happened to life in the real Fishtown.*

WHEN WE TALK about classes, we reflexively resort to stereotypes. It is hard to think about the white new upper class without envisioning big houses with Mercedeses parked under the porticos or to think about the white new lower class without envisioning broken-down cars rusting in front yards. But classes don't work that way in practice. The rich and the rednecks are mixed in with other people who qualify for the upper class or lower class but are nothing like the stereotypes.

This is especially true of the members of the new lower class. Most don't have anything obviously wrong with them. A better way to think about the new lower class is in terms of your own extended family or in terms of the stories your friends have told you about their families. At least a few relatives in those circles will be people who have never quite gotten their acts together and are the despair of the parents and siblings, even though they seem perfectly pleasant when you meet them. That's mostly what the new lower class involves. Individually, they're not much of a problem. Collectively, they can destroy the kind of civil society that America requires.

If one adult man lives with his hard-pressed sister and her family because he can't manage to hold on to a steady job, that puts a lot of stress on the sister's family. If many adult men in a community are living off relatives or girlfriends, that puts lots of stress on the community. A man who fathers a child without marrying the mother may be a nice guy who is sorry it happened, and he may be trying to do what he can to help out. But it remains true that only a small minority of unmarried men end up being fathers to their children. Children need fathers, and the next generation in a community with lots of children without fathers is in trouble. People who don't go to church can be just as morally upright as those who do, but as a group they do not generate the social capital that the churchgoing population generates—it's not "their fault" that social capital deteriorates, but that doesn't make the deterioration any less real. The empirical relationships that exist among marriage, industriousness, honesty, religiosity, and a self-governing society mean that the damage is done, even though no one intends it.

That's not to say that the new lower class doesn't also have a growing number of people who are problematic as individuals. Alongside the men who say they want to work but can't seem to hold a job are growing numbers of men who have no intention of working if they can avoid it, and who not only live off their girlfriends but sometimes bankrupt them. Alongside the men who fathered children by their girlfriends but make some effort to help are others who abandon their girlfriends as soon as they learn that a pregnancy is under way and are never seen again.

Alongside the women who didn't get married but are trying hard to be good mothers are those who are the horror stories that workers in the child protective services exchange—mothers who use three-year-olds to babysit for infants while they go out for the evening; homes where the children are brain damaged because the latest live-in boyfriend makes meth in the kitchen sink; and the many cases of outright physical and emotional abuse by never-married women who are not just overburdened mothers but irresponsible or incompetent ones.

To people who live in working-class communities, none of this comes as news. But readers who do not live in working-class communities need something more than statistics. As a way of understanding what the last four chapters have meant for real people, and for understanding why I will argue in part 3 that the consequences are so bad, it is time to step back from the numbers and listen to the voices of real people who live in the real Fishtown.

FISHTOWN CONSISTS OF a triangle of blocks alongside the Delaware River about two miles northeast of Independence Hall in Philadelphia. It has no formal legal existence. Some people think it was named by Charles Dickens, derisively, when he visited Philadelphia in 1842, but one of the voices you will hear, local historian Ken Milano, has tracked down a newspaper reference to the area as "Fish-town" as early as 1808.[1] The name may go all the way back to the Revolution, when the neighborhood was the center of the local shad fishing industry.

Its residents argue about Fishtown's boundaries. Everyone agrees that it is bounded by Frankford Avenue on the northwest and the river on the southeast, but some say that the northeast boundary is Norris Street, while those who take a more expansive view say that Fishtown goes up to York Street, three blocks farther to the northeast. In either case, Fishtown is small, not much more than a mile long on any of its three sides.

In 1960, it had a population of 12,077, all but 20 of whom were white.[2] Eighty percent of Fishtown men worked in blue-collar jobs, many of them the skilled jobs required by the specialty manufacturers that dominated the Philadelphia economy. Germans and Irish were the dominant ethnic groups in the nineteenth century, supplemented during the twentieth century by Poles and, in the 1990s, by an influx of people from other countries in eastern Europe. When the 2000 census was taken, Fishtown remained exceptionally white for an inner-city neighborhood—91.3 percent white.

Fishtown's persistence as an almost entirely white inner-city neighborhood is unusual, and it has attracted attention. In the early 1950s, sociologist Peter Rossi surveyed Kensington District (the officially recognized Philadelphia entity that contains Fishtown) as part of the research for his book *Why Families Move*, and was bemused to discover that even though Kensington was objectively deprived, its residents liked the place. Indeed, of the four Philadelphia neighborhoods that Rossi surveyed, Kensington's people had the fewest complaints about their neighborhood.[3]

In 1970, as the aftermath of the civil rights revolution created tension between urban whites and blacks in the North, *Philadelphia Inquirer* reporter Peter Binzen made Fishtown the subject of a book, *Whitetown U.S.A.: A First-Hand Study of How the "Silent Majority" Lives, Learns, Works, and Thinks.*[4] Binzen portrayed a tightly knit, family-oriented, hard-drinking, hardworking, hard-fighting blue-collar neighborhood that felt persecuted by the government and disdained by the elites. But Kensington was still inordinately proud of its community, much to the exasperation of the social service establishment. "Kensingtonians are psychologically unable to face up to their social, cultural, and economic deprivation," said one Philadelphia social services administrator. "Pride prevents them from taking advantage of social services. For them to accept these services might be to admit that they're not all they claim to be."[5] The director of Temple University's Student Community Action Center lamented that "nobody knows how to work in the white community. Kensington doesn't want us there. It refuses to admit it's a poverty area."[6]

More than twenty-five years later, in the last half of the 1990s, Patricia Stern, a PhD candidate at the University of Pennsylvania, decided to make the remaining white areas of Kensington the subject of her dissertation. She began to spend time in a parish adjacent to Fishtown, served by a church that she called St. Jude (all the names in her dissertation are altered to protect privacy). During the most intense year of her research, she lived full time in St. Jude's parish. In 2002, by then Patricia Stern Smallacombe, she completed her dissertation, "Why Do They Stay: Rootedness and Isolation in an Inner-City White Neighborhood."[7] It is a richly detailed ethnographic account, with many extended passages taken verbatim from field notes and interviews. Here, in the words of its residents, is how the dry statistics about the fictional Fishtown of the preceding chapters translate into the changes that occurred in the daily life of the real Fishtown.[8]

Marriage

In the real Fishtown as in the fictional Fishtown, the decline began in the 1970s. In the case of marriage, we cannot tell how many adults were married in the 1960 and 1970 censuses—the census tract data tell us only what percentage of persons ages 14 and older were married—but we do know that in 1970, 81 percent of families with children under age 18 were still headed by married couples. Over just the next ten years, that figure dropped to 67 percent.

The traditional norm in Fishtown had not necessarily been "get married and then get pregnant and have a baby." Quite frequently, it had been "get pregnant, then get married and have a baby." But the shift from either norm by the time Smallacombe did her research had been drastic. Jenny, one of seven children of prosperous working-class parents who divorced when she was a child (the father had physically abused the mother), turned twenty in the mid-1980s.

> I was twenty when I had [my son]. Nineteen pregnant and twenty when I had him. My older sister who was married at a young age was pregnant. I wanted to be married to the guy I meet, I'm going to get married and follow her footsteps. It didn't work out. Then my younger sister, we were pregnant all at the same time, which was great, all three of us being pregnant. My mother didn't believe any of us, that we were pregnant. The one was okay because she was married. It was okay for her. . . . We were all in competition. Me and my four sisters all had babies and only one *did it the right way*.[9] (Emphasis in the original.)

By the 1990s, more and more girls like Jenny's younger sister, still in their midteens, were getting pregnant. Carrie, a lunchroom staffer at St. Jude parochial school, had a sixteen-year-old daughter in a Catholic secondary school.

> My daughter has been to six baby showers in the last four months. . . . There's fifty-two pregnant kids in [the school].

Fifty-two. That's bad. Not to mention the ones that already have
kids. . . . Like I said, everybody makes mistakes and I don't condemn anybody for making a mistake, but what's happening here?
Why are there so many? When I went to school there was some
pregnancy, but I'd say probably four in the whole year.[10]

Why does it happen? Lack of information about family planning
doesn't seem to have been the problem. There are no testimonies in
"Why Do They Stay" from young women who are surprised and dismayed about getting pregnant and no reports that their Catholic beliefs prevented them from using birth control. A lot of pregnancies
just happened, in the same way they had in the past, except that the
pregnancies were not followed by marriage. Some pregnancies were
wanted—Smallacombe observed a certain amount of social status associated with having a baby.[11] Many pregnancies were welcomed as a
way to get out of the house, either by moving in with a boyfriend or
by going on welfare. Christina Quinn, herself a single mother, talked
about a friend who had her first baby at age fourteen.

I had a girlfriend when Joanie was born who had five kids. I was
twenty-one years old and she had five children. I was like, "You're
crazy," and she was like, "You're late." . . . She didn't want to live
at home. It was her way out of the house only to find herself back
with her parents with five kids because the guy she was with
wasn't ready for all these kids. Neither was she, really, so her
mother raised them. I see her every once in a while. She says that
today—that her mother had to raise her children. She didn't
even know how to raise children.[12]

Not knowing how to be mothers is a big problem, says a fourth-
grade teacher at a public school in St. Jude's parish:

Two-thirds of the parents of children in my classes do not
work. . . . Parents want kids to think of them as good parents,
they want to "*do*" for their kids but do not know how. . . . Or, if
the mothers are not strung out on drugs, they are mixed up with

men. . . . The children know how to take care of themselves in that they're streetwise, they can handle things out on the street. They learn responsibility, taking care of siblings. But, they don't know the distinction between *taking care* of a child and *raising* a child.[13] (Emphasis in the original.)

Christina Quinn's friend's five children are not the only ones being raised by grandparents. On the contrary, grandparents all over Kensington are raising their grandchildren. Sometimes these arrangements work well. A single mother named Marie talks about her son and their life:

Right now he's on it [she receives public assistance for her son]. I collect a check for him which pays our board, and I work under the table. I bartend. . . . I know I can't do it for the rest of my life, but as of right now I'm quite content with it. It pays our bills and we live very nicely on it. . . . Plus, I live with my mother who . . . he's her world. He is her world.

Sometimes not so well:

Field note: Bonnie [told] the sad tale of the Burns family. She began by recounting how the grandmother went to court against her daughter who is on drugs to get custody of the daughter's children. The grandmother won the suit, and the three grandchildren now live with her and her husband on Oak Street. Her daughter's husband is no longer alive, died from a drug overdose. Nevertheless, Mrs. Burns' daughter still comes around Oak Street. Bonnie said, "The kids, they love their mother. When she leaves, they are devastated." Bonnie claimed that the grandmother does not want her daughter to come around because it confuses the children. She noted that the grandmother has a lump on her breast and is not taking care of it. Bonnie repeated the question she asked Mrs. Burns to her face one day, "Who's going to be there for them kids if something happens to you?"[14]

Meanwhile, it's not as if the women who are married necessarily have a breadwinner to rely on. Sister Carol, who runs St. Jude's parochial school, explains:

> I guess what I see . . . is a lot of women who are taking care of the whole kit and caboodle. They almost got an extra son at home, better known as the husband, if they have one. . . . There are women with two bags of groceries in their hands, children hanging onto both sides of their coats, and the husband with his computer game walking behind her down the street. There's something wrong here![15]

Which brings us to the question of male industriousness.

Industriousness

In the 1960 census, about 9 percent of all Fishtown men ages 20–64 were not in the labor force. In the 2000 census, about 30 percent of Fishtown men in the same age range were not in the labor force.[16]

The phenomenal growth in the proportion of working-age Fishtown men out of the labor force from 1960 to 2000 raises the possibility that we are looking at larger numbers of discouraged workers who no longer think they have a chance of finding jobs. But the male unemployment rates in Fishtown in 1960 and 2000 were not much different—7.3 percent in 1960 and 8.9 percent in 2000. When they talked about jobs, the people of Fishtown lamented the loss of high-paying factory jobs, but they did not say there were no jobs to be had anymore. They talked about men who just couldn't seem to cope with the process of getting and holding a job.

Simon was one of the owners of a small factory located in Fishtown. Jenny, whom we met earlier, was his office manager. Phil was the quality technical manager. Simon was not prissy about whom he was willing to hire. He had a track record of giving chances to applicants with criminal records, substance-abuse problems, no high school diploma, and no work experience. He had a simple rule: He would give anyone a chance, but that person had to show up on schedule and do the job or he was out. Smallacombe inquired about the young men who hang out, apparently doing nothing.

Field note: I sat back in my chair and said with part cheek and part challenge, "Okay, what about the white guys on the corner. The white guys." Simon said, "The white guys around the corner [across from his factory]?" I said, "Metaphorically, The Corner." Jenny laughed—"The bums." Simon clarified, "Those guys couldn't work here, they can't hold a job. . . . They're not motivated to work." Jenny said, "They'll live on welfare, or any other income they got coming in. They don't want to work."[17]

Jenny had grown up around a lot of these guys, she said. They had no interest in holding a job or having a family, and now they were in their thirties.

A lot of them are sweethearts. They just don't have the ambition. I think it was the way they were brought up, watching their fathers and their uncles hang on the same corner, and they just take the tradition. It's a special feeling [at this moment she started hitting her hand on the table in a thumping rhythm along with each generation—indicated here by italics], that it went from *father* to *uncle* to *kids* and then their *kids*. . . . It's a trademark.[18]

Ken Milano, shown that quotation, recalled the Sunshine Club.

When I was growing up [in the 1970s], we had the "Sunshine Club," guys who were either not working or on unemployment. They were so proud of this fact, they had t-shirts made up— "Member of the Sunshine Club" or some such thing. The thing was usually to try and work during the summer down the shore at Wildwood [on the Jersey Shore], then get some stupid job for a couple of months just to get your time in to collect unemployment for the rest of the year, until summer rolled around again.[19]

Tammy, a native of Kensington who had become the president of the local credit union, reflected that the guys on the corner had helped mess up her brother.

> *Field note:* Tammy told the story about how her brother was working at a fast food restaurant. Apparently, his friends on the corner felt this job was beneath him, and advised the brother to ask for more money from his boss. He did, and was fired soon after the incident. Tammy revealed that her brother has never held a steady job in which he was paid by a check since this experience. Instead, he works odd jobs, "under the table," in the neighborhood to pay for what he needs—a TV here, something there.[20]

Welfare plays a big role as well. In chapter 9, I presented the graph showing rising disability, and observed that it was impossible that more men should be physically unable to work in 2010 than in 1960. Patricia Smallacombe noted that there are legitimate claims for disability payments because many men in Fishtown are in occupations such as roofing and construction where disabling injuries happen. But, she continued,

> At the same time, there are other men whose injuries come about in more dubious ways. . . . These residents get by on this income and other family resources; sometimes they continue working under the table doing odd jobs. In addition, social service and health providers in the neighborhood observe a higher frequency of families getting into the [disability] system by giving their children medication like Ritalin for ADHD to qualify the child for government disability support.[21]

Even when the men can't get welfare, the women can, and the men can live off them. Such men are known as "runners" or "fly-by-nights," because they are constantly on the move, avoiding debt collectors, child support collectors, their girlfriends or children, or the police. They, too, are active in the drug trade, which exploded in the ten to fifteen years before Smallacombe arrived in the last half of the 1990s.[22]

Honesty

Crime wasn't a problem in the Fishtown that Peter Rossi and Peter Benzin studied. Fistfights were a common way of settling disputes, but one of the pluses of living in a tight-knit working-class neighborhood was a high level of honesty within the community. If somebody stepped out of line, people weren't necessarily going to wait for the cops. "It used to be your car getting broken into was the only real crime, but everybody knew who did it," Ken Milano recalls. "It was usually the huffers [glue sniffers], so you went to where they hung out, bashed some heads and found out who did it easy enough." Even Fishtown's gangs helped maintain law and order (of a sort), Milano said. "Most gangs were kind of like vigilantes—beat the crap out of thieves, dopeheads, etc."

That kind of community cohesion had badly deteriorated when Smallacombe did her research. The changes in family structure meant that there were larger numbers of teenagers on the street and no one keeping track of where they were, and that had consequences. Marie, who lived near Pop's Playground, well known as someone who tried to intervene in the time-honored ways, talked about the limits she now had to put on herself.

> It's just hopeless. There's a handful of kids across the street. I sit there and I see them do these things and yes, I jump on them for certain things that I can. If they're being destructive to property or something like that, yeah, I can. But if they're sitting there and smoking weed, or drinking booze, and I know they're only 14 or 15 years old, there's nothing I can do about that. Nothing. . . . These parents know they're not home but they don't care. So why should I go out and put an effort into it when I'm only going to get retaliation on my home, my vehicle or my family? I'm not. There's only so far I'm going to go.[23]

A kind of unreasoning destructiveness had come to Fishtown. Bob was a Kensington native who worked for the Parks Department as director of Pop's Playground:

> I don't understand the destroying that goes on. Kids destroying areas that are for their benefit. I don't understand it. For instance, tearing up the matting, breaking into the playground, destroy the bathroom earlier in the year. The drinking. Hey, people have drank in this playground for decades. But they never broke bottles or they always made sure everything was thrown in the trash can.[24]

And the vandalism had been accompanied by an increase in real crime, much of it targeted toward older residents in the community who are the most easily frightened—in one case that Smallacombe relates, the offender's own mother. Her son needed the money for drugs.

Several Kensington residents commented on a change in parenting that they thought contributed to the rise in crime among teenagers. It wasn't just that the parents weren't home. It used to be that the parents didn't have to be home. If a neighbor saw a child misbehaving, it was considered appropriate for the neighbor to intervene. The parents would be grateful when they found out, and they would take the word of the neighbor if the child protested his innocence.

Unmarried and divorced parents tend not to behave that way, Smallacombe was told. Instead, they tend to try to be the good guy with their children. Here is Marie again:

> Then you hear why the discipline was only minimal—"Well, you know, I talked to them and they said this, that, and the other, and I figure 'Maybe he's right.' " And I'm like, "Well, no. You had the facts, you knew the facts, and now you're just trying to make yourself look like you're in the right. . . . You want to be the cool parent, the friend parent, the great parent that the kid does whatever he wants, however he wants, dresses great."[25]

These parents also tried to show their devotion by sticking up for their children no matter what. Carrie again:

> We had a neighbor [whom we called] "Not My Son Sue" because everything is "Not my kid." . . . Somebody actually watched her son throw a baseball bat through a car window and she stood there and she said, "Not my son." Twenty-five witnesses, including a policeman, and "Not my son." You have a lot of that.[26]

A counselor at St. Jude, observing this kind of thing daily, saw a pattern: "Kids are more challenging, [with] less fear of consequences. Parents have given power to children and this is destructive. . . . Parents feel they are getting what they deserve . . . 'I'm a rotten parent, I'm at work, and all sorts of excuses, so this is why I must deserve this.' "[27]

Religiosity

Fishtown had been an intensely Catholic neighborhood in earlier decades. Fishtown itself has two large churches, and the adjacent neighborhood where Smallacombe centered her fieldwork had the one she called St. Jude. As Smallacombe documents, it is hard to exaggerate the centrality of the Catholic Church in Fishtown's past. The churches of Fishtown were much more than places where people went once a week to worship. They were social centers and the places where most of the children of Fishtown were educated. The Catholic worldview pervaded the worldview of Fishtown's parishioners. The church's teachings—among others, that the home is a domestic church—gave validation to the core values of Fishtown.

All of that had faded by the time Smallacombe did her research. The role of the church was by no means gone—during the year she lived near St. Jude, the closing of the St. Jude novena featured 20 priests and seminarians and about 1,200 neighborhood people in the procession around the parish.[28] The church-run lottery, Chances, was still a major social event. The younger families who sent their children to the parochial schools were still active in the church. But for the rest of the younger generation in Fishtown, the connection with the church was growing tenuous even for those who went through the motions:

> *Field note:* I took a shortcut to the church, following other parish-
> ioners down Rowe Street. . . . There was a family trudging in front
> of me—a man, woman, and boy. The man and boy were dressed in
> blue jeans, sneakers, and "Eagles" jackets with hoods, typical attire
> for most men at mass. . . . By the time everyone trickled in, there
> were about a hundred people. Older people and some younger par-
> ents in their 20s and 30s genuflected before entering the pews.
> However, I did not see any children performing this ritual, or say-
> ing any prayers for that matter. Most were standing around with
> their coats on throughout the service; they looked rather blank.[29]

Even the children who attended the parochial school did not neces-sarily form a cohort for transmitting Fishtown's Catholic tradition to the next generation. Smallacombe concluded that "the same children who appear in Catholic school uniforms and comply with discipline in the school are more likely than their predecessors to be sexually active and drug and alcohol users even before they reach high school; these youths do not acknowledge the consequences of their actions as either morally wrong or potentially dangerous."[30] Sister Carol was matter-of-fact about the nature of the residual relationship of young Fishtown to the church: "There is a religious piece to it, though it's not what it used to be. When things are tough, they grab for God. When they're getting married, they want to be in upper church; when they're in the hospital, they want nuns and priests there."[31]

The New Lower Class

My use of the term *lower class* would not sound out of place to the people of Kensington. Some of them use it themselves, in contra-distinction to *family people*, a label for people who made a decent living and took care of their children and their extended families. People who didn't do those things were lower class. Angie, a lunchroom worker at the St. Jude parochial school, had recently moved across Trax Street, considered to be a dividing line between the family people and others. She was brought face-to-face with the lower class:

> Now I live over there and it actually is a lower class of people. . . . Don't get me wrong, there's some St. Jude's parishioners there and they're just like us, but there's more of a lower. . . . They're a lower class. I'm sorry. They definitely are. It's the nonworking, welfare, you know, where they don't care. To me that . . . Welfare is not bad, but if you're able to work you should work. These people, I feel, are able to work.[32]

For Americans who have been used to hearing about problems associated with welfare dependency and family breakup in terms of race, the testimony from the residents of Kensington serves as a useful corrective. The problems of the white new lower class sound just like the much more widely publicized problems of the black and Latino lower classes.

> *Field note:* From the end of the table, Bonnie added her two cents with a story about what she called a "white trash" family living next door to her mother's house in the Parish neighborhood. Bonnie vividly depicted a disturbing scene of underfed children in dirty diapers running around the house with no adult supervision. . . . Bonnie related this story with disgust and horror. I had never seen her become emotional about any such situation in the neighborhood before; she is far from shy about relating bad news and tales of delinquency and degeneration among white residents they all knew. This was personal, though. Everyone at the table fell silent.[33]

Epilogue

Fishtown has changed a lot since Patricia Smallacombe finished her fieldwork at the end of the 1990s. In the 2000s, gentrification came to Fishtown. It was an irresistible process. Fishtown had cheap housing compared to more fashionable neighborhoods, it was close to downtown Philadelphia, and it was reasonably safe. Juvenile crime and druggies might have become a problem by Fishtown's traditional standards, but you still didn't need to worry that you would be mugged walking home or that the convenience store would be robbed at gunpoint while you picked up a quart of milk late at night. And so first the pioneers—the artists and musicians without much money—started to move into Fishtown. In the last few years, affluent young professionals have expanded their beachhead.

If you go to Fishtown today, you will see a streetscape that is still much like it used to be, but with occasional differences. Bars that used to specialize in Bud and Seagram's Seven and (if you insisted on food) pig's feet and Slim Jims now have sophisticated lighting, bars glistening with bottles of every kind of boutique alcohol, and menus that you might find on South Broad Street.

Some of the abandoned factories have been turned into chic loft apartments. The five efficiency apartments in the house next to Ken Milano's are being renovated—hardwood floors, exposed brick, shiny new kitchens and bathrooms—and will reopen with commensurately higher rents. Houses that were worth $30,000 in the 1990s are selling for $200,000 and up. Skyrocketing property values mean that even the family people, who mostly own their homes, will find it tempting to sell their homes, bank part of their profit, and use the rest to move to the suburbs where friends have already settled. The new lower class in Fishtown who now rent will be unable to afford to remain, and they will have to find new places to live.

And so the old Fishtown is fading fast. Ken Milano doesn't see much to like in the new version. "With poor folks, you know what you got, or at least I do, as I grew up in these parts. New folks have all sorts of different ways of dealing with problems. It's not a fistfight, that's for sure. More like calling the cops on you and having your ass locked up, or worse, suing you." Ken Milano still loves Fishtown, what's left of it, but a few years ago he had to make a wrenching decision of his own. His son had just finished kindergarten at St. Jude's, but Milano knew that the school at one of the Fishtown parishes,

'Holy Name, had closed in 2006, and he could see that enrollment was declining at St. Jude's. He and his wife didn't want their children to have to lose all their friends halfway through elementary school, so they transferred their son to St. Mary's downtown. St. Jude's priest was dismayed—"Ken, I'm doing everything I can to keep this school open and you're taking your kid out?" But Milano decided he had to do what was best for his family. On February 28, 2011, the Office of Catholic Education announced that seven parishes would close their respective schools at the end of the current academic year because of low enrollment. One of them was the grade school at St. Jude's.

In a few years, there will no longer be a "real Fishtown." But there will still be thousands of working-class neighborhoods and towns across the nation. A dwindling number of them will be urban. Many more of them will be the working-class suburbs where the urban white working class has been moving for years. Others will be small towns in rural areas where the deterioration in the founding virtues has been spreading as rapidly as it spread in Fishtown.[34] There is nothing abstract or merely statistical about the human losses that the deterioration has caused.

13

The Size of the New Lower Class

In which ways of thinking about the nature and magnitude of the new lower class are presented.

BECAUSE THE NEW lower class consists of a continuum of people, there are no sharp edges for deciding who belongs and who doesn't. Still, it is possible to get a sense of the order of magnitude by considering three nonoverlapping groups that are problematic for America's civic culture.

Three Problematic Categories

Men Who Aren't Making a Living

I want to identify a population that is heavily populated by men who are economically ineffectual or worse. To do so, I use the idea of *making a living,* and put men who are not making a living into that population. I define making a living as earning an income large enough that it puts a household of two above the poverty line—in 2010, an income of $14,634.[1]

Failing to meet that goal is full of implications because it asks so little. As of 2010, a married man without children could have done it if he worked 50.5 weeks at a minimum-wage job. But the minimum wage is seldom relevant for men ages 30–49 who have stayed in the labor force. Only 6 percent of hourly paid workers have wages that low.[2] Suppose that in 2010 you held the job that is synonymous with low prestige and low pay—janitor. If you made exactly the average hourly wage of all janitors, $11.60, and you worked forty-hour weeks, your income in 2010 would have passed my definition of *making a living* in the thirty-first week of the year.[3]

My point is not that the poverty line is a good measure of poverty. Nor am I against women working to help put together an adequate family income.[4] Rather: Healthy men who aren't bringing home enough income to put themselves and one other adult above the poverty line are failing to pass a low bar. Among this population of men are a large proportion who are economically ineffectual.

Figure 13.1 shows the percentage of white males ages 30–49 who met that definition of making a living from 1959 through 2009. (Recall that CPS income figures are based on the year preceding the survey.)

FIGURE 13.1.   **MEN NOT MAKING A LIVING**

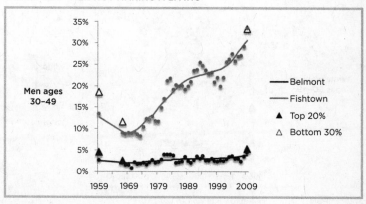

Source: IPUMS. Sample limited to white males ages 30-49.[5]

Things were getting better for Fishtown men between 1959 and 1967. Not only that; we can infer that they had been getting better since at least 1939. Scholars have retrospectively calculated the poverty rate back as far as the 1940 census, showing that poverty then stood at more than 50 percent of the American population.[6] For

Fishtown men, the percentage who weren't making a living started to increase in 1974 and continued to increase through good times and bad except for a dip in the late 1990s. In 2007, when unemployment was still low, that percentage had hit 27 percent, more than triple the proportion in 1973.

Single Women with Children

Being a single mother is tough, and it is appropriate to sympathize with women who are in that situation, but that doesn't make single parenthood any less problematic for the functioning of America's civic culture. In figure 13.2, I include all prime-age women with minor children living in the household. I ignore the white families with minor children headed by a parent and stepparent (whose children's outcomes are about the same as those of divorced parents who have not remarried), because the CPS does not break out this category.

FIGURE 13.2.   **SINGLE WOMEN RAISING MINOR CHILDREN**

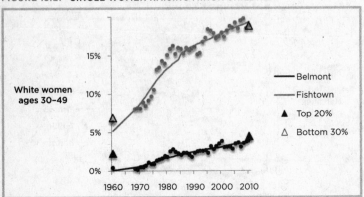

Source: IPUMS. Sample limited to white women ages 30–49.

The trends in the graph are not surprising given the similar information about single-parent households you have already seen in chapter 8. As of 2010, the percentage of prime-age white women in Fishtown who were single and raising minor children had quadrupled since 1960. Once again, the changing composition of Fishtown explains nothing. The proportion of single mothers among the bottom 30 percent in 1960 was almost identical to those among all Fishtown women.

Isolates

Men who aren't making a living and single women raising minors do not exhaust the problematic populations in Fishtown. Still another group consists of men who are making a living and women who are not single mothers, but who are disconnected from the matrix of community life. You probably recognize the type: They have friends, but purely for social purposes—friends good for going out and having a good time, not ones who are good for helping out in tough times. They live in the neighborhood, but are not of it. They don't get involved in anything—not so much as a softball league, let alone taking an active role in the PTA or chairing a civic fund drive.

The GSS offers a way of estimating the size of this population through its data on group memberships. Figure 13.3 shows the percentage of prime-age adults who belong to no organizations whatsoever (the GSS asked about fifteen specific categories, plus an "all other" category) and attend church no more than once a year.

FIGURE 13.3. **COMMUNITY ISOLATES**

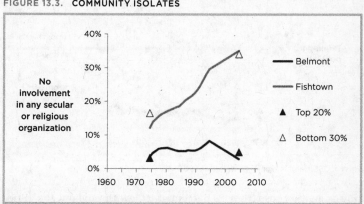

Source: GSS. Sample limited to whites ages 30–49.

Limitations on the GSS's income data and sample sizes prevent an accurate estimate of the overlap between the isolates and the other two populations I have discussed. But clearly the isolates add new people to the new lower class. As of the most recent GSS survey that asked these questions, in 2004, 24 percent of Fishtown women who were not single mothers were community isolates as I have defined them, compared to just 3 percent of such Belmont women. Twenty-seven percent of Fishtown men whose total income put them above the poverty threshold for two adults were community isolates, compared to 3 percent of such Belmont men.[7]

Adding Up the Categories

Figure 13.4 combines prime-age white males who weren't making a living and single mothers raising minor children, and assumes that a quarter of the isolates were not part of either of those populations.[8]

The percentage of Fishtown residents who are problematic in one

FIGURE 13.4.   **A WAY OF THINKING ABOUT THE SIZE OF THE WHITE NEW LOWER CLASS**

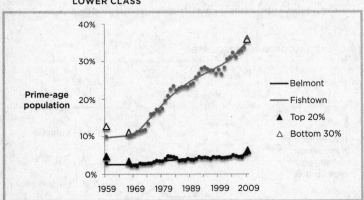

Source: GSS. Sample limited to whites ages 30–49.

way or another rose from 10 percent at its low throughout the 1960s to 33 percent in 2007, the last year before the recession, while remaining low in Belmont—4 percent in 2007.

If we include all whites ages 30–49 regardless of neighborhood, adding in the half of all whites who are in neither Belmont nor Fishtown, the percentage who qualified for the white new lower class more than doubled from 8 percent at its low in the late 1960s to 17 percent in 2007. In 2009, a year into the recession, that percentage had passed 19 percent and probably passed 20 percent in 2010.

My discussion of the size of the white new lower class should be treated as conservative in two senses. First, the percentages are arguably underestimated. If marriage with children is crucial to America's civic culture, it might plausibly be required that a man in his thirties and forties who is "making a living" be able to support a wife and at least one child above the poverty line, not just himself and another adult as my definition specified. I have also assumed that the entire criminal class is captured by my measure of men not making a living, when in fact criminals are underrepresented in the CPS. Second, the raw numbers implied by my presentation are too low. The prime-age adults include only a minority of the whites who fall into the new lower class. My presentation ignores all the men under thirty and older than forty-nine who are economically ineffectual, all the women under thirty and older than forty-nine who are raising children alone, and all of the social isolates under thirty and older than forty-nine.

Reaching an exact estimate of the white new lower class is neither feasible nor necessary, however. If the overall percentage of whites ages 30–49 who qualify for the new lower class has doubled since the 1960s and is moving anywhere close to the 20 percent of the white prime-age population indicated by the definition I have used, it is a lower class that is changing national life.

Part III

Why It Matters

THE ECONOMIST JOHN Maynard Keynes, accused of changing his mind about monetary policy, famously replied, "When the facts change, I change my mind. What do you do, sir?"[1] The honest answer to Keynes's question is "Often, nothing." Data can bear on policy issues, but many of our opinions about policy are grounded in premises about the nature of human life and human society that are beyond the reach of data. Try to think of any new data that would change your position on abortion, the death penalty, legalization of marijuana, same-sex marriage, or the inheritance tax. If you cannot, you are not necessarily being unreasonable.

So it has been with the evidence I have presented. A social democrat may see in parts 1 and 2 a compelling case for the redistribution of wealth. A social conservative may see a compelling case for government policies that support marriage, religion, and traditional values. I am a libertarian, and see a compelling case for returning to the founders' conception of limited government.

In the concluding chapter, I try to explain why I see the facts in this light. Since only a few percent of American adults are libertarians, most of you should expect to disagree. But the chapters leading up to the last one continue to add data to the conversation, and they may inform your positions without changing them.

If nothing else, I hope to convince you of this: The trends of the last half century do not represent just the passing of an outmoded way of life that I have identified with "the American project." Rather, the trends signify damage to the heart of American community and the ways in which the great majority of Americans pursue satisfying lives. The trends of the last half century matter a lot. Many of the best and most exceptional qualities of American culture cannot survive unless they are reversed.

14

The Selective Collapse of American Community

In which I argue that a central aspect of American exceptionalism, American civic life, is nearing collapse in Fishtown.

IN THE MID-1950S, Edward Banfield, who would become one of America's most distinguished political scientists, was an obscure young scholar who had spent nine months living in a southern Italian town that he would later call Montegrano. He came away from that experience with an insight into the nature of communities. The town where he had lived didn't work because it was run on the basis of what he called *amoral familism*. Amoral familism was based on a single decision rule that he decoded as follows: "Maximize the material, short-run advantage of the nuclear family; assume that all others will do likewise."[1] That insight and his elaboration of it made the book he wrote about the town, *The Moral Basis of a Backward Society*, a classic.

Amoral familism didn't leave much room for altruism or even co-operation. An order of nuns struggled to maintain an orphanage in an ancient monastery, but the people of Montegrano contributed nothing to its support, even though the children in the orphanage came from their region. The monastery needed work, and there were local stonemasons who had free time, but none of them donated even a day's work to help with repairs. Montegrano had two churches, but neither played any part in the secular life of the community. In fact, there was just one "association" in the whole town—twenty-five upper-class men who maintained a clubroom where they could play cards.

As he searched for a way to introduce Montegrano to his American readers of the 1950s, Banfield recalled another town where he had done fieldwork. It was an American town similar to Montegrano in population, climate, terrain, and isolation: St. George, Utah. He decided to open *The Moral Basis of a Backward Society* with an account of the activities reported in a single issue of St. George's weekly newspaper.

The Red Cross was conducting a membership drive that week. The Business and Professional Women's Club was raising funds to build a new dormitory for the local community college. The Future Farmers of America was holding a father-son banquet. A local business had donated a set of encyclopedias to the school district. The Chamber of Commerce was discussing the feasibility of building a road between two nearby towns. "Skywatch" volunteers were being signed up (for what purpose, Banfield doesn't say). A local church had collected $1,393.11 in pennies (worth more than $10,500 in 2010) for a children's hospital. There was an announcement of the meeting of the PTA, concluding with the words, "As a responsible citizen of our community, you belong in the PTA." All that, in a town of 4,562 people in the middle of the Utah desert, reported in a single issue of a weekly newspaper.

American Community and American Exceptionalism

The founding virtues operating under the freedoms guaranteed by the Constitution produced an American civic culture that was unique in all the world. Not only Americans thought so. All observers agreed that community life in the United States was unlike community life anywhere else. Its closest cousin was England's civic culture, but the pervasive effects of England's class system meant that "closest" was still quite different.

The first unparalleled aspect of American community life was the extent of its neighborliness. Neighborliness is not the same as hospitality. Many cultures have traditions of generous hospitality to strangers and guests. But widespread voluntary mutual assistance among unrelated people who happen to live alongside one another has been rare. In the United States, it has been ubiquitous. One of the things that made the real Fishtown in years past so dear to the people who lived there was its neighborliness—the way that residents routinely helped out one another, continually, in matters great and small: keeping an eye on a house when its family was away, loaning a tool or the proverbial cup of sugar, taking care of a neighbor's children while the mother was running errands, or driving a neighbor to the doctor's office. Neighborliness has often been identified with small towns and rural areas, but that's misleading. As the real Fishtown illustrated, urban neighborhoods in America often used to be as close as small towns, with identities so strong that their residents defined themselves by the neighborhood where they grew up.

The second unparalleled aspect of American community life has been vibrant civic engagement in solving local problems. Sometimes this meant involvement in local government, but even more often it has been conducted within the voluntary associations, which Americans historically formed at the drop of a hat. One of the most quoted passages in *Democracy in America* begins with Tocqueville's observation that "Americans of all ages, all stations in life, and all types of dispositions are forever forming associations." He goes on:

> There are not only commercial and industrial associations in which all take part, but others of a thousand different types— religious, moral, serious, futile, very general and very limited, immensely large and very minute. Americans combine to give fêtes, found seminaries, build churches, distribute books, and send missionaries to the antipodes. Hospitals, prisons, and schools take place in that way. Finally, if they want to proclaim a truth or propagate some feeling by the encouragement of a great example, they form an association. In every case, at the head of any new undertaking, where in France you would find the

government or in England some territorial magnate, in the United States you are sure to find an association.[2]

The reach and scope of these voluntary associations by the end of the nineteenth century and reaching into the first decades of the twentieth has been largely forgotten. Cultural historian Marvin Olasky pulled together data that give a sense of the profusion of activities. Here, for example, is the roster of activities conducted by associations affiliated with 112 Protestant churches in Manhattan and the Bronx at the turn of the twentieth century: 48 industrial schools, 45 libraries or reading rooms, 44 sewing schools, 40 kindergartens, 29 small-sum savings banks and loan associations, 21 employment offices, 20 gymnasia and swimming pools, 8 medical dispensaries, 7 full-day nurseries, and 4 lodging houses.[3] Those are just some of the Protestant churches in two boroughs of New York City, and it is not a complete list of the activities shown in the report. Try to imagine what the roster would look like if we added in the activities of the New York Catholic diocese, the Jewish charities, then the activities of a completely separate and extensive web of secular voluntary associations. Perhaps the numbers from a very different setting will indicate how long that list of activities sponsored by secular organizations might have been. When Iowa mounted a food conservation program in World War I, it engaged the participation of 9,630 chapters of thirty-one different secular fraternal associations. It is a number worth pausing to think about: 9,630, in one lightly populated state.[4]

The role of those secular fraternal associations has been even more completely forgotten than the role of the numberless small charities. Today, most people know of organizations such as the Elks, Moose, and Odd Fellows (if they know of them at all) as male lower-middle-class social clubs. They are actually the remnants of a mosaic of organizations that were a central feature of American civic life. We are indebted to Theda Skocpol for bringing their role back to life in her 2003 book, *Diminished Democracy*.[5] You need to read her entire account to get a sense of all the functions the fraternal organizations filled. For our purposes, one is particularly salient: They drew their membership from across the social classes, and ensured regular, close interaction among people of different classes. "Evidence to this effect is entirely consistent," Skocpol writes, "whether it comes from scholarly studies or from assorted old lodge or post rosters I have found that happen to list members' occupations."[6] One of her passages is worth quoting at length:

> Read biographical sketches of prominent men and women of the past . . . and you will see proudly proclaimed memberships and officerships in a wide array of the same fraternal, veterans', women's, and civic associations that also involved millions of non-elite citizens. . . . Those who were leaders had to care about inspiring large numbers of fellow members. Members counted; and leaders had to mobilize and interact with others from a wide range of backgrounds or they were not successful. To get ahead within associations, ambitious men and women had to express and act on values and activities shared with people of diverse occupational backgrounds.[7]

This does not mean that the people of Fishtown and Belmont participated equally in the good old days, but it does mean that they interacted. If you lived in Fishtown, you might or might not be a member of a fraternal organization, but you knew people who were, and they in turn knew people who lived in Belmont—not just by name but as lodge brothers or sisters.[8]

Social Capital and Class

The case for the ongoing collapse of American community was first made by Harvard political scientist Robert Putnam in his best-selling book *Bowling Alone*.[9] Adopting the social scientists' name for neighborliness and civic engagement, *social capital*, and assembling data from a multitude of sources, Putnam devoted a chapter each to six types of activity: volunteering and philanthropy, political participation, civic participation, religious participation, connections in the workplace, and informal social connections. In this chapter, I will omit religious participation, which was covered in chapter 11. Here is a sampling of indicators on the other issues, and how much they changed through the mid-1990s:[10]

- Voted in the presidential election: Down 22 percent from 1960 to 1996.[11]
- Attended a public meeting on town or school affairs: Down 35 percent from 1973 to 1994.
- Served as an officer of some club or organization: Down 42 percent from 1973 to 1994.
- Worked for a political party: Down 42 percent from 1973 to 1994.
- Served on a committee for some local organization: Down 39 percent from 1973 to 1994.
- Percentage of parents with children under age 18 who are members of the PTA: Down 61 percent from 1960 to 1997.
- Average membership rate in thirty-two national chapter-based associations: Down by almost 50 percent from 1960 to 1997.
- Times per year that people entertain friends at home: Down 45 percent from 1975 to 1997.
- "Our whole family usually eats dinner together." Percentage of married Americans who answer "disagree": Up 69 percent from 1977 to 1999.
- United Way contributions as a percentage of personal income: Down 55 percent from 1963 to 1998.
- Membership in men's bowling leagues per 1,000 men ages 20 and older: Down 73 percent from 1963 to 1998 (while the number of bowlers continued to increase).

There's much more, but these examples will serve to make the point. Measure it however he might, Putnam found the same thing: consistent and widespread evidence, direct and indirect, that America's social capital had seriously eroded.

Community and the New Upper Class

The good news, of a sort, is that civic life in the new upper class is as robust in many places as it was in Tocqueville's time. Burlington,

Vermont, is an example of a certain kind of small city that David Brooks calls "Latte Towns," enclaves of affluent and well-educated people, sometimes in scenic locales such as Santa Fe or Aspen and sometimes in university towns such as Ann Arbor, Berkeley, or Chapel Hill. Of Burlington, Brooks writes:

> Burlington boasts a phenomenally busy public square. There are kite festivals and yoga festivals and eating festivals. There are arts councils, school-to-work collaboratives, environmental groups, preservation groups, community-supported agriculture, antidevelopment groups, and ad hoc activist groups. . . . And this public square is one of the features that draw people to Latte Towns. People in these places apparently would rather spend less time in the private sphere of their home and their one-acre yard and more time in the common areas.[12]

Attendance at city council meetings in Latte Towns is high and residents who willingly take part in local politics are plentiful. The classic neighborly interactions vary. In new-upper-class neighborhoods filled with restored Victorian houses, neighbors often interact in traditional ways. Where homes are secluded on their own multi-acre lots, they don't. But the neighborliness can exist even then, with parents' associations in the schools often serving as a way for wealthy parents to develop local friendships.

Social capital in the new upper class is not confined to suburbs and small cities. Within Washington, DC, neighborhoods such as Cleveland Park are locally famous for their civic activism. In *The Big Sort*, Bill Bishop describes the intense neighborhood pride and activism in the Austin neighborhood of Travis Heights. Even in the most urban of SuperZips in Manhattan, San Francisco, Chicago, and Boston, you will find active neighborhoods engaged in their own version of community life.

Added to that are the forms of community life that the new upper class enjoys because of their professions and their affluence. Their best friends probably do not live in the same geographic neighborhood, perhaps not even in the same city. The same is true of the clubs to which they belong and the charities with which they are engaged. For the new upper class, the geographic neighborhood has become less and less relevant to the set of activities that fall under the rubric of social capital.

Has the new upper class, or Belmont more broadly, avoided the erosion of social capital altogether? It is frustratingly difficult to find data for answering that question. We know from *Bowling Alone* that the decline in social capital began in the 1960s, with 1964 being the modal year, and that the decline was rapid. The first data on social capital that can be disaggregated by class comes with the General Social Survey in 1974. The GSS continued to collect such data until 1994, when (*very* frustratingly) it stopped asking those questions with the single exception of the 2004 survey. So we don't know how much Belmont had already deteriorated before 1974, and we have just a single survey for estimating changes since 1994. With those limitations in mind, it looks as if Belmont has been doing pretty well. The details are given in appendix F. The short story goes like this:

Consider two indexes of decline in social capital: *social disengagement*, meaning that people no longer belong to sports clubs, hobby clubs, fraternal organizations, nationality groups (e.g., Sons of Italy), or veterans groups; and *civic disengagement*, meaning that people no longer belong to service groups, youth groups (e.g., being a scoutmaster), school service groups, or local political organizations. A person is defined as being socially or civically disengaged if he has no memberships whatsoever.

The index of social disengagement was effectively flat for Belmont from 1974 to 2004, with the percentage of the socially disengaged going from 35 percent in the surveys of the 1970s to 36 percent in the single survey in the 2000s. The index of civic disengagement in Belmont shows a U-turn. In the GSS surveys of the 1970s, 38 percent of Belmont had no memberships in civic groups. That percentage rose to 50 in the 1980s and 59 in the 1990s. Then, in that one lonely survey in 2004, the percentage dropped to 45, even lower than it had been in the 1970s. Are the 2004 results an anomaly or an indicator of revived civic engagement in Belmont? Your guess is as good as mine.

Combining the findings from the GSS with qualitative observations about life in upper-middle-class communities, there is reason to think that social capital in Belmont in general, and the new upper class in particular, has not taken the same downturn that it took elsewhere in America.

The Internet and New Forms of Social Capital

There's more good news for people who are deeply involved in the Internet. Putnam wrote *Bowling Alone* during the last half of the 1990s, when the Internet was just beginning to flower. Since then, the Internet has produced a variety of new ways for human beings to interact. Many of them have all of the characteristics of social capital, and the academic world has accordingly been building a literature to examine whether the Internet undermines social capital by competing with traditional social interactions or augments traditional social capital through new resources.[13] The answer, predictably, is "It depends." Sometimes, a community is formed through the Internet (e.g., mothers with small children in a big city form their own website for mutual support and to share information about local resources).[14] Sometimes, highly traditional forms of neighboring are facilitated by the Internet: The website lotsahelpinghands.com makes it easy for the friends of a family undergoing a crisis to cooperate during times of need (e.g., the friends of a mother undergoing chemotherapy create a schedule for preparing dinners every night for weeks). Sometimes, online friendships lead to the use of traditional resources (e.g., when a teenager realizes that an online friend a thousand miles away is sounding suicidal, he contacts the boy's school and mobilizes an intervention). All of these examples are drawn from experiences just within my own immediate family. There are dozens of other types of interactions fostered by the Internet that meet any reasonable definition of social capital.

How much is Fishtown participating in these new forms of social capital? The Pew Foundation's ongoing Internet & American Life Project has found that families with incomes of $75,000 or more were more likely (often close to twice as likely) to get their news online, bank online, seek out medical information online, shop online, pay bills online, and conduct research into products online than were families with incomes of less than $30,000.[15] Another study in the Internet & American Life Project found positive relationships of education to use of social-networking sites, in terms of both the size of the networks and the extensiveness of the activities on those networks.[16] Given those patterns, it is highly likely that Fishtown's use of the Internet in ways that augment social capital is much lower than Belmont's.

Community and the New Lower Class

The bad news involves Fishtown in general and the white new lower class in particular. By the time the GSS data began in 1974, social and civic disengagement in Fishtown were already much higher than they were in Belmont. In the 1970s surveys, 63 percent of Fishtown was socially disengaged compared to 35 percent of Belmont. For civic disengagement, the comparison was 69 percent to 38 percent. What had those figures been in 1960? I have been unable to find an answer. All we know is that the nationwide data assembled by Putnam show a steep decline in social capital in the 1960s. The decline surely hit Fishtown at least as hard as it hit other communities, and plausibly a lot harder.

By the 2000s, Fishtown had deteriorated even more. In the 2004 survey, 75 percent of Fishtown was socially disengaged, up from 63 percent in the 1970s surveys, and 82 percent of Fishtown was civically disengaged, up from 69 percent in the 1970s. These trends taken from the GSS could have been predicted just by looking at the severe declines in marriage and religiosity in Fishtown.

The role of marriage—specifically, marriage with children—is obvious. Some large proportion of the webs of engagement in an ordinary community are spun because of the environment that parents are trying to foster for their children—through the schools, but also in everything from getting a new swing set for the park to prompting the city council to install four-way stop signs on an intersection where children play. Married fathers are a good source of labor for these tasks. Unmarried fathers are not. *Of course* social capital declined in Fishtown. Meanwhile, single mothers who want to foster the right environment for their children are usually doing double duty already, trying to be the breadwinner and an attentive parent at the same time. Few single mothers have much time or energy to spare for community activities. *Of course* social capital declined in Fishtown.

The effects of the decline in religiosity are also obvious, especially after learning in chapter 11 via Robert Putnam that about half of all the kinds of social capital originate in the context of churches and, at least as important, that people who are involved in their churches also disproportionately engage in the secular kinds of social capital. *Of course* social capital declined in Fishtown.

Voting in Presidential Elections

Voting in presidential elections is a classic case of an indicator that doesn't mean much for any one person but has many implications in large samples. Voting is the most elementary act of participation in a democracy, and presidential elections are the most visible and, for most people, the most important election. In aggregates, people who do not bother with even this simplest form of civic engagement are unlikely to be civically engaged in other ways. Voting in presidential elections also offers one of the rare measures of social capital for which the GSS gives us an unbroken trendline, starting with the 1968 contest between Richard Nixon and Hubert Humphrey. Figure 14.1 shows voting turnout for prime-age whites in Belmont and Fishtown.[17]

The main story line is that turnout in Fishtown was already much lower than turnout in Belmont even in 1968—70 percent versus 96 percent—and remained so. But the contrast in the trends also has important implications. Belmont turnout never dropped below 86 percent and returned to more than 90 percent in the 2000s. Fishtown turnout dropped from 70 percent in 1968 to 51 percent in 1988. Except for a spike in the 1992 election, it remained in the low 50s or worse through the 2008 election of Barack Obama. We also know that the turnout in 1968 was lower than it had been in the 1950s, when the percentage of whites with less than a high school education (an approximation of the Fishtown of the 1950s) was at least

FIGURE 14.1.   **VOTING TURNOUT IN PRESIDENTIAL ELECTIONS, 1968-2008**

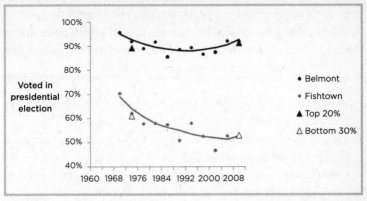

Source: GSS. Sample limited to whites ages 30–49. Data smoothed using locally estimated regression (LOESS).

75 percent.[18] I cannot be more precise, but it looks as if voting in presidential elections in Fishtown dropped by about a third from 1960 to 2008, while voting in Belmont remained extremely high.

Collapse of the Possibility of Community

The scariest message from the GSS does not consist of declines in specific activities that make up social capital, but this: The raw material that makes community even *possible* has diminished so much in Fishtown that the situation may be beyond retrieval.

That raw material is social trust—not trust in a particular neighbor who happens to be your friend, but a generalized expectation that the people around you will do the right thing. As Francis Fukuyama documented in *Trust: The Social Virtues and the Creation of Prosperity*, the existence of social trust is a core explanation of why some cultures create wealth and other cultures are mired in poverty.[19] At the community level, it is hard to think of any form of social capital that would exist without trust. Robert Putnam puts it in terms of reciprocity: "The touchstone of social capital is the principle of generalized reciprocity—I'll do this for you now, without expecting anything immediately in return and perhaps without even knowing you, confident that down the road you or someone else will return the favor."[20]

When social trust breaks down, social capital breaks down across the board. With that in mind, consider this set of three questions that the GSS has asked in almost every survey since 1972:

- Would you say that most of the time people try to be helpful, or that they are mostly just looking out for themselves?
- Do you think most people would try to take advantage of you if they got a chance, or would they try to be fair?
- Generally speaking, would you say that people can be trusted or that you can't be too careful in dealing with people?

The trends in the answers to these questions are alarming. Figure 14.2 begins the story with the results for the question on trust.

FIGURE 14.2.   WHITES' ESTIMATION OF THE TRUSTWORTHINESS OF
                OTHERS

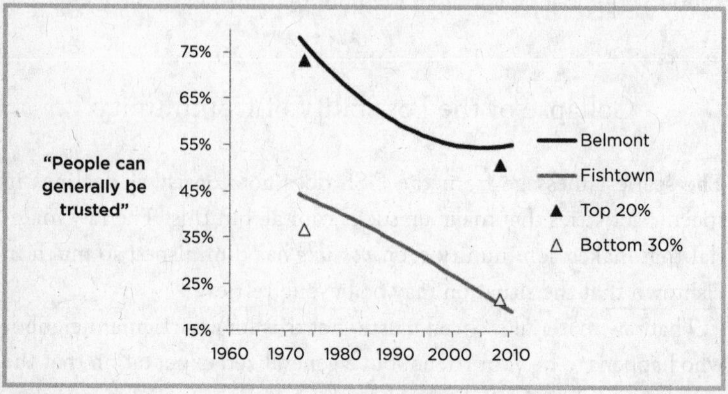

Source: Author's analysis of the GSS. Sample limited to whites ages 30–49. Data smoothed using locally estimated regression (LOESS).

Putnam's data indicate that social trust had declined prior to 1972, though we cannot know how or whether that decline affected Belmont and Fishtown differently.[21] In the GSS's surveys in the first half of the 1970s, around 75 percent of those in Belmont were still trusting. In the last half of the 2000s, that figure had dropped to about 60 percent. Fishtown in the 1970s was already much more distrustful than Belmont, with fewer than half of the respondents saying that most people can be trusted. Their pessimism only got worse. In the GSS surveys conducted from 2006 through 2010, only 20 percent of Fishtown respondents said that other people can generally be trusted.

Figure 14.3 shows the results for the fairness question.

FIGURE 14.3.   **WHITES' ESTIMATION OF THE FAIRNESS OF OTHERS**

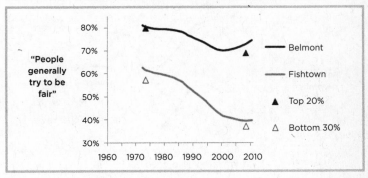

Source: Author's analysis of the GSS. Sample limited to whites ages 30–49. Data smoothed using locally estimated regression (LOESS).

In this case, we are back to the familiar picture of divergence between Belmont and Fishtown as well as overall decline. A gap between Belmont and Fishtown already existed when the first GSS surveys occurred in the early 1970s, but the gap grew substantially between the 1970s and the 2000s. Not much changed in Belmont, where almost 80 percent of people still believe in the fairness of others. As in the case of trust, the belief in the fairness of others in Fishtown has declined to a minority of people.

The results for both trust and fairness make sense in light of the other changes in life in Fishtown. If in recent decades you lived in a neighborhood that has become much more densely populated with people who will cheat, rob, assault, and perhaps even murder you, you would be a fool not to have become more untrusting and less likely to assume that other people will treat you fairly. Correspondingly, the people of Belmont live in a world where neighbors are pretty much as they always were, and it makes sense that their optimism about their fellow human beings has not fallen as much. But they also live in a society in which, once they leave the confines of Belmont, they have to watch their backs more carefully than they once did, so their trust in their fellow countrymen in general has dropped as well.

Figure 14.4 shows the situation for the assumption of helpfulness.

FIGURE 14.4.   WHITES' ESTIMATION OF THE HELPFULNESS OF OTHERS

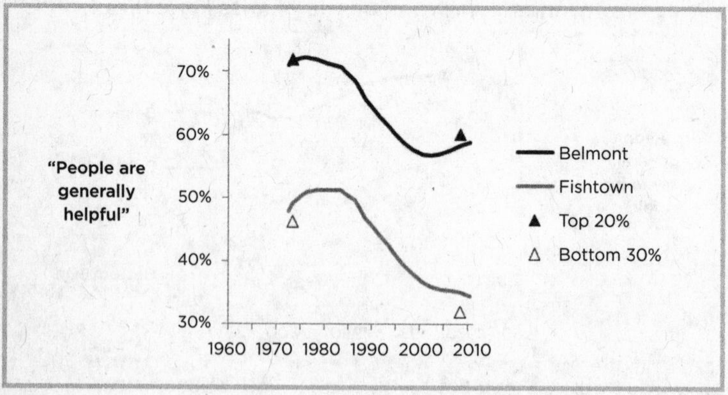

Source: GSS. Sample limited to whites ages 30–49. Data smoothed using locally estimated regression (LOESS).

The assumption of helpfulness was fairly stable in both neighborhoods during the 1970s, and then began a steep decline during the 1980s that continued until around 2000 for Belmont. The neighborhoods were about as far apart in the last half of the 1980s as they had been in the first half of the 1970s. Two troubling signs: In Fishtown, a substantial majority already agreed with "people are mostly just looking out for themselves" by the 2000s. And the belief in helpfulness continued to decline more shallowly through the 2000s, while it had stabilized at a much higher level in Belmont.

The decline in social trust in Belmont is not trivial. On the other hand, the declines on all three indicators have leveled out in Belmont, and it is possible to imagine a revival of community given the right circumstances. The big question is whether the remaining levels of social trust in Fishtown are enough to sustain anything approaching the traditional expectations of American neighborliness and local problem solving. There is no metric for specifying the tipping point at which all is lost. Looking at the whole picture for Fishtown, capped by what can only be called disastrous declines in social capital, it is hard for me to envision a revival in Fishtown unless Fishtown operates under a radically changed set of social signals.

Another problem regarding social trust, and one that may help explain the decline, has surfaced more recently: The key ingredient of social capital, social trust, is eroded by ethnic diversity. In the years after *Bowling Alone* appeared, Robert Putnam's research led him to a disturbing finding: Ethnic diversity works against social trust within a community—not only against trusting people of the other ethnicity, but against trusting even neighbors of one's own ethnic group. In addition, Putnam's research found that in areas of greater ethnic diversity, there was lower confidence in local government, a lower sense of political efficacy, less likelihood of working on a community project, less likelihood of giving to charity, fewer close friends, and lower perceived quality of life.[22] How is the corrosive effect of ethnic diversity on social capital to be reconciled with the reality of an increasingly diverse twenty-first-century America? I personally am optimistic that the distrust that has accompanied ethnic diversity will diminish—that the generations born in the last half century are comfortable with ethnic diversity in a way that their parents could not be—but that's still a hope, not a fact.

The Consequences of Collapsed Social Capital

I must anticipate a plausible reaction to this discussion:

We have just been treated to nostalgia for a world that was never as wonderful as the author tries to portray it. All those voluntary organizations and all that neighborliness existed side by side with widespread poverty and human suffering of all kinds, not to mention systemic discrimination against women and people of color. Most of the community activities that the author celebrates are actually boring, and the closeness of community can be suffocating. Hasn't he ever read Main Street?

Without doubt, high levels of social capital have downsides.

Small-town entertainments and conversations are not to everyone's taste. In a small, close-knit community, everybody knows just about everything you do, anonymity is impossible, and the pressure to conform can be oppressive.

High social capital may have other disadvantages. One point of view (which I do not share) argues that the hallmark of high social capital—neighbors helping neighbors cope with their problems—is inferior to a system that meets human needs through government programs, because only the government can provide help without the moral judgmentalism associated with charity. For my own part, I have argued that too much of certain kinds of social capital impedes the exercise of individual creativity and diminishes the production of great art, literature, and music.[23] Considerations like these explain why two of the basic texts on social capital have chapters identically titled "The Dark Side of Social Capital."[24]

But if we are talking about daily life for most people, the decay in social capital makes an important difference in quality of life, and this is as true in large cities as in small towns. A neighborhood with weak social capital is more vulnerable to crime than one with high social capital. A neighborhood with weak social capital must take its problems to police or social welfare bureaucracies because local resources for dealing with them have atrophied. In a neighborhood with weak social capital, the small daily pleasures of friendly interchange with neighbors and storekeepers dry up. The sum of it all is that people living in places with weak social capital generally lead less satisfying lives than people who live in places with high social capital—they are less happy. Which brings us to the topic of the next chapter.

15

The Founding Virtues and the Stuff of Life

In which it is argued that the founding virtues are inextricably bound up with the ways in which human beings acquire deep satisfactions in life—the ways in which they pursue happiness. Evidence about self-reported happiness is presented to support that position, and to document a steep drop in self-reported happiness in Fishtown.

THE DETERIORATION OF social capital in lower-class white America strips the people who live there of one of the main resources through which Americans have pursued happiness. The same may be said of the deterioration in marriage, industriousness, honesty, and religiosity. These are not aspects of human life that may or may not be important, depending on personal preferences. Together, they make up the stuff of life.

Aristotelian Happiness

Using the word *happiness* may seem to be asking for trouble—doesn't happiness mean many different things to different people? But the core nature of human happiness is widely agreed upon in the West. It goes all the way back to Aristotle's views about happiness in the *Nicomachean Ethics*. Distilling his discussion of happiness into a short definition leaves out a lot, but this captures the sense of Aristotle's argument well enough for our purposes: *Happiness consists of lasting and justified satisfaction with life as a whole*. The definition in effect says that when you decide how happy you are, you are thinking of aspects of your life that tend to define your life (not just bits and pieces of it); that you base your assessment of your happiness on deep satisfactions with the way things have gone, not passing pleasures; and that you believe in your heart of hearts that those satisfactions have been worth achieving. It is not really a controversial definition— try to imagine a definition of happiness you could apply to your own life that is much different.

What are these deep satisfactions that let us reach old age happy? We can begin by saying what they aren't. Few people reach old age satisfied with their lives because they were rich or famous. Film and music producer David Geffen—and a billionaire—once said in a television interview, a sad smile on his face, "Show me someone who thinks that money buys happiness, and I'll show you someone who has never had a lot of money."[1] Here's a variant: Show me someone who thinks deep satisfactions in old age come from having been rich or famous, and I'll show you someone who's never been old. Rich and famous people can reach old age deeply satisfied with their lives, but because of *how* they got the money or *how* they got the fame.

Once you start to think through the kinds of accomplishments that do lead people to reach old age satisfied with who they have been and what they have done, you will find (I propose) that the accomplishments you have in mind have three things in common. First, the source of satisfaction involves something important. We can get pleasure from trivial things, but pleasure is different from deep satisfaction. Second, the source of satisfaction has involved effort, probably over an extended period of time. The cliché "Nothing worth having comes easily" is true. Third, some level of personal responsibility for the outcome is essential. In the case of events close to home, you have to be able to say, "If it hadn't been for me, this good thing wouldn't have come about as it did."

There aren't many activities in life that satisfy the three requirements of importance, effort, and responsibility. Having been a good parent qualifies. Being part of a good marriage qualifies. Having done your job well qualifies. Having been a faithful adherent of one of the great religions qualifies. Having been a good neighbor and good friend to those whose lives intersected with yours qualifies. But what else?

Let me put it formally: If we ask what are the domains through which human beings achieve deep satisfactions in life—achieve happiness—the answer is that there are just four: family, vocation, community, and faith, with these provisos: *Community* can embrace people who are scattered geographically. *Vocation* can include avocations or causes.

It is not necessary for any individual to make use of all four domains, nor do I array them in a hierarchy. I merely assert that these four are all there are. The stuff of life occurs within those four domains.

The Four Domains and Self-Reported Happiness

The simplest way of making the point that the four domains are in fact related to happiness is to use the social scientists' measure of

FIGURE 15.1.   **"HOW HAPPY ARE YOU?"**

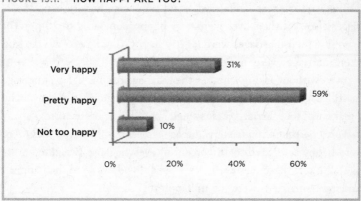

Source: Author's analysis of the GSS surveys from 1990–2008. Sample limited to whites ages 30–49.

happiness: asking people "How happy are you?" It is not a perfect measure—I'm sure that many people tell an interviewer they are happy for reasons that have nothing to do with "lasting and justified satisfaction with life as a whole." But the empirical relationship between self-reported happiness and the four domains is worth examining. The data come from the General Social Survey, combining the surveys conducted from 1990 through 2010.[2]

People were given the choice of answering "not too happy," "pretty happy," and "very happy." Figure 15.1 shows the results.

About one out of three whites ages 30–49 said they were "very happy"—the only answer of the three that means much. You might answer "pretty happy" when what you really mean is "I'm doing okay, can't complain" or "Things could be a lot worse." People don't answer "very happy" so haphazardly. It is likely to be a sign that a person really does assess his life positively.

Family

The relationship of marriage to happiness is simple as can be. There's hardly anything better than a good marriage for promoting happiness and nothing worse than a bad one. Fifty-eight percent of white prime-age GSS respondents who said they were in very happy marriages also said their lives were very happy, compared to 10 percent who said their marriages were "pretty happy" and 8 percent who said their marriages were "not too happy."

Even without asking whether the marriage itself is happy, marriage is still a good bet for achieving happiness. Figure 15.2 shows the breakdown for marriage versus singlehood in its various forms.

Forty percent of married prime-age whites reported that they were very happy compared to 18 percent of everyone else (weighted average). Among those who were not married, widows were the happiest and never-marrieds were the unhappiest.

During three surveys in the 2000s, the GSS also asked about cohabitation. In terms of happiness, cohabitation is a little bit better than living alone, but not much. In those three surveys, 43 percent of all

FIGURE 15.2. **SELF-REPORTED HAPPINESS AND MARITAL STATUS**

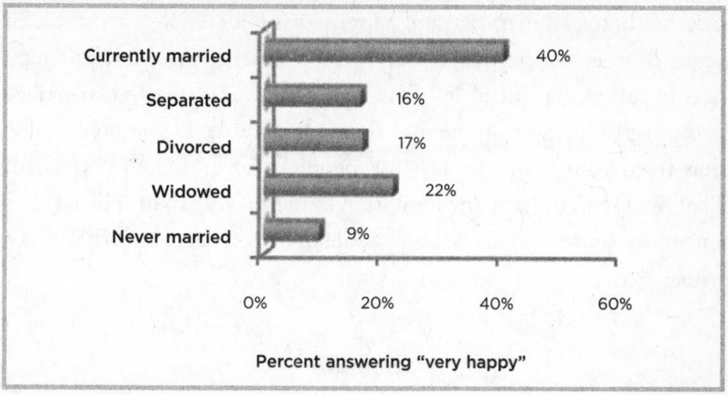

Source: GSS surveys from 1990 to 2010. Sample limited to whites ages 30–49.

prime-age whites who were legally married said they were very happy, compared to 29 percent of those who were cohabiting with a partner and 22 percent of those who had a partner and were not cohabiting. Even the 29 percent has an artifact in it. It is a lot easier to end an unhappy cohabitation than to end an unhappy marriage. In effect, the pool of cohabitating people is drained of unhappy potential respondents much more quickly than is the pool of married people.

Do children make people happy? As any parent can testify, that's a complicated question. Infants are a source of joy, but they are a lot of work, especially for the mother, and they disrupt pleasant patterns of life that prevailed before the birth. Teenagers are notoriously a source of anxiety and unhappiness for the parents. And yet it is also true that most parents see their children as a defining aspect of their lives, often *the* defining aspect. When the children turn out well, they are also the source of perhaps the deepest of all human satisfactions. These many complications account for the fact that married whites in their thirties and forties report that they are about equally happy whether or not they have children. Among unmarried people (combining those who are separated, divorced, widowed, and never married), those with children are notably *less* happy than those without children—a finding that reflects the many economic and emotional difficulties of being a single parent.

Before leaving the topic, I must emphasize that the statistical relationship between marriage and happiness is not completely causal. To some degree, happy people self-select into marriage and unhappy people self-select out of it.[3] However, the causal role that marriage plays in producing happiness is also indisputable. If you don't know that from your own life, just ask people who are happily married. They will seldom have any hesitation in identifying their marriages as a primary cause of their lasting and justified satisfaction with life as a whole.

Vocation

Direct evidence for the relationship of vocation to happiness comes via a GSS question that asks, "On the whole, how satisfied are you with the work you do?" The relationship of the answers to that question and self-reported happiness is unambiguous and strong, as shown in figure 15.3.

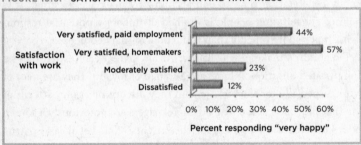

FIGURE 15.3.   **SATISFACTION WITH WORK AND HAPPINESS**

Source: GSS surveys from 1990 to 2010. Sample limited to whites ages 30–49.

The results support using the concept of *vocation* instead of *job* when thinking about what makes people happy. The highest proportion of people with high work satisfaction who also reported that they were very happy consisted of women whom the GSS called housewives. I have substituted the old-fashioned term *homemakers* in the figure, reflecting my assumption that the source of their satisfaction had a lot more to do with making a home than with keeping house.

Whether the satisfaction came from making a home or working at paid employment, the percentages of very happy people halved for those who were only moderately satisfied with their work, and halved again for those who were dissatisfied with their work.

Faith

Figure 15.4 sums up the bemusing situation facing social scientists, who as a group are predominantly secular. It shows the GSS data regarding religious attendance and self-reported happiness.

FIGURE 15.4.   **ATTENDANCE AT RELIGIOUS SERVICES AND HAPPINESS**

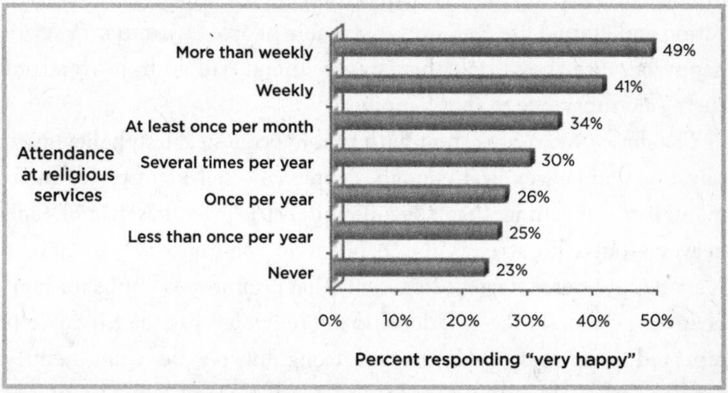

Attendance at religious services

More than weekly	49%
Weekly	41%
At least once per month	34%
Several times per year	30%
Once per year	26%
Less than once per year	25%
Never	23%

Percent responding "very happy"

Source: GSS surveys from 1990 to 2010. Sample limited to whites ages 30–49.

Social scientists rarely find such an orderly relationship over so many categories. At the top, 49 percent of those who attend worship services more than once a week report they are very happy. At the bottom, only 23 percent of the white adults who never attend worship services report they are very happy.

It is hard for me to find an artifact that might explain this result. It does not seem plausible (by any logic I can think of) that people who are already happy more likely to attend worship services than unhappy people. If anything, any artifact in the data would seem to work the other way—people who are unhappy go to church in search of solace.

Is it the act of going to worship services or the content of the religious faith that is associated with the happiness? The answer appears to be that you have to believe *and* attend. Forty-three percent of people who are believers and attend at least once a week said they were happy, about twice the percentage who say they believe but never attend church. People who attend services without believing don't get much advantage either—the percentage of nonbelievers reporting they were very happy stayed stuck at around 20 percent regardless of their attendance.

Explaining why this relationship between religiosity and happiness persists using a nonreligious explanation is a problem. Is it a matter of self-delusion? It might be argued that in America religion still refers overwhelmingly to Christianity, Christianity promises believers salvation and eternal life, and impressionable people buy into it. They're happy because they think they are saved and will go to heaven, but there's no substance to that happiness.

The data are not consistent with that hypothesis. First, believing in salvation and heaven isn't enough. People who self-identify as fundamentalists—meaning that they definitely believe in salvation and heaven—but who attend church no more than once a year have a "very happy" percentage (22 percent) that is almost as low as for non-believers. Second, the relationship of religious attendance to self-reported happiness is almost as strong for people who identify themselves as religious moderates or liberals (meaning that their confidence in salvation and heaven is likely to be dodgy) as it is for fundamentalists—47 percent of fundamentalists who attend church weekly or more report they are very happy, compared to 42 percent of religious moderates and 41 percent of religious liberals.

Community

The GSS has items measuring the level of community activity, as reported in the previous chapter, but those items were seldom given to the same respondents who were asked how happy they are for the GSS surveys conducted during the 1990s and 2000s (any given subject of the GSS is not asked about all the items for that year's survey). Happily, there is an alternative source of data in the form of the Social Capital Benchmark Survey (SCBS) conducted under the auspices of the Saguaro Seminar organized by Robert Putnam. The survey was conducted in 2000. Its total sample of 29,233 included 8,895 whites ages 30–49, and it contained a comprehensive set of measures of level of community activity along with a question about self-reported happiness.[4] The Social Capital Benchmark Survey also created indexes for different types of social capital. I used five of them for the comparison with happiness, made up of indicators described in the box.[5]

Indicators Used in the Social Capital Benchmark Survey Indexes

The *group involvement index* counts memberships in fraternal, ethnic, political, sports, youth, literary, veterans, or other kinds of clubs or organization other than religious ones.

The *organized group interactions index* combines measures of actual attendance at public meetings, club meetings, and local community events.

The *giving and volunteering index* combines indicators of volunteering for various organizations, frequency of volunteering, and charitable contributions.

The *informal social interactions index* combines measures of visits with relatives, having friends to the home, socializing with coworkers, hanging out with friends in public places, and playing cards and board games.

The *electoral politics index* combines indicators of voting, voter registration, interest in politics and national affairs, political knowledge, and frequency of newspaper reading.

In table 15.1, I grouped these indexes into five categories running from "very low" to "very high." For indexes with many values, the cutoff points for the categories were the 10th, 33rd, 67th, and 90th centiles of the distribution. For indexes with fewer values, I followed those guidelines as closely as possible.[6]

TABLE 15.1. PERCENTAGE OF WHITES AGES 30-49 WHO REPORT THAT
THEY ARE VERY HAPPY

	Index category	
Social capital index	Very low	Very high
Group involvement	32%	47%
Organized group interactions	29%	49%
Giving and volunteering	32%	57%
Informal social interactions	29%	48%
Electoral politics	29%	48%

Source: Social Capital Benchmark Survey. Sample limited to whites ages 30–49.

High levels of community involvement were consistently associated with much higher levels of "very happy" people than low levels of community involvement. Furthermore, each of the different types of involvement seemed to be about equally related to happiness, with "giving and volunteering" having a modest edge.[7]

The Social Capital Benchmark Survey also created an index of social trust combining responses to questions about trusting neighbors, coworkers, congregants, store workers, local police, and others in general. The relationship of self-reported happiness to their level of social trust was unusually high, as shown in figure 15.5.

FIGURE 15.5. RELATIONSHIP OF SOCIAL TRUST TO HAPPINESS

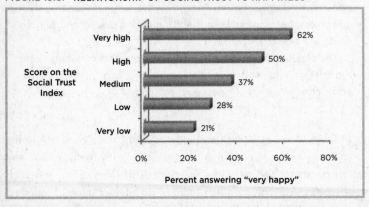

Source: Social Capital Benchmark Survey. Sample limited to whites ages 30–49.

If people in the Social Capital Benchmark Survey were very high in social trust, 62 percent of them reported being very happy. If they were very low in social trust, only 21 percent of them reported being very happy.

Putting the Pieces Together

Each of the four domains—family, vocation, faith, and community—has a direct and strong relationship to self-reported happiness. But which is the most important? Multivariate analysis can help answer that question. Appendix G gives the details, but essentially we are asking what the role of each is after controlling for the others and also asking about how they interact with one another.[8]

Figure 15.6 shows some of the results when the effects of the "high" level of each measure (a very happy marriage, high work satisfaction, strong religious involvement, and high social trust) are added to the probability that people say they are very happy.

At baseline—unmarried, dissatisfied with one's work, professing

FIGURE 15.6.   **THINGS THAT INCREASE THE LIKELIHOOD THAT SOMEONE REPORTS BEING VERY HAPPY, IN ORDER OF THEIR IMPORTANCE**

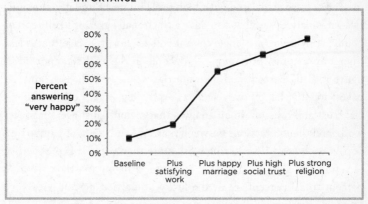

Source: GSS surveys from 1990–2010. Sample limited to white adults ages 30–49. Results of a logit analysis, fitted for a person age 40.

no religion, and with very low social trust—the probability that a white person aged 30–49 responded "very happy" to the question about his life in general was only 10 percent. Having either a very satisfying job or a very happy marriage raised that percentage by almost equal amounts, to about 19 percent, with the effect of a very satisfying job being fractionally greater. Then came the big interaction effect: having a very satisfying job *and* a very happy marriage jumped the probability to 55 percent. Having high social trust pushed the percentage to 69 percent, and adding strong religious involvement raised the probability to 76 percent.

The details are not etched in stone. Different specifications of the model (for example, using three categories for the variables instead of four) sometimes gave a very happy marriage a greater independent effect than a very satisfying job, and gave strong religion a greater independent effect than high social trust. What remained unchanged under all the variations was the primacy of marriage and vocation and the secondary role of social trust and religion in raising the probability of responding "very happy."

How much difference does it make to be in a happy marriage instead of just being married? In one sense, a lot, as I described earlier in the discussion of family. Unhappy marriages were associated with a low probability of being happy with life in general, whereas happy marriages were associated with high probabilities. Similarly, the multivariate analyses say that you have a fractionally greater likelihood of being happy if you are single than if you are in a marriage that is less than "very happy." But among the people in the analysis reported in figure 15.6, 67 percent said their marriages *were* "very happy," and the payoff for that happy marriage was extremely large. Let's ignore social trust and religion. In an analysis that includes just age, marriage, work, and the interactions between marriage and work, an unmarried person with very dissatisfying work more than triples his probability of reporting "very happy" if he can enter a happy marriage, from 9 percent to 30 percent. Even the lucky unmarried person with very satisfying work more than doubles his probability of reporting "very happy" if he marries, from 28 percent to 63 percent. So marriage is a risk, but the downside is much smaller than the upside, and for most people the risk pays off.

What Happens When Income Is Added to the Equation?

The analyses reported so far have not included income as a control variable, and yet it has consistently been found that, at any given slice of time, rich people are more likely than poor people to say they are happy. I have ignored that consistent relationship because it has just as consistently been found that the relationship is not causal after abject poverty has been left behind. Longitudinal evidence reveals that people don't get happier as they go from a modest income to affluence.[9]

The relationship exists in a cross section of the population because the qualities in individuals that make them happy in their marriages, satisfied with their work, socially trusting, and strongly involved with their religion are also qualities that are likely to make them successful in their jobs. In addition, marriage itself, independent of the personal qualities that produced the marriage, increases income—both by combining two incomes in some cases and because of the marriage premium discussed in chapter 9. Conversely, people who have a failed family life, are dissatisfied with their jobs, are disengaged from their communities, and have no spiritual life tend not to be happy because of those failures—and the same qualities that produced those failures also mean that, as a group, they are likely to have depressed incomes. Controlling for income as an explanation of happiness is as likely to mislead as to inform, wrongly attributing to income effects that are actually the result of qualities that produce both happiness and high income.

For the record, however, all of the relationships between the four domains and happiness that I describe in this chapter, bivariate and jointly in the multivariate analysis, persist after controlling for family income.[10] The absolute magnitude of the relationships are attenuated because of the cross-sectional correlation that exists between happiness and income. But the *incremental* effects on the probability of being very happy as shown in figure 15.6 are about the same. For example, in figure 15.6, having very satisfying work increased the baseline probability of answering "very happy" by 9 percentage points. For someone with the median income, the same change in work satisfaction increased the baseline probability by even more, 16 percentage points.[11] Without controlling for income, adding a happy marriage to very satisfying work boosted the probability by 36 percentage points. For a person at the median income, the comparable boost was 31 percentage points.

THE ARGUMENT UNDERLYING these many graphs and analyses has been that the founding virtues are instrumental to the domains for achieving deep satisfactions in life. Decay in the founding virtues is problematic for human flourishing. Those statements may have been self-evident to many readers without all the graphs and tables, but empirical support for them is readily available.

Divergence in Self-Reported Happiness

We are now in a position to ask what happened to self-reported happiness over time and by neighborhood.

The roles of the four domains of happiness are somewhat different in Belmont and Fishtown, but they add up to a remarkably similar total. In figure 15.7, I repeat the exercise of figure 15.6, showing the increment in the probability of being very happy as the effects of each domain are added in the order of their importance, but reporting the results separately for Belmont and Fishtown.

Belmont and Fishtown have somewhat different profiles. Give the people of Belmont very satisfying work and a very happy marriage, and social trust doesn't add much to the probability of reporting being

FIGURE 15.7.   **DIFFERENCES AND SIMILARITIES IN THE ACHIEVEMENT OF HAPPINESS IN BELMONT AND FISHTOWN**

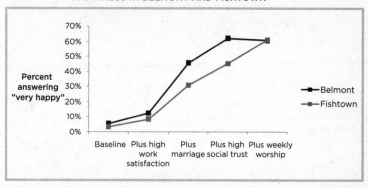

Source: GSS surveys from 1990–2010. Sample limited to white adults ages 30–49. Results of a logit analysis, fitted for a person age 40.

"very happy," and strong religion actually lowers the probability—statistically at least (it is appropriate to accept counterintuitive results of complex quantitative analyses provisionally). For the people of Fishtown, the effects of the four domains are more evenly spread, with the addition of a happy marriage, high social trust, and strong religion each adding a roughly equal increment to the probability of reporting being "very happy."

In the end, people who are high on all four measures have a remarkably similar probability of reporting they are very happy, regardless of whether they belong to Belmont or Fishtown. This is worth pondering. There is no inherent barrier to happiness for a person with a low level of education holding a low-skill job. The domains for achieving happiness *can* work as well for the people of Fishtown as for the people of Belmont. But they haven't been working as well over the course of the last half century, which leads to a predictable result when we examine the trendline of happiness in figure 15.8.

FIGURE 15.8. SELF-REPORTED HAPPINESS OVER TIME IN BELMONT AND FISHTOWN

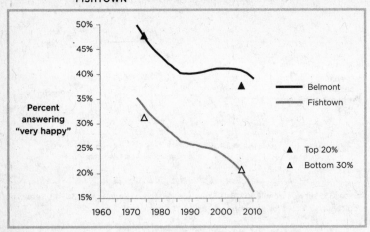

Source: GSS. Sample limited to whites ages 30–49. Data smoothed using locally estimated regression (LOESS).

When the GSS surveys began in the first half of the 1970s, the percentages of people in Belmont and Fishtown who reported they were very happy already showed a substantial gap of about 15 percentage points. There is no way of knowing what the proportions were in 1960.

In Belmont, the pattern is familiar from the trendlines in part 2: deterioration during the 1970s, stabilization thereafter. In Fishtown, self-reported happiness dropped from about 33 percent in the 1970s to an average of 22 percent in the 2000s. It is not a surprising finding, given the trendlines for Fishtown presented in part 2 and the testimony of the people of the real Fishtown in chapter 12, but it is an important finding. The trendlines for the founding virtues were not merely showing changes in social institutions and norms. They were saying things about the deterioration of life in Fishtown at the level of human happiness.

16

One Nation, Divisible

In which the numbers are expanded to include all Americans,
and it is shown that what you see in white America is what is
happening throughout all of America.

THIS BOOK HAS focused on the fortunes of whites as a way of stripping away distractions and concentrating on my thesis: Our nation is coming apart at the seams—not ethnic seams, but the seams of class. Having made that case in terms of whites, we cannot try to peer into the future without examining the picture when everyone else is brought into it.

Intuitively, it would seem that adding in the rest of America must make the situation even bleaker for Fishtown, and the separation with Belmont even greater. Problems in white working-class America may have been worsening under the radar, but problems in black America have attracted coverage for decades, and many of the numbers that have gotten so much publicity—the breakdown of marriage, dropout from the labor force, and crime—have used the same measures that I presented in part 2.

It was a surprise to me and perhaps it will be a surprise to you: Expanding the data to include all Americans makes hardly any difference at all. I will not replicate all of the graphs in part 2, but a representative sampling of the indicators will illustrate the point.

Marriage

Figure 16.1 shows what happens to the marriage numbers when blacks, Latinos, and everyone else are added to Belmont and Fishtown according to the same assignment rules that governed the assignment of whites. The lines in the graphs labeled "All Fishtown" thus refer to the entire American working class (and below), and "All Belmont" refers to the entire American upper-middle class (and above). As before, I focus on adults ages 30–49.

FIGURE 16.1.   **MARRIAGE FOR ALL PRIME-AGE ADULTS**

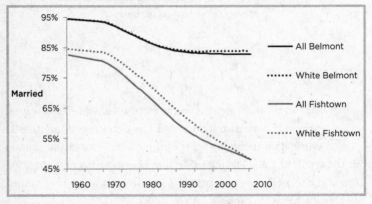

Source: IPUMS CPS. Samples limited to persons ages 30–49.

It is no surprise that the lines for All Belmont and White Belmont are so close together—as of 2010, whites constituted 76 percent of the population of All Belmont, and another 10 percent were East Asians, Southeast Asians, and South Asians, whose demographic characteristics among the college-educated are similar to those of whites.

But All Fishtown was only 63 percent white in 2010. Yet the percentage of married people in All Fishtown in 2010 was the same as in White Fishtown—about 48 percent. How is this possible, when only 42 percent of prime-age Fishtown blacks were married in 2010? The answer for marriage applies to other indicators as well. The racial

composition of All Fishtown in 2010 was 63 percent white, 12 percent black, 16 percent Latino, and 9 percent "other." Fishtown blacks
had a somewhat lower marriage rate than whites, but 50 percent of
Fishtown Latinos were married and 56 percent of the "Others" were
married. Both percentages were higher than the 48 percent among
Fishtown whites. Net result: a marriage rate for All Fishtown that was
about the same as the marriage rate for White Fishtown.

The same picture emerges for the other indicators in the chapter
on marriage. All Fishtown and White Fishtown were not identical as
of 2010 on trends in divorce and the never-married population, but
they were only a few percentage points apart. Even when we turn to
the most notorious of the family problems in the African American
community, children being raised by mothers without the father
present, All Fishtown and White Fishtown are quite similar, as shown
in figure 16.2.

FIGURE 16.2.   **CHILDREN STILL LIVING WITH BOTH BIOLOGICAL PARENTS
WHEN THE MOTHER IS AGE 40, FOR ALL MOTHERS**

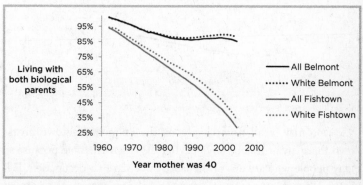

Source: NLS Mature Women, NLS Young Women, NLSY-79.

As of 2005, 37 percent of children in White Fishtown were still
living with both biological parents when the mother was age 40, compared to 30 percent of children in All Fishtown—a minor difference.
The main story line is that the baseline figures in 1960 were 95 percent and 95 percent, respectively, and that the disaster has struck
Fishtown no matter which racial aggregation is used—and that the

intact family remained strong in Belmont, no matter which racial aggregation is used.

Industriousness

Figure 16.3 shows the story for labor force participation among males ages 30–49.

FIGURE 16.3. **MALE LABOR FORCE PARTICIPATION BY EDUCATION FOR ALL PRIME-AGE MEN**

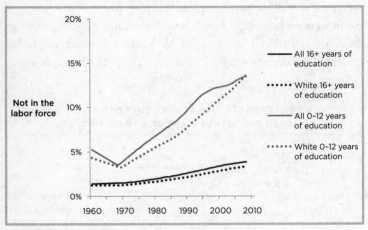

Source: IPUMS CPS. Samples limited to persons ages 30–49.

As you may recall from chapter 9, the Belmont-Fishtown breakdown for analyzing labor force participation isn't feasible because so many people who are out of the labor force have no occupation. Figure 16.3 therefore compares men with no more than twelve years of education with those who have at least sixteen years of education. Once again, the percentage for whites as of 2010 was virtually identical with the percentage for the whole population, and for the same reason that the marriage rates were so close: Blacks have a much higher proportion of low-education males out of the labor force than whites, but the growing proportion of Latinos, who have higher labor force participation than whites, made up the difference.

In the chapter on industriousness, the summary indicator was the percentage of households in which the head of household or the spouse worked at least forty hours in the preceding week. Figure 16.4 shows how that indicator looks when we expand the population to include everybody.

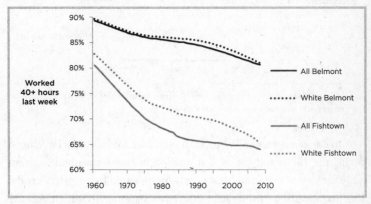

FIGURE 16.4. **HOUSEHOLD IN WHICH THE HEAD OR SPOUSE WORKED 40 HOURS IN THE PRECEDING WEEK FOR ALL PRIME-AGE ADULTS**

Source: IPUMS CPS. Samples limited to persons ages 30–49.

In this case, a noticeable gap opened up between White Fishtown and All Fishtown in the 1980s and 1990s, but it closed to nearly zero in the 2000s.

Honesty

At last, we have an indicator that looks considerably worse when we include everybody than when the analysis is limited to whites: imprisonment, as shown in figure 16.5.

As of the 2004 inmate survey (the most recent one), the imprisonment rate was 63 percent higher for all males than for white males. But when we turn from imprisonment to arrest rates, we're back to a picture of minor differences between white Fishtown and multiracial Fishtown in the most recent data. Figure 16.6 shows the trends for violent crime.

FIGURE 16.5.   INMATES IN STATE AND FEDERAL PRISONS FOR ALL
               PRIME-AGE MALES

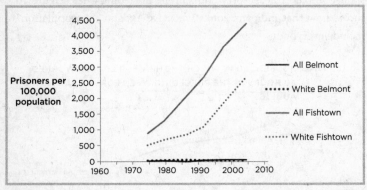

Source: The state and federal inmate surveys. Prisoner sample limited to males ages 20–49.
The denominator is based on persons ages 30–49.

A major gap between White Fishtown and All Fishtown developed
during the 1970s and 1980s, but by 2009 it had diminished substantially for violent crime and had nearly disappeared for property crime.
The juxtaposition of the racial discrepancy in imprisonment and the
closing of the racial gap in arrests lends itself to two narratives. One
argues that we are currently overimprisoning blacks and Latinos,
given the similarity of current arrest rates in Fishtown. The other

FIGURE 16.6.   ARREST RATES WHEN THE SAMPLES ARE EXPANDED TO
               INCLUDE ALL PRIME-AGE ADULTS

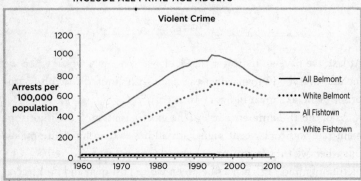

Source: FBI Uniform Crime Reports.

narrative argues that the reason we have seen arrests drop more among Fishtown blacks and Latinos than among Fishtown whites is because they were imprisoned at higher rates. I will leave it to others to debate the merits of the alternative narratives.

Religiosity

In chapter 11, I summarized the difference between Belmont and Fishtown by defining the religious core of a community as the percentage of people who both attended worship services regularly and said they had a strong religious affiliation. The result when other ethnic groups are added to Fishtown is shown in figure 16.7.

FIGURE 16.7.   **THE RELIGIOUS CORE FOR ALL PRIME-AGE ADULTS**

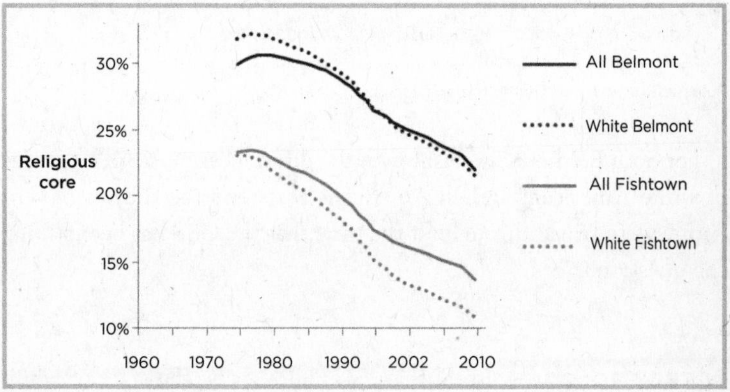

Source: GSS. Samples limited to persons ages 30–49.

Not only is the religious core as large in All Belmont as it is in White Belmont, it is larger in All Fishtown than it is in White Fishtown. Unfortunately, the difference is not great—14 percent of All Fishtown consisted of people with a strong religious affiliation who also attended church regularly, compared to 11 percent of White Fishtown, and both proportions are quite small.

Happiness

Finally, what about the numbers of Americans who consider themselves to be "very happy"? Once again, being white has little to do with it, as shown in figure 16.8.

FIGURE 16.8. **HAPPINESS FOR ALL PRIME-AGE ADULTS**

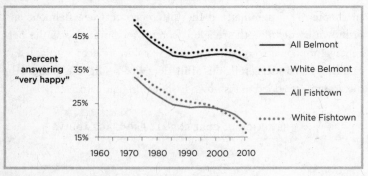

Source: GSS. Samples limited to persons ages 30–49.

For both Belmont and Fishtown, the differences in the percentages of white Americans and all Americans who reported they were very happy were trivial throughout the time that the GSS has been asking the question.

IN THE PROLOGUE, I said that I would describe the state of white America from 1960 through 2010. That purpose is even proclaimed in the subtitle of the book. No matter how I explained my reasons for doing so, there had to remain some sense among many of you that this was an odd thing to do, and perhaps disturbing, when the United States is moving from a white-dominated culture to one in which whites are just the most numerous of many different races and ethnicities. Now, as we turn to the final chapter and a consideration of where the nation might go from here, it can be said:

We are one nation, indivisible, in terms of whites and people of color. Differences in the fortunes of different ethnic groups persist, but white America is not headed in one direction and nonwhite America in another. We are divisible in terms of class. The coming apart at the seams has not been confined to whites, nor will its evil effects be confined to whites. *Coming Apart* may have told the story of white America, but its message is about all of America.

17

Alternative Futures

In which it is asked whether the divergence of American classes foreshadows the end of the American project. Two models for thinking about that prospect are presented, one pessimistic and the other optimistic.

GREAT NATIONS EVENTUALLY cease to be great, inevitably. It's not the end of the world. Britain goes on despite the loss of its onetime geopolitical preeminence. France goes on despite the loss of its onetime preeminence in the arts. The United States will go on under many alternative futures. "There is a great deal of ruin in a nation," Adam Smith wisely counseled a young correspondent who feared that Britain was on its last legs in the 1700s.[1] As a great power, America still has a lot of ruin left in it.

But how much ruin does the American project have left? The historical precedent is Rome. In terms of wealth, military might, and territorial reach, Rome was at its peak under the emperors. But Rome's initial downward step, five centuries before the eventual fall of the Western Roman Empire, was its loss of the republic when Caesar became the first emperor. Was that loss important? Not in material terms. But for Romans who treasured their republic, it was a tragedy that no amount of imperial splendor could redeem.

The United States faces a similar prospect: remaining as wealthy and powerful as ever, but leaving its heritage behind. The successor state need not be one ruled by emperors. We may continue to have a President and a Congress and a Supreme Court. But the United States will be just one more in history's procession of dominant nations. Everything that makes America exceptional will have disappeared.

The American Project Versus the European Model

I have used the phrase *the American project* frequently. It refers to national life based on the founders' idea that the "sum of good government," as Thomas Jefferson put it in his first inaugural address, is a state that "shall restrain men from injuring one another [and] shall leave them otherwise free to regulate their own pursuits of industry and improvement."

At this point in our history, more and more people, including prominent academics, the leaders of the Democratic Party, and some large portion of the American electorate, believe that history has overtaken that original conception. Over the course of the twentieth century, western Europe developed an alternative to the American model, the advanced welfare state, that provides a great deal of personal freedom in all areas of life except the economic ones. The restrictions that the European model imposes on the economic behavior of both employers and employees are substantial, but, in return, the citizens of Europe's welfare states have (so far) gotten economic security.

I think it is a bad trade. In chapter 15, I indirectly described why. Let me be more explicit here.

The European model assumes that human needs can be disaggregated when it comes to choices about public policy. People need food and shelter, so let us make sure that everyone has food and shelter. People may also need self-respect, but that doesn't have anything to do with whether the state provides them with food and shelter. People may also need intimate relationships with others, but that doesn't have anything to do with policies regarding marriage and children. People may also need self-actualization, but that doesn't have anything to do with policies that diminish the challenges of life.

More Sanguine Views

This indictment of the European model represents a minority position, at least among intellectuals, and so do my perspective on happiness and my conclusion that the American project is disintegrating.

For an evocation of the European model as the ideal, I recommend Jeremy Rifkin's *The European Dream: How Europe's Vision of the Future Is Quietly Eclipsing the American Dream.*[2] Two companion volumes reflecting the European perspective on religion and happiness are Phil Zuckerman's *Society Without God: What the Least Religious Nations Can Tell Us About Contentment* and Richard Layard's *Happiness: Lessons from a New Science.*[3]

For the case that American culture shows great continuity over the last two centuries, enduring to the present, I recommend Claude Fischer's *Made in America: A Social History of American Culture and Character.*[4] Fischer and Michael Hout also wrote *Century of Difference: How America Changed in the Last One Hundred Years,* which takes many social and economic trendlines in this book further back than 1960.[5]

These are all thoughtful and useful analyses that I will not try to engage in a data-driven debate. With regard to advocacy of the European model: If you think that providing economic equality and security are primary functions of government, you should be a social democrat. You can easily find evidence on behalf of social democracy (given that pair of priorities) that you think is dispositive. I look at the same evidence and judge it to be peripheral, irrelevant, or wrong-headed—not because the numbers are wrong, but because of differences on first principles. With regard to Claude Fischer's optimism about the continuity of American culture, I share much of it if we are talking about Belmont, not if we are talking about Fishtown—but that is not a distinction that Fischer set out to explore, so our positions largely pass in the night, neither directly in conflict with the other.

The tacit assumption of the advanced welfare state is correct when human beings face starvation or death by exposure. Then, food and shelter are all that count. But in an advanced society, the needs for food and shelter can be met in a variety of ways, and at that point human needs can no longer be disaggregated. The ways in which food and shelter are obtained affects whether the other human needs are met.

People need self-respect, but self-respect must be earned—it cannot be self-respect if it's not earned—and the only way to earn anything is to achieve it in the face of the possibility of failing. People need intimate relationships with others, but intimate relationships that are rich and fulfilling need content, and that content is supplied only when humans are engaged in interactions that have consequences. People need self-actualization, but self-actualization is not a straight road, visible in advance, running from point A to point B. Self-actualization intrinsically requires an exploration of possibilities for life beyond the obvious and convenient. All of these good things in life—self-respect, intimate relationships, and self-actualization—require freedom in the only way that freedom is meaningful: freedom to act in all arenas of life coupled with responsibility for the consequences of those actions. The underlying meaning of that coupling—freedom *and* responsibility—is crucial. Responsibility for the consequences of actions is not the price of freedom, but one of its rewards. Knowing that we have responsibility for the consequences of our actions is a major part of what makes life worth living.

Recall from chapter 15 the four domains that I argued are the sources of deep satisfactions: family, vocation, community, and faith. In each of those domains, responsibility for the desired outcome is inseparable from the satisfaction. The deep satisfactions that go with raising children arise from having fulfilled your responsibility for just about the most important thing that human beings do. If you're a disengaged father who doesn't contribute much to that effort, or a wealthy mother who has turned over most of the hard part to full-time day care and then boarding schools, the satisfactions are diminished accordingly. The same is true if you're a low-income parent who finds it easier to let the apparatus of an advanced welfare state take over. In the workplace, getting a pay raise is pleasant whether you deserve it or not, but the deep satisfactions that can come from a job promotion are inextricably bound up with the sense of having done things that merited it. If you know that you got the promotion just because you're the boss's nephew, or because the civil service rules specify that you must get that promotion if you have served enough time in grade, deep satisfactions are impossible.

When the government intervenes to help, whether in the European welfare state or in America's more diluted version, it not only diminishes our responsibility for the desired outcome, it enfeebles the institutions through which people live satisfying lives. There is no way for clever planners to avoid it. Marriage is a strong and vital institution not because the day-to-day work of raising children and being a good spouse is so much fun, but because the family has responsibility for doing important things that won't get done unless the family does them. Communities are strong and vital not because it's so much fun to respond to our neighbors' needs, but because the community has the responsibility for doing important things that won't get done unless the community does them. Once that imperative has been met—family and community *really do* have the action—then an elaborate web of expectations, rewards, and punishments evolves over time. Together, that web leads to norms of good behavior that support families and communities in performing their functions. When the government says it will take some of the trouble out of doing the things that families and communities evolved to do, it inevitably takes some of the action away from families and communities. The web frays, and eventually disintegrates.

Through November 21, 1963, the American project demonstrated that a society can provide great personal freedom while generating strong and vital human networks that helped its citizens cope.[6] America on the eve of John Kennedy's assassination, while flawed, was still headed in the right direction.

In some ways, the United States continued in the right direction, bringing us closer to the ideals that animated the nation's creation. The leading examples are the revolutions in the status of African Americans and women. The barriers facing them in 1963 represented a continuing failure of America to make good on its ideals. In every realm of American life, those barriers had been reduced drastically by 2010.

In other ways, it has been downhill ever since. The trendlines of part 2 and chapter 14 constitute the gravamen of that charge. Family, vocation, community, and faith have all been enfeebled, in predictable ways.

The problems these changes have engendered are different in kind from the problems of poverty. The problems that children suffer *because* of poverty disappear when the family is no longer poor. The problems that poor communities suffer *because* of poverty disappear when the community is no longer poor. The first two-thirds of the twentieth century saw spectacular progress on that front. But when families become dysfunctional, or cease to form altogether, growing numbers of children suffer in ways that have little to do with lack of money. When communities are no longer bound by their members' web of mutual obligations, the continuing human needs must be handed over to bureaucracies—the bluntest, clumsiest of all tools for giving people the kind of help they need. The neighborhood becomes a sterile place to live at best and, at worst, becomes the Hobbesian all-against-all free-fire zone that we have seen in some of our major cities.

These costs—enfeebling family, vocation, community, and faith— are not exacted on the people of Belmont. The things the government does to take the trouble out of things seldom intersect with the life of a successful attorney or executive. Rather, they intersect with life in Fishtown. A man who is holding down a menial job and thereby supporting a wife and children is doing something authentically important with his life. He should take deep satisfaction from that, and be praised by his community for doing so. If that same man lives under a system that says the children of the woman he sleeps with will be taken care of whether or not he contributes, then that status goes away. I am not describing a theoretical outcome, but American neighborhoods where, once, working at a menial job to provide for his family made a man proud and gave him status in his community, and where now it doesn't. Taking the trouble out of life strips people of major ways in which human beings look back on their lives and say, "I made a difference."

Europe has proved that countries with enfeebled family, vocation, community, and faith can still be pleasant places to live. I am delighted when I get a chance to go to Stockholm or Paris. When I get there, the people don't seem to be groaning under the yoke of an oppressive system. On the contrary, there's a lot to like about day-to-day life in the advanced welfare states of western Europe. They are great places to visit. But the view of life that has taken root in those same countries is problematic. It seems to go something like this: The purpose of life is to while away the time between birth and death as pleasantly as possible, and the purpose of government is to make it as easy as possible to while away the time as pleasantly as possible—the Europe Syndrome.

Europe's short workweeks and frequent vacations are one symptom of the syndrome. The idea of work as a means of self-actualization has faded. The view of work as a necessary evil, interfering with the higher good of leisure, dominates. To have to go out to look for a job or to have to risk being fired from a job are seen as terrible impositions. The precipitous decline of marriage, far greater in Europe than in the United States, is another symptom. What is the point of a lifetime commitment when the state will act as surrogate spouse when it comes to paying the bills? The decline of fertility to far below replacement is another symptom. Children are seen as a burden that the state must help shoulder, and even then they're a lot of trouble that distract from things that are more fun. The secularization of Europe is yet another symptom. Europeans have broadly come to believe that humans are a collection of activated chemicals that, after a period of time, deactivate. If that's the case, saying that the purpose of life is to pass the time as pleasantly as possible is a reasonable position. Indeed, taking any other position is ultimately irrational.

The alternative to the Europe Syndrome is to say that your life can have transcendent meaning if it is spent doing important things—raising a family, supporting yourself, being a good friend and a good neighbor, learning what you can do well and then doing it as well as you possibly can. Providing the best possible framework for doing those things is what the American project is all about. When I say that the American project is in danger, that's the nature of the loss I have in mind: the loss of the framework through which people can best pursue happiness.

The reasons we face the prospect of losing that heritage are many, but none are more important than the twin realities that I have tried to describe in the preceding chapters. On one side of the spectrum, a significant and growing portion of the American population is losing the virtues required to be functioning members of a free society. On the other side of the spectrum, the people who run the country are doing just fine. Their framework for pursuing happiness is relatively unaffected by the forces that are enfeebling family, community, vocation, and faith elsewhere in the society. In fact, they have become so isolated that they are often oblivious to the nature of the problems that exist elsewhere.

The forces that have led to the formation of the new lower class continue as I write. In the absence of some outside intervention, the new lower class will continue to grow. Advocacy for that outside intervention can come from many levels of society—that much is still true in America—but eventually it must gain the support of the new upper class if it is to be ratified. Too much power is held by the new upper class to expect otherwise. What are the prospects of that happening? I conclude this tangled story by offering two alternative ways of thinking about what comes next.

A Hollow Elite

The first alternative is that the new upper class is in just as much trouble as the new lower class, albeit in different ways, and the American project is doomed. The new upper class has vast resources, both in wealth and in human capital. The modern economy is ideally suited to their strengths. They are doing an excellent job of co-opting the new intellectual talent in each generation, much as classical China co-opted the new intellectual talent in each generation through its examination system. But the new upper class is showing signs of becoming an elite that is hollow at the core.

A Collapse of Self-Confidence

In the late 1940s and early 1950s, Arnold J. Toynbee's *A Study of History* had a public vogue in the United States.[7] Toynbee identified twenty-six distinct civilizations in recorded history and propounded a grand theory that explained their trajectories of growth and decline. The academics pounced on *A Study of History*—Toynbee's sweeping, moralistic approach was at odds with the academic temper of the time—and after a few years it became intellectually unfashionable. But in 2001, while working on a book about the history of human accomplishment, I decided that I should take a look at a work so rich in material. Eventually I reached the chapter titled "Schism in the Soul," and experienced a shock of recognition.[8]

In that chapter, Toynbee took up the processes that lead to the disintegration of civilizations. His argument went like this: The growth phase of a civilization is led by a creative minority with a strong, self-confident sense of style, virtue, and purpose. The uncreative majority follows along. Then, at some point in every civilization's journey, the creative minority degenerates into a dominant minority. Its members still run the show, but they are no longer confident and no longer set the example. Among other reactions are a "lapse into truancy"—a rejection of the obligations of citizenship—and "surrender to a sense of promiscuity"—vulgarization of manners, the arts, and language—that "are apt to appear first in the ranks of the proletariat and to spread from there to the ranks of the dominant minority, which usually succumbs to the sickness of 'proletarianization.' "[9]

The shock of recognition that I experienced in 2001 came because of the adoption by the middle class and upper-middle class of behaviors that used to be distinctly lower class. When Tipper Gore, the wife of senator and later vice president Al Gore, attacked the incontestable violence and misogyny of rock and rap lyrics, why was she so roundly scolded by so many of her social and political peers? Why were four-letter words, which formerly were seen by the upper-middle class as déclassé, appearing in glossy upscale magazines? How had "the hooker look" become a fashion trend among nice girls from the suburbs? How had tattoos, which a few decades ago had been proof positive that one was a member of the proletariat, become chic? Toynbee would have shrugged and said that this is what happens when civilizations are headed downhill—America's creative minority has degenerated into a dominant minority, and we are witnessing the universal next step, the proletarianization of the dominant minority.

There are many reasons to bridle at that characterization. For one thing, civilizations that see a coarsening of the culture are sometimes in their heyday. Why shouldn't America in recent decades be seen as something like Regency England? The early 1800s were a time of haphazard morals and mindless extravagance in the aristocracy, but also the era when England defeated Napoleon and English science, technology, literature, art, and industry were in a golden age. We should remember, too, that cultures sometimes do an abrupt about-face. Within a few decades of the end of the Regency, England had become Victorian.

For another thing, how is America's new upper class vulnerable to a charge of imitating the proletariat, when, as this book has just documented, the new upper class and, more broadly, Belmont, have more or less held the line on marriage, industriousness, and honesty— even religiosity, comparatively speaking—while the proletariat has deteriorated?

All good points. But, nonetheless, the signs that America's new upper class has suffered a collapse of self-confidence are hard to ignore. There is, for example, the collapse of confidence in codes of honorable behavior.

The Collapse of a Sturdy Elite Code

In *The Philadelphia Story*, Tracey (Katharine Hepburn) is unable to recall what happened between her and Mike (Jimmy Stewart) the night before, because she had been so drunk that she passed out. She is relieved to learn that Mike had carried her to her bedroom, deposited her on her bed, and departed, but worries about why he had been so gallant. "Was I so unattractive, so distant, so forbidding, or something?"

she asks. That wasn't the problem, Mike replies. "You were also a little the worse—or better—for wine, and there are rules about that."

Mike was observing the code. Codes of behavior exist in every nook of society, and they are powerful determinants of the social order within that nook. Doctors have a code and cops have a code. Teenagers have a code. Prisoners have a code. The elite has a code. The difference between the elite's code and the others is the breadth of its influence. The history of England in the last half of the nineteenth century can be seen as the Victorian elite's success in propagandizing the entire English population into accepting its code of morals.[10] A degenerate elite code can inspire contempt and encourage revolution among the rest of the population, with France in the mid-eighteenth century and Russia in the early twentieth as cases in point.

In keeping with its democratic tradition, America did not have different codes for socioeconomic classes.[11] To be a decent person was to adhere to a code that applied to all, rich and poor. In effect, Mike in *The Philadelphia Story* was observing the code of behavior that was taught to every American child who attended school, usually through the McGuffey Readers I described in chapter 6, reinforced by the larger American civic religion that gave rise to the McGuffey Readers in the first place. Here is a passage from the *Fourth Reader*, 1901 edition, that a man of Mike's generation would have read when he was in the fourth grade: "Tom Barton never forgot the lesson of that night; and he came to believe, and to act upon the belief, in after years, that true manliness is in harmony with gentleness, kindness, and self-denial."[12]

By the time *The Philadelphia Story* was released in 1940, the McGuffey Readers weren't being used anymore, but the code survived and it was still being communicated. Growing up in the 1940s and 1950s, I understood the code for males to go something like this:

> To be a man means that you are brave, loyal, and true. When you are in the wrong, you own up and take your punishment. You don't take advantage of women. As a husband, you support and

protect your wife and children. You are gracious in victory and a good sport in defeat. Your word is your bond. Your handshake is as good as your word. It's not whether you win or lose, but how you play the game. When the ship goes down, you put the women and children into the lifeboats and wave good-bye with a smile.

It is hard to imagine a paragraph more crammed with clichés. My point is that they were clichés precisely because boys understood that this was the way they were supposed to behave. A code existed that was energetically propagated by the people who ran America and it was taken seriously. If you see or hear any of those clichés used today among the new upper class, it is probably sarcastically. The code of the American gentleman has collapsed, just as the parallel code of the American lady has collapsed.

In today's new upper class—what Toynbee would surely see as a dominant minority—the code that has taken its place is a set of mushy injunctions to be nice. Call it the code of ecumenical niceness. Children are supposed to share their toys, not hit one another, take turns . . . to be nice. And, by and large, the children of the new upper class grow up to be nice. But they are also taught that they should respect everyone else's way of doing things, regardless of gender, race, sexual preference, cultural practices, or national origin, which leads to the crucial flaw in ecumenical niceness. The code of the dominant minority is supposed to set the standard for the society, but ecumenical niceness has a hold only on people whom the dominant minority is willing to judge—namely, one another.

That's what I mean by loss of self-confidence. The new upper class still does a good job of practicing some of the virtues, but it no longer preaches them. It has lost self-confidence in the rightness of its own customs and values, and preaches nonjudgmentalism instead.

Nonjudgmentalism is one of the more baffling features of the new-upper-class culture.[13] The members of the new upper class are industrious to the point of obsession, but there are no derogatory labels for adults who are not industrious. The young women of the new upper class hardly ever have babies out of wedlock, but it is imper-missible to use a derogatory label for nonmarital births. You will probably raise a few eyebrows even if you use a derogatory label for criminals. When you get down to it, it is not acceptable in the new upper class to use derogatory labels for anyone, with three excep-tions: people with differing political views, fundamentalist Chris-tians, and rural working-class whites.

If you are of a conspiratorial cast of mind, nonjudgmentalism looks suspiciously like the new upper class keeping the good stuff to itself. The new upper class knows the secret to maximizing the chances of leading a happy life, but it refuses to let anyone else in on the secret. Conspiratorial explanations are unnecessary, however. Nonjudgmen-talism ceases to be baffling if you think of it as a symptom of Toyn-bee's loss of self-confidence among the dominant minority. The new upper class doesn't want to push its way of living onto the less fortu-nate, for who are they to say that their way of living is really better? It works for them, but who is to say that it will work for others? Who are they to say that their way of behaving is virtuous and others' ways of behaving are not?

Toynbee entitled his discussion "schism in the soul" because the dis-integration of a civilization is not a monolithic process. While part of the dominant minority begins to mimic the culture of the proletariat, remnants of it become utopians, or ascetics, or try to invoke old norms (as I am doing here). To recognize a disintegrating civilization, Toyn-bee says, look for a riven culture—riven as our culture is today. For every example of violence and moral obtuseness coming out of Hollywood, one can cite films, often faithful renderings of classic nov-els, expressing an exquisite moral sensibility. On television, the worst-of-times, best-of-times paradox can be encompassed within the same television series—wonderful moral insights in one plotline, moral ob-tuseness in another, sometimes occurring within the same episode. Some parents of the new upper class are responsible for producing and distributing the content that represents the worst of contemporary culture, while others are going to great lengths to protect their chil-dren from what they see as a violent and decadent culture. Sometimes those parents are one and the same people. The only common thread

that I claim in all of this is an unwillingness on the part of any significant portion of the new upper class to preach what they practice.

Unseemliness

The collapse of a sturdy code (ecumenical niceness is not sturdy) also
means that certain concepts lose their power to constrain behavior.
One of those concepts is unseemliness.

The Random House Dictionary of the English Language defines *unseemly* as "not in keeping with established standards of taste or proper
form; unbecoming or indecorous in appearance; improper in speech,
conduct, etc.; inappropriate for time or place." The ultimate source,
The Oxford English Dictionary, requires just three words: "Unbecoming, unfitting; indecent."[14]

Some examples? Unseemliness is television producer Aaron Spelling building a house of 56,500 square feet and 123 rooms. Unseemliness is Henry McKinnell, the CEO of Pfizer, getting a $99 million
golden parachute and an $82 million pension after a tenure that saw
Pfizer's share price plunge.[15] They did nothing illegal. Spelling had
the money to build his dream house, just as millions of others would
like to do, and got zoning approval for his plans. McKinnell's separation package was paid according to the contract he had signed with
Pfizer when he became CEO. But the outcomes were inappropriate
for time or place, not suited to the circumstances. They were unbecoming and unfitting. They were unseemly.

I chose two examples so extreme that only people who deny that
unseemly is a valid concept can argue with me. But as soon as I move
to less extreme examples, that phrase, "established standards of taste
or proper form," comes into play. Since my two examples involved
money, let's stick with that topic. The final figure in this book, 17.1,
shows the trend in the total compensation received by CEOs of large
corporations since 1970.

Where does unseemliness begin? Even in 1970, the average CEO
made about $1 million. Was that unseemly, given what good CEOs
contribute to the success of their company? If that wasn't unseemly,
is it unseemly that the average compensation doubled to $2 million

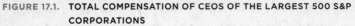

FIGURE 17.1.   **TOTAL COMPENSATION OF CEOS OF THE LARGEST 500 S&P
CORPORATIONS**

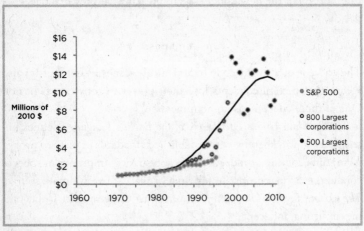

Source: Murphy, 1999, fig. 1. Forbes Annual Executive Compensation Reports.[16]

by 1987? That it doubled again to $4 million by 1992? That it doubled again to $8 million by 1998? That it doubled again to $16 million by 2006?

I am not asking whether the increases were economically rational. The technical literature hotly debates this issue, but it does not reach the question I am asking. To clarify that question, it may help if I stipulate for purposes of argument that these increases *were* economically rational. I will further stipulate that the dynamics producing those increases promoted economic growth and, ultimately, a better life for people all the way down the line. Now return to the question: Is there anything unseemly about the story told in figure 17.1?

At the individual level, accepting a big compensation package is seldom unseemly. You're the CEO; you've worked hard to get where you are; you think that your contribution is valuable to the company; you know that your compensation package is in line with what CEOs of comparable companies are getting. It is hard to see any ethical obligation to negotiate a smaller deal for yourself than the board of directors is willing to give you.[17]

But what about all those boards of directors, themselves composed of many people who are or have been CEOs themselves? They have a fiduciary responsibility to the stockholders, not to the employees of the company. To what extent are they handing out these compensation packages because, like it or not, that's what it takes to get the kind of person they need to run the company? Or to what extent have the boards of directors of corporate America—and nonprofit America, and foundation America—become cozy extended families, scratching one another's backs, happily going along with a market that has become lucrative for all of them, taking advantage of their privileged positions—rigging the game, but within the law.[18]

It looks suspiciously as if there's a lot of unseemliness going on, but I cannot prove it. People within the corporate world with whom I have discussed the issue vary in their assessment of how much the cozy-little-club phenomenon applies, though all acknowledge that it exists to some extent. Finding hard data on the how-much question is as difficult as finding hard data on the criminal aspects of corporate malfeasance that I discussed in chapter 10.

Even without hard data, I won't get any argument from people on the Left, who are inclined to view corporate America suspiciously in the absence of any data whatsoever. But it is not really an issue that is decided by political views. Recently, I asked a successful entrepreneur, an ardent proponent of free markets, what he thought about the bonus of several hundred million dollars that a board had decided to award to the departing CEO of a large company as a thank-you gift. He looked at me sharply and said, "It's obscene." That is a reasonable way for people to react whether they are liberal, conservative, or libertarian—the issue is not what should be legal, but what is seemly.

I have focused on the economic manifestations of unseemliness in the private sector because they have such broad ramifications for the United States—the great majority of the new upper class are involved in the corporate, nonprofit, and foundation worlds, all of which have instances of the kind of unseemliness that I think is reflected in figure 17.1. But if you're looking for egregious examples of unseemliness, you can do no better than look at contemporary American government.

It's not new. The crafting of legislation by the Congress has always been like the making of sausage. But when the federal government

did not have much to sell except contracts for roads, military equipment, and government buildings, the amount of energy devoted to
scrambling for government spoils was commensurate with the size of
the pot. The pot has grown, with hundreds of billions of dollars of
goodies now up for grabs for whoever knows the right people, can
convince the right committee chairman to insert a clause in the legislation, convince the right regulatory bureaucrat to word a ruling in a
certain way, or secure the right appointment to a key government
panel. Perhaps unseemliness per unit of government has not increased
in the last half century, but the number and size of those units has
increased by orders of magnitude, and the magnitude of unseemliness
has increased along with them. Washington is in a new Gilded Age of
influence peddling that dwarfs anything that has come before.

Unseemliness is a symptom of the collapse of codes of behavior
that depend not on laws and regulations, but upon shared understandings regarding the fitness of things, and upon an allegiance to
behave in accordance with those shared understandings. Unseemliness is another symptom of hollowness at the core.

MY PROPOSITION IS that the hollow elite is as dysfunctional in its
way as the new lower class is in its way. Personally and as families, its
members are successful. But they have abdicated their responsibility
to set and promulgate standards. The most powerful and successful
members of their class increasingly trade on the perks of their privileged positions without regard to the seemliness of that behavior. The
members of the new upper class are active politically, but when it
comes to using their positions to help sustain the republic in day-to-
day life, they are AWOL.

The Prognosis

If the case I have just made for a hollow elite is completely correct, all
is lost. Think ahead to the situation in, say, 2020, assuming that the
trends we have examined in this book continue. The United States is

stuck with a large and growing lower class that is able to care for itself only sporadically and inconsistently. Its concentration in Fishtown puts more and more pressure on the remaining Fishtown families who are trying to hold the line.

The new upper class has continued to prosper as the dollar value of the talents they bring to the economy has continued to grow. With increased wealth, the prices that members of the new upper class are willing to pay for a home in the right kind of place have risen even more, less affluent residents who still provided some diversity within the SuperZips in 2010 have moved out, and the uniformity of very affluent, very highly educated populations within the SuperZips has increased. The proportion of the new upper class who are in the third generation of upper-class upbringing has increased, and with that increase has come increasing ignorance of the world outside their bubble.

Liberals in the new upper class continue to support adoption of the European model, as they have for decades. Conservatives in the new upper class still contribute to conservative candidates, but they are no more willing to preach what they practice than are those on the Left. Those in the new upper class who don't care about politics don't mind the drift toward the European model, because paying taxes is a cheap price for a quiet conscience—much cheaper than actually having to get involved in the lives of their fellow citizens.

The new laws and regulations steadily accrete, and America's governing regime is soon indistinguishable from that of an advanced European welfare state. The American project is dead.

A Civic Great Awakening

The alternative future has a chance to the extent that the following four predictions are borne out. First, we in America will be watching what happens in Europe, and it will not be pretty. Second, science will undermine the moral underpinnings of the welfare state. Third, it will become increasingly obvious that there is a simple, affordable way to replace the entire apparatus of the welfare state. Fourth, the persistence of Americans' allegiance to the American project will turn out to be far greater than my argument so far has acknowledged.

Watching the European Model Implode

The simplest way in which the advanced welfare state will lose attractiveness is the looming bankruptcy of the European welfare states.

The financial bankruptcy is not anything that even the cleverest planner can avoid. As publicly financed benefits grow, so do the populations who find that they need them. The more people who need benefits, the more government bureaucracy is required. The more people who rely on support from the government and the larger the government, the fewer the people in the private sector who pay for the benefits and for the apparatus of the state.[19] The larger the number of people who depend on government either for benefits or for their jobs, the larger the constituency for voting for ever-larger government.

These are arithmetical realities that have become manifest in every advanced Western country. They have brought some European welfare states within sight of bankruptcy as I write. Fertility rates that are far below replacement throughout western Europe ensure that the productive native-born population will fall still more in the years to come.

There is no permanent way out of the self-destructive dynamics of the welfare state, but Europe has a tempting palliative—encouraging large-scale immigration of younger populations who work in the private sector and pay taxes that make up the revenue deficit. It won't work forever—sooner or later, the immigrants, too, will succumb to the incentives that the welfare state sets up. But the more immediate problem is that most of the new workers come from cultures that are radically different from those of western Europe. In some cases, those cultures despise the values that led to the welfare state. The United States will have a chance to watch these events unfold before our own situation becomes as critical, and the sight will be a powerful incentive to avoid going down the same road.

Watching the Intellectual Foundations of the Welfare State Implode

The founders believed that certain aspects of human nature were immutable and that they tightly constrain what is politically and culturally possible. Madison's observation in *The Federalist*, no. 51, that "if men were angels, no government would be necessary" is famous, but the preceding two sentences get more directly to the point: "It may be a reflection on human nature that such devices should be necessary to control the abuses of government. But what is government itself, but the greatest of all reflections on human nature?"[20]

The advocates of the welfare state in both Europe and the United States reject this view, substituting instead the belief that human nature can be changed. The purest expression of optimism about the plasticity of human beings comes from Marxism, which held that, given the right social setting, humans could become selfless and collectivist, making it possible for Marx's goal—from each according to his ability, to each according to his needs—to become a reality in a communist society.[21] The social democrats of the twentieth century who created the modern welfare state did not have the same aggressive agenda that the Soviet Union adopted, but the long-term workability of their creation depended equally on the premise that human beings are plastic. The first operational implication of this premise was that the welfare state could be designed in ways that would lead people not to take advantage of the incentives that the welfare state sets up—for example, generous unemployment benefits would not importantly affect how hard people tried to keep old jobs or how hard they looked for new ones. The second operational implication of this premise was that properly designed government interventions could correct problems of human behavior.

As the welfare state evolved over the twentieth century, two more specific beliefs about the nature of *Homo sapiens* were woven into its fabric. The first of these was the belief that people are equal not just in the way that the American Declaration of Independence meant—equal in the eyes of God and before the law—but equal, or nearly so, in their latent abilities and characteristics. To some extent, this belief

applies to individuals—the idea that all children should aspire to get
a college degree reflects a kind of optimistic view that all children are
naturally smart enough for college if only they get the right kind of
instruction. But the strict interpretation of the equality premise applies to groups of people. In a fair society, it is believed, different
groups of people—men and women, blacks and whites, heterosexuals
and homosexuals, the children of poor people and the children of
rich people—will naturally have the same distributions of outcomes
in life: the same mean income, the same mean educational attainment, the same proportions who become janitors and CEOs, the
same proportions who become English professors and theoretical
physicists, the same proportions who become stand-up comedians
and point guards. When that doesn't happen, it is because of bad
human behavior and an unfair society. For the last forty years, the
premise that significant group differences *cannot* exist has justified
thousands of pages of government regulations and legislation reaching
into everything from the paperwork required to fire someone to the
funding of high school wrestling teams. Everything that we associate
with the phrase "politically correct" eventually comes back to this
premise.

The second of the beliefs about *Homo sapiens* that became an intellectual underpinning of the welfare state is that, at bottom, human
beings are not really responsible for the things they do. People who do
well do not deserve what they have gotten—they got it because they
were born into the right social stratum. Or if they did well despite
being born poor and disadvantaged, it was because the luck of the
draw gave them personal qualities that enabled them to succeed. People who do badly do not deserve it either. They were born into the
wrong social stratum, or were handicapped by personal weaknesses
that were not their fault. Thus it is morally appropriate to require the
economically successful to hand over most of what they have earned
to the state, and it is inappropriate to say of anyone who drifts in and
out of work that he is lazy or irresponsible.

During the next ten or twenty years, I believe that all of these intellectual foundations of the modern welfare state will be discredited
by a tidal change in our scientific understanding of human behavior

that is already under way. The effects of that tidal change will spill over into every crevice of political and cultural life. Harvard's Edward O. Wilson anticipated what is to come in a book titled *Consilience*.[22] As the twenty-first century progresses, he argued, the social sciences are increasingly going to be shaped by the findings of biology—specifically, the findings of the neuroscientists and the geneticists.

What are they finding so far? Nothing surprising. That's the point. For example, science is proving beyond a shadow of a doubt that males and females respond differently to babies for reasons that have nothing to do with the way they were raised.[23] It is not a finding that should surprise anyone, but it is fundamentally at odds with a belief that, in a nonsexist world, men and women will find caring for infants equally rewarding. And so it is with many topics that bear on policy issues. We are still at the beginning of a steep learning curve.

But we do know already that the collapse of these moral pillars of the welfare state must eventually have profound effects on policy. An illustration may serve to make the point. For many years, I have been among those who argue (as I have in this book) that the growth in births to unmarried women has been a social catastrophe. But while those of us who take this position have been able to prove that other family structures *have not* worked as well as the traditional family, no one has been able to prove that alternatives *could not* work as well. And so the social planners keep coming up with the next new ingenious program that will compensate for the absence of fathers.

I am predicting that over the next few decades advances in evolutionary psychology are going to be conjoined with advances in genetic understanding, leading to a scientific consensus that goes something like this: There are genetic reasons, rooted in the mechanisms of human evolution, why little boys who grow up in neighborhoods without married fathers tend to reach adolescence not socialized to the norms of behavior that they will need to stay out of prison and to hold jobs. These same reasons explain why child abuse is, and always will be, concentrated among family structures in which the live-in male is not the married biological father. These same reasons explain why society's attempts to compensate for the lack of married biological fathers don't work and will never work.

There is no reason to be frightened of such knowledge. We will still be able to acknowledge that many single women do a wonderful job of raising their children. Social democrats may be able to design some outside interventions that do some good. But they will have to stop claiming that the traditional family is just one of many equally valid alternatives. They will have to acknowledge that the traditional family plays a special, indispensable role in human flourishing and that social policy must be based on that truth.

The same concrete effects of the new knowledge will make us rethink every domain in which the central government has imposed its judgment about how people ought to live their lives. Here are some more examples of things I think the neuroscientists and geneticists will prove over the next few decades:

- Human beings enjoy themselves when they are exercising their realized capabilities at the limit of those capabilities.
- Challenge and responsibility for consequences is an indispensable part of human motivation to exercise their realized capabilities at the limit of those capabilities.
- People grouped by gender, ethnicity, age, social class, and sexual preference, left free to live their lives as they see fit, will produce group differences in outcomes, because they differ genetically in their cognitive, psychological, and physiological profiles.
- Regardless of whether people have free will, human flourishing requires that they live in an environment in which they are treated as if they did.
- Actually, it turns out that humans *do* have free will in a deep neurological sense.

All of these questions will be answered long before the end of the twenty-first century, and the direction the answers are taking will be evident within the lifetimes of most of us. I have entitled this section "Watching the Intellectual Foundations of the Welfare State Implode" to reflect my confidence that the more we learn about how human beings work at the deepest genetic and neural levels, the more that many age-old ways of thinking about human nature will be vindicated. The institutions surrounding marriage, vocation, community, and faith will be found to be the critical resources through which human beings lead satisfying lives. It will be found that those institutions deteriorate in the advanced welfare states for reasons that are intrinsic to the nature of the welfare state. It will be found that those institutions are richest and most robust in states that allow people to work out their lives on their own and in company with the people around them.

The Increasing Obviousness of an Alternative

It has been muttered by some conservatives since the 1960s: "If we'd just divide up all the money we're spending on poor people and give them the cash, they wouldn't be poor." For most of that period, doing that wasn't really feasible. Now it is.

You may find the calculations and the arguments in *In Our Hands*, a book published in 2006, proposing that the government provide a basic income for all Americans ages 21 and older, to be financed by cashing out all income transfer programs. I wrote then that the projected costs of the current system and my plan for a basic income would cross in 2011, as indeed they did.[24] But the situation in 2011 or over the next few years is not relevant. Rather: At some point over the next decade or two, the finances of the welfare state must become ridiculous to everyone.

To some of us, it was already ridiculous when I wrote *In Our Hands*. The United States is one of the richest countries on earth. Most Americans—the precise percentage will vary depending on one's definition of "enough"—make enough money for themselves and their families that the entire welfare state could be dismantled tomorrow and they would do just fine. And yet in 2002, as I was writing *In Our Hands*, the federal government alone spent about $1.5 trillion in transfer payments, including Social Security, Medicare, and all forms of corporate welfare. The states spent another few hundred billion dollars in transfer payments. And yet we still had millions of people in need.

That's what I mean by ridiculous. How, in a country where most people don't need a penny of income transfers to begin with, can we spend $1.5 trillion on income transfers and still have material want?

Stand back from the day-to-day debates about how we can tweak Social Security here and tweak Medicare there and contemplate how
crazy the current system is. Only a government could spend so much
money so inefficiently.

Readers of different political persuasions can come up with reasons
why the situation in 2002 wasn't as crazy as it looked to me. But
sooner or later, at some budgetary figure, the amount of money we
are spending to achieve easily achievable goals will eventually persuade everyone that using armies of bureaucrats to take trillions of
dollars, spend a lot of it on themselves, give back a lot of it to people
who don't need it, and dole out what remains with all sorts of regulations and favoritism is not reasonable or necessary. Wealthy nations
can accomplish the core goal of the advanced welfare state—the economic wherewithal for people to provide for their basic needs—without the apparatus of the welfare state. Sooner or later, that truth has
to make radical change possible. A question remains—how can support be provided in a way that leaves people responsible for the consequences of their actions?—but that question has an answer, as I try
to persuade my readers in *In Our Hands*.

The Resilience of American Ideals

Finally, thankfully, the United States has a history of confounding
pessimists. Whenever the American project has suffered a wounding
blow or taken a wrong turn that looked as if it might be fatal, things
have eventually worked out, more or less. Can it happen again?

Nobel economist Robert Fogel argued the affirmative in a book titled *The Fourth Great Awakening & the Future of Egalitarianism*
(2000). His thesis drew upon a curious feature of American history.
Since colonial days, America has periodically been swept by religious
movements known as "Great Awakenings." Before Fogel, historians
agreed that there were three of them, each characterized by powerful
preachers, revivalism, and evangelical enthusiasm. The first began in
the mid-1720s and reached its apex in the late 1730s. The second
began around 1800 and lasted until 1840. The beginning of the Third

Great Awakening is dated variously from the 1860s to 1890 and continued into the early 1900s.

Each of the first three Great Awakenings had a political aftermath, Fogel argued, "a phase in which the new ethics precipitates powerful political programs and movements."[25] The First Great Awakening set the stage for the American Revolution. The Second Great Awakening was instrumental in the spread of the temperance movement, compulsory elementary education, abolitionism, and the beginning of the women's suffrage movement. The Third Great Awakening laid the ethical basis for the reforms of the New Deal and, later, the civil rights movement.

Fogel then made a case that the United States experienced a Fourth Great Awakening beginning around 1960 and continuing through the time that Fogel was writing his book in the late 1990s. Even as the mainline denominations began to lose membership in the 1960s, the growth of "enthusiastic religion"—people who believed in the doctrines of born-again Christianity—increased. Adding in members of mainline churches and the Roman Catholic Church who share the beliefs of the evangelical Christian churches, Fogel put the adherents of enthusiastic religion at about 60 million people at the end of the 1980s, representing a third of the electorate.[26] Fogel saw the early political phase of the Fourth Great Awakening in the right-to-life movement, the tax revolts of the 1970s, and the criticism of the media in the 1980s.

The eventual result will not be a straight-line extrapolation of the agenda of the Christian Coalition or any other specifically religious influence, in Fogel's view, but the emergence of a "postmodern egalitarian agenda," as the new century sees "two mighty camps of egalitarians . . . arrayed against each other"—the political disciples of the Third Great Awakening and those of the Fourth Great Awakening. The new egalitarian agenda cannot be based on the social and economic goals of the welfare state (the product of the Third Great Awakening), Fogel argued, because in large part those goals have been achieved. Poverty no longer has the resonance it had in the first half of the twentieth century. He continued:

Now, at the dawn of the new millennium, it is necessary to
address such postmodern concerns as the struggle for self-
realization, the desire to find a deeper meaning in life than the
endless accumulation of consumer durables and the pursuit of
pleasure. . . . Unlike the reform agenda of the Third Great
Awakening, that of the Fourth emphasizes the spiritual needs of
life in a country where even the poor are materially rich by the
standards prevailing a century ago and where many of those who
are materially rich are spiritually deprived.[27]

Fogel characterized the political agenda of the Fourth Great Awakening as an attempt to reinstate the principle of equality of opportunity versus the continuing attempt of the disciples of the Third Great
Awakening to extend the principle of equality of condition.

What struck me forcibly is Fogel's confidence that the postmodern
egalitarian agenda is not the exclusive property of political conservatives, just as the agenda of the Third Great Awakening was not the
exclusive property of political liberals. In both cases, the power of the
movement transcended partisan politics. I see the same transcen-
dence with regard to many of the issues raised in this book. My evidence is anecdotal. I have friends of various political persuasions who
are part of the new upper class. When we discuss issues such as the
increasing isolation of our children from the rest of America, I hear
from all sides that this has already been worrying them. When I talk
about these issues with students in elite colleges who are the offspring of families affluent for two or three generations, the charge
that they are disconnected from the rest of America is something
they are willing to take seriously.

On the other side of the class divide, my family has lived for more
than twenty years in a blue-collar and agricultural region of Maryland
where all the problems of Fishtown have been visibly increasing. Politically, our neighbors span the range. But there remains a core of civic
virtue and involvement that could make headway against those problems if the people who are trying to do the right things get the rein-
forcement they need—not in the form of government assistance, but
in validation of the values and standards they continue to uphold.

It is my impression—I do not claim any more systematic evidence—that people across the political spectrum are ready to respond quickly and positively as soon as the issues raised in this book are acknowledged. A large part of the problem consists of nothing more complicated than our unwillingness to say out loud what we believe. A great many people, especially in the new upper class, just need to start preaching what they practice.

And so I am hoping for a civic Great Awakening among the new upper class. It starts with a question that I hope they will take to heart: How much do you value what has made America exceptional, and what are you willing to do to preserve it?

As I have remarked throughout the book, American exceptionalism is not just something that Americans claim for themselves. Historically, Americans have been different as a people, even peculiar, and everyone around the world has recognized it. I am thinking of qualities such as American industriousness and neighborliness discussed in earlier chapters, but also American optimism even when there doesn't seem to be any good reason for it, our striking lack of class envy, and the assumption by most Americans that they are in control of their own destinies. Finally, there is the most lovable of exceptional American qualities: our tradition of insisting that we are part of the middle class, even if we aren't, and of interacting with our fellow citizens as if we were all middle class.

The exceptionalism has not been a figment of anyone's imagination, and it has been wonderful. But nothing in the water has made us that way. We have been the product of the cultural capital bequeathed to us by the system the founders laid down: a system that says people must be free to live life as they see fit and to be responsible for the consequences of their actions; that it is not the government's job to protect people from themselves; that it is not the government's job to stage-manage how people interact with one another. Discard the system that created the cultural capital, and the qualities we have loved about Americans will go away.

In addition to preaching what they practice, America's new upper class must take a close look at the way they are living their lives, ask whether those lives are impoverished in some of the ways that Fogel describes, and then think about ways to change. I am not suggesting that people in the new upper class should sacrifice their self-interest. I just want to accelerate a rediscovery of what that self-interest is. Age-old human wisdom has understood that a life well lived requires engagement with those around us. A civic Great Awakening among the new upper class can arise in part from the renewed understanding that it can be pleasant to lead a glossy life, but it is ultimately more rewarding—and more fun—to lead a textured life, and to be in the midst of others who are leading textured lives.

What it comes down to is that America's new upper class must once again fall in love with what makes America different. The drift away from those qualities can be slowed by piecemeal victories on specific items of legislation or victories on specific Supreme Court cases, but only slowed. It is going to be stopped only when we are all talking again about why America is exceptional and why it is so important that America remain exceptional. That requires once again seeing the American project for what it has been: a different way for people to live together, unique among the nations of the earth, and immeasurably precious.

Acknowledgments

Coming Apart is the final expression of thoughts that were planted by my experiences in the villages of northeast Thailand in the 1960s. They germinated through the 1970s as I evaluated American social programs to help the disadvantaged. Then in 1980, events in my personal life led me to reflect on how little success and money have to do with happiness. That prosaic insight, combined with my evolving ideas about government, made me decide to write a book about the relationship of happiness to public policy.

It turned out that I couldn't jump right into that topic. Losing Ground, published in 1984, looked to its readers like a stand-alone book. To me, it was the underbrush that had to be cleared away before I could write the book that I had originally intended. That book, titled In Pursuit: Of Happiness and Good Government, was published in 1988. I am sure all authors have a favorite among the books they write. In Pursuit has remained mine.

The content of In Pursuit has been a backdrop to most of what I have written since. Its influence on the last two chapters of The Bell Curve is obvious. In Pursuit's themes are threaded throughout What It Means to Be a Libertarian. The Aristotelian Principle that figured prominently in part 2 of *In Pursuit* frames part 4 of *Human Accomplishment* and lies behind the argument of *Real Education*. My advocacy of a guaranteed minimum income in *In Our Hands* is explained in terms of the pursuit of happiness. Twenty-three years after *In Pursuit* appeared, I remain devoted to its central policy thesis: The framework created by the American founders, stripped of its acceptance of slavery, is the best possible way to enable people of all kinds to pursue happiness.

I have been aware from the outset that *Coming Apart* would be my valedictory on the topic of happiness and public policy, and have also recognized the possibility that it would be my valedictory, period—I am sixty-eight as I write this, and nothing is promised. Since so much that I was writing grew from thoughts and themes that have evolved for the last forty-five years, I began to take pleasure in embedding bits and pieces of earlier writings—a phrase here, a trope there, sometimes whole sentences—wondering if anyone but me would ever notice.

I will give away a few important examples here. The prologue of *Coming Apart* uses the same literary device that opened *Losing Ground*, and a few of its sentences echo sentences in *Losing Ground*. The discussion of the foundations of the new upper class in chapter 2 draws heavily on the analysis I wrote with Richard J. Herrnstein in *The Bell Curve*. I came across Toynbee's "Schism in the Soul" because of work I was doing for *Human Accomplishment*, and my discussion of it in chapter 17 draws directly from an article I wrote about it for the *Wall Street Journal*. The Europe Syndrome was first described in *In Our Hands*. The conclusion of chapter 17 draws from the Irving Kristol lecture "The Happiness of the People," which I delivered while writing *Coming Apart*. Most obviously, the discussion of the stuff of life in chapter 15 and the application of that material to an argument for limited government in chapter 17 draw from *In Pursuit*. To some, all this may seem to be a form of plagiarism. I prefer to think of it as requiring me to make my first acknowledgment to the bright ideas of my younger self.

Bill Bennett deserves a special acknowledgment. We had decided to write a book together and prepared a proposal on the same broad topic as *Coming Apart*. At the last minute—and I do mean the last minute—I realized that the book I wanted to write would be such a personal statement that I couldn't collaborate with anyone, not even someone as simpatico as Bill. He didn't let my abrupt about-face damage our friendship, and generously told me to go ahead and write the book on my own.

I asked a variety of scholars to review portions of *Coming Apart* that either referenced them or dealt with matters on which they were expert. I will not name most of them. Being included in my acknowledgments can cause trouble for people in academia. This has led a few of them to make a public show of denouncing their acknowledgment lest their colleagues think they agree with anything I have written. But I nonetheless want to thank, even if anonymously, those who responded to my queries. I can safely thank by name colleagues who are also friends: Tom Bouchard, Arthur Brooks, John Dilulio, Greg Duncan, Earl Hunt, Irwin Stelzer, and James Q. Wilson. Thanks go as well to my guides to Fishtown: Mike DiBerardini, Chuck Valentine, and especially Ken Milano.

Karlyn Bowman, who directs the American Enterprise Institute's Social Processes Group, gave me unstinting support, moral and material, throughout the project. Andrew Rugg provided prompt and efficient logistic support. Many AEI staff members responded to my request to take a draft version of the quiz in chapter 4, and greatly improved the revised version through their comments.

Thanks once again—how many times does this make in the last quarter century?—to Amanda Urban, the Platonic ideal of the literary agent. Sean Desmond provided seasoned editorial guidance and was uncomplainingly patient when the schedule slipped. Maureen Clark was an amazingly meticulous copyeditor. Catherine wielded her red pen lovingly but unsparingly.

Charles Murray
Burkittsville, Maryland
July 18, 2011

Appendix A

Data Sources and Presentation

Data Sources

The 1960 Census and 1968–2010 Current Population Survey (CPS)

The main source for marital and employment data is a data series that starts with a 1 percent sample of the decennial census for 1960 and continues from 1968 through 2010 using the March editions of the CPS. The CPS surveys for 1961 through 1967 are not used because the coding for occupations in those years was inadequate to identify who met the Belmont and Fishtown occupational criteria.

The 1960 census sample for persons ages 18–65 was 986,917, of whom 402,889 were whites ages 30–49 (the primary sample for analysis). Annual sample sizes for the CPS for persons ages 18–65 from 1968 through 2010 ranged from 130,124 to 209,802, with the samples of whites ages 30–49 ranging from 22,345 to 48,134.

Both the census data and the CPS data are available online through IPUMS (Integrated Public Use Microdata Series), managed by the Minnesota Population Center, which is always cited as the source for the census and CPS data in the graphs. The URL for IPUMS is http://cps.ipums.org/cps/.

General Social Survey (GSS)

The GSS has been conducted since 1972 by the National Opinion Research Center at the University of Chicago. Available online, the GSS surveys include a wide variety of demographic, behavioral, and attitudinal questions, including many that have been asked identically for all of the surveys. It is the most widely used American attitudinal database.

Sample sizes for the GSS are much smaller than for the CPS. From 1972 through 1993, the entire sample ranged from 1,372 to 1,860. From 1994 through 2008, it ranged from 2,023 to 2,992, with a special augmented sample of 4,510 in 2006. The number of whites ages 30–49 has ranged from 413 to 1,176. The URL for the GSS is http://www.norc.org/GSS+Website/.

Vital Statistics, National Center for Health Statistics (NCHS)

The NCHS collects data on all births in the United States. For the analyses of out-of-wedlock births in chapter 8, I used random samples of 200,000 cases drawn from every other year. The URL for the Vital Statistics system at NCHS is http://www.cdc.gov/nchs/nvss.htm.

Zip Code and Census Tract Data

For the zip code analyses of the 2000 decennial census, I employed the American FactFinder tool provided on the website of the Bureau of the Census. This resource enables anyone to download census data broken down by zip code (or many other aggregations). As I write, the Census Bureau is in transition from an old to a new version of American FactFinder, but you can easily find it on the Census Bureau's main web page, http://www.census.gov/. For locating the geographic borders of zip codes, I used hipcodes.com, supplemented by Google Maps.

For the 1960 data on census tracts, I used the PDFs of the 1960 census volumes, available on the Bureau of the Census website, and the ASCII files for the 1960 census available from the Interuniversity

Consortium for Political and Social Research (ICPSR). The ICPSR's URL is http://www.icpsr.umich.edu/icpsrweb/ICPSR/.

The day after submitting the draft of *Coming Apart*, I was shown the Social Explorer website, which I recommend to all other scholars who want to do this kind of analysis, and which would have saved me weeks of work. Its URL is http://www.socialexplorer.com/pub/home/home.aspx

National Longitudinal Surveys (NLS)

The NLS comprise a family of surveys sponsored by the Bureau of Labor Statistics and conducted by the Center for Human Resource Research at Ohio State University. For constructing the trendline for children still living with both biological parents when the mother was age 40, I integrated data from the Young Women sample (initial sample size was 5,159) and the Mature Women sample (initial sample was 5,083), both of which were followed from 1968 to 2003, and the Fertility sample of the 1979 cohort of the National Longitudinal Survey of Youth (initial sample size was 6,283), which is still being followed as I write in 2011. All of the surveys are available online. The NLS's URL is https://www.nlsinfo.org/.

The Uniform Crime Reports (UCR)

The UCR is an ongoing compilation of national offense and arrest statistics conducted by the Federal Bureau of Investigation and published annually since 1935. Data for the years from 1995 onward are available online. The UCR's URL is http://www.fbi.gov/about-us/cjis/ucr/ucr.

Surveys of Inmates in State and Federal Correctional Facilities

Inmate surveys, designed by the Bureau of Justice Statistics and conducted by the Bureau of the Census, have been conducted in 1974 (state), 1979 (state), 1986 (state), 1991 (federal), 1997 (state and federal), and 2004 (state and federal). The samples of males used in the analysis were 8,741 in 1974, 9,142 in 1979, 11,556 in 1986, 11,163 in 1991, 14,530 in 1997, and 11,569 in 2004. The surveys are available online at http://www.icpsr.umich.edu/icpsrweb/ICPSR/.

Conventions for the Presentation of Graphics

As noted in chapter 8, the vertical axis in a graph is based on the minimum and maximum values of the variables being plotted in a given graph, with a minimum range of 20 percentage points.

The smoothed curve that runs through the actual data points on each graph using the CPS serves the same purpose as a moving average, to give a visual sense of the overall trend. They are created by a procedure known as "locally weighted scatterplot smoothing," originated by W. S. Cleveland in 1979 and abbreviated as *LOESS* or *LOWESS*.[1] In an ordinary moving average, the smoothed value is the mean of however many data points are specified. In a LOESS plot, the smoothed value is calculated by giving the most weight to the adjacent points in the data and less weight to distant ones (or no weight, depending on the bandwidth that the analyst has specified).

For the CPS data, LOESS serves the cosmetic purpose of smoothing the annual data. For the GSS, with its much smaller sample sizes, LOESS serves a more important function of maximizing the available information, producing trendlines that are more confidently interpretable than ordinary least squares (OLS) regression trendlines or moving averages. I follow the procedure used by Claude Fischer and Michael Hout in *Century of Difference*. It has three steps, as summarized by Fischer and Hout in their appendix A, which describes the procedure in detail:

1. Obtain a LOESS fit for the general trend (without regard to subpopulations or covariates).
2. Generate a new variable that assigns the LOESS fitted values to each time point.
3. Enter the trend variable (per step 2), interesting covariates, and

terms for the interaction between natural time (not recoded) and the covariates into a multivariate parametric regression.[2]

In graphs using GSS data, I do not show the survey-by-survey data points. The sample sizes are too small, especially for Belmont, to produce reliable estimates for a given survey.

ONE FINAL NOTE on presentation: In *Coming Apart*, I continue to treat singular third-person pronouns according to a rule I have been unsuccessfully advocating for more than a quarter of a century: Absent a reason to do otherwise, use the gender of the author or, in a coauthored book, the gender of the principal author.

Appendix B

Supplemental Material for the Segregation Chapter

The 2000 Census

Decennial census data by zip code for the 2000 census were downloaded using the American FactFinder tool on the Census Bureau's website. Zip codes for Puerto Rico, the Virgin Islands, and military installations were deleted, leaving data for 31,720 zip codes.

Calculation of the Zip Code Centile Scores

The centile score is based on the sum of standardized scores for a zip code's percentage of adults with college educations and its median family income, weighted by population. This would be a simple matter of creating standardized scores and weighting the sum of those scores by population, except for a complication: The centile was to represent where individuals within a zip code fit within the national population of individuals, not where the zip code as a whole fit within the national set of zip codes.

Standardized Scores

Standardized scores provide a way to compare apples and oranges. For example, suppose you want to know who is taller relative to their reference groups: a 5'4" female gymnast or a 6'10" player in the National Basketball Association. You need to place the gymnast and the basketball player in the distribution of heights of their respective groups. The way you do that is by a simple arithmetic formula, $z = (X - M)/S$, where z is the standardized score, X is the value for the individual, M is the mean of the group, and S is the standard deviation of the group. Wikipedia has a straightforward explanation of what a standard deviation is.

The creation of the zip code index variable, *centile*, began with a Stata database with a line for each zip code. The variables in the database were the percentage of persons in the zip code with a BA *(pbabin)*, the median family income of persons in that zip *(medianinc)* in thousands of 2010 dollars, and the population ages 25 and older in that zip code *(pop25)*.

The database of the nation's zip codes was expanded by a tenth of the size of the population ages 25 and older using Stata's EXPAND command (so that, for example, a zip code with 1,000 persons ages 25 and older had 100 lines in the expanded database), resulting in a database of 18,216,898 lines. Each of these lines included the two indicators in the index, *pbabin* and *medianinc*, for the zip code in which the individual lived. Standardized scores were computed for both indicators. The index is the sum of the two standardized scores. The RANK function in Stata calculated ranks from low to high, with the highest ranks signifying the highest combined levels of education and income in that census tract. Thus the centile score consists of the rank of the index score divided by the total sample of the population ages 25 and older, then multiplied by 100 so that it ranges from 0 to 99.

I prepared two versions of centile score, one of which used the actual median income and the other of which used the logged value of median income, which reduces the value of extremely high medians.

An examination of the two versions, which had a correlation of 0.998, revealed that the version using actual median income gave greater weight to education than to minor changes in income for zip codes that were in the bottom half of the distribution, which seemed to me to be a more realistic representation of the relative importance of the two at low levels of both. Given the focus of the book, the more important question was whether the two versions had importantly different scores at the top. They did not. With only a few exceptions, the two versions of *centile* were within less than 2 percentage points of each other. I chose to use the version using actual median income, which gave more interpretable results at the low end.

The SuperZips consist of all zip codes with centile scores of 95 or higher.

Linking Zip Codes with the Political Ideology of the Congressional Representative

The database I employed to link congressional districts with zip codes was the Congressional District Database sold by zipinfo.com. Zip codes that fell into more than one district were assigned to the district that contained a majority of the zip+4 codings, which take the breakdown of zip codes to the block level.

As the measure of the political orientation of a congressional district, I averaged the liberal quotient calculated annually by the Americans for Democratic Action (ADA) for each congressperson for the 108th through 111th Congresses (those elected in 2002, 2004, 2006, and 2008). I used the ratings for only one year of each Congress (2004, 2005, 2007, and 2009), since the correlation within the two years of a Congress is close to perfect.

Census Tracts in the 1960 Census

Census tract data for the 1960 census were taken from the Elizabeth Mullen Bogue file (hereafter "Bogue"), available from the ICPSR. The data comprised 175 metropolitan areas that included 104,010,696 people out of the total resident population (all ages) in the 1960 census of 179,323,175. The population not included in the database was exclusively rural or lived in towns that were not part of metropolitan areas.

The Bogue file does not include the Census Bureau's calculation of median income, but I was able to replicate the census values through the standard formula for computing medians from grouped income, *median* = $l + h((n/2 - cf)/f)$, where l is the lower limit of the median class (the interval within which the median must lie), n is the total number of cases, cf is the cumulative number of cases in intervals prior to the median class, f is the number of cases in the median class, and h is the width of the median class (e.g., if the median class represents people with incomes of $5,000–$5,999, the width is 1,000).

For the twenty-three census tracts with a median income higher than the top code of $25,000, the census reports simply "$25,000+." Using the 1 percent sample of the 1960 census provided through IPUMS, I knew that if the distribution of incomes beyond $25,000 followed the same logarithmic trend as exhibited for incomes of $15,000–$24,999, I could expect half of those above $25,000 to make $28,000 or less. But I also knew that the number of those with incomes greater than $25,000 was almost three times as large as we would have predicted knowing the distribution from $15,000 through $24,999. I used $50,000 as my estimate of the point at which half of the $25,000+ population would be reached. This is probably too high, but it is better to err on the high side (given the thrust of my argument, which stresses the separation of the new upper class in 2000, compared to the high-income population in 1960).

The Alumni Sample

The elite schools keep careful track of their alumni for fund-raising purposes, which means that their periodic anniversary reports and alumni directories have close to 100 percent data on the whereabouts of their living alumni. Using the anniversary report of my own

Harvard class (1965) and volumes provided by friends and colleagues, I recorded the zip codes of the home addresses for alumni from Harvard, Princeton, Yale, and Wesleyan in the following classes and years to which the home zip codes apply:

Harvard/Radcliffe. Classes/zip code years: 1965/1990, 1968/1993, 1990/2010

Princeton. Classes: 1980, 1981, 1982, 1985, 1987, 1989, 1990, 1991; zip code year: 2009

Yale. Classes/zip code years: 1964/1989, 1970/2000, 1979/2004

Wesleyan. Classes: randomly selected graduates from 1970 to 1979; zip code year: 1996

For persons who were at a typical age for college graduation, 22, the zip codes apply to their home residence at the ages of 40–52 for the HPY sample and 39–48 for the Wesleyan sample.

Table B.1 shows the sample sizes, and centile means and standard deviations by school.

TABLE B.1. **BASIC STATISTICS FOR THE ALUMNI ZIP CODE SAMPLES**

| School | N | Centile scores | |
		Mean	Standard deviation
Harvard	3,499	84.0	21.2
Princeton	8,049	84.7	20.9
Yale	2,769	82.8	21.3
Wesleyan	1,588	79.9	22.4
Total	**15,905**	**83.7**	**21.2**

The mean centile scores of the zip codes for the three iconic schools were remarkably close, and Wesleyan wasn't far behind. The overall percentage of HPY graduates living in SuperZips was 43.6, with Yale having a slightly lower percentage of 40.9 compared to 43.9 percent for Harvard and 44.4 percent for Princeton. The higher percentages for Harvard and Princeton are plausibly attributable to a hometown effect—the Boston area was more attractive to Harvard graduates, and the Princeton area to Princeton graduates, than the New Haven area was to Yale graduates. Since the zip codes of Cambridge westward from Boston, and the zip codes surrounding Princeton, are dense with SuperZips, this tendency to stay near their college gave an upward push to the overall mean for Harvard and Princeton that Yale did not share. The proportion of Wesleyan graduates living in Super-Zips was 31.5 percent.

Appendix C

Supplemental Material for the Chapter on Belmont and Fishtown

How Subjects Were Assigned to Belmont or Fishtown

The Occupations Qualifying for Belmont and Fishtown

The definition of occupations is based on the 1990 occupational classification system of the Bureau of Labor Statistics. The IPUMS census and CPS databases both include a consistent variable across time based on the 1990 classification. For the GSS and NLS databases, I converted the 1960, 1970, 1980, and 2000 classifications to the 1990 coding.

Occupations were then classified into eight categories, shown below with examples of the occupations that fall within them.

1. *High-status professions and symbolic-analyst occupations* (physicians, attorneys, architects, engineers, university faculty, scientists, and content-production occupations in television, film, publishing, and the news media)
2. *Managerial positions* (in business, government, education, foundations, nonprofits, and service organizations)

3. *Mid-level white-collar positions* (e.g., underwriters, buyers, agents, inspectors, real estate sales, advertising sales, human resources specialists)

4. *High-skill technical occupations* (e.g., K–12 teachers, police, nurses, pharmacists, physical therapists, technicians in the sciences and engineering)

5. *The blue-collar professions* (e.g., farm owners and managers, electricians, plumbers, tool and die makers, machinists, cabinet-makers)[1]

6. *Other skilled blue-collar occupations* (e.g., mechanics, heavy-equipment operators, repairers, cooks, welders, paperhangers, glaziers, oil drillers)

7. *Low-level white-collar occupations* (e.g., file clerks, typists, mail and paper handlers, bank tellers, receptionists)

8. *Low-skill service and blue-collar occupations* (e.g., cashiers, security guards, kitchen workers, hospital orderlies, porters, parking lot attendants, drivers, construction laborers)

The Belmont occupations consist of those in categories 1 and 2. The Fishtown occupations consist of those in categories 5 through 8.

The Assignment Rules

The socioeconomic status (SES) of an unmarried adult living alone is determined by that person's education, occupation, and income. For adults who are part of a married couple, the situation is more complicated.

In 1960, SES was almost always determined by the status of the husband both because of custom and because so few married women had a job in a higher-status occupation than the husband's. Both factors changed over time, reflected in the designation of "head of household" in the Current Population Survey. The wife was designated as the head of household for only 1 percent of married couples in the 1960 census. By 2010, women were designated as the head of household for 42 percent of married couples in the CPS.

What then is the SES of a couple in which the husband works on an assembly line and the wife is manager of the company's payroll department? No answer works for all cases, but I chose to assign people who are part of a married couple to Belmont or Fishtown based on the person who has the higher-ranking occupation, with "higher" based on the order of the eight occupational categories listed above. If only one spouse has an occupation, assignment is based on the person with an occupation. If both spouses have a Belmont occupation or both have a Fishtown occupation, I used the educational data for the spouse with the higher level of education.[2] *These criteria also define "head of household" as I use the phrase in the text.*

Within the framework described above, persons were assigned to Belmont or Fishtown according to the following decision rules:

Unmarried heads of households with occupations:

- Assign to Belmont if educational attainment is a college degree or higher and the person is in a Belmont occupation.
- Assign to Fishtown if educational attainment is no more than a high school diploma and the person is in a Fishtown occupation.

Unmarried heads of household without known occupations:

- Assign to Fishtown if educational attainment is no more than a high school diploma.[3]

Married persons with occupations:

- Assign to Belmont if at least one spouse is in a Belmont occupation and the educational attainment of that person is a college degree or higher.
- Assign to Fishtown if both spouses are in Fishtown occupations and neither has more than a high school diploma.
- Assign to Fishtown if one spouse is in a Fishtown occupation, the other has no occupation, and the spouse with an occupation has no more than a high school diploma.

Married persons without known occupations:

- Assign to Fishtown if both spouses have no more than a high school diploma.[4]

Persons ages 21 and older living in a household in which they are neither the head of household nor the spouse:

- Assign to Fishtown or Belmont based on their own occupation and education.[5]

With regard to the last category, adults who are neither the head of household nor the spouse, I again did not have the option of choosing a perfect rule. A twenty-three-year-old who is living with his affluent parents probably still enjoys their socioeconomic status even if he is working as a bartender. But the rule becomes more consistently appropriate when dealing with persons ages 30–49, as almost all of the analyses in part 2 do. The older you get, the more your status depends on your own education and job, no matter with whom you live.

For a few tabulations, I needed to classify persons under the age of 21 who were neither the head of household nor the spouse. They were assigned to a neighborhood based on the occupation and education of the head of household.[6]

Why Wasn't Income Used in Assigning People to Neighborhoods?

The three standard components of socioeconomic status are occupation, educational attainment, and income, and yet I created the neighborhoods without using income as a criterion. The reason is that including income in the definition of a neighborhood exaggerates tendencies that already exist. For example, if I require that everyone in Fishtown have a family income in the bottom quintile, I guarantee that Fishtown has a high percentage of single-parent homes (not all people with low incomes are single parents, but single parents disproportionately have low family incomes). If I require that everyone in Belmont have an income in the top 20 percent, I guarantee that almost every head of household is in the labor force (few households have high family income without the head of household being in the labor force).

By not using income, the people in Fishtown can include the blue-collar couple who both work and have a combined income of $90,000. The people in Belmont can include the divorced mother with a PhD on a college faculty who has a modest income because she is working only half time. Using an income criterion would have excluded both kinds of people. Some degree of artifact is unavoidable even using just education and occupation, because education and occupation are related to income. But omitting income reduces the artifact.

Taking the Changing Composition of Belmont and Fishtown into Account

Trendlines running from 1960 to 2010 have to consider a major technical issue: The compositions of Belmont and Fishtown presumably changed.

The Shifting Ground of Social Class

The national numbers on the variables used to assign people to Belmont and Fishtown shifted radically from 1960 to 2010. Figure C.1 shows the situation with regard to education.

The proportion of prime-age whites without a high school diploma dropped from one out of two to one out of twenty-five. The proportion with a college degree grew from one out of ten to one out of three. It has to be assumed that high school dropouts in 1960 consisted of a pool that was very different from the pool of high school dropouts in 2010, and that the same is true of the pool of college graduates.

FIGURE C.1.   **CHANGES IN EDUCATIONAL ATTAINMENT**

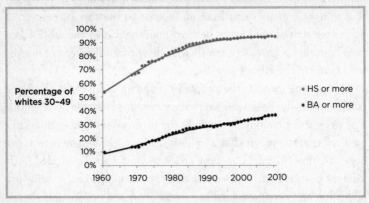

Source: IPUMS. Sample limited to whites ages 30–49.

FIGURE C.2.   **CHANGES IN THE PREVALENCE OF TWO BASIC JOB CATEGORIES**

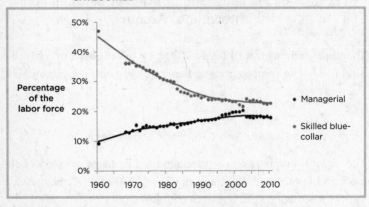

Source: IPUMS. Sample limited to whites ages 30–49 in the labor force.

The same thing happened with occupations. Figure C.2 illustrates this through two basic job categories: managerial jobs and skilled blue-collar jobs (categories 5 and 6 combined).

In 1960, 47 percent of prime-age white American workers were working at blue-collar jobs. By 2010, that proportion had been halved to 23 percent. Meanwhile, managerial jobs went from only 9 percent of the workforce to 18 percent.

The result is that the distribution of prime-age whites into the two neighborhoods also changed drastically from 1960 through 2010, as shown in figure C.3:

FIGURE C.3.   THE CHANGING BALANCE OF THE TWO NEIGHBORHOODS

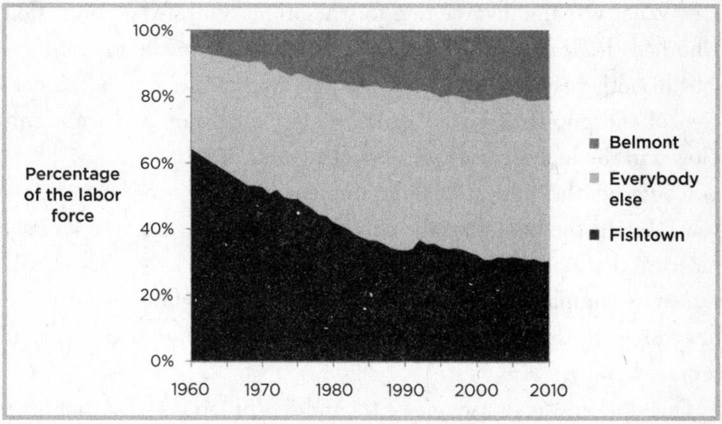

Source: IPUMS. Sample limited to whites ages 30–49.

In 1960, 64 percent of prime-age white Americans qualified for Fishtown, a number that had fallen to 30 percent by 2009. In 1960, only 6 percent of prime-age white Americans qualified for Belmont, a number that had risen to 21 percent by 2010.

This raises a question: Isn't it possible that Fishtown didn't really deteriorate at all? The hypothesis is that behavior in Fishtown changed from 1960 through 2010 because the composition of the neighborhood changed. In effect, more than half of the people in Fishtown in 1960 had moved out by 2010. Which people left Fishtown? Presumably those with the most ability to move up in the world. The cream was skimmed from Fishtown. A similar artifact might be working in Belmont, which more than tripled as a proportion of the population between 1960 and 2010. Perhaps changes in Belmont merely reflect a dilution of the quality of its population, as people who formerly wouldn't have completed college or entered the professions moved in.

Creation of the Top 20 Percent and Bottom 30 Percent

These hypotheses are likely to explain something, so we need a constant yardstick based on the proportions of people in Belmont and Fishtown as of 2010—in round numbers, 20 percent and 30 percent, respectively. For example, suppose we are looking at divorce, a trend-line that begins in 1960 and ends in 2010. The questions to be asked are "What was the divorce rate for the 30 percent of the population who had the least education and were employed in the lowest-level jobs in both years?" and "What was the divorce rate for the 20 percent of the population who had the most education and were employed in the highest-level jobs in both years?"

Choosing the educational attainment measure was straightforward. I used the highest grade completed. Choosing an occupational measure that ranks occupations from "lowest-level" to "highest-level" was more complicated. The eight occupational categories listed at the beginning of this appendix are too broad. A continuous scale is required.

One option was to use one of the indexes of job prestige that have been created over the years, based on the answers that social scientists get when they ask large samples of people to say which of two occupations has more prestige in their eyes. With enough people making enough comparisons, it is possible to combine the results into a continuous scale. I used one of the best of those scales, created by Keiko Nakao and Judith Treas, for analyses conducted early in the research for this book.[7] But it was ultimately unsatisfying. The orderings even in the best indexes often don't pass the face-validity test— we don't look at them and say, "Yes, that makes sense." On the Nakao-Treas scale, for example, a sociology teacher has higher prestige than a judge, a math instructor has higher prestige than a chief executive, an air traffic controller has higher prestige than an electrical engineer, and a registered nurse has higher prestige than a space scientist. Actors and professional athletes—people who are idolized in our celebrity culture—have lower occupational prestige than all of the above. Any scale of occupational prestige is riddled with such examples. Robert Hauser and John Warren, creators of another major occupational prestige index, reviewed the evidence for measures of occupational prestige and concluded that the educational level required for an occupation was a more useful indicator than composite measures of occupational prestige and that "the global concept of occupational status is scientifically obsolete."[8]

But sticking with the educational level required for occupations is not much help for discriminating among the people who held a large variety of blue-collar occupations in 1960. The number of years of formal K–12 education required to be a carpenter and a menial laborer are probably about the same—many stevedores and highly skilled carpenters in 1960 had identical levels of education, having dropped out of school as soon as the law allowed—but the cognitive demands of the two jobs are quite different. Of those who were carpenters and stevedores in 1960, we would expect that the proportion of carpenters who had the capacity to move into technical or white-collar occupations was higher than the proportion of stevedores who had the capacity to do so.

To use information about a person's occupation for assigning him to the top 20 percent or bottom 30 percent, I adapted the work of psychometricians Earl Hunt and Tara Madhyastha, who used the Department of Labor's O*NET ratings to assign cognitive requirements to the entire range of jobs.[9] The O*NET database in the years used for the analysis contained ratings by the incumbents of jobs of the skills required for 801 jobs, using anchored questions. For example, for the characteristic "arm-hand steadiness," the incumbent was asked to rate the requirements for that job on a 1–7 scale in which 2 was "light a candle" and 6 was "cut facets in a diamond." Hunt and Madhyastha focused on twenty cognitive demands covering verbal abilities, idea generation, reasoning abilities, quantitative abilities, memory, perceptual abilities, spatial abilities, and attentiveness. A factor analysis of these twenty cognitive demands produced the generic result that has characterized factor analyses of batteries of mental measures for a century: The first factor, representing the general mental factor known as *g*, dominated the results. I used the factor loading for each occupation—its "*g*-loading," expressed in the IQ metric, with a mean of 100 and a standard deviation of 15—as the measure of the cognitive demands of that occupation.[10]

Why is a measure of the cognitive demands of a job useful for discriminating among blue-collar jobs? Because it has been determined that cognitive ability affects job productivity throughout the range of jobs, from nuclear physicist to janitor.[11] This doesn't negate the importance of small-motor skills in being, say, a carpenter, but being an outstanding carpenter also requires good visual-spatial skills, which are part of what IQ tests measure, and also the problem-solving abilities that are part of what IQ tests measure.

The results using the cognitive demands of a job have a few anomalies of their own—are the cognitive demands of being a veterinarian really higher (if only slightly) than those of being a physician, as the *g*-loadings of the two jobs say? There are also problems produced by the way that the 1990 Census Bureau job categories are defined— directors and producers are in the same occupational category as actors, even though the skill sets required by those jobs are different. But the orderings work reasonably well, especially for the blue-collar jobs that are most important for understanding whether Fishtown was subject to a creaming effect.[12]

The index for ranking people from high to low on this combination of education and occupation was created as follows:

Educational attainment. Educational attainment was expressed as the standardized score for highest grade completed, based on the mean and standard deviation of whites ages 30–49 in the year in question.

Cognitive demands of an occupation. A standardized score based on the *g*-loadings was computed for the distribution of occupations among whites ages 30–49 who had occupations in the year in question.

The standardized scores for educational attainment and cognitive demands of the occupation were combined. For persons without an occupation, the standardized score for educational attainment was doubled. The combined scores were rank-ordered, from lowest to highest. These were the assignment rules:

Head of household or spouse:

- Assign to the top 20 percent or bottom 30 percent based on the educational attainment and occupation of the head of household.

Persons who are neither the head of household nor the spouse:

- Assign to the top 20 percent or bottom 30 percent based on their own educational attainment and occupation.

Because of its large and nationally representative samples, the CPS was used as the template for determining the cutoffs for the top 20 percent and bottom 30 percent when other databases were used. That is, the means and standard deviations for educational attainment and cognitive demands of the CPS sample were applied to the data from other databases that were smaller or with less representative samples. For the GSS, with its comparatively small sample sizes, I did not use a single year in determining cutoffs. I combined the four surveys from 1972 through 1975 to use as the opening baseline and all four surveys from 2004 through 2010 as the closing baseline.

The exercise created a shadow population for Fishtown in the opening year of a data series that plausibly represents the people who would have remained in Fishtown even in 2010. Take 1960, the opening year I use whenever I can, as an example. The bottom 30 percent was an amazingly badly educated group of people by today's standards. Fifty-nine percent of people in the bottom 30 percent in 1960 had no more than eight years of education. Only 12 percent of the bottom 30 percent had high school diplomas.

The high proportion of the bottom 30 percent with just an eighth-grade education is especially indicative of a shadow Fishtown with low levels of ability. As noted in chapter 9, everyone in their thirties and forties in 1960 had grown up at a time when children were already legally required to remain in school until age sixteen. In the ordinary course of events, children finish eighth grade when they are fourteen. A high proportion (an exact estimate is not possible) of those with no more than eight years of education had repeated a grade in elementary school or junior high, which is a strong indicator of serious learning difficulties.

The exercise produced parallel results for Belmont, drastically lowering the educational distribution. Everybody assigned to Belmont in 1960 had a college degree, compared to just 53 percent of those in the top 20 percent. Forty-one percent in the top 20 percent had no more than twelve years of education.

Why Are the Outcomes for the Top 20 Percent and Bottom 30 Percent So Similar to the Outcomes for Belmont and Fishtown?

In almost all of the graphs in part 2, you can see from the markers for the top 20 percent and bottom 30 percent that changes in the composition of the neighborhoods make remarkably little difference. How can this be?

It is easy to see why the increase in the percentage of people qualifying for Belmont between 1960 and 2010 didn't make much difference. In 1960, the people ages 30–49 had been of college age from the late 1930s to the early 1950s, when many people who had the ability to get college degrees were not even trying to go to college. The college sorting machine discussed in chapter 2 had not yet kicked in, and a large pool of college-qualified students was not being tapped. Thus the increased number of people who qualified for Belmont by 2010, decades after the college sorting machine had been doing its work, didn't necessarily mean that the upper-middle class as a whole consisted of much smarter people (the effects of the sorting machine are strongest for people at the very top of the ability distribution). The case of managerial jobs makes the point. In 1960, 80 percent of people holding managerial jobs and who therefore qualified for Belmont occupationally did not have college degrees and didn't qualify for Belmont educationally. By 2010, that proportion had dropped to 47 percent. Many of the people in Belmont in 2010 were holding the same jobs that their counterparts held in 1960; the only difference was that in 2010 they had a piece of paper saying they had been awarded a college degree. In terms of ability, the pool of people in Belmont was not necessarily diluted.

Similarly, Fishtown surely suffered some loss of talent as it went from 64 percent of the prime-age population to 30 percent, but that loss wasn't necessarily huge. The NLSY-79, with its large nationally representative sample of whites with a good measure of IQ, helps make that point. The occupational data for the following numbers refer to the early 2000s, when all the members of the sample were in their late thirties through mid-forties.

If we look at mean IQ by occupational category, the relationship is as we would expect, as shown in table C.1.

TABLE C.1.   *g*-LOADINGS OF JOBS AND THE MEAN IQ OF THE PEOPLE WHO HOLD THEM

Occupational category	Mean *g*-loading of the occupations	Mean IQ of the job holders
High-status professions	120	117
Managerial positions	116	107
Mid-level white-collar occupations	111	107
High-skill technical occupations	107	109
The blue-collar professions	109	100
Low-level white-collar occupations	92	103
Other skilled blue-collar occupations	89	98
Low-skill service and blue-collar occupations	83	94

Source: NLSY-79. Sample limited to whites.

The ordering of the *g*-loadings is about what one would expect, with the high-status professions on top, the low-skill service and blue-collar jobs at the bottom, and others spaced with modest differences. The similarity of the requirements for the mid-level white-collar jobs, high-skill technical jobs, and the blue-collar professions also makes sense. Intuitively, there is no reason to think that you need to be smarter to be a paramedic than to be an electrician, nor that there should be a difference between them and people holding down mid-level jobs in an office.

The ordering of the mean IQ of whites in the NLSY-79 who actually held those jobs generally follows the same order, but with much more bunching. The people who held managerial positions, mid-level white-collar jobs, and high-skill technical jobs were all about the same. In part, this probably reflects measurement error—people who actually hold mid-level white-collar jobs can easily give their job a description that leads the interviewer to code it as a managerial job. In part, it reflects the aggregation of different kinds of jobs. Except for "chief executives and public administrators," the 1990 occupational categories for managers do not discriminate between senior managers and junior ones, and no one in the NLSY-79 sample had become a chief executive. The fifty-one "accountants and auditors" had a mean of 113, suggesting that, not surprisingly, jobs have an IQ gradient within the managerial category.

Despite these problems, the important pair of points from table C.1 are that (1) yes, occupational sorting by IQ exists, but (2) it is very far from perfect. While a higher percentage of carpenters than stevedores have the capacity to become paramedics, as I wrote a few pages ago, table C.1 indicates that the difference in those percentages are modest.

Thus part of the explanation for the generally small differences in the results using the Belmont-Fishtown method and the Top 20 Percent–Bottom 30 Percent method is that there was a great deal of slack in the sorting of people by SES in 1960, and that many of the people who moved out of Fishtown between then and 2010 moved into jobs that were no more demanding than the jobs they had left. But that is unlikely to be the whole story. It remains remarkable that even when we limit the sample in 1960 to people who not only qualified for Fishtown but were in the lower half of Fishtown with regard to both their education and the cognitive demands of the jobs they held, their records on marriage, employment, crime, and religiosity were about the same as those in the rest of Fishtown. The result suggests that powerful norms of social and economic behavior in 1960 swept virtually everyone into their embrace.

Sample Sizes in the GSS

The Current Population Survey sample is so large that restricting the analyses to whites ages 30–49 poses no problems with sample sizes, but the same cannot be said of the General Social Survey. The Belmont samples for individual survey years had a median of only 81, and dipped as low as 48. For Fishtown, the comparable figures were 216 and 143. I therefore originally conducted the GSS analyses with a broader age group that included everyone from ages 25 to 64. This had the effect of expanding the Belmont and Fishtown samples for individual survey years to medians of 122 and 373, respectively, but I discovered that the results were virtually identical to analyses

TABLE C.2. **GSS RESULTS FOR BELMONT USING AGES 30–49 COMPARED TO AGES 25–64**

Indicator	Survey years	Age range				
		30–49	n	25–64	n	Difference
"Extramarital sex is always wrong"	1972–76	51.7%	174	51.1%	282	0.6
	2006–10	70.6%	221	69.9%	408	0.7
"Very happily married" (% of married respondents)	1972–76	73.0%	215	74.9%	338	-1.9
	2006–10	73.0%	259	71.7%	474	1.3
No religion	1972–76	9.0%	278	10.6%	470	-1.6
	2006–10	21.2%	397	22.1%	725	-0.9
De facto secular	1972–76	27.0%	278	31.1%	470	-4.1
	2006–10	41.8%	397	41.4%	724	0.4
Regular attendance among believers	1972–76	62.6%	203	60.8%	324	1.8
	2006–10	53.4%	232	54.5%	426	-1.1
The religious core	1972–76	31.5%	168	28.1%	270	3.4
	2006–10	22.5%	387	24.6%	704	-2.1
Voted in presidential election	1972–76	92.8%	276	91.5%	461	1.3
	2006–10	92.2%	385	93.7%	700	-1.5
"People can generally be trusted"	1972–76	74.8%	218	70.5%	376	4.3
	2006–10	55.9%	315	57.3%	572	-1.4
"People generally try to be fair"	1972–76	79.6%	216	76.7%	374	2.9
	2006–10	75.0%	236	75.5%	429	-0.5
"People are generally helpful"	1972–76	69.9%	216	65.9%	375	4.0
	2006–10	59.3%	236	62.1%	430	-2.8
"Very happy"	1972–76	48.2%	278	45.3%	468	2.9
	2006–10	40.1%	339	40.2%	625	-0.1

restricted to ages 30–49. Table C.2 illustrates, showing the beginning values for Belmont (combining results from the 1972 to 1976 surveys), the ending values (combining results from the 2006 to 2010 surveys), and the difference between the two.

The results for Fishtown, with its larger sample sizes, were even closer. Because the results for ages 30–49 were so similar, I decided to maintain consistency in the presentation, using the 30–49 age range for the GSS as I did for the CPS.

Appendix D

Supplemental Material for the Marriage Chapter

Notes to the Figures in Chapter 8

Figure 8.1 on the Woman's Role in Marriage

Regarding my estimate that 95 percent of people in the early 1960s would have agreed with the GSS item "It is much better for everyone involved if the man is the achiever outside the home and the woman takes care of the home and family":

The 1962 Gallup survey of women asked whether a woman is happier if she is married and caring for a family or if she is unmarried with a career. Ninety-six percent of ever-married women and 77 percent of never-married women said she is happier married and caring for a family, which, given the marriage statistics for 1960, implies that 94 percent of all women in the Gallup age range would have given that answer. It must be assumed that virtually all women giving that answer would (to be consistent) also agree with the statement "It is much better for everyone involved if the man is the achiever outside the home and the woman takes care of the home and family."

The Gallup survey was limited to women. We know from answers to the GSS question in the 1970s that (not surprisingly) men were even more likely than women to say that the woman's place was in the home—there was an average 8-point differential. Given the indirect evidence that roughly 94 percent of women would have agreed with that item in the early 1960s and that an even higher proportion of men would have agreed with it, the 95 percent estimate seems to be a minimum for both sexes combined.

I also examined age differences in the responses in responses to the Gallup question, but they were trivial. The results for women ages 21–29 and 50–60 were within a percentage point of the one for white women ages 30–49.

Figure 8.2 on Extramarital Sex

Regarding the GSS item "What about a married person having sexual relations with someone other than his or her husband or wife?" and my estimate that 80 percent of people in the early 1960s would have answered that it is always wrong:

The item asked in the 1962 Gallup survey specified extramarital sex by wives and the sample consisted exclusively of women. Eighty-four percent of the ever-married sample and 85 percent of the never-married sample said no. The GSS item did not specify which spouse cheats on whom, asking simply about sex with a person other than one's spouse, and asked the question of both sexes.

In the GSS surveys, there was no significant age-related difference among white women. The gender differential on this item ran at about 7 percent, with more women than men saying extramarital sex was always wrong. My 80 percent estimate assumes that women would have answered only slightly differently in 1962 if the item had been worded to include both spouses, and splits the gender differential observed in the GSS surveys. This estimate also has face validity. In the GSS surveys conducted in 2000, 2002, 2004, 2006, and 2008, combining the sexes, 78 percent of all whites ages 30–49 gave the "always wrong" answer to this item. It does not seem plausible that more whites ages 30–49 thought extramarital sex was always wrong in 2000–2008 than in the first half of the 1960s, and it is accordingly hard to believe that the 80 percent estimate for 1960–64 is too low.

Figure 8.3 on Marriage Rates

A plausible hypothesis about figure 8.3 is that much of the apparent decline in marriage is an artifact of the rising age at first marriage: It reflects the increased number of people in their thirties who are still not married, but will marry eventually. It turns out, however, that even though the average age of first marriage went up from 1960 to 2010, the percentage who put off marriage until after age 30 still constituted a small part of the overall population. Graphs limited to whites ages 40–49 looks almost exactly the same as the trendlines shown in figure 8.3. Limited to ages 40–49, married whites in Belmont went from 94.5 percent in 1960 to 84.3 percent in 2010, compared to 94.0 percent and 82.7 percent for those ages 30–49. Limited to ages 40–49, married whites in Fishtown went from 83.1 percent in 1960 to 49.6 percent in 2010, compared to 84.2 percent and 48.0 percent for those ages 30–49.

Figure 8.5 on Divorce Rates

Figure 8.5 includes separated people. The percentage of whites who are married-but-separated in the CPS did not change markedly from 1960 to 2010, remaining in a range from 1.3 to 2.4 percent. Separation usually means divorce. The probability that a separation will result in a divorce is more than 50 percent after a one-year separation, and quickly rises to more than 90 percent for separations lasting longer than that.[1]

Figure 8.6 on "Very Happy" Marriages

Regarding my estimate that 63 percent of respondents would have said they were in very happy marriages in the first half of the 1960s:

In the 1962 Gallup survey, women had been asked how happy their marriages were, and given the options of "extremely happy," "fairly happy," and "not so happy." Fifty-seven percent of the married women said their marriages were extremely happy, while 39 percent said "fairly happy" and 4 percent said "not so happy." The corrections for gender differential and persons outside the 30–49 age range are small and in opposite directions, canceling each other out.

The imponderable is the difference in the wording of the options: "extremely happy" in the Gallup survey versus "very happy" in the GSS; "fairly happy" in the Gallup versus "pretty happy" in the GSS; and "not so happy" in the Gallup versus "not too happy" in the GSS. The last two pairs of choices seem roughly equivalent. But, in my judgment, asking that a marriage be "extremely happy" sets a higher bar than asking that it be "very happy." (*Extremely* evokes for me something in addition to the quiet contentment that could justify a "very happy" answer.) How much higher? Adding just 3 points to the 1962 result to make it an even 60 percent felt like too little. Adding 8 points to make 65 percent felt like too much. So you see 63 (62.5 would have been ridiculous). If anyone has a better idea, I'll be happy to entertain it.

Table 8.1 on the Nonmarital-Birth Ratio by Mother's Education

Table 8.1 adjusts the Vital Statistics data based on education at the time of the birth to the best estimate of the ultimate educational attainment of women who give birth. The case of women with twelve years of education will illustrate the procedure I applied to all the educational levels.

In the 1979 cohort of the NLSY, the nonmarital-birth ratio for women with twelve years of education was 12.10 percent if based on education at birth (the measure given by the National Center for Health Statistics) and 12.83 percent if based on education at age 40 (the appropriate measure for an analysis based on women's final educational attainment). I therefore weighted the National Center for Health Statistics' nonmarital-birth ratios for women with twelve years of education by 1.060 (the result of 12.83/12.10) to reach an estimate for women whose final educational attainment was twelve years. I then applied these adjusted figures to the distribution of educational attainment of women in Belmont and Fishtown in a given year.

The Effect of Class Differences in Age at Marriage and Childbearing

People with lower levels of education marry at younger ages and have babies at younger ages than people who are busy with school through most of their twenties. If we control for these differences, how much would the apparent class differences in divorce be diminished?

Using the NLSY-79, the chances that a Fishtown child would have experienced a divorce by the time his mother was age 40 was 44 percent, compared to 12 percent for a Belmont child. Suppose that Fishtown women married and had babies at the same ages that Belmont women do (averaging at ages 25 and 31, respectively). Then the chances of divorce would have been 32 percent for the Fishtown child and 10 percent for the Belmont child—still a big difference, but reduced.[2]

If the question is how children are being socialized in today's America, it makes no difference. Age at marriage and at giving birth may explain something about *why* the percentages of children experiencing divorce differ across classes, but the fact remains that people in the upper socioeconomic classes *do* marry and have their children at older ages than people in the lower socioeconomic classes. If we can figure out a way to change that situation, then we will reduce the future divergence between the ways children of different classes are socialized. But right now, it's irrelevant.

Supplemental Material for the Honesty Chapter

Notes to the Figures in Chapter 10

Figure 10.1 on Where White Prisoners Come From

When I report that 80 percent of federal and state prisoners are drawn from the working class, a natural reaction is to wonder whether that figure is exaggerated by statistical artifacts, and yet I say in the text that 80 percent is more likely to be an underestimate than an overestimate.

Let's start with the artifacts that might exaggerate that percentage. One possibility is that we're looking at an artifact of education. Prison inmates have disproportionately high dropout rates from secondary school. In 2004, the year of the last inmate survey, 62 percent of white male inmates ages 20–49 had fewer than twelve years of education, quadruple the 15 percent of white males ages 20–49 in the general population. Because becoming a high school dropout is likely to consign a person to Fishtown, perhaps the prison population includes many young men who grew up in middle-class or affluent neighborhoods, got in trouble, dropped out of school, worked at blue-collar jobs, and look as if they come from Fishtown.

But this cannot possibly be a large artifact, because parents outside Fishtown have so few children who do not complete high school. Consider the 1979 cohort of the National Longitudinal Survey of Youth, born in 1957–64. Among white males who were the children of Belmont parents, only 2.5 percent dropped out of high school. Of all the white males who dropped out of high school, 85 percent had Fishtown parents. White high school dropouts in prison who were raised outside Fishtown can account for only a small proportion of the prison population.

Another possibility is that the prison data underrepresent white-collar crime. Let's assume that when people in Belmont commit crimes, they are mostly crimes involving embezzlement or fraud—the only two offenses in the Uniform Crime Reports that might be characterized as white-collar crime—and such crimes result in prison sentences less frequently than crimes such as robbery or burglary.

This cannot represent a large artifact, because embezzlement and fraud constitute such a small proportion of serious crime. In 2008, the FBI reported 117,217 arrests of whites for fraud and 10,517 for embezzlement. The percentage of arrests for serious crime this represents depends on how you define *serious*. The offenses in the crime index are murder, forcible rape, robbery, aggravated assault, burglary, arson, larceny-theft, and motor vehicle theft. If you count just index crimes plus fraud and embezzlement as serious, then they represent 10 percent. If you add in some other crimes that are not index crimes but seem as serious as fraud and embezzlement—assault, forgery and counterfeiting, and dealing in stolen property—then the percentage is 6 percent. If you add in drug offenses, the percentage drops to 4 percent.

Furthermore, fraud, for which whites were arrested ten times more frequently than for embezzlement, often consists of traditional con-man frauds. People doing bait-and-switch cons on the street are not what we have in mind when we think of white-collar crime. Consider also that the numbers I just gave are based on 2008, when about 18 percent of the people classified as white by the FBI were Latino whites. Even if we assume that the Latino crime rate is no higher than the non-Latino crime rate (an incorrect assumption), the estimated total arrests for non-Latino whites must be adjusted down-ward accordingly.

Taken together, it is impossible to postulate a rate for white-collar crime committed by non-Fishtown residents that would materially affect their responsibility for all serious crime, unless you assume, with no corroborating evidence, that there is serious undetected white-collar crime of mammoth proportions.

A third possibility is that people outside Fishtown have better lawyers and so go to prison less often than people from Fishtown who are accused of the same type of crime. There is no exact way to estimate the size of that effect, but a few observations are possible. Some offenders from Belmont probably avoid prison time because they (or Mom and Dad, in the case of young offenders) hire a good lawyer—but even the best lawyers have a hard time getting proba-tion for their clients if the court is looking at the second or third ar-rest for a class 1 felony. By the same token, the prevalence of sentencing guidelines means that first-time offenders often avoid prison sentences even without good lawyers. One may accept that Belmont offenders come to the criminal justice system with better representation than many Fishtown offenders without having a basis for thinking that the discrepancies in sentencing will produce statis-tically important changes in the proportions of offenders who appear to come from Fishtown.

Now let's turn to the other side of the ledger, and the opposite hy-pothesis: The estimated percentage of white criminal activity coming out of Fishtown is underestimated, perhaps grossly underestimated, because I am counting prisoners instead of crimes.

Ever since criminologist Marvin Wolfgang's pioneering longitudi-nal study of all of the males born in Philadelphia in 1945, scholars have found that a small proportion of those who are ever arrested ac-count for about half of all offenses.[1] The exact size of that proportion has varied by study, but it has usually been in the neighborhood of 7 percent, leading to a term of art in the criminological literature, "the dirty seven percent." Since people are incarcerated partly be-cause of their past criminal history as well as their current offense, people in prison have a much higher mean number of arrests than do members of an entire birth cohort, but the pattern is the same. Figure E.1 shows the story graphically.

FIGURE E.1.   **CONCENTRATION OF ARRESTS AMONG A MINORITY OF PRISONERS**

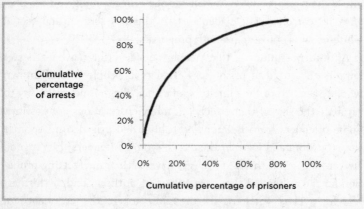

Source: 2004 survey of state and federal inmates. Sample limited to white males ages 20–49.

That seemingly perfect mathematical function represented in figure E.1 is not a fitted line. It was drawn from the raw data. In the 2004 inmate survey, more than half of all prior arrests of white male prisoners ages 20–49 were accumulated by just 13 percent of them. More than three-quarters of all their prior arrests were accumulated by just 31 percent of them.

Prisoners from the different neighborhoods had different arrest histories. Those from Belmont averaged 4.0 arrests prior to the one that landed them in prison and those from Fishtown had 6.3. The differences are actually even greater than that, because age is strongly related to number of prior arrests (as one would expect), and the average ages of prisoners from Belmont and Fishtown were 38.0 and 33.6, respectively. After controlling for those differences in age, the number of prior arrests for a typical prisoner age 30 from Fishtown was 2.4 times that of a typical prisoner age 30 from Belmont.[2] These differences alone would make the proportion of crimes coming out of Fishtown much larger than it appears from counting prisoners.

Consider next that offenders are arrested for only a fraction of the crimes they commit. The typical prisoner is believed to commit somewhere in the neighborhood of twelve to fifteen non-drug-related crimes in the year prior to his imprisonment.[3] That distribution is highly skewed. In a study of Wisconsin prisoners by John Dilulio and Anne Piehl, the median of non-drug-related crimes is 12, but the mean is 141.[4] In an earlier Rand study of self-reported crimes, 50 percent of convicted robbers reported fewer than 5 robberies in the year prior to incarceration, but 10 percent said they had committed more than 87 that year. Among active burglars, 50 percent had committed fewer than 6 in the year prior to incarceration, while 10 percent said they had committed more than 230.[5] Even if we discount for braggadocio, members of the top quartile of prisoners probably committed dozens of crimes in the year before they were locked up. If you have to predict which prisoners fall into that top quartile based on their prior arrests, the logical expectation is that the arrests and self-reports are correlated. Since Fishtown prisoners have substantially more prior arrests than prisoners from Belmont, an estimate of the proportion of total crimes coming out of Fishtown would once again rise.

All in all, it is a lot easier to make the case that 80 percent is too low, not too high, as an estimate of the degree to which white male crime is produced by men with very low education and working (when they work at all) in blue-collar jobs.

Figure 10.3 on White Arrests for Index Crimes

There are two main technical questions that arise about figure 10.3: Can we legitimately use arrest rates as a proxy measure for criminal activity? Can we use the profile of the prison population to draw inferences about the profile of the arrestee population? I discuss each in turn.

Using the white arrest rate as a proxy for the white crime rate. In the FBI's Uniform Crime Reports (UCR), statistics on reported offenses do not include the race of the offender (which is often unknown, especially for property crimes), let alone the educational and occupational background of the offender. But we do have arrests reported by race, and we do have the neighborhood breakdown of prison inmates; using those resources, we can establish a plausible estimate of the white crime rate by neighborhood.

We begin with the fact that reported offenses and arrests of whites are highly correlated. From 1960 to 2008, the correlation between the overall violent crime rate and white arrests for violent crime was +0.92. For property crime, the correlation was +0.91.[6] Figure E.2 shows how the proportional changes look for violent crime, using 1960 as the baseline equal to 1.

FIGURE E.2. WHITE ARREST RATE FOR VIOLENT CRIME AND THE OVERALL VIOLENT CRIME RATE

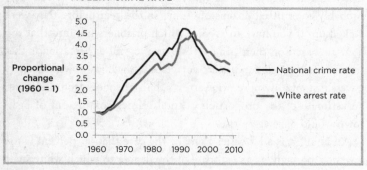

Source: UCR crime data.

There is good reason to think that changes in white arrest rates tell us a lot about changes in white criminal activity.

Using the socioeconomic profile of prisoners as the basis for estimating the neighborhood distribution of whites arrested for index crimes. The next question is what percentage of whites who are arrested for index crimes comes from Belmont and what percentage comes from Fish-town. We know what the profile of white prisoners looks like and that the profile did not change appreciably from 1974 to 2004. Is it reason-able to assume that the educational and occupational profile of per-sons arrested for index crimes is similar to the educational and occupational profile of prisoners? The answer is not only yes, it is once again quite possible that the educational and occupational profiles of persons arrested for index crimes are more heavily skewed toward Fishtown than the prison population is.

The key to that conclusion is the specification of arrests for *index* crimes. If we were talking about a minor offense such as drivers who are stopped for speeding, the socioeconomic profile of offenders would probably be not that much different from the profile of the general population of the same age and sex. If we were talking about a somewhat more unusual offense such as arrest for possession of marijuana, the population of offenders would deviate further from the general population of the same age and sex, but it wouldn't be like the profile of the prison population. But an arrest for an index offense means an arrest for murder, forcible rape, robbery, aggravated assault, burglary, arson, larceny-theft, and motor vehicle theft. In 2008, arrests for violent index offenses amounted to only 4 percent of all arrests and arrests for the property index offenses amounted to only 12 percent of all arrests. This is a highly selective group of arrestees.

Meanwhile, the educational and occupational profile of prisoners is based on everybody who is in prison, many of whom did not commit index offenses. In the 2004 survey, for example, the offenses for which the prisoners were serving time were split almost evenly between index and nonindex crimes (53 percent were incarcerated for an index offense), and the educational and occupational levels were both higher for prisoners found guilty of nonindex offenses. The differences were small (for example, 18 percent imprisoned for a nonindex offense had education beyond high school, compared to 13 percent of those imprisoned for an index offense), but the data do indicate that persons imprisoned for index crimes are more intensely concentrated in Fishtown than persons imprisoned for nonindex crimes.

Integrity in the Business World

The text of chapter 10 references my exploration of data from the Securities and Exchange Commission and the Internal Revenue

Service and states that the evidence from them cannot be used to demonstrate systematic changes in business integrity. The following summarizes the results of those efforts.

Evidence from the Securities and Exchange Commission (SEC)

The SEC is responsible for policing securities markets. They identify and prosecute wrongdoers, which would seem to make the SEC an excellent source of data. But the SEC has not published anything comparable to the FBI's Uniform Crime Reports data for assessing changes in corporate malfeasance over time.

The one partial exception to this is the Accounting and Auditing Enforcement Release (AAER) that the SEC issues at the completion of an investigation of alleged wrongdoing. But the annual number of AAERs did not pass 100 until 1994, and has never been higher than 232. The number of publicly traded companies is about 15,000.[7] With a numerator in the low hundreds and a denominator in five figures, trends are uninterpretable—they could as easily reflect changes in staffing or administrative policy as real changes in corporate malfeasance, or simply represent random noise.[8]

Evidence from the Internal Revenue Service (IRS)

The most serious violation of the tax code is tax fraud. As of 2005, tax returns were filed for almost 6 million corporations and 25 million proprietorships and partnerships. That same year the IRS assessed 217 civil penalties for corporate income tax fraud. It is impossible to interpret trends with such data, for the same reason that trends in AAERs are uninterpretable.[9]

The data on lesser tax infractions are a little more interpretable, but not much. Two categories of offense have consistent definitions over the years: delinquency, which refers to the failure to file tax returns on their due date, and failure to pay, which can include any amount short of the total that the IRS eventually decides you really owed the federal government. Figure E.3 shows the trends for corporations.

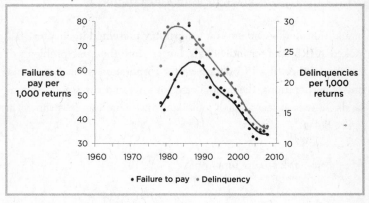

FIGURE E.3. **TRENDS IN DELINQUENCY AND FAILURE TO PAY FEDERAL INCOME TAXES: CORPORATIONS**

Source: 2009 *IRS Data Book,* table 17, and comparable tables from earlier editions.

For corporations, the picture since the mid-1980s has been one of steady decline in both the rate of delinquencies and failures to pay.

Other Ways of Identifying Corporate Malfeasance

Scholars have tested other indicators of corporate malfeasance with varying degrees of success, but all of the reliable ones use financial measures that must be extracted from the detailed financial statements filed by corporations, not ones that are reported in aggregate data about U.S. corporations. See Cecchini et al., 2010, for a description of one of the most recent ideas and a literature review of other attempts. The simplest measure, applied in Prechel and Morris, 2010, is to use a restatement of corporate finances given to the SEC within a given year (for reasons other than a change in accounting standards) as suggestive of malfeasance. Apart from the merits and shortcomings of that measure, I was unable to find a way of assembling a longitudi-

nal database using that measure with anything short of a major research project.

Integrity in Personal Finances

In addition to the evidence on bankruptcy presented in chapter 10, I
looked at IRS data for individuals, but ran into the same problems of
interpretability that IRS data have for corporations. For individuals,
unlike corporations, the annual cases of tax fraud run into the thousands, so it is at least worth looking at the trendline. It is shown in
figure E.4.

FIGURE E.4.   **TAX FRAUD: INDIVIDUALS**

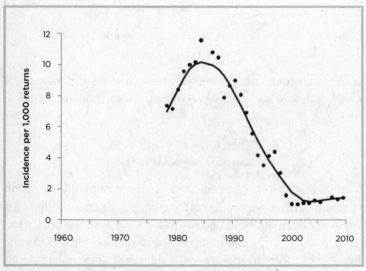

Source: 2009 *IRS Data Book*, table 17, and comparable tables from earlier editions.

From 1984 to 2000, the rate of tax fraud dropped steeply, leveling
off thereafter. Perhaps this reflects reductions in IRS investigative resources or other administrative artifacts but, at the least, there is certainly no evidence of increased dishonesty.

For the much lesser but also more common offenses of delinquency

**FIGURE E.5.   TRENDS IN DELINQUENCY AND FAILURE TO PAY FEDERAL
INCOME TAXES: INDIVIDUALS**

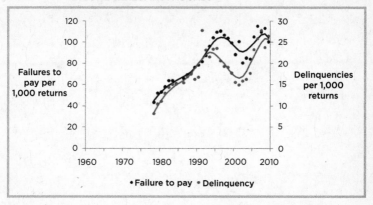

Source: 2009 *IRS Data Book*, table 17, and comparable tables from earlier editions.

and failure to pay, the trends go in the opposite direction. The trends since 1978 are shown in figure E.5.

In contrast to the corporate trends, both delinquency and failure to pay rose over the period. The problem is that delinquencies and failure to pay on the part of individuals coping with a notoriously complex American tax code can reflect carelessness, procrastination, or an honest mistake, with no implications for integrity. They can also reflect a decline in integrity. There is no way to untangle which causes play what role.

Appendix F

Supplemental Material for the American Community Chapter

In chapter 14, I summarize the results for measures of social, civic, and political disengagement. This appendix lays out the data on which those summaries were based.

Social Disengagement

The measure of social disengagement uses GSS questions asking about membership in sports clubs (e.g., a kayaking club), hobby clubs (e.g., a stamp collectors' club), fraternal organizations (e.g., Elks), nationality groups (e.g., Sons of Italy), veterans' groups (e.g., VFW), literary or art groups (e.g., the Baker Street Irregulars), or school fraternities. Belonging to *none* of these groups is scored as an indicator of social disengagement. Figure F.1 shows the results.

These data are only suggestive. We know from Putnam's work that disengagement began to rise in the 1960s, so in figure F.1 we are probably looking at lines that have started to level off after a rapid increase. At the right-hand side of the graph, we have results from just a single GSS survey after 1994, in 2004, to give us estimates of social

FIGURE F.1.   SOCIAL DISENGAGEMENT

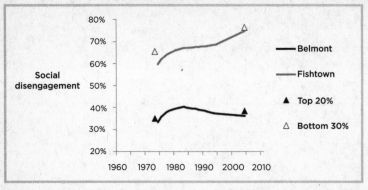

Source: Author's analysis of the GSS. Sample limited to whites ages 30–49. Data for 1972 through 1994 smoothed using locally estimated regression (LOESS). Data for 2004 represent percentages for that survey.

disengagement in the 2000s. If we take the data at face value, Fishtown has been far more socially disengaged than Belmont at least since the 1970s, and that gap has widened even more. In the 2004 survey, 36 percent of those in Belmont were socially disengaged compared to 75 percent of those in Fishtown.

Civic Disengagement

The second composite index measures membership in civic organizations. It asks if someone is a member of a service group (e.g., Kiwanis), a youth group (e.g., coaches Little League), school service group (e.g., PTA), or a political club. Belonging to none of those groups is scored as an indicator of civic disengagement. Note that I do not include church groups, which would double-count for religiosity, covered in chapter 11. Once again we have a frustrating shortage of data after 1994, with the one survey in 2004 that asked the right questions. Figure F.2 shows the results.

Once again, divergence between Belmont and Fishtown was already high when we pick up the trendlines in the 1970s. Civic disen-

FIGURE F.2. CIVIC DISENGAGEMENT

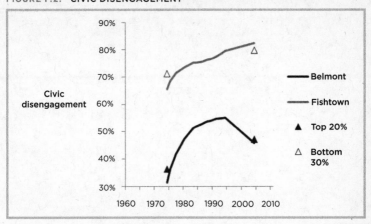

Source: Author's analysis of the GSS. Sample limited to whites ages 30–49. Data for 1972 through 1994 smoothed using locally estimated regression (LOESS). Data for 2004 represent percentages for that survey.

gagement increased in Belmont through the early 1990s and then showed a decrease in the lone 2004 survey. In Fishtown, civic disengagement rose throughout the period. The combination of trends meant a wide gap between Belmont and Fishtown in the 2004 survey—45 percent in Belmont versus 85 percent in Fishtown.

Appendix G

Supplemental Material for the Chapter About the Founding Virtues and the Stuff of Life

The happiness question in the General Social Survey asks, "Taken all together, how would you say things are these days—would you say that you are very happy, pretty happy, or not too happy?" The dependent variable in the logit analyses that are presented in figures 15.6 and 15.7 used a binary variable in which 1 stood for responses of "very happy" and 0 stood for "pretty happy" or "not too happy." The sample was limited to the GSS surveys from 1990 through 2010. The independent variables and their codings were as follows:

Age. Age in years.

Family. Since children don't have much effect on happiness independently of marital status, and those who are unmarried have similar relationships to happiness whether they are never married or formerly married, the variable for family has just three values: (1) unmarried, (2) married and saying their marriage was "pretty happy" or "not too happy," and (3) married and saying that their marriage was "very happy."

Vocation. The main effect of vocation on happiness is satisfaction with the work one does. Working longer hours also has some independent relationship, but for presentational purposes I have ignored it.

Analyses were originally conducted using four values of vocation: (1) dissatisfied with work, any number of hours and any kind of work; (2) moderately satisfied with work, any number of hours and any kind of work; (3) a woman who is very satisfied with being a full-time home-maker; and (4) very satisfied with work and working at paid employ-ment, any number of hours and either sex. Discriminating between satisfied people in paid employment and satisfied homemakers did not add to the analysis, so categories (3) and (4) were collapsed for the analyses shown in the text.

Faith. This variable has three values, drawing on the categories used in chapter 11: (1) de facto seculars—those either with no reli-gion or professing a religion but attending worship services no more than once a year; (2) believers who profess a religion and attend ser-vices at least several times a year but do not qualify for the third cat-egory; and (3) those who attend services at least nearly every week and say that they have a strong affiliation with their religion.

Community. Because of the GSS's sparse data on measures of social and civic engagement during the 1990s and 2000s, we are restricted to an index of social trust, which sums the optimistic responses to the helpfulness, fairness, and trustworthiness questions discussed in chapter 14. The three items were coded so that the negative answer (e.g., "most people try to take advantage of you") is scored as 0, the "it depends" answer is scored as 1, and the positive answer is scored as 2. The combined scores formed an index with a minimum score of 0 and a maximum score of 6. The three categories used in the analysis were low social trust (0–2), moderate social trust (3–4), and high social trust (5–6).

The presentation in the text summarizes logit analyses that ex-plored all the permutations of interactions among these four indepen-dent variables.

Notes

Internet Sources

Standards for citing online materials are still evolving. I have followed the Chicago style with a few simplifying adaptations. Major institutional websites such as the College Board or the Bureau of Labor Statistics are more easily found by Googling than by typing in a URL. I do not give URLs for the specific page I used unless finding it required significant searching once I reached the website (and even then, websites are so constantly in flux that you will often find a "page not found" message when you enter the URL that worked for me). Regarding books and other documents in the public domain that have been accessed online, you can find the context for any specific quote by going to the institutional website giving access to that book, searching for the book, then entering a short phrase from the quotation into the search function. In accordance with Chicago's guidelines, I do not include the date when I accessed the website. If it no longer exists when you read this book, knowing that it did at some date in the past does not seem helpful.

Frequently Used Abbreviations

BLS	Bureau of Labor Statistics
CPS	Current Population Survey
GSS	General Social Survey

IPUMS	Integrated Public Use Microdata Series
NCHS	National Center for Health Statistics
NLSY	National Longitudinal Survey of Youth
SAUS	Statistical Abstract of the United States
UCR	Uniform Crime Reports

Prologue: November 21, 1963

1. Deadline Hollywood website, http://www.deadline.com/2010/05/full-series -rankings-for-the-2009-10-broadcast-season/. Televisionista website, http:// televisionista.blogspot.com/2008/06/tv-ratings-2007-2008-season-top -200.html.
2. The Current Population Survey didn't yet ask about children in the house, but we know from later years that wives without young children are more than twice as likely to work full time than wives who do have young children.
3. The Motion Picture Association of America Production Code website, http://productioncode.dhwritings.com/multipleframes_productioncode .php.
4. *Time* magazine website, http://www.time.com/time/magazine/article/0,9171, 898033,00.html.
5. Author's analysis of data from Gallup poll #1963-0678, obtained from the Roper Center for Public Opinion Research website.
6. FBI, *Crime in the United States 1963*.
7. Ross, 1987.

Part I: The Formation of a New Upper Class

1. Reich, 1991.
2. Herrnstein and Murray, 1994.
3. Brooks, 2000, 10.
4. Florida, 2002, xxvii.
5. SAUS-2011, table 509.
6. The age range of 25 and older is chosen to be coordinate with the available census breakdown for zip codes. But it is also convenient as an age range for embracing the new upper class. No one except in the entertainment industry or sports rises to the top 5 percent of an occupation under the age of 25, and many people in the new upper class who are still employed after age 65 remain in their prominent positions.
7. The calculation was as follows: BLS statistics for 2010 indicate that 121,987,000 Americans ages 25 and older were employed (Employment and Earnings Online, table 8, January 2011). The March CPS for 2010

indicates that 23.4 percent were in the professions or managerial positions. That leads to a top 5 percent of employed persons in those occupations in 2010 consisting of 1,427,248 persons (Occupations and Earnings 2010, table A3, available online at the Bureau of Labor Statistics' website).

8. This number needs a correction that I won't try to make. In 2010, 16 percent of the spouses of people in the professions and managerial positions ages 25 and older were also in one of those occupations. But trying to estimate what percentage of these couples consisted of two people in the most successful 5 percent would be pushing this attempt to develop a ballpark figure much too far.

9. In Eisenhower's time, the cabinet consisted of ten posts: the heads of the Departments of State; Treasury; Defense; Justice; Interior; Agriculture; Commerce; Health, Education, and Welfare; Labor; and the Postmaster General. Postmaster General has not been a cabinet position since 1971, so I used the nine cabinet departments as the basis for comparing the Eisenhower and Kennedy cabinets with those of George W. Bush and Barack Obama (as of 2011). Forty-six percent of the cabinet members in the Eisenhower and Kennedy years (1953–63) grew up in lower-middle-class or working-class families compared to 27 percent in the Bush and Obama cabinets (2001–10). Thirty-two percent of the cabinet members in the Eisenhower and Kennedy years grew up in upper-middle-class, rich, or politically influential families, compared to 54 percent in the Bush and Obama cabinets.

1: Our Kind of People

1. The campuses were the University of California at Berkeley, Stanford, the University of Chicago, the University of Michigan, Michigan State, Ohio State, and Swarthmore. Qualifying census tracts are limited to those with at least 500 adults ages 25 and older and 250 families or more.

2. Department of Housing and Urban Development website, http://www .huduser.org/periodicals/USHMC/spring2001/histdat2.html.

3. Los Angeles Public Library website, http://dbase1.lapl.org/.

4. The estimate of 80,000 is for 1961–62, in Phillips, 1991, appendix A.

5. The full account of how this apocryphal exchange entered literary history is told in a letter to the editor of the *New York Times Book Review* by Eddy Dow for November 13, 1988. Obtained from the archives of the *New York Times* website.

6. I am indebted to the current owner of Topridge for access to materials about Mrs. Post's lifestyle at Topridge and her other homes.

7. By the 2000 census, 66 percent of the residents of Cambridge had college degrees and the median income for Cambridge as a whole stood well above the national average at $80,565.

8. Brooks, 2000, 55–57.

9. In 2010, 55 percent of all new cars sold in the United States were foreign (www.goodcarbadcar.net). In the parking lot of the Walmart in predominantly working-class Newton, Iowa (centile score 47), on June 10, 2011, 83 percent of the cars were American makes (n=200). In the shopping center and surrounding streets of predominantly working-class Brunswick, Maryland (centile score 41), on the afternoon of May 27, 2011, 64 percent of the cars were American makes (n=200). In the parking lots of Wildwood Shopping Center and Georgetown Square in affluent Bethesda, Maryland (centile 99), on the morning of June 27, 2011, 23 percent (n=171) and 17 percent (n=150) of the cars were American makes, respectively.

10. Author's analysis of data from the Centers for Disease Control's Behavioral Risk Factor Surveillance System (BRFSS), annual survey for 2009. Data downloaded from the Centers for Disease Control website.

11. The data are available from the Saguaro Seminar's Civic Engagement in America website, *Bowling Alone*, http://www.bowlingalone.com/data.htm.

12. Author's analysis of data for the population as a whole. Data are from the Pew Research Center's Diet/Gambling/Movies survey, released November 13, 2007. Data available from the Pew Research Center website, http://pewsocialtrends.org/category/data-sets/.

13. In the Centers for Disease Control's Behavioral Risk Factor Surveillance System for 2009, 35 percent of the respondents said that they smoked some days or every day.

14. Pew Research Center, "Americans Spending More Time Following the News," September 12, 2010, available online at the Pew Research Center for the People & the Press website, http://people-press.org/2010/09/12/americans-spending-more-time-following-the-news/.

15. For a review of the studies relating socioeconomic status to television viewing, see Gorely, Marshall, and Biddle, 2004.

16. This number is based on Nielsen data for the first two quarters of 2010, continuing a shallow long-term upward trend: http://blog.nielsen.com/nielsenwire/media_entertainment/state-of-the-media-tv-usage-trends-q2-2010/.

17. For the relationship of socioeconomic status to breast-feeding, see Heck, 2006.

18. See, for example, Aronson and Huston, 2004; Mcloyd, 1998; Parcel and Menaghan, 1989.

19. For a sampling of resources for New York parents applying to preschool, see http://blogs.urbanbaby.com/newyork/2010/08/17/a-league-of-your-own-for-school-admissions/.

20. An excellent summary of the technical literature for the general reader is Bronson, 2009.

21. *U.S. News & World Report* website, http://colleges.usnews.rankingsand reviews .com/best-colleges.

22. Brooks, 2000, chapter 3; Florida, 2002, chapters 5–9.
23. Florida, 2002, quoting office architect Don Carter, 123.

2. The Foundations of the New Upper Class

1. Quoted in Karlgaard, 2005.
2. Herrnstein and Murray, 1994, chapters 2 and 3. For a more recent survey of the literature on this topic, see Gottfredson, 2003.
3. Goldberg, 2003, 51–52.
4. All the Fortune 500s since 1955 can be found on the CNN Money website, http://money.cnn.com/magazines/fortune/fortune500/2011/. The corporations ranked 100 in 1960 and 2010 were McDonnell Douglas and Amazon, respectively. The 500th-ranked corporations were Masonite and Blockbuster.
5. Eberstadt, 2008. Broda and Weinstein, 2008, make the case that the Consumer Price Index has systematically understated real gains in purchasing power.
6. For an examination of whether a change in CPS methodology could have produced the jump in 1994–95, see Raffalovich, Monnat, and Hui-shien, 2009, which concludes that it probably did not. For the analysis using IRS data, see Piketty and Saez, 2006. Data in figure 2.1 use one income figure per family unit.
7. Brooks, 2000, 178–85.
8. For a full presentation of the data on college stratification as of the early 1990s, see Herrnstein and Murray, 1994, chapter 1.
9. Herrnstein and Murray, 1994, 38. The schools were Brown, Bryn Mawr, Columbia, Harvard, Mount Holyoke, Princeton, Radcliffe, Smith, University of Pennsylvania, Vassar, Wellesley, Williams, and Yale.
10. Herrnstein and Murray, 1994, 30.
11. Bender, 1960, 4.
12. Soares, 2007, 38.
13. In absolute numbers, the four largest concentrations of students with admissions test scores in the top 5 percent were all in public universities—the state universities of California at Berkeley, Illinois at Urbana-Champaign, Michigan at Ann Arbor, and Wisconsin at Madison (Geiger, 2002, table 2). It would seem that the high-scoring students in these schools would be exposed to a much more diverse set of classmates than those in the Ivies. But taking such students as a percentage of the entire entering class in those universities is misleading. All of the public universities that were part of Geiger's 105 schools have honors programs, and all of them are described in the same way: They try to replicate the experience of the small liberal arts college within the framework of the large state university. Students in honors colleges have access to special courses, with small classes filled with

other honors students and taught by specially selected faculty. Many of the programs also have housing set aside for the honors students. The University of Michigan recently opened the Perlman Honors Commons—in effect, a separate student union for honors students. These programs go a long way toward replicating the cognitive profile and much of the social interaction found at elite private schools. They are also increasingly competitive. As of 2010, getting into the honors programs of the top public universities required credentials similar to those required for many elite private colleges.

14. The website for the *U.S. News & World Report* rankings is http://colleges .usnews.rankingsandreviews.com/best-colleges.

15. Espenshade and Radford, 2009, chapter 4.

16. Soares, 2007, tables 1.1 and 6.1.

17. Ibid., 3.

18. Ibid., table 6.6.

19. The figure for private schools is specifically for non-Catholic private schools.

20. Golden, 2006.

21. Soares sees four factors as evidence that admissions committees are still admitting the "right" kind of people: (1) having a parent with a postgraduate or professional degree, (2) graduating from a non-Catholic private school, (3) coming from a family in which both parent and student have visited an art museum, and (4) being an officer in high school government. The first three lend themselves to interpretations involving academic merit. A parent with a PhD, medical degree, or law degree from a reputable university is virtually guaranteed to have a high IQ (obtaining a postgraduate or professional degree screens very effectively for high IQ). Students who have obtained entrance to competitive private schools have undergone a screen for IQ, and students who graduate from private schools are likely to be academically better prepared than students from public schools. The young person who has gone to an art museum with a parent may have done so in blind obedience to the parent, but there is likely to be a correlation with the child's IQ and whether, being given an opportunity to go to the art museum, he actually did. As for the fourth variable, being an officer in high school government, an admissions office that takes such nonacademic achievements into account would seem to be giving points for the student's actual accomplishments, not a penumbra of cultural capital.

22. I continue to use "math" and "verbal" for what are now called the critical reading and math reasoning tests. The percentages on parental education are unpublished figures provided to me courtesy of the College Board.

23. Since so many people reading this book, especially parents with children nearing college, assume that coaching can raise their children's SAT scores by large amounts, discussion of this issue is warranted. From 1981 to 1990, three separate analyses of all the prior studies were published in peer-reviewed journals. They found a coaching effect of 9 to 25 points on the SAT verbal and of 15 to 25 points on the SAT math. See Herrnstein

and Murray, 1994, 400–402. Derek Briggs, using the National Education Longitudinal Study of 1988, found effects of 3 to 20 points for the SAT verbal and 10 to 28 points for the SAT math (Briggs, 2004). Donald Powers and Donald Rock, using a nationally representative sample of students who took the SAT after its revisions in the mid-1990s, found an average coaching effect of 6 to 12 points on the SAT verbal and 13 to 18 points on the SAT math (Powers and Rock, 1999). These effects are not large enough to sway many college admissions decisions.

No study published in a peer-reviewed journal shows average gains approaching the fabled 100-point and 200-point jumps you hear about in anecdotes. When investigating this issue in 2007, I asked Kaplan and Princeton Review for such evidence. Kaplan replied that it chooses not to release data for proprietary reasons. Princeton Review did not respond (Murray, 2007).

The illusion of large gains arises mainly from two artifacts. The first is self-selection. The students who seem to profit from a coaching course tend to be those who, if the course had not been available, would have worked hard on their own to prepare for the test. The second is the conflation of the effect of coaching with the effect of preparation that students can do on their own. No student should walk into the SAT cold. It makes sense for students to practice some sample items and to review their algebra textbook if it has been a few years since they have taken algebra. But once a few hours have been spent on these routine steps, most of the juice has been squeezed out of preparation for the SAT. Combine self-selection artifacts with the role of basic preparation, and you have the reason that independent studies using control groups show such small average gains from formal coaching.

24. The transmission works through both genes and environment, but the distinction is blurred because cognitive ability in the parents is associated with parenting practices that promote the child's cognitive ability. In addition, it has been found that the shared environment among siblings—which includes the things that parents do to promote cognitive development in their children—has a small long-term role independent of genes. See Plomin et al., 2001; Rowe, Vazsonyi, and Flannery, 1994; Rowe, 2003.

25. The correlation of spousal IQ has been in the region of +0.4 since spouses have been tested (Jensen, 1998, 183), indicating an underlying role of cognitive ability in mate selection that probably has always existed. But a correlation alone is not enough for understanding the kind of phenomenon discussed in the text, in which people with high IQs marry each other. A positive correlation reflects the degree to which two phenomena vary together, but nothing more. If every woman married a man whose IQ score was exactly equal to hers, the correlation of spousal IQ would be +1.0, and it would also be +1.0 if every woman married a man whose IQ score was exactly 20 points higher than hers—but the implications for the IQ of offspring would be radically different.

26. Schwartz and Mare, 2005.
27. This statement is true for public universities and unselective private colleges, where gaining admission is easier than graduating. It is not necessarily true of selective colleges. "The hardest thing about Harvard is getting in" was already a commonplace when I was there in the early 1960s.
28. Murray, 2008, chapter 3.
29. The original Coleman Report is Coleman, Campbell, and Hobson, 1966. For a collection of reanalyses of the Coleman Report, see Mosteller and Moynihan, 1972.
30. In the NLSY-79, the means for whites obtaining bachelors, masters, and PhDs or professional degrees by the year 2000 (when the NLSY-79 subjects were ages 36–43) were 113.3, 116.9, and 125.6, respectively. For blacks, the comparable means were 99.1, 101.7, and 112.2. The Latino means were 106.7, 106.4, and 115.2. See Murray, 2009, for a full discussion of the stability of IQ scores for various degree levels.
31. The whiteness of the broad elite is discussed in chapter 3, pp. 79–80, relative to the racial composition of the most affluent and best-educated zip codes. The narrow elite in the private sector is also still overwhelmingly white. A few examples: Among the Fortune 500 CEOs as of 2011, 98 percent were white (as always, meaning non-Latino whites). Among the 51 directors nominated for Academy Awards from 2000 to 2011, 92 percent were white. Among the 123 syndicated columnists in 2008 with the largest number of outlets, 95 percent were white. My search on senior executives in major television networks, both news and entertainment, did not produce examples of nonwhite executives in jobs that shape content, but the ethnicity of many of those executives could not be identified.

    The whiteness of the narrow elite in government jobs varies. Statewide offices are still overwhelmingly held by whites. For example, as of the end of 2010, 45 of the 50 governors and 96 out of 100 senators were whites of European origin. Elections at the district and municipal level are more likely to produce ethnically diverse officeholders (the House of Representatives as of the end of 2010 was 83 percent white), but they also contribute few members of the narrow elite. Presidential appointments are also ethnically diverse. For example, federal judges serving as of the end of 2010 were 78 percent white. Data for these statements were collected from a large number of websites, including person-by-person web searches. The data on federal judges were obtained from www.uscourts.gov/JudgesAndJudgeships/BiographicalDirectoryOfJudges.aspx.
32. For a discussion of the psychometric properties of the AFQT, see Herrnstein and Murray, 1994, appendix 2. The scores used here are normed by age using comparable procedures for the 1979 and 1997 cohorts of the NLSY.
33. Kalmijn, 1994; Kalmijn, 1998.

34. Arum, Roksa, and Budig, 2008.

35. The standard linear regression equation

$$\hat{Y} = r_{xy}\frac{s_y}{s_x}(X - \overline{X}) + \overline{Y}$$

predicts the magnitude of regression to the mean independently of whatever causal mechanism may be involved (Humphreys, 1978). In the case of parental-child regression to the mean in IQ, $\hat{Y}$ is a given child's expected IQ, X is the midpoint parental IQ for a given pair of parents, $\overline{X}$ is the sample mean for midpoint parental IQ, $\overline{Y}$ is the sample mean for offspring IQ, r_{xy} is the sample correlation of midpoint parental and offspring IQ, and s_x and s_y are the sample standard deviations of midpoint parental IQ and offspring IQ, respectively.

To fill in these parameters, I use a white mean of 103 and standard deviation of 14.5. These are based on the mean of the array of sample means produced by standardizations for the Stanford-Binet (version 5, subjects ages 12–23, 2001); the Wechsler Adult Intelligence Scale (version III, subjects ages 16–64, 1995); the Wechsler Intelligence Scale for Children (version IV, subjects ages 14–16, 2002); and the Armed Services Vocational Aptitude Battery (NLSY-97, subjects ages 13–17, 1997). The mean standard deviation of those same data sets was 14.5. Data for the Stanford-Binet and Wechsler standardizations were provided courtesy of William Dickens, and reported in Dickens and Flynn, 2006. In the calculations of the variance of midpoint parental IQ (the equation for doing so is given in the appendix of Humphreys, 1978), I specified a correlation of spousal IQ of +0.5, which, given a standard deviation of 14.5 for the white population standard deviation, produced an expected standard deviation of midpoint parental IQ of 12.6. For a review of the literature on familial IQ correlations that leads to these specifications, see Bouchard, 1981.

36. An IQ of 135 assumes that the average graduate of an elite college is at the 99th centile of IQ of the entire population of seventeen-year-olds. This is consistent with the median combined Critical Reading and Mathematics scores of 1400 or more among the top dozen schools in the most recent *U.S. News & World Report* rankings (http://colleges.usnews.rankingsandreviews .com/best-colleges). In 2010, a combined score of 1400 put a student at about the 97th percentile of all students who took the SAT (based on the distribution produced by the known means and standard deviations for the two tests and a correlation of +0.7 between them). But the number of test-takers in 2010 represented only 36 percent of the seventeen-year-olds in the country. Any plausible assumptions about the proportion of the 62 percent of seventeen-year-olds who didn't take the SAT who could have gotten a combined score of 1400 or more puts a student who actually does score 1400 well into the 99th centile of the seventeen-year-old population.

For 2010 SAT test data, see *College-Bound Seniors 2010*, available at the College Board website. For a discussion of estimating SAT scores for those who don't take the test, see Murray, 2008, 70, and the associated notes.

37. Murray, 2009, 102.
38. Gottfredson, 2003.
39. The following numbers are not statistically derived, but represent the results of a simulation that used Stata's DRAWNORM command to create a sample of 10 million normally distributed values of two variables with means of 103, standard deviations of 14.5, and a correlation of +0.5.

3: A New Kind of Segregation

1. Massey, 2009.
2. Ibid., figure 5.
3. Ibid., figure 8.
4. Ibid., 85.
5. Four times the median poverty threshold for the CPS (based on persons of all ages and races) in 1999, the income year for the 2000 census, was $67,824, cutting off the 58th centile of family income in the CPS for 1999.
6. In the comparisons of 1960 and 2000, I use census tracts for 1960 and zip codes for 2000. The 1960 census tract data are taken from the Elizabeth Mullen Bogue file (hereafter Bogue), named for the woman who did much of the keypunching of the data published in the printed publications of the Bureau of the Census. Those published data in 1960 included 175 metropolitan areas with 104,010,696 people, or 58.0 percent of the resident population. Zip codes, which didn't yet exist in 1960, are a much more easily understood unit than census tracts, so I use zip codes for the 2000 census, using complete national data downloadable from the American FactFinder tool on the Bureau of the Census's website. In those instances when I directly compare 1960 and 2000 data, I restrict the comparison to the metropolitan areas covered by the Bogue file.
7. The figure in the text is the median of the median family income in the four census tracts, weighted by the number of families in each census tract. Parallel weighting is used for other statistics that aggregate across census tracts or zip codes. The $60,700 threshold would be passed by an Austin teacher with a bachelor's degree, eighteen years of experience, working a 230-day year. Salary schedules are from http://www.austinisd.org.
8. Weighted mean based on the population ages 25 and older.
9. Not all of the high-education zip codes were rich. The zip code for the University of Texas campus (78705) had the third-highest proportion of BAs, 73 percent, but a median income of only $46,480 dollars, reflecting the presence of lots of grad students who had BAs but hardly any income. Otherwise, however, education and wealth went together.
10. Moll, 1985. The others were William and Mary, Miami University of Ohio,

University of California (all campuses), University of Michigan, University of North Carolina at Chapel Hill, University of Vermont, and University of Virginia.

11. For the 2000 census, what I am calling for convenience "north of Central Park" consisted of all the zip codes from Ninety-Fourth Street northward on the West Side and from Ninety-Sixth Street northward on the East Side. The Upper East Side included the zip codes that encompassed East Sixtieth to Ninety-Sixth streets and Fifth Avenue to the East River. The 1960 census tracts used for the analysis were consistent with these zip code borders within two blocks.

12. The salary schedule for the New York City Department of Education can be found at http://schools.nyc.gov/NR/rdonlyres/EDDB658C-BE7F-4314 -85C0-03F5A00B8A0B/0/salary.pdf.

13. The three-block radius also included my family in one direction and my wife's family in another. Our fathers were both mid-level executives at Maytag.

14. The other 4 percent of the SuperZip population consists of Native Americans, Americans with origins in the Pacific islands, and people classified as mixed race.

15. In 2011, for example, Asian applicants made up 18 percent of the acceptances at Harvard. *Harvard Gazette*, May 11, 2011, http://news.harvard.edu/ gazette/story/2011/03/an-unprecedented-admissions-year/. For a complete analysis of trends in minority admissions since the 1980s, see Espenshade, 2009. The most detailed presentation of the evidence that Asian students have an admissions disadvantage—Asian applicants have to have higher SAT scores than other students (including whites) to have an equal probability of being admitted—is in Espenshade, Chung, and Walling, 2004.

16. The phrase "honorary whites" is associated with Hacker, 1992, but it does not occur in that book. Although Hacker has used the phrase in many talks, he cannot recall ever consigning it to print (Andrew Hacker, personal communication, May 14, 2011).

17. Census Bureau, http://2010.census.gov/2010census/data/index.php.

18. The American FactFinder tool was transitioning to a new version in 2011, but the link to it appears on the home page of the Census Bureau, www.census.gov. The ethnic profiles of the six zip codes in the 2000 census were as follows:

Zip code	% White	% Black	% Hispanic	% Asian
02461	82.0	1.0	2.1	11.8
10583	81.8	2.1	2.7	11.4
20007	82.5	4.0	4.2	5.7
60657	82.4	3.4	4.4	5.0
90212	82.4	1.7	2.2	8.3
94301	81.7	1.9	2.1	9.4

19. This number is based on the zip code classifications as of 2000, and does not include zip codes associated exclusively with a post office.

20. The class numbered 776 students. As of the twenty-fifth reunion, information was available for 743 of them (96 percent). Fifteen were deceased and 135 were living abroad. For those living in the United States, the twenty-fifth reunion profiles showed the town or city in which they lived but not the zip code. Many of the smaller towns had a single zip code. For those with multiple zip codes, I used online white pages to determine the home address and its zip code. Since the names almost always included a middle initial and the name of the spouse or partner, I was able to determine home zip codes for all but 45 of those living in the United States. The numbers in the text are based on the 547 who were known to be living in the United States and for whom a home zip code could be determined. The zip codes of those for whom data could not be obtained were probably even more heavily concentrated in the elite zip codes than those whose zip codes were obtained— almost all of those 45 names could be found in online white pages, and they had work addresses in the most exclusive zip codes of New York City, Los Angeles, San Francisco, Chicago, or Boston, but their home phone numbers and addresses were unlisted.

21. It is worth noting that the reviewers of *Bobos in Paradise* for the *New York Times*, *Wall Street Journal*, and *Washington Post* were Janet Maslin, Emily Prager, and Jonathan Yardley, respectively, all of whom had spent their adult lives intimately familiar with members of the new upper class, and all of them thought that Brooks nailed it.

22. For details of the sample, see appendix B.

23. You may be wondering about the three isolated SuperZips: two little ones in the top left quadrant of the map and one large one on the right center. The two little ones are the zip code that contain the tiny Maryland towns of Barnesville, with a population of 138 adults, and Beallsville, with 76. The large one is zip code 20721, adult population 14,451, part of Bowie, Maryland, one of three SuperZips in the nation with a majority African American population (82 percent black). The other two are the tiny zip code 45384, adult population 123 (95 percent black) of Wilberforce, Ohio, near Dayton; and zip code 60461, adult population 3,347 (55 percent black), the Chicago suburb of Olympia Fields, Illinois.

24. In a few cases, a SuperZip was separated from a cluster of other SuperZips by a single zip code with a centile score of 90 or higher. I included such SuperZips in the cluster.

25. Including San Francisco with New York, Washington, and Los Angeles is a judgment call based on the enormous influence that the information technology sector has acquired in the last three decades, not just technologically and economically but culturally. To the CEOs of multibillion-dollar businesses who do not live in the cities I listed and are incensed at being omitted from the narrow elite, I can only observe that lots of large corporations could go bust without making a ripple on the national scene.

26. For literature reviews and original data, see Cardiff, 2005, and Mariani, 2008. The Left's faculty dominance varies widely by type of both school and department. The humanities and social sciences have the most drastic tilt. Here are examples of Left:Right ratios from Mariani, 2008, table 3, going from highest to lowest: English 7.4:1, history/political science 6.2:1, social sciences 5.8:1, humanities 5.4:1, physical sciences 4.1:1, biological sciences 4.0:1, engineering 1.5:1, health sciences 1.0:1, business 0.8:1. Faculties of highly selective schools are even further to the Left (3.7:1) than schools that are not highly selective (2.7:1).

27. In a survey of five hundred journalists that the Pew Project for Excellence in Journalism conducted in 2007, Pew reported the results for three levels of the national media: executives (CEOs, general managers, and publishers), senior editors and producers, and working journalists and editors. The least liberal tilt was found for executives, who had a Left:Right ratio of 1.6:1. For senior editors and producers, the ratio was 2.1:1. For working journalists and editors, it was 6.7:1. Among the latter group, 12 percent described themselves as very liberal, 28 percent as liberal, 3 percent as conservative, and 3 percent as very conservative (Project for Excellence in Journalism, 2008, 55). The PDF of the report is available at http://www.stateofthemedia.org/2008/Journalists%20topline.pdf. See also Groseclose, 2005.

28. Source: almost any Academy Awards show.

29. Callahan, 2010, chapter 1.

30. The percentages in the text represent town-level results when a SuperZip represented the only zip code for the town, or when SuperZips represented at least half of the zip codes when a town had more than one. Data were obtained by going to the websites of state boards of election. Some of them present data by town; some of them don't.

31. Bishop, 2008, 1–8.

32. Data downloaded from the ADA website.

4: How Thick Is Your Bubble?

1. Tocqueville, 1840, vol. 2, Google Books.

2. The idea for creating a test and items 7 and 11 (and perhaps a few others I've forgotton) came from reading Brooks, 2000.

3. "Chief breadwinner" is defined as the person with the higher-rated occupational category in a household headed by a married couple.

4. Author's analysis, based on persons in the NLSY-79 sample followed from 1979 through 2006 with no more than two missing interview waves.

5. The Pew Forum on Religious and Public Life website, http://religions.pewforum.org/affiliations.

6. Bishop, 2008.

7. Murray, 2008, chapter 2.

8. These assume that the standard deviation for a school with a mean IQ of 115 is 12 instead of the national standard deviation of 15, consistent with what is empirically observed with subgroups that score substantially higher or lower than a national mean.

9. Centers for Disease Control, http://www.cdc.gov/BRFSS/.

10. Chinni, 2010, introduction, Kindle edition.

11. Pickuptrucks.com, http://news.pickuptrucks.com/2011/01/2010-year-end -top-10-pickup-truck-sales.html.

12. In the DDB Life Style data for 1995–98: If you did not have a college degree and were anywhere under $100,000 per year in income, you had a 14 percent chance of fishing five or more times per year. With a college degree and an income greater than $100,000, you had a 4 percent chance. Extrapolate that relationship to people who are in the top few centiles of socioeconomic status, and the percentage presumably drops accordingly.

13. My basic source was http://en.wikipedia.org/wiki/List_of_casual_dining_ restaurant_chains. I went to the specific websites of restaurants with worldwide outlets to estimate the number of outlets in the United States.

14. Some of the chains are privately held, and revenues must be estimated. Twelve billion dollars is an extremely conservative estimate.

15. Box Office Mojo website, http://www.boxofficemojo.com/yearly/chart/ ?yr=2009&p=.htm.

16. Deadline Hollywood website, http://www.deadline.com/2010/05/full-series -rankings-for-the-2009-10-broadcast-season/.

17. SBJNet website, http://sbj.net/main.asp?SectionID=18&SubSectionID=2 3&ArticleID=86519.

5: The Bright Side of the New Upper Class

1. Herrnstein, Bekle, and Taylor, 1990.

2. Herrnstein and Murray, 1994, 34.

Part II: The Formation of a New Lower Class

1. U.S. Bureau of the Census, 1975, vol. 1, series D, table nos. 182–232. These figures refer to workers of both sexes, all ages, and all races.

6: The Founding Virtues

1. Grund, 1837, Google Books.

2. Quoted in Adams, 1889, Google Books.

3. Quoted in ibid.

4. Quoted in ibid.

5. Quoted in ibid.
6. Kurland, 1986, vol. 1, chapter 13, document 36, http://press-pubs.uchi cago.edu/founders/documents/v1ch13s36.html.
7. Benjamin Franklin to William Strahan, February 16, 1784, in Murphy, 1906, Google Books.
8. Quoted in Spalding, 1996, 30.
9. Adams, 1889, Google Books.
10. Tocqueville, 1840, vol. 2, Google Books.
11. Grund, 1837, Google Books.
12. Adams, 1889, Google Books.
13. Hamilton, 1833, Google Books.
14. Grund, 1837, Google Books.
15. Thomas Jefferson to Nathaniel Macon, in *The Works of Thomas Jefferson*, federal ed., vol. 12 (New York and London: G. P. Putnam's Sons, 1904–5), Online Library of Liberty.
16. The other virtues were piety, philanthropy, industry, and economy in one list and harmony, industry, and frugality in the other. George Washington to the General Assembly of Presbyterian Churches, May 1789, in Allen, 1988, 181; and George Washington to the Marquis de Lafayette, January 29, 1789, in Allen, 1988, 161, Online Library of Liberty.
17. John Adams to Secretary Jay, September 23, 1787, in Adams, 1856, vol. 8, Online Library of Liberty.
18. Thomas Jefferson to William Duane, August 4, 1812, in Ford, 1904, Online Library of Liberty.
19. For historical crime data, see Gurr, 1989.
20. The data on prosecutions for theft come from Nelson, 1967. The data on the population of Middlesex County come from Chickering, 1846, Google Books.
21. By way of comparison: The rate of reported larceny-thefts in the United States in 2008 was 319 per 10,000 people, a number that doesn't add in all the other forms of property crime or consider all the larceny-thefts that go unreported. Uniform Crime Reports for 2008.
22. In the cities, there is also the peculiar role of mobs in the nineteenth century. This is a rich topic unto itself, but, like frontier fighting, the activities of mobs only occasionally fell into the categories of crime or dishonesty as we normally think of it.
23. Tocqueville, 1840, vol. 1, Google Books.
24. Hamilton, 1833, Google Books.
25. Grund, 1837, Google Books.
26. James Wilson, "Of the Natural Rights of Individuals," in *Collected Works of James Wilson*, vol. 2, ed. Kermit L. Hall and Mark David Hall (Indianapolis: Liberty Fund, 2007), Online Library of Liberty.
27. John Adams, *Diary*, June 2, 1778.

28. John Adams, "John Adams to the Young Men of the City of New York," in Charles Francis Adams, ed., *The Works of John Adams, Second President of the United States: With a Life of the Author, Notes and Illustrations*, vol. 9 (Boston: Little, Brown and Co., 1856), Online Library of Liberty. Even Benjamin Franklin, whose extramarital liaisons were many and enthusiastic, observed that "a bachelor is not a complete human being. He is like the odd half of a pair of scissors, which has not yet found its fellow, and is therefore not even half so useful as they might be together." Benjamin Franklin to Thomas Jordan, London, May 18, 1787, in Murphy, 1906, Google Books.

29. Martineau, 1837, part 2, Google Books.

30. Tocqueville, 1840, vol. 2, Google Books.

31. Ibid.

32. Ibid.

33. Grund, 1837, Google Books.

34. Novak, 2002, 34.

35. Washington's Farewell Address, Online Library of Liberty.

36. John Adams to the officers of the first brigade of the third division of the militia of Massachusetts in *The Works of John Adams*.

37. John Adams to F. A. Vanderkemp, quoted in Novak, 2002, epigraph.

38. James Madison to Frederick Beasley, November 20, 1825, quoted in Novak, 2002, 33.

39. Thomas Jefferson, *Notes on the State of Virginia*, Online Library of Liberty.

40. The anecdote is given in the diary of the Reverend Ethan Allen, now held by the Library of Congress, and is quoted in full in Novak, 2002, 31. Its authenticity is unverified. Allen was a child during Jefferson's presidency, so it is probably a secondhand account at best. But this passage from a letter written in 1807 reflects a sensibility consistent with the anecdote: "The practice of morality being necessary for the well-being of society, [our Creator] has taken care to impress its precepts so indelibly on our hearts that they shall not be effaced by the subtleties of our brain. We all agree in the obligation of the moral precepts of Jesus, and nowhere will they be found delivered in greater purity than in His discourses. It is, then, a matter of principle with me to avoid disturbing the tranquility of others by the expression of any opinion on the innocent questions in which we schismatize." Thomas Jefferson to James Fishback, in Foley, 1900, Google Books.

41. Thomas Jefferson to William Canby, September 18, 1813, http://www .beliefnet.com/resourcelib/docs/57/Letter_from_Thomas_Jefferson_to_ William_Canby_1.html.

42. Quoted in Clark, 1983, 413.

43. Quoted in Novak, 2002, 37. See the rest of Novak's chapter 2 for examples of links between Christianity and the needs of a self-governing society.

44. Tocqueville, 1840, vol. 1, Google Books.

45. *New York Times*, April 22, 1910, p. 1, New York Times Archives.

8: Marriage

1. For an excellent treatise on that proposition, see Hymowitz, 2006.
2. Roper Center for Public Opinion Research website, http://www.roper center.uconn.edu/. USGALLUP.556POS.R137M.
3. Roper Center for Public Opinion Research website.
4. This calculation multiplies the "happily married among those married" percentage from the GSS with the percentage of persons married in the CPS, with its much larger and nationally representative sample.
5. Aronson and Huston, 2004.
6. Fomby and Cherlin, 2007; Cavenagh and Huston, 2006.
7. Bronte-Tinkew et al., 2006; Harper and McLanahan, 1998.
8. Sourander et al., 2006.
9. Bauman, Silver, and Stein, 2006; Denise et al., 2005.
10. Warner and Hayward, 2006.
11. Pearson, Muller, and Frisco, 2006.
12. Carlson, 2006.
13. Brown, 2006.
14. The citations of specific journal articles are only illustrative of a large literature. Some major review sources are McLanahan and Sandefur, 1994; Mayer, 1997; McLanahan, 2001; Aronson and Huston, 2004; and Hymowitz, 2006.
15. In making this calculation, I exclude children living with a widowed parent.
16. Malinowski, 1930, Google Books.
17. Laslett, Oosterveen, and Smith, 1980.
18. Brown and Manning, 2009.
19. Bumpass and Lu, 2000.
20. Ibid.
21. Aronson and Huston, 2004, table 1.
22. Ibid., table 2.
23. Brown, 2004, table 1.
24. Summarized in Bumpass and Lu, 2000.

9: Industriousness

1. For whites ages 16 and older, the unemployment rate was 5.1 percent in 1960–64 and 4.5 percent in 2008. I use 2004–8 instead of the most recent five-year period, 2006–10, to avoid clouding the comparison with the high unemployment rates of 2009 and 2010. Bureau of Labor Statistics website.
2. The slight declines in labor force dropouts between the 1960 measure, based on the decennial census, and 1968, based on the CPS, should be ignored. Overall, we know that white male labor force participation among prime-age males during the decade remained flat, and the slight decline

is prudently attributed to the difference in the sources. There could be some incomparability, despite the identical labor force question used in both surveys, because the CPS data all come from the March survey, whereas the census data are collected over a broader span of time. Another issue is the assignment of occupations for people who are out of the labor force. The census of 1960 was significantly more likely than the CPS surveys to identify someone out of the labor force with an occupation.

3. Another peculiarity of the graph is the sudden jump for men with no more than a high school education in 1993–94. I have satisfied myself that it is not a result of miscoding or other data errors, but I have no explanation for it.

4. Herrnstein and Murray, 1994, chapters 7–8.

5. I use the national unemployment rate for the civilian noninstitutional population ages 16 and older as reported by the Bureau of Labor Statistics to reflect the overall state of the labor market.

6. Logit analysis regressing a binary variable (employed or unemployed) on year and the national unemployment rate.

7. The CPS reports hours in intervals (1–14, 15–29, 30–34, 35–39, 40, 40–48, 49–59, and 60+). I used the midpoint of each interval, and 65 for those in the 60+ group, to reach my estimate of hours per week.

8. Sundstrom, 1999, presents evidence that time-diary estimates of hours per week show smaller weekly totals than the CPS estimates, and that the college-educated show the greatest discrepancy. Whether this discrepancy represents a real overestimate of time spent working or differences in the kinds of work captured by the two measures is not known.

9. Bureau of Labor Statistics website, www.bls.gov. Occupational Employment Statistics for 2009, http://www.bls.gov/oes/current/oes_nat.htm. Converted to 2010 dollars.

10. Bureau of Labor Statistics website.

11. The leisure hours were 104.3 for college men and 101.9 for men without a high school diploma, a 2 percent difference. Aguiar and Hurst, 2009, table 2-2.

12. Ibid., 2.

13. Ibid., tables 3-2B, 3-3B, 3-3C.

14. The 1985 study did not have a race variable. These results apply to men of all races.

15. Nakosteen and Zimmer, 1987.

16. Becker, 1981.

17. Gilder, 1973. Gilder, 1986, is an expanded and revised version.

18. The seminal article arguing for an increase in male productivity is Korenman and Neumark, 1991. Some ingenious evidence supporting this position is Ginther and Zavodny, 2001, which uses shotgun weddings (men marrying pregnant women whom they might not have married absent the pregnancy)

as a way of diminishing selection effects. Arguing against the increase in male productivity are Cornwell and Rupert, 1997; Krashinsky, 2004; and Dougherty, 2006.

19. The results are based on a logit analysis regressing a binary variable (in or out of the labor force) on year, marital status (binary), the unemployment rate for white males ages 30–49, categorical variables for education (college degree or more, no more than a high school diploma, and in between), and an interaction term for education and marriage. The fitted values for 1960 and 2010 set the unemployment rate for prime-age white males at the 1960/1968–2010 mean of 4.1 percent.

20. Author's analysis, IPUMS based on white women ages 18–64 not in school.

21. I set the minimum size for computing a percentage at 100. The CPS data for Belmont had small numbers of single women in their thirties and forties through the mid-1970s. This means that the Belmont percentage for 1969 is based on 1968–70, the percentage for 1972 is based on 1971–72, the percentage for 1974 is based on 1973–74, and the percentage for 1976 is based on 1975–76.

22. From 1960 to 2008, the mean for all employed white women ages 30–49 was 36.5 hours, showing an upward trend from about 35 hours at the end of the 1960s to more than 37 hours for all but one of the years from 1988 through 2008.

23. More formally, the trendline shows the percentage of homes in the CPS in which, for married households, one of the spouses had worked at least forty hours during the week preceding the interview or, for unmarried households, in which the person designated as head of household had worked at least forty hours during the week preceding the interview. The sample is restricted to persons coded as either head of household or spouse of head of household.

10: Honesty

1. High school dropouts with blue-collar occupations ages 30–49 usually live in working-class neighborhoods even if they spent their childhoods in Belmont. The reason for the Belmont-Fishtown classification is to have a way of characterizing the existing population of a neighborhood, not the socio-economic class of their parents. But crime is exceptional, since so much of it is committed by young men in their teens or twenties, hence I inquire into the probable socioeconomic backgrounds of prison inmates, as described in appendix E. There is no basis for thinking that a substantial number of prisoners who qualify for Fishtown as adults actually were born to middle-class or upper-middle-class parents.

2. The data on inmates' occupations were sparse. The survey asked several different questions about the job that the probationer had held at the time of the interview or before the arrest, but even combining all of those

answers produced occupational data for fewer than half of the respondents. Among those who did give occupations, 79 percent were in occupations that qualified them for Fishtown, while only 7 percent were in occupations that qualified them for Belmont. Among all white males ages 20–49, the comparable proportions were 59 percent and 25 percent.

3. Joe Nocera, "Still Stuck in Denial on Wall St.," *New York Times*, October 1, 2010.

4. Declarations of bankruptcy under Chapter 13 include a repayment plan for some or all of the debt.

5. From 1972 through 2005, the figure is based on "nonbusiness" filings. In the SAUS prior to 1981, filings were reported in terms of the occupation of the debtor. Combining all the published data, we have both measures from 1972 to 1980. The total for lines for "employees" and "other, not in business" in the pre-1981 coding were within a few hundred cases of the number for "nonbusiness" during those years, so I used that total as a proxy for nonbusiness cases for 1960–71.

6. Domowitz and Eovaldi, 1993, lists thirteen "prodebtor" provisions of the 1978 act, including, among others, an expansive list of exemptions (property that the bankrupt can keep) and restrictions on the rights of creditors.

7. Domowitz and Eovaldi, 1993, tested multivariate regression models using data from 1961 through 1985 and concluded the effect of the bill in its first years was not significant.

8. Michelle White (White, 1998) describes how this works in terms of two types of people: Type A, who would file for bankruptcy only if misfortune creates unmanageable financial distress, and Type B, who "plan in advance to take advantage of the possibility of bankruptcy in the same way that many households plan in advance to reduce their tax liability" (p. 693). She then works through the financial calculations for bankruptcy laws with different exemption levels, and demonstrates that it is indeed possible under American bankruptcy law to plan for bankruptcy to pay—if you are a person who doesn't much care if you stiff your creditors.

9. Sullivan, Warren, and Westbrook, 2000.

10. Zhu, 2011.

11: Religiosity

1. Putnam, 2000, 66.

2. Ibid., 67.

3. Leege and Kellstedt, 1993; Verba, Schlozman, and Brady, 1995; McKenzie, 2001.

4. Levin, 1994.

5. Hummer et al., 1999.

6. Idler and Kasl, 1992.

7. Lehrer and Chiswick, 1993.

8. Koenig, McCollough, and Larson, 2001.

9. See, for example, Donahue and Benson, 1995; Muller and Ellison, 2001; Regnerus, 2000.

10. Hutchinson, 1986.

11. Hoge, Johnson, and Luidens, 1994, 1.

12. Ibid., 2–6.

13. Ibid., 1994, 1–4. The percentage of people who said they had attended a worship service in the last seven days had moved within the 47–52 percent range from the mid-1950s through 1963, then dropped to the 40–42 percent range in the first half of the 1970s.

14. Hadaway and Marier, 1998.

15. International Social Survey Program: Religion 2, 1998, cited in Hunsberger and Altemeyer, 2006, 13, table 1.

16. Larson and Witham, 1998.

12: The Real Fishtown

1. Milano, 2008, 76–77. Milano, a lifelong resident of Fishtown, has also written two other histories about Fishtown.

2. Upon reading that twenty people in Fishtown in 1960 were not white, Ken Milano wrote, "Twenty? Wow, sounds like a lot. I'm surprised." Data for 1960 are based on Philadelphia census tracts 18A and 18B. For subsequent censuses through 2000, they were Philadelphia census tracts 143 and 158. The borders of the census tracts correspond closely with the local definition of the boundary of Fishtown—the Delaware River, Frankford Avenue, and halfway between Norris Street and York Street.

3. Rossi, 1955.

4. Binzen, 1970.

5. Quoted in ibid., 103.

6. Quoted in ibid., 103.

7. Smallacombe's research also covered Fishtown as locally defined, but her center of activity was in the adjacent area to the north.

8. A literature on white working-class culture exists that I have not tried to review here. Much of it—Binzen's book on Fishtown is a journalistic example—was written in the 1960s and 1970s, prompted by the white working-class backlash against what was seen as government favoritism toward African Americans at the expense of white working-class Americans. Examples are Sennett and Cobb, 1972, and Rubin, 1976. Much of the literature on the white working class since the 1960s has dwelt on racial issues, but other useful descriptions of white working-class society independently of race are Kornblum, 1974; Hirsch, 1983; Halle, 1984; and MacLeod, 1987. Smallacombe's work is uniquely valuable for this book

partly because it serendipitously uses the Kensington District as its locale (when I chose Fishtown as the name for my fictional working-class community, I had no idea that Smallacombe's dissertation existed) and partly because it describes life in the late 1990s, after the trends I describe in part 2 had taken hold.

9. Smallacombe, 2002, 206.

10. Ibid., 209.

11. Ibid.

12. Ibid., 208.

13. Ibid., 210.

14. Ibid., 165.

15. Ibid., 220.

16. The census tract data for 1960 show labor force participation for males ages 14 and older, while the census tract data for 2000 use the age range of 16 and older. I chose 20–64 as an age range at which Fishtown males would be expected to be in the labor force both in 1960 and in 2000 (college attendance for Fishtown men ages 20 and over was still very low as of 2000). I applied the national labor force participation rates in 1960 for white males ages 14–18 and those ages 65 and older to the number of actual Fishtown males in those age ranges to obtain the estimate of labor force participation among males ages 20–64. For 2000, I followed a parallel procedure, except that the age range for the younger males was 16–19 instead of 14–19. I double-checked the extremely high 2000 figure (30 percent) by replicating the national statistics limited to white males who came from working-class families. That exercise produced an estimate of 29 percent.

17. Smallacombe, 2002, 194.

18. Ibid.

19. This and following quotations from Ken Milano are taken from conversations and e-mails in the spring of 2011.

20. Smallacombe, 2002, 214.

21. Ibid., 85.

22. Ibid., 166.

23. Ibid., 239

24. Ibid., 238

25. Ibid., 227.

26. Ibid., 227–28.

27. Ibid., 233

28. Ibid., 254.

29. Ibid., 259.

30. Ibid., 271–72.

31. Ibid., 264.

32. Ibid., 148.

33. Ibid., 147.

34. For an account set in Oelwein, Iowa, see Reding, 2009.

13: The Size of the New Lower Class

1. *Income* is defined as money from private sources in the form of wages, income from a business, dividends, interest, rent, or other income that does not come from government benefits. I am using the poverty threshold for a household consisting of just two adults, with the household head under the age of 65 as of the 2010 CPS, expressed in constant dollars for calendar 1959–2009. I use this procedure instead of the actual thresholds for each year because of changes in the reporting and calculation of the poverty threshold that make the actual thresholds not quite comparable across time. But the differences are minor. For example, the actual threshold for a two-adult household headed by a male (a distinction no longer made in the calculation of poverty thresholds) in 1959 was $1,965. The threshold based on the 2010 CPS is $1,960 (1959 dollars).

2. Six percent overstates the prevalence of minimum-wage jobs, since many of those are jobs such as waitperson or dealer in a casino where tips are the major source of net income. Bureau of Labor Statistics website, http://www.bls.gov/cps/minwage2010.htm.

3. Bureau of Labor Statistics website, http://www.bls.gov/oes/current/oes_nat.htm#00-0000. Occupation 37-1012, converted to 2010 dollars.

4. I also am not saying that authentic stay-at-home full-time fathers are not as honorably occupied as stay-at-home full-time mothers. But there are still too few of them to affect the statistics.

5. The source of income is not given in the 1960 census. The calculation for 1959 thus assumes that none of the income for males ages 30–49 came from government benefits. This is not technically correct, but the sources and amounts of government assistance for males were still extremely rare (mostly veteran's and disability benefits) and small as of 1959, so the degree of error is unlikely to be more than a percentage point.

6. Ross, Danziger, and Smolensky, 1987. The reductions in poverty in the 1940s and 1950s continued but did not accelerate in the 1960s. See Murray, 1984, for the details about the indictment of the policies of the 1960s.

7. This figure is based on total income including government benefits, because the GSS doesn't split out that category—one of the technical issues that prevent trustworthy calculation of the nonoverlapping part of the community isolate population.

8. Figure 13.4 extrapolates the trendline for isolates observed in the GSS data from 1974 to 2004 back to 1960. The assumption behind this is based on Robert Putnam's trendlines for social capital from the 1950s onward in Putnam, 2000, which shows steeply falling organizational membership from the early 1960s onward. Putnam's findings are discussed in more detail in chapter 14.

Part III: Why It Matters

1. Quoted in Alfred L. Malabre Jr., *Lost Prophets: An Insider's History of the Modern Economists* (Cambridge, MA: Harvard Business School Press, 1994), 220.

14: The Selective Collapse of American Community

1. Banfield, 1958, 85.
2. Tocqueville, 1840, 514.
3. Olasky, 1992, 86. Chapters 5 and 6 of *The Tragedy of American Compassion* have a wide range of similar data.
4. Pollock, 1923, in Skocpol, 2003, 63–64.
5. Skocpol, 2003, especially chapters 2 and 3.
6. Ibid., 108–9.
7. Ibid., 110–11.
8. When Robert and Helen Lynd conducted their classic study of Muncie, Indiana, in the mid-1920s, they reported the memberships in organizations among their samples of "business-class" and "working class" respondents, effectively representing the white-collar and blue-collar occupations. Fifty-seven percent of working-class men and 36 percent of working-class wives (all of the respondents were married) belonged to at least one organization, numbers that are higher than any observed for Fishtown in the data present, but they pale in comparison to the percentages for the business class: 97 percent among the men and 92 percent among their wives. B. Lynd and H. Lynd, 1929, appendix table 19.
9. Putnam, 2000.
10. Ibid., chapters 2, 3, 6, 7.
11. This actually understates the real decrease in participation, Putnam points out, because voting in the South after 1965 represents many black votes that do not reflect a new propensity to participate in the election, but the ability to do so in the aftermath of the civil rights movement and the Voting Rights Act of 1965. Putnam, 2000, 31–33.
12. Brooks, 2000, 106.
13. See, for example, Nie, 2001; Wellman et al., 2001; Hampton and Wellman, 2003; Bargh, 2004; Williams, 2006.
14. This and the next two examples are ones that have directly involved members of my family, and they are only a few of the many examples our family has experienced. If you reach blindfolded into a bowl of marbles and the first three you pick at random are purple, chances are high that the bowl has a lot of purple marbles. When the examples of social capital via the Internet are so plentiful, both from members of my own family and from the families of friends, it seems extremely likely to me that we are witnessing a

transformation of traditional social capital that goes far beyond anything that the scholarly literature has yet documented.

15. Jim Jansen, "Use of the Internet in Higher-Income Households," November 24, 2010, Pew Research Center's Internet & American Life Project, www.pewinternet.org.

16. Keith N. Hampton et al., "Social Networking Sites and Our Lives," June 16, 2011, Pew Research Center's Internet & American Life Project, www.pewinternet.org.

17. Unlike most graphs using GSS data, this one shows data points for the individual election years, since sample sizes were adequate (in all but the 1968 and 2008 elections, at least two GSS surveys could be combined to produce the samples for Belmont and Fishtown).

18. Approximately 72 percent of all adults of all races without a high school diploma voted in the 1952 and 1956 election samples used for the analyses in *The American Voter* (Campbell, 1960, table 15-1, p. 252). Interpolating the white voting turnout among those who hadn't completed high school is imprecise, but it could not have been lower than 75 percent and may have approached 80 percent.

19. Fukuyama, 1995.

20. Putnam, 2007, 134.

21. Putnam used a variety of data sources to obtain comparable measures of pre-1972 trust. For adults as a whole, all races, the proportion of trusting people had dropped from about 53 percent to 49 percent from 1960 to 1972. Putnam, 2007, table 38, p. 140.

22. Ibid., 149–50.

23. Murray, 2003, chapter 19.

24. Field, 2003; Putnam, 2000.

15: The Founding Virtues and the Stuff of Life

1. I cannot retrieve the name of the show or the date of the interview—I saw it many years ago, and Google has been no help—but that sad smile on Geffen's face made his words stick.

2. The relationships of self-reported happiness to family, vocation, community, and faith in the surveys from 1990 to 1998 and 2000 to 2010 were examined separately to see if they had changed. They had not, except for minor variations. Combining the surveys expands the sample sizes and provides greater stability for the multivariate analyses. For a more extensive discussion of the relationship of the quantitative measure of happiness to work, marriage, religion, income, and a variety of other topics, see Brooks, 2008.

3. For a review of the literature and evidence showing an independent effect of marriage on happiness, see Stutzer, 2006.

4. The happiness item offered four alternatives instead of the three offered by

the GSS, and the wording of the alternatives is not quite the same as the wording of the GSS alternatives: "not happy at all," "not very happy," "happy," and "very happy." Accordingly, the absolute percentages of people who identified themselves as "very happy" in the Social Capital Benchmark Survey cannot be compared to those in the GSS data. To give a sense of the difference in the results: In the GSS data for the 2000s, 32 percent of prime-age whites said they were "very happy" compared to 42 percent in the Social Capital Benchmark Survey. In the GSS data for the 2000s, 9 percent said they were "not too happy" compared to a combined total of 4 percent in the Social Capital Benchmark Survey who said they were "not happy at all" or "not very happy."

5. The SCBS also had a "protest activities index" that combined measures of nonelectoral forms of political participation—signing petitions, attending political meeting or rallies, membership in political groups or labor unions, and engaging in a demonstration, protest, boycott, or march. But 46 percent of the sample had a score of zero, making it impossible to establish "very low" and "very high" categories that resembled the cutoffs for the other index. For the record, 39 percent of those who had a protest activities index score of zero answered that they were "very happy," compared to 46 percent of those who got the top scores on that index.

6. All cutoffs were calculated using sample weights applied to the entire SCBS sample (all races, all ages).

7. I should note that the giving and volunteering index includes an indicator based on religion-based volunteering and charity, which might have tapped into the high levels of happiness already discussed among the very religious. You may be wondering whether all these indexes are catching the same people in the "very low" and "very high" categories, which would account for the similarity in results. The answer is no. The correlations among the indexes are moderate, mostly in the +0.3 to +0.5 range, which means that people fall into different parts of the range for different indexes. Take, for example, the pair of indexes with the highest correlation (+0.54) among prime-age whites, the group involvement index and the giving and volunteering index. For the giving and volunteering index, 1,219 people fell into the highest category, but only 413 of them also fell into the highest category on the group involvement index. And those results are for the most highly correlated pair. It seems fair to conclude that different types of community engagement are each (largely) independently associated with higher levels of self-reported happiness.

8. The simple version of a multivariate analysis considers each independent variable separately (an independent variable is a hypothesized cause of the dependent variable). In the type of analysis used here, known as logit, the simple version shows you the size of boost given to the probability of answering "very happy" by every category of every independent variable. Take, for example, the work satisfaction variable, which has four categories: "very

dissatisfied," "a little dissatisfied," "moderately satisfied," and "very satisfied." The analysis gives you a separate number—the size of the boost—for each of the four categories.

The more complicated version of multivariate analysis asks what happens when we consider how permutations interact—a happy marriage with no religion, high social trust with high job satisfaction, and so on. The problem is that the number of permutations grows exponentially with the addition of variables. It is easily possible to calculate analyses that contain every permutation of several variables—the computer doesn't get tired—but the great majority of the numbers associated with the interaction terms are not only going to be statistically nonsignificant, they are going to be so small that they have no discernible effect on the probability of responding "very happy." Furthermore, you must remember that the computer is not worried about whether there is a good reason to expect that an interaction effect may exist or whether the sample size for a given permutation is large enough to be interpretable; it just blindly follows its instructions. In doing so, it assigns an "effect" to every interaction no matter what. The program has no capacity for saying, "This is just noise obscuring real relationships," so the analyst has to make that judgment. In the analysis reported in the text, only marriage and vocation had nontrivial interaction effects. The results are thus based on categorical variables for marriage, work satisfaction, social trust, and strength of religious involvement, and the interactions between marriage and work satisfaction. The equation also includes age as a control variable.

9. See Brooks, 2008, chapter 5, for a recent review of the literature on happiness and income and chapter 6 for a review of the literature on happiness and income inequality.

10. The analysis was conducted using interaction terms of income with the categorical independent variables, but all of the interaction effects were substantively tiny and did not approach statistical significance. The results reported in table 15.2 replicated the one reported in figure 15.6 with the addition of a continuous variable expressing family income in constant dollars.

11. These figures are fitted to age 40 and $50,500, the rounded median income ($50,499) of the sample used in the multivariate analyses.

17: Alternative Futures

1. Vol. 2 of the *Glasgow Edition of the Works and Correspondence of Adam Smith* (Indianapolis: Liberty Fund, 1981). Chapter: *[IV.vii.c] part third: Of the Advantages which Europe has derived from the Discovery of America, and from that of a Passage to the East Indies by the Cape of Good Hope*. Online Library of Liberty.

2. Rifkin, 2004.

3. Zuckerman, 2008; Layard, 2005.

4. Fischer, 2010.

5. Fischer and Hout, 2006.

6. Many libertarians would quarrel with that statement, arguing that the New Deal was the beginning of the end. I agree that it was the thin edge of the wedge that rationalized the later expansions of federal power, but, for practical purposes, the American project was still alive and well until the next inflection point after Kennedy's assassination.

7. Toynbee's vogue came about because of D. C. Somervell's abridgment of volumes 1–6, published in 1946. The six volumes themselves were published from 1934 to 1939. In 1957, Somervell published his abridgment of volumes 7–10, which Toynbee had published between the end of World War II and 1954.

8. Toynbee, 1946, chapter 19.

9. Ibid., 439.

10. Himmelfarb, 1984.

11. I ignore the quasi-aristocratic code that might be said to have existed among the very small northeastern elite in the late nineteenth century.

12. "True Manliness," in *The New McGuffey Fourth Reader*, 1901, 42–47. Available online at Google Books.

13. Nonjudgmentalism is even more extreme in western Europe than it is in the United States, but I am not sufficiently familiar with the data from western Europe to be confident that the discrepancy between the behavior and the words of the European upper class are as great as they are in the United States.

14. *The Oxford English Dictionary* gives a secondary meaning that is now archaic: "uncomely, unhandsome."

15. Regarding the Spelling mansion: Jeannine Stein, "The House of Spelling: Massive Construction Project in Holmby Hills Flusters Some Neighbors," *Los Angeles Times*, April 8, 1988. Regarding Henry McKinnell's departure from Pfizer: CNBC News, December 22, 2006, "Pfizer's McKinnell—The $200 Million Man," CNBC News website; "Golden Parachutes: Bosses Who Walked Away with Large Payouts," the online version of *The Economist*, July 27, 2010.

16. Both the Murphy and the Forbes data include bonuses, stock options, and other forms of compensation along with salary. The Forbes chart used for figure 17.1, from http://www.forbes.com/lists/2011/12/ceo-pay-20-year-historical-chart.html, purports to show pay from 1989 to 2011, but those years refer to the year of publication, not the year of compensation. I have moved all of the numbers back one year, so that, for example, I assign to 2010 the $9.026 million mean that Forbes assigns to 2011.

17. I think an ethical issue does arise for CEOs who want a deal that will pay them handsome separation packages even if they drive the company over a cliff, but that's peripheral to the discussion here.

18. Bizjak, 2011.

19. In the advanced countries of the West, the private sector accounts for either all the production of wealth or all but a trivial proportion. The taxes paid

by government employees in advanced countries amount, with the rarest exceptions, to a partial clawback of their salaries, not a contribution to the financing of the welfare state.

20. *The Federalist*, no. 51, http://www.foundingfathers.info/federalistpapers/.
21. The slogan was first stated by Marx in *Critique of the Gotha Programme*, April or early May 1875. Available online at http://www.marxists.org/archive/marx/works/download/Marx_Critque_of_the_Gotha_Programme.pdf.
22. Wilson, 1998.
23. Murray, 2005.
24. Murray, 2006, 21.
25. Fogel, 2000, 17.
26. Ibid., 25.
27. Ibid., 176–77.

Appendix A: Data Sources and Presentation

1. Cleveland, 1979.
2. Fischer and Hout, 2006, 253.

Appendix C: Supplemental Material for the Chapter on Belmont and Fishtown

1. "Blue-collar professions" refer to high-skill blue-collar jobs that lend themselves to self-employment or have a natural career path to supervisory positions on blue-collar work sites.
2. This stipulation means that a person whose spouse has an AA degree or higher is not assigned to Fishtown even if both the husband and wife are in Fishtown occupations.
3. For databases that show a person's years of completed education rather than highest degree completed, persons who have completed a thirteenth year of schooling are categorized as "no more than a high school diploma." Persons who have completed fourteen years of schooling are considered equivalent to those who have achieved an associate's degree.
4. Married couples in which both had a college degree, the head of household was ages 30–49, but neither had an occupation were not assigned to a neighborhood, because of the likelihood of missing data or some other problems with the data (there are few circumstances in which neither person in such a couple would not even have an occupation). In the CPS database, there were only 471 such couples among the 691,942 married white couples in which the head of household was ages 30–49.
5. The rule in the text includes married persons who are living in households in which neither is the head—for example, married children still living with one of the spouse's parents. People in such circumstances are identified only in the CPS or census data, and constitute a minuscule portion of the population.

6. Age 21 is chosen for the cutoff because of its traditional standing as the age of majority.

7. Nakao and Treas, 1994.

8. Hauser and Warren, 1997.

9. Unpublished data provided courtesy of Earl Hunt.

10. In practice, using one of the prestige scales would have produced about the same results as using the measure of cognitive demands. The correlation of the *g*-loadings with the Nakao and Treas occupational prestige index was +0.74 and the correlation with the Hauser and Warren index was +0.76. Based on the 1990 occupational coding used by the Census Bureau.

11. For a discussion of the literature on job productivity and cognitive ability as of the early 1990s, see Herrnstein and Murray, 1994, chapter 3. For an update on the literature as of the early 2000s, see Gottfredson, 2003.

12. The bottom-ranked occupations were loggers, graders and sorters of agricultural products, operators of construction equipment, miners, stevedores and other materials movers, stock handlers, packers and wrappers, packagers, and equipment cleaners.

Appendix D: Supplemental Material for the Marriage Chapter

1. Bramlett and Mosher, 2002, table 35.

2. These results are produced by logit analyses in which a binary variable (whether the child experienced a divorce by the time his mother was age 40) was regressed on neighborhood in the first model and on neighborhood, mother's age at marriage, and mother's age at giving birth in the second model.

Appendix E: Supplemental Material for the Honesty Chapter

1. The results for the original cohort born in 1945 were published in Wolfgang, Figlio, and Sellin, 1972. The study was replicated with the 1958 Philadelphia birth cohort; see Tracy, 1990.

2. These results are produced by regressing the number of prior arrests on age, years of education, occupational class, and the interaction of education and occupational class for white male prisoners ages 20–49. Age was fitted to 30 for both neighborhoods. Educational values were fitted based on the average education attainment among prisoners from the two neighborhoods— seventeen and ten years for Belmont and Fishtown, respectively. The fitted numbers of prior arrests resulting from this procedure were 2.46 and 5.92 for Belmont and Fishtown, respectively.

3. Levitt, 1996; Dilulio and Piehl, 1991; Dilulio and Piehl, 1995.

4. Dilulio, 1991.

5. Greenwood and Abrahamse, 1982, xiii.
6. In this statistic and the others that follow, I do not use UCR arrest data from 1974 to 1980. During those years, a significant number of law enforcement agencies reported results that did not cover the full twelve months, and those were included in the published UCR volumes.
7. Bloomberg LP.
8. For the record, the incidence of SEC Accounting and Auditing Enforcement Releases rose from 1983 to 2003 and subsequently declined.
9. For the record, the incidence of IRS fraud cases declined from the first data in 1978 through 2009.

Bibliography

Adams, Charles Francis, ed. 1856. *The Works of John Adams, Second President of the United States: With a Life of the Author, Notes and Illustrations.* Boston: Little, Brown & Co.

Adams, Henry. 1889. *History of the United States During the First Administration of Thomas Jefferson.* New York: Charles Scribner's Sons.

Aguiar, Mark, and Erik Hurst. 2009. *The Increase in Leisure Inequality: 1965–2005.* Washington, DC: AEI Press.

Allen, W. B., ed. 1988. *George Washington: A Collection.* Indianapolis: Liberty Fund.

Aronson, Stacey R., and Aletha C. Huston. 2004. The mother-infant relationship in single, cohabiting, and married families: A case for marriage? *Journal of Family Psychology* 18 (1):5–18.

Arum, Richard, Josipa Roksa, and Michelle J. Budig. 2008. The romance of college attendance: Higher education stratification and mate selection. *Research in Social Stratification and Mobility* 26:107–21.

Banfield, Edward C. 1958. *The Moral Basis of a Backward Society.* Glencoe, IL: The Free Press.

Bargh, John A., and Katelyn Y. A. McKenna. 2004. The Internet and social life. *Annual Review of Psychology* 55 (1):573–90.

Bauman, Laurie J., Ellen J. Silver, and Ruth E. K. Stein. 2006. Cumulative social disadvantage and child health. *Pediatrics* 117:1321–27.

Becker, Gary S. 1981. *A Treatise on the Family.* Cambridge, MA: Harvard University Press.

Bender, Wilbur J. 1960. Final report of W. J. Bender, Chairman of the Admission and Scholarship Committee and Dean of Admissions and Financial Aids, 1952–1960. Harvard University.

Binzen, Peter. 1970. *Whitetown USA: A First-Hand Study of How the "Silent Majority" Lives, Learns, Works, and Thinks.* New York: Random House.

Bishop, Bill. 2008. *The Big Sort: Why the Clustering of Like-Minded America Is Tearing Us Apart.* Boston: Houghton Mifflin.

Bizjak, John, Michael Lemmon, and Thanh Nguyen. 2011. Are all CEOs above average?: An empirical analysis of compensation peer groups and pay design. *Journal of Financial Economics* (June):538–55.

Bouchard, Thomas J., Jr. 1981. Familial studies of intelligence: A review. *Science* 212 (May 29):1055–59.

Bramlett, M. D., and W. D. Mosher. 2002. Cohabitation, marriage, divorce, and remarriage in the United States. In *Vital Health Statistics* 23 (22): National Center for Health Statistics.

Briggs, Derek C. 2004. Evaluating SAT coaching: Gains, effects, and self-selection. In *Rethinking the SAT: The Future of Standardized Testing in University Admissions,* edited by R. Zwick. New York: Routledge Falmer.

Broda, Christian, and David E. Weinstein. 2008. *Prices, Poverty, and Inequality: Why Americans Are Better Off Than You Think.* Washington, DC: AEI Press.

Bronson, Po, and Ashley Merryman. 2009. *Nurture Shock: New Thinking About Children.* New York: Hachette Book Group.

Bronte-Tinkew, Jacinta, Kristin A. Moore, and Jennifer Carrano. 2006. The influence of father involvement on youth risk behaviors among adolescents: A comparison of native-born and immigrant families. *Social Science Research* 35:181–209.

Brooks, Arthur C. 2008. *Gross National Happiness.* New York: Basic Books.

Brooks, David. 2000. *Bobos in Paradise: The New Upper Class and How They Got There.* New York: Simon & Schuster.

Brown, Susan L. 2004. Family structure and child well-being: The significance of parental cohabitation. *Journal of Marriage and the Family* 66 (May): 351–67.

———. 2006. Family structure transitions and adolescent well-being. *Demography* 43:447–61.

Brown, Susan L., and Wendy D. Manning. 2009. Family boundary ambiguity and the measurement of family structure: The significance of cohabitation. *Demography* 46 (1):85–101.

Bumpass, L.L., and Hsien-Hen Lu. 2000. Trends in cohabitation and implications for children's family contexts in the United States. *Population Studies* 54 (1):29–41.

Campbell, Angus, Philip E. Converse, Warren E. Miller, and Donald E. Stokes. 1960. *The American Voter.* New York: Wiley.

Cardiff, Christopher, and Daniel B. Klein. 2005. Faculty partisan affiliations in all disciplines: A voter-registration study. *Critical Review* 17 (3–4):237–55.

Carlson, Marcia J. 2006. Family structure, father involvement, and adolescent outcomes. *Journal of Marriage and the Family* 68:137–54.

Cavenagh, Shannon E., and Aletha C. Huston. 2006. Family instability and children's early problem behavior. *Social Forces* 85:551–80.

Chickering, Jesse. 1846. *A Statistical View of the Population of Massachusetts from 1765 to 1840.* Boston: Charles C. Little & James Brown.

Chinni, Dante, and James Gimpel. 2010. *Our Patchwork Nation: The Surprising Truth About the "Real" America.* New York: Gotham Books.

Clark, Ronald W. 1983. *Benjamin Franklin: A Biography.* New York: Random House.

Cleveland, W. S. 1979. Robust locally weighted regression and smoothing scatterplots. *Journal of the American Statistical Association* 74 (368):829–36.

Coleman, James S., Ernest Q. Campbell, and Carol J. Hobson. 1966. *Equality of Educational Opportunity.* Washington, DC: National Center for Educational Statistics.

Cornwell, C., and P. Rupert. 1997. Unobservable individual effects, marriage, and the earnings of young men. *Economic Inquiry* 35 (2):285–94.

Denise, Kendrick, et al. 2005. Relationships between child, family, and neighbourhood characteristics and childhood study. *Social Medicine* 61:1905–15.

Dickens, William T., and James R. Flynn. 2006. Black Americans reduce the racial IQ gap: Evidence from standardization samples. *Psychological Science* 17 (10):913–20.

Dilulio, John J., Jr., and Anne Morrison Piehl. 1991. Does prison pay?: The stormy national debate over the cost-effectiveness of imprisonment. *Brookings Review* 9 (4):28–35.

Dilulio, John J., and Anne Morrison Piehl. 1995. Does prison pay?: Revisited. *Brookings Review* 13:21–25.

Domowitz, Ian, and Thomas L. Eovaldi. 1993. The impact of the Bankruptcy Reform Act of 1978 on consumer bankruptcy. *Journal of Law and Economics* 36 (2):803–35.

Donahue, Michael J., and Peter L. Benson. 1995. Religion and the well-being of adolescents. *Journal of Social Issues* 51 (2).

Dougherty, Christopher. 2006. The marriage premium as a distributed fixed effect. *Journal of Human Resources* 41 (2):433–43.

Eberstadt, Nicholas. 2008. *The Poverty of the Poverty Rate: Measure and Mismeasure of Material Deprivation in Modern America.* Washington, DC: AEI Press.

Espenshade, Thomas J., Chang Y. Chung, and Joan L. Walling. 2004. Admission preferences for minority students, athletes, and legacies at elite universities. *Social Science Quarterly* 85 (5):1422–46.

Espenshade, Thomas J., and Alexandria Walton Radford. 2009. *No Longer Separate, Not Yet Equal: Race and Class in Elite College Admission and Campus Life*. Princeton, NJ: Princeton University Press.

Field, John. 2003. *Social Capital*. New York: Routledge.

Fischer, Claude S. 2010. *Made in America: A Social History of American Culture and Character*. Chicago: University of Chicago Press.

Fischer, Claude S., and Michael Hout. 2006. *Century of Difference: How America Changed in the Last One Hundred Years*. New York: Russell Sage Foundation.

Florida, Richard. 2002. *The Rise of the Creative Class*. New York: Basic Books.

Fogel, Robert W. 2000. *The Fourth Great Awakening and the Future of Egalitarianism*. Chicago: University of Chicago Press.

Foley, John P., ed. 1900. *The Jeffersonian Cyclopedia*. New York: Funk & Wagnalls.

Fomby, Paula, and Andrew J. Cherlin. 2007. Family instability and child well-being. *American Sociological Review* 72 (April):181–204.

Ford, Paul Leicester, ed. 1904–5. *The Works of Thomas Jefferson*. Vol. 11, *Federal Edition*. New York: G. P. Putnam's Sons.

Fukuyama, Francis. 1995. *Trust: The Social Virtues and the Creation of Prosperity*. New York: The Free Press.

Geiger, Roger L. 2002. The competition for high ability students: Universities in a key marketplace. In *The Future of the City of Intellect: The Changing American University*, edited by S. Brint. Stanford, CA: Stanford University Press.

Gilder, George. 1973. *Sexual Suicide*. San Antonio: Quadrangle.

———. 1986. *Men and Marriage*. Gretna, LA: Pelican Publishing.

Ginther, Donna K., and Madeline Zavodny. 2001. Is the male marriage premium due to selection?: The effect of shotgun weddings on the return to marriage. *Journal of Population Economics* 14 (2):313–28.

Goldberg, Steven. 2003. *Fads and Fallacies in the Social Sciences*. Amherst, NY: Humanity Books.

Golden, Daniel. 2006. *The Price of Admission: How America's Ruling Class Buys Its Way into Elite Colleges—and Who Gets Left Outside the Gates*. New York: Random House.

Gorely, Trish, Simon J. Marshall, and Stuart Biddle. 2004. "Couch Kids: Correlates of Television Viewing Among Youth." *International Journal of Behavioral Medicine* 11 (3):152–63.

Gottfredson, Linda S. 2003. g, jobs, and life. In *The Scientific Study of General Intelligence: A Tribute to Arthur R. Jensen*. Oxford: Pergamon.

Greenwood, Peter W., and A. Abrahamse. 1982. *Selective Incapacitation*. Santa Monica: Rand Corp.

Groseclose, Tim, and Jeffrey Milyo. 2005. A measure of media bias. *Quarterly Journal of Economics* 120 (4):1191–237.

Grove, Robert D., and Alice M. Hetzel. 1968. *Vital Statistics Rates in the*

United States, 1940–1960. Washington, DC: National Center for Health Statistics.

Grund, Francis J. 1837. *The Americans in Their Moral, Social, and Political Relations*. Vol. 1. London: Longman, Rees, Orme, Brown, Green, and Longman.

Gurr, Ted R. *Violence in America: The History of Crime*. Newbury Park, CA: Sage.

Hacker, Andrew. 1992. *Two Nations: Black and White, Separate, Hostile, Unequal*. New York: Charles Scribner's & Sons.

Hadaway, C. Kirk, and P. L. Marier. 1998. Did you really go to church this week?: Behind the poll data. *The Christian Century*, May 6, 472–75.

Halle, David. 1984. *America's Working Man*. Chicago: University of Chicago Press.

Hamilton, Thomas. 1833. *Men and Manners in America*. London: T. Cadell.

Hampton, K., and B. Wellman. 2003. Neighboring in Netville: How the Internet supports community and social capital in a wired suburb. *City & Community* 2 (4):277–311.

Harper, Cynthia C., and Sara S. McLanahan. 1998. Father absence and youth incarceration. Presented at the American Sociological Association, 1998.

Hauser, Robert M., and John Robert Warren. 1997. Socioeconomic indexes for occupations: A review, update, and critique. *Sociological Methodology* 27:177–298.

Heck, Katherine E., Paula Braveman, Catherine Cubbin, Gilberto Chavez, and John Kiely. 2006. Socioeconomic status and breastfeeding initiation among California mothers. *Public Health Reports* 121 (1):51–59.

Herrnstein, Richard J., Terry Belke, and James Taylor. 1990. New York City Police Department Class of June 1940: A Preliminary Report. Cambridge: Harvard University.

Herrnstein, Richard J., and Charles Murray. 1994. *The Bell Curve: Intelligence and Class Structure in American Life*. New York: Free Press.

Himmelfarb, Gertrude. 1984. *The Idea of Poverty: England in the Early Industrial Age*. New York: Alfred A. Knopf.

Hirsch, Arnold R. 1983. *Making the Second Ghetto*. Cambridge, UK: Cambridge University Press.

Hoge, Dean R., Benton Johnson, and Donald A. Luidens. 1994. *Vanishing Boundaries: The Religion of Mainline Protestant Baby Boomers*. Louisville: Westminster/John Knox Press.

Hummer, R. A., Richard G. Rogers, Charles B. Nam, and Christopher G. Ellison. 1999. Religious involvement and U.S. adult mortality. *Demography* 36 (2):273–85.

Humphreys, Lloyd G. 1978. To understand regression from parent to offspring, think statistically. *Psychological Bulletin* 85 (6):1317–22.

Hunsberger, Bruce E., and Bob Altemeyer. 2006. *Atheists: A Groundbreaking Study of America's Nonbelievers*. Amherst, NY: Prometheus Books.

Hutchinson, William R. 1986. Past imperfect: History and the prospect for liberalism. In *Liberal Protestantism: Realities and Possibilities*, edited by R. S. Michaelson and W. C. Roof. New York: Pilgrim Press.

Hymowitz, Kay S. 2006. *Marriage and Caste in America: Separate and Unequal Families in a Post-Marital Age*. Chicago: Ivan R. Dee.

Idler, Ellen, and Stanislav V. Kasl. 1992. Religion, disability, depression, and the timing of death. *American Journal of Sociology* 97 (4):1052–79.

Jensen, Arthur R. 1998. *The g Factor: The Science of Mental Ability*. Westport, CT: Praeger.

Kalmijn, Matthijs. 1998. Intermarriage and homogamy: Causes, patterns, trends. *Annual Review of Sociology* 24:395–421.

———. 1994. Assortative mating by cultural and economic occupational status. *American Journal of Sociology* 100:422–52.

Karlgaard, Richard. 2005. Talent wars. *Forbes*, October 31.

Koenig, Harold G., Michael E. McCullough, and David B. Larson. 2001. *Handbook of Religion and Health*. New York: Oxford University Press.

Korenman, Sanders, and David Neumark. 1991. Does marriage really make men more productive? *Journal of Human Resources* 26 (2):282–307.

Kornblum, William. 1974. *Blue-Collar Community*. Chicago: University of Chicago Press.

Krashinsky, Harry A. 2004. Do marital status and computer usage really change the wage structure? *Journal of Human Resources* 29 (3):774–91.

Kurland, Philip B., and Ralph Lerner, eds. 1986. *The Founders' Constitution*. Chicago: University of Chicago Press.

Larson, Edward J., and Larry Witham. 1998. Leading scientists still reject God. *Nature* 394 (6691):313.

Laslett, Peter, Karla Oosterveen, and Richard M. Smith, eds. 1980. *Bastardy and Its Comparative History: Studies in the History of Illegitimacy and Marital Nonconformism*. Cambridge, MA: Harvard University Press.

Leege, David, and Lyman A. Kellstedt, eds. 1993. *Rediscovering the Religious Factor in American Politics*. New York: M. E. Sharpe.

Lehrer, Evelyn L., and Carmel U. Chiswick. 1993. Religion as a determinant of marital stability. *Demography* 30 (3):385–404.

Levin, Jeffrey S. 1994. Religion and health: Is there an association, is it valid, and is it causal? *Social Science and Medicine* 38 (11):1475–82.

Levitt, Steven D. 1996. The effect of prison population size on crime rates: Evidence from prison overcrowding litigation. *Quarterly Journal of Economics* 3:319–52.

Lynd, Robert, and Helen M. Lynd. 1929. *Middletown: A Study in American Culture*. New York: Harcourt, Brace and Co.

MacLeod, Jay. 1987. *Ain't No Makin' It: Leveled Aspirations in a Low-Income Neighborhood*. Boulder: Westview Press.

Malabre, Alfred L., Jr. 1994. *Lost Prophets: An Insider's History of the Modern Economists*. Cambridge, MA: Harvard Business School Press.

Malinowski, Bronislaw. 1930. *Sex, Culture, and Myth*. 1962 ed. New York: Harcourt, Brace & World.

Mariani, Mack D., and Gordon J. Hewitt. 2008. Indoctrination U? Faculty ideology and changes in student orientation. *PS: Political Science and Politics* 41:773–83.

Martineau, Harriet. 1837. *Society in America*. Vol. 3. London: Saunders and Otley.

Massey, Douglas S., Jonathan Rothwell, and Thurston Domina. 2009. The changing bases of segregation in the United States. *Annals, American Academy of Political and Social Science* 626:74–90.

Mayer, Susan E. 1997. *What Money Can't Buy: Family Income and Children's Life Chances*. Cambridge, MA: Harvard University Press.

McKenzie, David J. 2001. Self-selection, church attendance, and local civic participation. *Journal for the Scientific Study of Religon* 40 (3):479–88.

McLanahan, Sara S. 2001. Life without father: What happens to the children? Princeton, NJ: Center for Research on Child Wellbeing.

McLanahan, Sara, and Gary Sandefur. 1994. *Growing Up with a Single Parent*. Cambridge, MA: Harvard University Press.

Mcloyd, Vonnie C. 1998. Socioeconomic disadvantage and child development. *American Psychologist* 53 (2):185–204.

Milano, Kenneth W. 2008. *Remembering Kensington and Fishtown: Philadelphia's Riverward Neighborhoods*. Charleston: History Press.

Moll, Richard. 1985. *Public Ivies: A Guide to America's Best Public Undergraduate Colleges and Universities*. New York: Penguin.

Mosteller, Frederick, and Daniel P. Moynihan, eds. 1972. *On Equality of Educational Opportunity*. New York: Random House.

Muller, Chandra, and Christopher G. Ellison. 2001. Religious involvement, social capital, and adolescents' academic progress: Evidence from the National Educational Longitudinal Study of 1988. *Sociological Focus* 34 (2).

Murphy, John J., ed. 1906. *The Wisdom of Benjamin Franklin*. New York: Brentanos.

Murphy, Kevin J. 1999. Executive compensation. In *Handbook of Labor Economics*, edited by O. Ashenfelter and D. Card. North Holland: Elsevier.

Murray, Charles. 1984. *Losing Ground: American Social Policy, 1950–1980*. New York: Basic Books.

———. 2003. *Human Accomplishment: The Pursuit of Excellence in the Arts and Sciences, 800 B.C. to 1950*. New York: HarperCollins.

———. 2005. The inequality taboo. *Commentary*, September 13–22.

———. 2006. *In Our Hands: A Plan to Replace the Welfare State*. Washington, DC: AEI Press.

———. 2007. Abolish the SAT. *The American*, July/August.

———. 2008. *Real Education: Four Simple Truths for Bringing America's Schools Back to Reality*. New York: Crown Forum.

———. 2009. Intelligence and College. *The National Interest* 1 (1):95–106.

Nakao, Keiko, and Judith Treas. 1994. Updating occupational prestige and socioeconomic scores: How the new measures measure up. *Sociological Methodology* 24:1–72.

Nakosteen, Robert A., and Michael A. Zimmer. 1987. Marital status and earnings of young men: A model with endogenous selection. *Journal of Human Resources* 22 (2):248–68.

National Center for Health Statistics. 1941. Vital Statistics of the United States, 1939, Part I. Washington, DC: National Center for Health Statistics.

Nelson, William E. 1967. Emerging notions of modern criminal law in the Revolutionary era: An historical perspective. *N.Y.U. Law Review* 450.

Nie, N. H. 2001. Sociability, interpersonal relations, and the Internet: reconciling conflicting findings. *American Behavioral Scientist* 45:420.

Novak, Michael. 2002. *On Two Wings: Humble Faith and Common Sense at the American Founding*. San Francisco: Encounter Books.

Olasky, Marvin. 1992. *The Tragedy of American Compassion*. Washington, DC: Regnery Gateway.

Parcel, Toby L., and Elizabeth G. Menaghan. 1989. Child home environment as a mediating construct between SES and child outcomes. Department of Sociology, The Ohio State University.

Pearson, Jennifer, Chandra Muller, and Michelle L. Frisco. 2006. Parental involvement, family structure, and adolescent sexual decision making. *Sociological Perspectives* 49:67–90.

Phillips, Kevin. 1991. *The Politics of Rich and Poor: Wealth and the American Electorate in the Reagan Aftermath*. New York: HarperPerennial.

Piketty, T., and E. Saez. 2006. The evolution of top incomes: A historical and international perspective. *American Economic Association Papers and Proceedings* 96:200–205.

Plomin, Robert, Kathryn Asbury, P. G. Dip, and Judith Dunn. 2001. Why are children in the same family so different? Nonshared environment a decade later. *Canadian Journal of Psychiatry* 46:225–33.

Pollock, Ivan L. 1923. *The Food Administration in Iowa*. Vol. 1. Iowa City: State Historical Society of Iowa.

Powers, Donald E., and Donald A. Rock. 1999. Effects of coaching on SAT I: Reasoning test scores. *Journal of Educational Measurement* 36 (2):93–118.

Putnam, Robert D. 2000. *Bowling Alone: The Collapse and Revival of American Community*. New York: Simon & Schuster.

———. 2007. *E pluribus unum*: Diversity and community in the twenty-first century. *Scandinavian Political Studies* 30 (2):137–74.

Raffalovich, Lawrence E., Shannon M. Monnat, and Tsao Hui-shien. 2009. Family income at the bottom and at the top: Income sources and family characteristics. *Research in Social Stratification and Mobility* 27:301–9.

Reding, Nick. 2009. *Methland: The Death and Life of an American Small Town*. New York: Bloomsbury.

Regnerus, Mark D. 2000. Shaping schooling success: Religious socialization and educational outcomes in metropolitan public schools. *Journal for the Scientific Study of Religion* 39:363–70.

Reich, Robert B. 1991. *The Work of Nations: Preparing Ourselves for 21st-Century Capitalism*. New York: Alfred A. Knopf.

Rifkin, Jeremy. 2004. *The European Dream: How Europe's Vision of the Future Is Quietly Eclipsing the American Dream*. New York: Penguin.

Ross, Christine, Sheldon Danziger, and Eugene Smolensky. 1987. The level and trend of poverty in the United States, 1939–1979. *Demography* 24 (4): 587–600.

Rossi, Peter H. 1955. *Why Families Move: A Study in the Social Psychology of Urban Residential Mobility*. Glencoe, IL: The Free Press.

Rowe, David, A. T. Vazsonyi, and D. J. Flannery. 1994. No more than skin deep: Ethnic and racial similarity in developmental process. *Psychological Review* 101 (3):396–413.

Rowe, David C. 2003. Assessing genotype-environment interactions and correlations in the postgenomic era. In *Behavioral Genetics in the Postgenomic Era*, edited by R. Plomin, J. C. DeFries, I. W. Craig, and P. McGuffin. Washington, DC: American Psychological Association.

Rubin, Lillian B. 1976. *Worlds of Pain: Life in the Working Class Family*. New York: Basic Books.

Schwartz, Christine R., and Robert D. Mare. 2005. Trends in educational assortative marriage from 1940 to 2003. *Demography* 42 (4):621–46.

Sennett, Richard, and J. Cobb. 1972. *The Hidden Injuries of Class*. New York: Vintage.

Skocpol, Theda. 2003. *Diminished Democracy: From Membership to Management in American Life*. Norman: University of Oklahoma Press.

Smallacombe, Patricia Stern. 2002. Why do they stay: Rootedness and isolation in an inner-city white neighborhood. PhD dissertation, Sociology, University of Pennsylvania, Philadelphia.

Soares, Joseph. 2007. *The Power of Privilege: Yale and America's Elite Colleges*. Stanford, CA: Stanford University Press.

Sourander, Andre, et al. 2006. Childhood predictors of male criminality: A prospective population-based follow-up study from age 8 to late adolescence. *Journal of the American Academy of Child and Adolescent Psychiatry* 45:578–86.

Spalding, Matthew, and Patrick J. Garrity. 1996. *A Sacred Union of Citizens: George Washington's Farewell Address and the American Character*. New York: Rowman & Littlefield.

Stutzer, Alois, and Bruno S. Frey. 2006. Does marriage make people happy, or do happy people get married? *Journal of Socio-Economics* 35:326–47.

Sullivan, Teresa A., Elizabeth Warren, and Jay Lawrence Westbrook. 2000. *The Fragile Middle Class: Americans in Debt*. New Haven, CT: Yale University Press.

Sundstrom, William A. 1999. The overworked American or the overestimated workweek? Trend and bias in recent estimates of weekly work hours in the United States. Santa Clara, CA: Santa Clara University.

Tocqueville, Alexis de. 1840. *Democracy in America*. Translated by H. Reeve. New York: J. & H. G. Langley.

Toynbee, Arnold J., and D. C. Somervell. 1946. *A Study of History: Abridgment of Volumes I–VI*. 1987 ed. Oxford: Oxford University Press.

Tracy, P. E., Marvin E. Wolfgang, and Robert M. Figlio. 1990. *Delinquency Careers in Two Birth Cohorts*. New York: Plenum Press.

U.S. Bureau of the Census. 1975. *Historical Statistics of the United States, Colonial Times to 1970*. 2 vols. Vol. 1. Washington, DC: U.S. Bureau of the Census.

Verba, Sidney, Kay L. Schlozman, and Henry E. Brady. 1995. *Voice and Equality: Civic Voluntarism in American Politics*. Cambridge, MA: Harvard University Press.

Warner, David F., and Mark D. Hayward. 2006. Early-life origins of the race gap in men's mortality. *Journal of Health and Social Behavior* 47:209–26.

Wellman, B., A. Q. Haase, J. Witte, and K. Hampton. 2001. Does the Internet increase, decrease, or supplement social capital? *American Behavioral Scientist* 45:436.

White, Michelle J. 1998. Why it pays to file for bankruptcy: A critical look at the incentives under U.S. personal bankruptcy law and a proposal for change. *University of Chicago Law Review* 65 (3):685–732.

Williams, Dmitri. 2006. On and off the 'Net: Scales for social capital in an online era. *Computer-Mediated Communication* 11 (2):593–628.

Wilson, Edward O. 1998. *Consilience: The Unity of Knowledge*. New York: Alfred A. Knopf.

Wolfgang, Marvin E., R. M. Figlio, and T. Sellin. 1972. *Delinquency in a Birth Cohort*. Chicago: University of Chicago Press.

Zhu, Ning. 2011. Household consumption and personal bankruptcy. *Journal of Legal Studies*:1–37.

Zuckerman, Phil. 2008. *Society Without God: What the Least Religious Nations Can Tell Us About Contentment*. New York: New York University Press.

Index

Page numbers in *italics* refer to figures.

ABOUT THE AUTHOR

CHARLES MURRAY is the W. H. Brady Scholar at the American Enterprise Institute. He first came to national attention in 1984 with *Losing Ground*. His subsequent books include *In Pursuit*, *The Bell Curve* (with Richard J. Herrnstein), *What It Means to Be a Libertarian*, *Human Accomplishment*, *In Our Hands*, and *Real Education*. He received a bachelor's degree in history from Harvard and a Ph.D. in political science from the Massachusetts Institute of Technology. He lives with his wife in Burkittsville, Maryland.